We Were Burning

WE WERE BURNING

JAPANESE ENTREPRENEURS AND THE FORGING OF THE ELECTRONIC AGE

Bob Johnstone

BASIC
BOOKS

A Member of the Perseus Books Group

℞ A CORNELIA AND MICHAEL BESSIE BOOK

℞ A CORNELIA AND MICHAEL BESSIE BOOK

Copyright © 1999 by Basic Books,
A Member of the Perseus Books Group.

Published in 1999 in the United States of America by Westview Press, 5500 Central Avenue, Boulder, Colorado 80301-2877, and in the United Kingdom by Westview Press, 12 Hid's Copse Road, Cumnor Hill, Oxford OX2 9JJ

Library of Congress Cataloging-in-Publication Data
Johnstone, Bob.
  We were burning : Japanese entrepreneurs and the electronic
revolution / Bob Johnstone.
      p. cm.
  Includes bibliographical references and index.
  ISBN 0-465-09117-2 (hc.)
  1. Electronic industries–Japan–History. 2. Electronic
industries–Technological innovations–Japan–History. I. Title.
HD9696.A3J36176   1998
338.4'7621381'0952–dc21   98-41188
                                                                                            CIP

Design by Heather Hutchison

98 99 00 01 02   10 9 8 7 6 5 4 3 2 1

For Setsuko

CONTENTS

LIST OF ILLUSTRATIONS

Author's Note:
In this book, Japanese names are presented in
their Japanese order, family name followed by
given name.

PREFACE:
PEOPLE, NOT POLICY

... the strength of government intervention has not been the decisive factor behind Japan's success. ... everything that has occurred in this country has stemmed ultimately from the cumulative strength of the people themselves.
                                    —Kikuchi Makoto[1]

I WAS BORN IN SCOTLAND IN SEPTEMBER 1951, the month that Bell Laboratories threw open transistor technology to the world. By the time I arrived at boarding school in Edinburgh ten years later, transistors in the shape of pocket-sized radios were ubiquitous.

My school prided itself on having nurtured Scotland's greatest novelist, Robert Louis Stevenson, author of such classics as *Treasure Island.* Many years later I was surprised to learn that another pupil there had been Scotland's greatest scientist, James Clerk Maxwell, author of famous equations that encompass all electromagnetic phenomena, including transistors. No prizes for guessing which of the two cultures my school held in higher esteem.[2]

I got my first transistor radio from a fellow boarder returning from summer holidays spent with his parents in Singapore. This boy usually brought back a case of mangoes—an impossibly exotic fruit in those days. One year, instead of mangoes, he arrived at school with a box full of duty-free transistor radios, which he proceeded to give away. He gave one to me, and I wasn't even one of his friends. They were *that* cheap.

That pocket radio—a National—was the first Japanese product I ever owned. It made a big difference to my otherwise miserable life at school. During breaks, I would wander around with it glued to my ear, listening to the cricket commentary. In the dormitory after lights out at night, I would plug in its tiny earphone and listen furtively to pop music on Radio Luxembourg. Little did I know it, but that radio was just the first of many Japanese electronic products that in the years to come would make a big difference, to all of our lives.

Pop music was one of the few highlights of growing up in 1960s Britain. In that immediately postimperial era, a palpable sense of decline pervaded the country. Shoddy goods of local manufacture seemed symptomatic of the decline.

In Japan during the same period, a very different mood prevailed. The 1960s were the decade of Prime Minister Ikeda Hayato's ambitious plan to double national income.[3] In 1968 the Japanese reached their goal, two years ahead of schedule.

I left Britain in early 1974, during the first Arab oil embargo. In the wake of the oil crisis came the longest recession of the postwar period. Of course, the Japanese were also hard hit by what they called the *oiru shyokku*. But for Japanese manufacturers of consumer electronic products, the 1970s were also glory days.

The decade kicked off with the introduction by Sharp and Seiko of the pocket calculator and the quartz watch, mass-market products that catapulted the electronics industry from transistors to microchips. In 1974 Matsushita—makers of my little National radio—overtook RCA to become the world's largest manufacturer of televisions. The following year saw the launch by the Japan Victor Company of the VHS video cassette recorder. Rounding out the decade would be that other quintessentially Japanese electronic icon, the Walkman portable stereo, introduced by Sony in 1979.

I went to Japan under the spell of artists like Hokusai and Kurosawa. Through a series of happy accidents, I stumbled into technology journalism. In 1982, I began writing about the Japanese electronics industry. At that time, Western analysts and policy makers were scratching their heads trying to figure out the causes of Japan's phenomenal success as a manufacturer, in particular of radios, televisions, cameras, and motorcycles. Then came publication of Chalmers Johnson's seminal work, *MITI and the Japanese Miracle*.[4] This book posited the notion that industrial policy, as applied by elite bureaucrats at the Ministry of International Trade & Industry, deserved much of the credit.

Though the most influential, Johnson was by no means the only one to point the finger at the ministry. "Japan's dominant position in consumer electronics today is no accident," asserted *Business Week*. "In the late 1950s," the magazine continued, "MITI's planners decided that the electronics industries should be the leading edge of growth for the Japanese economy."[5]

It seemed that the Japanese government had been sponsoring research and development consortia to help groups of local manufacturers catch up with their U.S. rivals. One initiative appeared to have been especially successful in achieving this aim. This was the so-called VLSI consortium, which brought together NEC, Toshiba, Fujitsu, Hitachi, and Mitsubishi—five of the Japanese electronics industry's largest firms.[6] The VLSI consortium ran from 1976 to 1980, a period which also saw Japan's initial inroads into the U.S. market for integrated circuits, in particular computer memory chips. It is worth noting, however, that Johnson's book covers the period 1925–75. It makes just one reference each to electronics and semiconductors.

Western observers were nonetheless quick to deduce a direct connection between the government-sponsored consortium and market penetration. In particular, editors thousands of miles away scented conspiracy. Collaboration, eh? So that was their little game. MITI stood revealed as the headquarters of Japan Inc.[7]

One of my first journalistic assignments was to interview a manager at a Japanese machine tool company about some recent technological breakthrough they had made. The editor specifically instructed me to ask whether in achieving this breakthrough, the company had merely been following MITI's instructions. The manager's reply, as I recall, was an indignant denial. I noted that R&D managers at other Japanese companies tended to respond to this question in similarly dismissive fashion.

My first big assignment was to cover the Fifth Generation Computer Project, an initiative that kicked off in earnest in 1982. This was the hubristic MITI-sponsored R&D consortium that was intended to leapfrog IBM, giving Japanese computer makers pole position in the world computer market. In retrospect, it is astonishing how seriously this threat was taken, and how earnestly Western governments endeavored to replicate the Japanese consortium-based approach to research.

"Japan provided a contrast for our own shortcomings," one U.S. observer concluded. "Japanese companies and government-business partnerships were effectively profiting from U.S.-generated innovations such as liquid crystal displays and semiconductor memories, and seemed to offer a superior model for gaining leadership in high-technology industries."[8]

Following the conspicuous failure of the Fifth Generation project (ended 1992) to meet its objectives, the industrial policy model has lost some of its luster, at least as a vehicle for overtaking rather than catching up. But as Endymion Wilkinson has argued, once stereotypes become established, they are notoriously long lived.[9] The myth of MITI the miracle-working ministry remains potent to this day. Well into the 1990s the United States and Europe continue to form R&D consortia, in misguided emulation of Japan's perceived success.

For example, in May 1994 the U.S. Department of Defense announced a half-billion-dollar program designed to boost America's moribund flat-panel display industry. Centerpiece of the program is the U.S. Display Consortium, a cooperative research organization whose ten corporate members include huge firms like AT&T and Xerox. Or, to take a more recent example, no fewer than three Pentagon-funded consortia are attempting to make blue light emitters: Their members include Kodak, Hewlett-Packard, and (once again) AT&T and Xerox. It is ironic to see such companies struggling in what they believe to be the Japanese mode to replicate a breakthrough made by a single researcher at a small, entrepreneurial Japanese firm.

Happily, recent work has shed new light on the subject of the effectiveness of Japan's R&D consortia. In particular, Scott Callon has convincingly demonstrated that (a) the VLSI consortium was in fact not much of a joint effort–the companies did most of the research in their own labs–and that (b) MITI's goal was–and is–not so much domination of world markets as "regulatory and budgetary control over what appear to be lucrative 'growth' areas for the future."[10]

Like all bureaucracies everywhere, MITI's major concern is to protect and, if possible, extend its turf. Thus, Callon argues, MITI's primary objective in establishing the VLSI project was to preempt a prior research program initiated by one of the ministry's archrivals, Nippon Telegraph & Telephone.

It is also ironic that, by the early 1980s, when Western analysts first became aware of MITI, the ministry's glory days were over. In 1979 MITI lost its primary instrument of control over Japanese firms—allocation of foreign currency. The power, that is, to decide who could—and who could not—import technologies.

In this connection, the well-known story of how MITI bureaucrats attempted to deny a fledgling Sony the $25,000 the company needed to license transistor technology from Western Electric is worth rehearsing here. Sony—in those days still known as Tokyo Tsushin Kogyo—had made initial approaches to the American firm without first consulting the ministry—a serious affront to bureaucratic dignity.

In October 1953, Sony cofounder Morita Akio flew to New York to sign the transistor license agreement, a copy of which he mailed back to Tokyo. But when his partner Ibuka Masaru took the document to the ministry to apply for the cash to make good on this arrangement, the section chief in charge of allocating foreign exchange at MITI was furious. It was "inexcusably outrageous" for Sony to have gone ahead and agreed to a contract without the ministry's say-so. It took poor Ibuka several months to smooth the bureaucrat's ruffled feathers. On 2 February 1954, he finally gained formal authorization to proceed.

Meanwhile Sony's competitors were not standing still. An American company called Regency Electronics made the world's first transistor radio, the TR-1, which it began marketing in December 1954. One month later, in January 1955, Sony produced a prototype transistor radio. "They had tried to be first. The thought crossed Ibuka's mind: if only MITI had issued their permit a little sooner . . . ."[11] As Morita would later grimly remark, "MITI has not been the great benefactor of the Japanese electronics industry that some critics seem to think it has."[12]

"The episode," commented Stanford University political scientist Daniel Okimoto, "belies the myth of MITI's prescience. It also brings to light the fact that some of Japan's most successful export industries—consumer electronics, cameras, watches, and other precision equipment—have managed to grow up strong and healthy outside MITI's incubator for targeted infant industries."[13]

So much for MITI. But to say that bureaucrats do not deserve the credit for the success of these industries is to invite the question: Who does?

It is hard to imagine a similar question being asked in the West. We are so accustomed to giving credit for commercial success to the entrepreneurs and visionaries whose determined features confront us every week on the covers of business magazines. In the case of U.S. electronics companies, we know that the prime movers at RCA were David Sarnoff; at Texas Instruments, Pat Haggerty; at Hewlett-Packard—well, Bill Hewlett and Dave Packard, of course. More recently we have hailed Steve Jobs at Apple, Bill Gates at Microsoft, and Andy Grove at Intel.

But what about Japanese entrepreneurs and visionaries? How many of them can we name? To be sure, Sony's Morita and Honda Soichiro of Honda Motors come to mind, but ... aren't they the exceptions that prove the rule? The rule, that is, which states that the Japanese are simply not entrepreneurial. Indeed, since we see entrepreneurs as quintessentially individualistic—that is to say, Western—the very expression "Japanese entrepreneur" sounds to our ears like a contradiction in terms.

And we find ourselves back in stereotype country. Our stereotypical image of the Japanese, as historian John Dower has pointed out, is "as mere prints off the same photographic negative, devoid of individuality," all looking exactly alike in their dark blue suits and gold-rimmed glasses.[14] It is hard to imagine such faceless clones as brave risk takers, betting their companies on some new and unproven technology. And yet, as this book will demonstrate, beyond question that is what they have repeatedly done.

There are, I think, several reasons why the crucial role played by entrepreneurs in the Japanese electronics industry has long gone unrecognized. One is that following Chalmers Johnson, the *a priori* assumption on the part of most Western investigators has been that industrial policy was itself the proper object of study. Since the hunters have been political scientists, we should not be surprised that policy has been their target.

A second reason for the oversight is that the focus of most study has been the computer industry. Given that the United States dominates this industry, that is a quite natural bias for American investigators to have. And to be sure MITI, understandably eager to prevent IBM achieving the same hegemony in Japan as the giant U.S. firm had established in Europe, was indeed at pains to nurture a strong domestic computer industry, using all the policy tools at its disposal.

But Japan's strength in electronics has historically been the *consumer* rather than the computer sector and, as we have seen, consumer electronics developed largely without government intervention. Remember that the first mass application of transistors was in a consumer product—the radio—and not the computer.

Indeed, IBM engineers were reluctant to switch to the new and unproven devices, but in 1955 IBM chairman Thomas Watson, Jr., bought over a hundred transistor radios and distributed them among key IBM executives. Eventually, Watson wrote a memo stating that, after 1 June 1958, IBM would build no more machines based on vacuum tubes.[15]

The casual observer may object that in Japan the consumer and computer sectors overlap, that giant firms like Hitachi, Mitsubishi, and Toshiba make both computers and consumer goods. That is true, but the Japanese industry also musters a second tier made up of smaller, specialist consumer electronics firms.

In this tier, Sony can be seen as the *primus inter pares* among a cluster of companies that includes Canon, Casio, Sharp, Seiko, and Yamaha. These quick-witted firms typically behave in a much more entrepreneurial fashion than the lumbering giants.

What tends to happen, though, is that when the smaller firms make a breakthrough the big companies, scenting profits, come piling in after the fact. In the ensuing struggle, the dust that surrounds the kill can make it hard to tell the lions from the hyenas.

Indeed, from a distance, it can be difficult to differentiate Japanese firms at all. And yet, as a recent Harvard study has demonstrated, Japanese firms may actually exhibit greater variance in corporate culture than their U.S. counterparts.[16] "U.S. employees enjoy a high degree of mobility throughout their careers, often switching jobs every few years," the study's authors explained. With the result that "corporate cultures tend to blend into a near-uniform code of behavior and expectations. Frequent acquisitions and sales of businesses, a common training ground for executives in the nation's schools of business—all tend to bring U.S. firms to a common culture."

In Japanese firms, by contrast, "new employees come in not yet fully trained; the corporation accepts responsibility for their training and socialization into the corporate culture. The resulting isolation of each firm from the next allows for a degree of differentiation that requires great caution about generalizations on Japanese management, technology strategy and the like."

Highly distinct corporate cultures, the study speculates, "serve to bring all employees together as a cohesive group of people, rather than a collection of individuals, as [is] characteristic of American firms."

This argument leads us to a third reason why Japanese entrepreneurs have been overlooked–that surprisingly little mention of them is made in Japan itself. Surprising, that is, unless you consider cultural factors such as the Japanese emphasis on the group, which discourages singling out individuals for praise. Indeed, as Dower pointed out, the Japanese (positive) self-stereotype is of themselves as a homogeneous people dedicated to maintaining the Confucian ideals of order and harmony.

Japan is also a rigidly hierarchical society in which media attention tends to focus on the elderly figureheads who make up top management, rather than on the young turks who often champion new technology. At the same time, Japanese companies are reluctant to open themselves up for scrutiny by outsiders, domestic as well as foreign. They feel that what goes on inside their gates is nobody's business but their own.

A final distinction is that in striking contrast to their U.S. counterparts, Japanese entrepreneurs typically do not seek to attract attention to themselves. Indeed, given their achievements, many of them exhibit a truly remarkable lack of ego. Sony's Morita is unusual both in his flair for publicity and his ability to speak English. His peers for the most part seem content with the approbation of their coworkers. Plus, of course, the incomparable satisfaction that comes from getting successful products out the door.

In writing this book, I did not set out with the intention of singing the praises of Japanese entrepreneurs. Rather, my starting point was a curiosity about the origins of key semiconductor devices and technologies. The more I wrote about semiconductors–by which I mean mostly the transistor and its direct descendent, the microchip–the more fascinated I became.

To a nonscientist like myself semiconductors seem to possess almost magical powers. For one thing, they almost never go wrong. People used to be delighted if a vacuum tube lasted five years. On my desk in front of me as I write is a point-contact transistor–the earliest form of the device–made by RCA in the mid-1950s. Forty years on, it still works perfectly.

For another, in microchip form semiconductor devices are so small as to be almost invisible. You can cram millions of transistors onto a slice of silicon no bigger than a shirt button. According to Intel chairman emeritus Gordon Moore, there are more transistors made each year than raindrops fall in California. In 1997, the industry produced about one quintillion of them–by Moore's calculation, at least as many as all the ants on earth.[17]

Such abundance gives chips the power to shrink formerly huge machines into something you can hold in the palm of your hand. Or to square the circle, by enabling the design of products that are not only more versatile than their predecessors, but also less expensive.[18]

Semiconductors are by their very nature a democratizing technology, because in volume they cost next to nothing to produce. Indeed, it costs less to make a transistor than it does to print a character on this page. Semiconductors thus eventually make even the most sophisticated appliances cheap enough for anyone to afford. Finally, in the form of lasers and light-emitting diodes, semiconductors produce light of exquisite brightness, purity, and hue.

The semiconductor is surely *the* invention of the twentieth century. Without semiconductors, many products that we take for granted in our daily lives would simply not exist. Today, we depend totally on the tiny devices. As U.S. semiconductor pioneer Nick Holonyak, Jr., put it, "If the transistor went away for one hour, I guarantee you–everything stops."

Obviously, you cannot make a transistor radio without transistors. To take a more recent example, the compact disc player (introduced by Sony in 1982) would not be compact without the tiny semiconductor laser that reads the information off the disc. By the same token, the Handycam (Sony's name for the camcorder, introduced in 1985) would not be handy without the microchip video camera that takes its pictures.

This tiny camera, known as the charge-coupled device, was the one that first aroused my curiosity about origins. Where had it come from? The answer was Bell Laboratories, where the CCD was invented in 1969. So how did it find its way into a Japanese camcorder in 1985?

It turned out that there were other, similar cases of key devices invented in the United States during the 1960s that had somehow ended up as enabling components in Japanese products a decade or more later. Often these devices were made *only* by Japanese companies. What had caused these extraordinary slips 'twixt cup and lip? Why had the inventors failed to capitalize on their own ingenuity? I was curious to find out.

The conventional, stereotypical, answer was that it was all part of a grand design hatched by MITI, aimed at achieving global predominance for Japan in strategic industries. This scenario runs roughly as follows. Huge Japanese conglomerates licensed from gullible or greedy U.S. firms full-fledged technologies, which the Japanese then plugged into their ultra-efficient production lines and turned the crank. Market domination was achieved through a combination of deep pockets, superior manufacturing, and, on occasion, illegal trading practices like dumping.

As time went by and I accumulated firsthand experience, I found this explanation less and less convincing. In 1990, I went to MIT on a journalism fellowship. There, as a participant in a seminar on the history of technology, I was assigned to report on a book that documented the application to machine tools of numerical controls, a pairing that greatly improved manufacturing precision.[19] The book offered a convincing explanation of why this technology had been such a sorry failure in the U.S. But by the same token, its argument could not be used to explain why numerical controls had been such a resounding success in Japan. Indeed the book made only two passing references to Japan, one of them in a footnote.

As it happened, I knew the answer to this question. I had met and interviewed Inaba Seiuemon, founder of Fanuc, the company that dominates the world market for numerical controls. Inaba, once memorably described as "a pint-sized Genghis Khan," turned out to be a remarkable individual. He had taken the numerical controls developed at MIT, stripped the unnecessary bells and whistles, and made the devices reliable. Inaba had also marketed the technology in an innovative way—by appealing over the heads of the machine tool companies to their customers, telling the latter how much more precisely they would be able to manufacture parts if their tools were equipped with his controllers.

By the mid-1980s Fanuc had become the most profitable company in Japan. The bright yellow factory on the slopes of Mount Fuji that Inaba built was a showpiece where visiting heads of state like Margaret Thatcher were taken, to marvel at the spectacle of robots making robots. If Inaba were not a major-league entrepreneur, then I was a Dutchman.

Inspired by Inaba's example, I reasoned that there had to be other Japanese entrepreneurs out there. As it happened, at the time I was intrigued by multimedia, a buzzword back in the early '90s. What did "multimedia" actually mean? About the only concrete manifestations of multimedia I could find were the boards that plugged into personal computers, allowing them to produce sound.

It turned out that these boards produced their sounds using a synthesizer chip, and that this chip was made only by the Japanese firm Yamaha. Investigating further, I found out that while the principle on which they were based was an American invention, the chips themselves were very much the result of the efforts of an extraordinary individual called Mochida Yasunori (whose story is told in chapter 7).

As time went by, I collected the stories of other remarkable individuals: men like Sasaki Tadashi at Sharp, Morozumi Shinji at Seiko, Kuwano Yukinori at Sanyo, Iwama Kazuo at Sony, and Teshima Toru at Stanley. My methodology was simple: Start by identifying a key device in which Japanese companies have a monopoly or near monopoly of the market, then trace the course of its development from invention through commercial application.

Most of the stories told in this book take place in the 1970s and 1980s. As time went by, I began to wonder whether the phenomenon of Japanese entrepreneurship in the consumer electronics segment of the semiconductor industry was peculiar to the immediately postwar generation. Then in 1993 Nichia Chemical, a small, previously unknown Japanese company, unexpectedly announced that it had developed a bright blue light emitting diode.

For reasons that are made clear in chapter 10, this was a momentous achievement. It was also something that some of the biggest firms in the electronics business had been trying without success to do for almost a quarter of a century. And, as the folks at Nichia were proud to point out, they had done it entirely under their own steam, without any government support whatsoever. For me, this little blue light was proof positive that the entrepreneurial dynamic in Japan was alive and kicking.

The stories I collected led me to develop a model of my own. In this model, I argue that technologies were not transferred fully developed for Japanese corporations to copy. Rather, they were often adopted, after they had been abandoned by their originators, by visionary and highly motivated Japanese entrepreneurs, for very specific reasons, at small and medium-size firms, when there was still much research and development work remaining to be done. For the technologies they licensed, these firms paid the asking price—often sizable sums. And from their government, they received little encouragement or financial support. In no sense was this, as is often charged, a "free ride" on other people's ideas.

This book is the story of these entrepreneurs, their motivations, and the technologies they adopted. It is a collection linked in several ways:

- thematically, in that the technologies all come from (or, as in the case of the liquid crystal display, are intimately related to) the semiconductor industry;
- chronologically, in that almost all of the technologies were invented during the 1960s, mostly at the central research laboratories of large U.S. companies; and
- practically, in that most of the technologies are now in the late 1990s used or about to be used in multimedia personal computers.

In a sense this book is also—and again, this was not my original intention—a history of the Japanese semiconductor industry, or at least those parts of it which do not make computer chips.

I should emphasize, however, that this book is not about technology per se. Readers who seek technical explanations about the devices and processes mentioned here will be referred elsewhere. Rather, it is an attempt to shed light on the question of why inventions flourish in one place and not in another. Or in a larger sense, of how technology happens, how inventions take root and bear fruit—whether in Japan or anywhere else for that matter. And it seems to me that the most important driver of this dynamic is—and always has been—not policy, but people.

We Were Burning

INTRODUCTION:
A NATION OF
TRANSISTOR SALESMEN?

Our true capital was our knowledge and our ingenuity and our passion . . .

–Akio Morita[1]

IT WAS, BY ANY MEASURE, a marvelous Christmas present. The transistor, born at Bell Telephone Laboratories on 16 December 1947, was the tiny seed from which today's trillion-dollar electronics industry would grow.

From a Japanese point of view, the advent of the transistor was not so much marvelous as miraculous. For one thing, the timing of the invention could hardly have been better. In late 1947 Japan was a phoenix about to begin its rise from the ashes of World War II. By 1951, when Western Electric began licensing transistor technology, the country was enjoying an economic boom brought about by billions of dollars of "divine aid," as the then governor of the Bank of Japan described it–procurements for United Nations forces fighting in neighboring Korea.

Had the transistor been invented a few years earlier, during World War II, there would have been no question of publishing word of the discovery, let alone licensing it to the enemy. By the end of the 1940s, however, with the communists taking over in China and North Korea and threatening to do likewise all across the Far East, Japan the former foe had become Japan the favored friend. As the threat of communism loomed, the Occupation forces abandoned their attempt to reform Japan. Their new imperative: to rebuild the country as a bulwark against the Red Menace.

In addition to Japan's newfound strategic importance, a second concern for the United States at this time was to lessen the burden of providing economic assistance to an impoverished nation. In 1947, the year of the transistor's invention, American aid to Japan exceeded $400 million. To help pull Japanese industry back onto its feet, the U.S. would provide technological assistance and encourage Japan to undertake research and development. Japanese scientists and engineers would be allocated scarce foreign currency to travel to the U.S. to visit American corporate laboratories and production lines. Paths would be cleared for the importation to Japan of new technologies—such as the transistor.

Japan is a country virtually devoid of natural resources. To pay for imports of food and raw materials like oil and iron ore, the Japanese must manufacture goods for export. But in the early days of economic recovery the question was, what sort of export goods should Japanese companies make?

In Tokyo to negotiate the first United States–Japan Security Treaty (1950), soon-to-be U.S. Secretary of State John Foster Dulles offered his hosts some tips. No doubt mindful that silk had been Japan's largest prewar export, Dulles suggested shirts and pyjamas as two likely export winners. The diplomat added helpfully that cocktail napkins might also be worth looking into.

Dulles's patronizing suggestion revealed a lamentable but by no means unusual ignorance of Japan's historical prowess as a manufacturer of sophisticated goods. During his 1953 European trip, in a restaurant in Düsseldorf, Sony cofounder Akio Morita was served an ice cream decorated with a miniature parasol. "This is from your country," the German waiter smiled. "That was the extent of his knowledge of Japan and its capabilities," Morita reflected miserably, "and maybe he was typical."[2]

An excellent example of Japan's historical prowess is the samurai sword. As early as the eighth century, Japanese swordsmiths had mastered the essentials of their craft. Over the next four hundred years they proceeded to hone their skills to "a level of perfection that connoisseurs have described as incomparable."[3] Nor were domestic warriors their only customers. During the succeeding centuries, Japanese blades were exported in huge quantities all over the Far East. In 1483, for example, Japan shipped 67,000 swords to China alone.[4]

Then came guns, first brought to Japan by Portuguese explorers in 1543. The Japanese responded to the arrival of this alien technology in characteristic fashion. Namely, with "a quite indefatigable curiosity, a passion to learn, and an aptitude for choosing, borrowing, adapting and 'japanizing' foreign ideas and techniques."[5]

Japanese armorers quickly learned how to make the European weapons. Then, with a knack for which they would become famous some four hundred years hence, the Japanese improved them. "They developed a serial firing technique to speed up the flow of bullets. They increased the caliber of the guns to increase each bullet's effectiveness, and they ordered waterproof lacquered cases to carry the matchlocks and gunpowder in. . . . Japanese gunmakers were busy refining the comparatively crude Portuguese firing mechanism—developing, for example, a helical mainspring and adjustable trigger-pull. They also devised a gun accessory unknown in Europe which enabled a matchlock to be fired in the rain."[6]

Ignorance of the swords and matchlocks of antiquity is understandable. But in recent memory, too, the Japanese had demonstrated that they were no slouches when it came to the design and manufacture of world-class weaponry. Had Secretary Dulles forgotten the Mitsubishi Zero?—the Japanese navy's famous fighter, whose lightweight construction enabled it to make the round trip to Pearl Harbor? The deadly Zero, whose superb engineering, superior speed, and swallowlike maneuverability made it the scourge of Allied fliers in the Pacific War?

To be sure, the Japanese would not henceforth be building any more fighters, or indeed weapons of any sort. Japan's American-drafted constitution, which went into effect in 1947—the year of the transistor's invention—explicitly renounced war and prohibited the export of any goods with military potential. Designed to prevent a resurgence of Japanese military ambitions, this prohibition would have an enormously important—and completely unintentional—side effect.

Engineering talent is not an unlimited commodity; each nation possesses only so much of it. Thus, how to apply this finite and precious resource is of considerable strategic significance. Throughout the Cold War period, 1945–1990, Western nations in general and the United States in particular would allocate, for better or worse, a very large fraction of their engineering skills to military ends. David Rubinfien, a former Raytheon engineer based in Japan during the 1960s, summed up the situation thus: "In America, the supply of engineers for [consumer electronics] dried up, because the needs of the defense activity became enormous. As rapidly as people showed promise of any kind, they were dragged into defense work, and that was sort of inevitable, because the salaries that could be paid were far better than private industry could pay, and that just absorbed the available people. . . ."

(On the other hand, there were some talented engineers like Israel Kalish, who joined RCA because, as he put it "I didn't want to work for a military supplier–at RCA, you could go home and tell your family what you were working on and they could relate to it . . . .")

During this same period, their Japanese counterparts were willy-nilly engaged in the design and manufacture of products exclusively intended for the consumption of the commercial marketplace.

Japan's renunciation of militarism was by no means entirely an external imposition. Among the generations that either fought or grew up in the war, or during its aftermath, there persists a deep and widespread revulsion for all things military. In their founding articles, some Japanese companies make their antimilitary stance explicit. For example, the first of Canon's "Five Principles for R&D Activities" states: "We reject research and development themes for military purposes." The third of Sony's "Management Policies" promises to "focus on highly sophisticated technical products that have great usefulness in society . . . ."

One of the first of these useful products was the transistor radio. By 1958, radios represented 77 percent of Japan's total electronics exports of ¥6.3 billion ($175 million).[7] In 1959, Japanese companies exported over 6 million portable radios–the majority of them transistor sets–to the United States, the largest individual market.[8]

For Japan the timing of the transistor's invention was propitious indeed. But other factors would also combine to ensure that the tiny seed would flourish when planted in Japanese soil. First, while prewar, science-based industry had been dominated by such products of chemistry as synthetic fertilizers, the transistor–like the atomic bomb–was an offshoot of physics. This was a field where the Japanese had already demonstrated themselves capable of producing world-class results.

Back in 1935 Yukawa Hideki, a young researcher at Kyoto University, had predicted the existence of a new elementary particle later dubbed the meson. For this discovery, Yukawa received the 1949 Nobel Prize for Physics, becoming Japan's first Nobel laureate. Sixteen

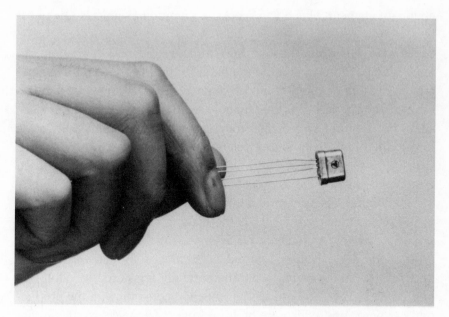

The first transistor manufactured by Totsuko in 1954. (Courtesy of Sony)

years later, Yukawa's contemporary and friend Tomonaga Shin-ichiro won for Japan a second physics Nobel Prize (which he would share that year with his rather better-known American counterpart, Richard Feynman).

In 1953, just as commercial production of transistors was getting underway in the United States, some of the world's top scientists would feel it worth their while to make what was then a long and tedious trip to Tokyo for an international conference on theoretical physics. They included one of the transistor's coinventors, John Bardeen. There, in addition to presenting a paper at the conference, Bardeen gave a lecture on the surface physics of semiconductors to a small but eager audience consisting of about fifty young Japanese physicists.

Intellectually the Japanese were thus well equipped to take the transistor on board. In terms of raw materials, too, the transistor could almost have been tailor-made for a resource-poor nation. All that was needed to make a transistor—in addition to brains—was a few grams of germanium or, later and more significantly, silicon, the world's most abundant element, plus a few specks of common chemicals like phosphorus.

The materials would have to be ultrapure, of course, containing no more than one foreign atom in a million. To produce such purity would require mastery of complex industrial processes. But complex processes were something at which the Japanese had long excelled, witness once again the samurai sword. The long, curved blade of this weapon is forged, then repeatedly folded, rehammered, and welded to produce a structure consisting of as many as 10,000 layers of steel. The finished weapon has an edge that is exceptionally tough and exceedingly sharp.

A traditional Japanese production process that bears more similarity to the semiconductor industry is the making of the woodblock prints known as *ukiyoe*. A collaborative art involving the combined efforts of artist, woodcarver, printer, and publisher, *ukiyoe* are made using a sequence of as many as ten separate, carefully registered woodblocks, one for each color. The process has much in common with the production of microchips, which are built up from many layers of silicon, oxide, and other materials, each of which must be aligned with exquisite precision on top of its predecessor.

Of course, swords and woodblock prints were handcrafted, not mass produced. But by another happy accident, 1947 also saw the arrival in Japan of a lanky American statistician called W. Edwards Deming, who had come to assist the Occupation with housing and population studies. Deming brought with him revolutionary ideas about statistical quality control as the basis for manufacturing excellence–ideas that had fallen on stony ground in his native land.

In Japan, Deming found an audience made receptive by criticism of the quality of its products–an audience, moreover, in the grip of a still untarnished admiration for all things American. During a speech in Tokyo at the Industry Club of Japan on 26 July 1950, Deming made the astonishing prophesy that, before long, Japanese quality would be the best in the world.[9] In this, as in many things, he would be proved right. Japanese manufacturers would apply Deming's notions of QC across the industrial spectrum, but nowhere more successfully than in the semiconductor industry.

In the industry's early days, when wires had to be soldered onto individual devices under a microscope, the manual dexterity of young

Japanese "transistor gals" played an important role. As the number of transistors that could be crammed onto a single silicon chip grew from a few, to a few hundred, to a few thousand and beyond, it would become essential to manufacture chips in dust-free clean rooms. Before entering such rooms, workers must take elaborate precautions and don special clothing. Many observers have commented that such procedures were readily adopted by a people accustomed to removing their shoes before entering their houses and to bathing before eating.

The tiny size of transistors and chips was another cultural factor that seemed to play to Japanese strengths. Forced by an unaccommodating geography to squeeze dwellings into less than a quarter of their country's total land area, the Japanese had long been masters at the arts of miniaturization. In the interests of compactness they rolled up their beds, folded their screens, stacked their tables, and nested their lunch boxes.

Lack of space may also account for Japanese attention to detail. Or perhaps this meticulousness results from the characteristic, sometimes obsessive, Japanese pursuit of perfection. While the rest of the world may be content with something that gets the job done, the Japanese tendency is to go whole hog (witness yet again the 10,000-layer sword blade). Often there is no economic rationale for such behavior, the only justification being the sense of satisfaction the individual derives from knowing he has done his utmost. But as one observer pointed out, in the semiconductor industry, "the way you're successful in getting high yields is to pay enormous attention to detail."

However you choose to explain it, attention to detail would be instrumental in winning Japan's third Nobel Prize for physics. In 1957, Esaki Leona, a 32-year-old physicist at a small Japanese electronics firm, was brought in to determine the cause of a problem holding up production of high-frequency transistors for radios.[10] His firm was called Tokyo Tsushin Kogyo, which some years earlier had begun applying to its products the easier-to-remember brand name Sony.

The transistors worked well until a wire was attached to them, at which point they ceased to function. In the United States, engineers confronted with a similar situation would conclude that the problem was simply a bad contact causing a short circuit and throw the dud devices away. But for Sony this particular transistor was key to the suc-

Transistor radio, 1957. (Courtesy of Sony)

cess a new line of radios they were planning to produce. The company simply had to know what was going wrong.

After about a month of painstaking experiments, Esaki and his young colleagues noticed something very strange happening inside these transistors. Normally as you apply more voltage to a circuit, the amount of current also increases. But in these devices, the opposite was happening. It was like stepping on the gas only to have your car slow down.

How to explain this startling effect? Esaki eventually concluded the only way was to resort to the bizarre logic of quantum mechanics. The electrons were not flowing downstream in the form of discrete particles; rather, they were tunneling upstream in the form of a continuous wave. And they were doing it very quickly, too.

To exploit this strange new phenomenon, Esaki went on to build what he called a tunnel diode, a device that was of tremendous scientific interest but that turned out to have little practical utility. (After Esaki won the 1973 Nobel Prize for his work, Kikuchi Makoto recalled Japanese reporters asking him what tunnel diodes were useful for. "They're not really useful for anything," Kikuchi replied truthfully. Esaki's mother never forgave him for this comment.) More important from Sony's point of view, however, was that having understood the basic science underlying the holdup in transistor production, they were able to fix the problem and move on.

For upstart firms like Sony, founded 7 May 1946, the transistor was a great leveler. Such a radically new technology meant that all firms, no matter how big, had to start from scratch. Indeed, the transistor gave the edge to small firms because of their ability to move more quickly than the lumbering giants that made up much of Japan's manufacturing industry.

Following the destruction of defeat and the attempt by the Occupation to break them up, the *zaibatsu* conglomerates that had dominated Japan's prewar and wartime industrial landscape were still in the process of regrouping. Overall the situation in Japan during the late 1940s and early 1950s was thus uncharacteristically favorable to newcomers, like a pine forest where fire has created gaps in which aspens can shoot up.

U.S. policy was to get Japan back on its feet. Transfer of technology was a key plank in that policy. Getting the official nod was of course important for facilitating technology transfer. But in terms of actual outcomes, a second, completely unrelated, development was of far greater importance in enabling Japanese firms to acquire the technology they needed.

In 1949, less than two years after the invention of the transistor, the U.S. Justice Department initiated an antitrust suit against American Telephone & Telegraph, alleging the phone company was giving preferential treatment in the procurement of equipment to its manufacturing arm, Western Electric. The suit demanded that the manufacturer be spun off from the parent company.

This was the first of several federal antitrust suits brought against major American technology companies, most notably RCA and IBM. During the 1950s, all three firms were forced to sign consent decrees that, among other things, obliged them to license their technology to all comers. Foreign firms also benefited from this unprecedented openness. The only difference was that, though the technology would henceforth be available to everyone, the foreigners would have to pay for it.

AT&T was thus obliged to throw open transistor technology to the world. Bell Labs vice president Jack Morton later tried to put a more positive spin on the phone company's 1951 decision: "We realized that if this thing was as big as we thought," he wrote, "we couldn't keep it to ourselves and we couldn't make all the technical contributions. It was in our interest to spread it around. If you cast your bread on the water, sometimes it comes back as angel food cake."[11]

On the other hand, hoarding your bread and—more to the point—not letting anyone else have the recipe, might well have seemed to the Justice Department like the action of a recalcitrant monopolist. AT&T knew that failure to license a potentially exciting new technology like the transistor could cost the company its case, which in turn would mean the loss of Western Electric.

In any event, by the consent decree of January 1956, AT&T was allowed to keep its manufacturing arm but obliged to license all existing patents royalty free to any interested domestic firm. In the interests of fairness, Western Electric was not permitted to sell semiconductors in the commercial marketplace. As far as licensing nondomestic firms was concerned, since AT&T did not participate in overseas markets, the firm had no incentive to exclude foreign manufacturers from access to the technology.[12]

In this way was established the liberal licensing policy which, for the most part, the semiconductor industry has practiced ever since. AT&T was able to set the pattern simply because the phone company owned most of the important device and process patents.

The second largest holder of semiconductor patents was RCA. Together with Bell Labs, RCA's David Sarnoff Research Center would be the other main source for an outpouring of inventions that subsequently found fulfillment in Japanese products. From Bell Labs came the transistor, along with most of the basic semiconductor production processes, the semiconductor laser (in practical form), and the microchip camera known as the charge-coupled device. RCA inventions included C-MOS, today's mainstream microchip process technology, the liquid crystal display, and the amorphous silicon solar cell.

For the Radio Corporation of America, the antitrust stakes were even higher than for AT&T. RCA was a firm that owed its very origin to patents, beginning with those on radio technology. The company was formed in October 1919 by pooling the radio patents owned by three corporations: General Electric, Westinghouse, and United Fruit, which depended on radio to link its plantations in Central America with its banana boats. During the 1920s, RCA adopted a restrictive form of access to these patents called "package licensing." That is, if you wanted to make radios, instead of licensing patents piecemeal, you could buy all the rights you needed from RCA in the form of a package. Licensing would become a major source of revenue for the corporation, which used the money to underwrite the research and development of new technologies like television. "RCA," wrote historian Margaret Graham, "was effectively in the business of selling research."[13]

In 1958, the Justice Department cracked down hard on the corporation, ruling that package licensing violated antitrust law. Henceforth RCA would have to open its TV patents to domestic rivals free of charge. To avoid further antitrust problems RCA had to walk a thin line. Israel Kalish recalled that when he joined the corporation as a researcher in 1953, "they told me RCA had thirty-three and a third percent of the TV picture tube market; the lawyers worried when they got to 35 percent, and the business managers worried when they got to 31 percent."

But there was nothing in the consent decree to stop sales of package licenses to companies overseas. The corporation's visionary chairman, David Sarnoff, was an avid promoter of international technology transfer. "It is my conviction," he told a group of Japanese businessmen in Tokyo on 20 October 1960, "that the wisest policy of electronic research is one that is based not upon concealing knowledge, but upon the widest and swiftest dissemination of knowledge, so that all may benefit."[14]

Like AT&T, RCA was unconcerned with the possibility that this policy could lead to future competition from foreign firms. To avoid competing against its licensees, the corporation chose not to participate in overseas markets. It was a decision RCA would ultimately come to regret.

By 1960 Japan was already RCA's number one market in terms of licensing, accounting by one estimate for perhaps 80 percent of royalty income. The company had granted patent licenses—most of them related to television, production of which began in Japan in 1953—to no fewer than eighty-two Japanese manufacturers.

RCA also had technical aid agreements in place with three Japanese manufacturers in television picture tubes, and four others in transistors. Technical aid was more important than licensing, according to Kalish, "because licensing said, you can use our patents, but technical aid said, you can look at the details of our process."

Sarnoff himself, one of his employees speculated, was probably the best-known American in Japan, short of President Eisenhower, General MacArthur, and John D. Rockefeller III. On his two-week visit to Japan in 1960—which was timed to coincide with the beginning of color television broadcasting there—Sarnoff was treated like royalty. He was met upon arrival at Haneda Airport by Prime Minister Ikeda Hayato and given the keys to the City of Tokyo by the mayor. RCA hosted a garden party for him at Frank Lloyd Wright's Imperial Hotel which was attended by 500 people, including all the company's licensees. The visit would climax on 28 October with Sarnoff receiving from Emperor Hirohito the Order of the Rising Sun (third class), the highest distinction ever bestowed by Japan on a foreign businessman.

Ownership of key patents enabled RCA's licensing group to operate at the highest level in Japan. The group was extremely active. "The licensing people had a network over there you couldn't believe," recalled Bernie Vonderschmitt, who saw it in action during the 1970s as general manager of RCA's semiconductor manufacturing division, "and when they smelled someone getting into the business, they would be there."[15]

RCA researchers and operating division executives like Vonderschmitt had a love-hate relationship with the licensing people. On the one hand, the latter were supportive of the former because, as Vonderschmitt explained, "they knew that unless the product divisions were successful, the value perceived by licensees would be slowly but surely attenuated. So they were favorably inclined to the divisions being successful and getting resources because that meant that their asset was being fed, and they could offer more to the Japanese."

Joe Castellano, a former researcher at the Sarnoff Center, recalled that around 1971, when RCA management axed the center's liquid crystal display development program, "the licensing people screamed and yelled, and it was back in two days."

On the other hand, Vonderschmitt continued, "the operating division people generally took the stance that the licensing people were giving everything [away] and producing our future competitors." Kalish added that "the [research] people involved really felt, we're doing this good work, but we're being sold down the drain by our patent people, they're selling our future."

In addition, it was galling to see these slick marketing guys take the credit for all the royalties that were rolling in. Adding injury to insult was the fact that the operating divisions themselves had to contribute to those royalties, in the wake of the 1958 consent decree, paying exactly the same rates as the licensees. It was indeed, as Vonderschmitt recalled, "a *weird* arrangement." Rubbing salt in the wounds was the lavish lifestyle that RCA's licensing people enjoyed. They had opulently furnished offices with thick-pile carpets, they ate in the best restaurants, and when they traveled they flew first class, while the lowly research and operating division grunts huddled back in coach.

New York–based licensing executives would make frequent trips to Japan, the main market for RCA research. In addition, there were also two or three licensing people stationed permanently in Tokyo. Operating division managers and scientists from the David Sarnoff Research Center would be flown in to help sell RCA product. Vonderschmitt and his counterparts would brief the Japanese licensees on what was going on in the U.S. marketplace, and what the future directions were likely to be. The researchers would describe what they had been working on and their latest results.

"The licensing people always wanted you to visit the licensees," Vonderschmitt said, "from the standpoint of trying to make an impression on them that RCA was still doing new developments, and that therefore made their [five-yearly renewal] negotiations easier." Back home, RCA facilities like the Sarnoff Research Center and the semiconductor factory in Somerville played host to a seemingly never-ending stream of camera-toting Japanese visitors.

Licensing of technology to the Japanese became, according to Sarnoff Center vice president Jim Clingham, "one of the best businesses

RCA had." Clingham estimated the royalty stream as being "worth $200–300 million a year." Accurate figures on exactly how much RCA earned from licensing have always been hard to get–even (or perhaps especially) for the people who generated the patents. According to former Sarnoff Center researcher and liquid crystal pioneer Richard Williams: "It was always insulated–like the CIA budget–you could never really tell how much money came from patent licensing, the way the budget was reported in [RCA's] annual report, so that nobody really knew–except that it was clear that there was a lot of money."

The gravy train continued to flow well into the 1990s. But by then, following the corporation's acquisition by General Electric in December 1985, RCA itself had long since been broken up, its R&D center let go for a derisory $1. Sarnoff's once-proud enterprise is today little more than a brand name, a pale orange afterglow of its glorious past.

Liberal semiconductor licensing policies were driven by a mixture of global strategic considerations, domestic antitrust pressures, and commercial interests. There was, however, still another reason why U.S. concerns were prepared to transfer their technology to Japan so blithely: Simply, in their wildest dreams, the Americans never imagined that the Japanese would catch up with them so quickly.

Victory had gone to America's head. As historian John Dower wrote, ". . . the war in the Pacific ended much as it had begun: in American underestimation of the technical capability of the Japanese."[16] Americans dismissed Japanese minds as "prerational and prescientific." At this time, a common perception of the Japanese was that they were like children.

Dower explained: "To Westerners, Oriental adults in general looked younger than their actual years. At an average height of five feet three inches, the Japanese was considerably shorter" than his Western counterpart.

The Americans saw themselves as teachers; the Japanese, as their pupils. These were images with which both felt comfortable. For their part, with their indefatigable curiosity, the Japanese were determined to learn everything they could from their oversized occupiers.

The first awareness in Japan of the transistor's existence came by word of mouth, probably via the science officers at the Occupation's

GHQ in Tokyo. In the early days, however, written sources were the most important channel through which information about the new technology filtered through to Japan.

The main font of American knowledge was the library of the cultural center at the headquarters of the Occupation forces. This was located in the Dai-Ichi Seimei Building by Hibiya Park, near the heart of downtown Tokyo. Magazines made available by the library included scientific publications like *Physical Review* and *Journal of Applied Physics*. Having been shipped by surface mail, they reached Japan after a considerable delay.

As soon as they arrived, these journals would be pounced upon when the library opened each morning by bright-eyed, tousle-headed young men like Kikuchi Makoto. "I'd flick through the contents," Kikuchi recalled, "and whenever I saw the word 'semiconductor' or 'transistor,' I'd go 'Found one!' and my heart would start to pound."

Then the youngsters would sit down and, in those pre-copier days, painstakingly transcribe entire articles by hand. Paper was scarce, remembered another Japanese transistor tyro, Nishizawa Jun'ichi, so they had to write in small letters, leaving no space for margins.

To study these exciting new developments, an informal group was hastily organized. It met for the first time in October 1948–a scant three months after the public announcement of the transistor–at the Electro-Technical Laboratory's headquarters in Nagata-cho, Tokyo. This building was just down the street from the old Sanno Hotel, where U.S. officers were billeted, and the nightclubs of Akasaka, where they frolicked. The organizers of the group were Kikuchi's boss, Komagata Sakuji, the director of the Electro-Technical Laboratory, a government institute, and Nishizawa's professor, Watanabe Yasushi, of Tohoku University in northern-central Japan. This study group, and the personal network that grew out of it, provided a very effective channel for pooling the latest information and disseminating it throughout the country.

The start of their careers happily coinciding with the dawn of modern electronics, Kikuchi and Nishizawa would become the leading researchers at their respective institutes. There, they would play a key role in educating engineers and diffusing semiconductor technology to industry–in particular, to smaller Japanese companies, which could not afford to send their employees off to learn at universities and corporate laboratories in the United States, the style which big firms like Hitachi and Toshiba adopted.

Early research on semiconductors was conducted in primitive conditions. "We had nothing in our laboratory," Nishizawa recalled, "if it rained, we had to use umbrellas because the roof leaked onto the benches." The Electro-Technical Laboratory had no heating, so in winter everybody had to wear overcoats. But the enthusiasm of these young men was unquenchable: "We were afire, totally afire," Kikuchi said, "and we poured ourselves into our work." Unable to afford expensive imported equipment for their research, Japan's transistor pioneers had to make everything themselves, improvising, scrounging, and cannibalizing wherever they could.[17]

A particular problem in the early '50s was how to produce single-crystal silicon of unprecedentedly high (99.999999%) purity. Here, young Japanese researchers showed particular ingenuity.

Key to success in producing single crystals is maintaining the temperature of the material constant, $\pm 1°C$. But the only temperature-measuring gear Kikuchi and his coworkers had was calibrated in degrees, not tenths of a degree. So, to increase the sensitivity of the readout, they attached a mirror to the needle of the meter. Shining a lamp on this mirror reflected a bar of light onto an enlarged scale drawn on the wall of the laboratory. This enabled the researchers to monitor small variations in temperature for which they could then compensate. The improvised scheme worked very well.

With their greater purchasing power, researchers at the laboratories of Nippon Telegraph & Telephone at Musashino in western Tokyo could afford to buy more sensitive temperature gauges. Their problem was refining the material, which involved passing a heating coil slowly and smoothly up the ingot. The solution, devised by a researcher called Iwase Shingo, was to attach the coil via a pulley to a wooden block floating in a bucket of water, in which he punched a small hole. As the level of the water went down, so the coil rose.[18]

In the early days of the semiconductor era—that is, between the public announcement of the transistor on 1 July 1948 and the first Bell Labs symposium for licensees in September 1951—in Japan, mostly national laboratories and universities were in the running. Once licensing began, however, the onus switched to the private sector. Big companies like Hitachi and Toshiba opened their own channels, licensing the lat-est knowhow from U.S. counterparts such as RCA and General Electric.

Sony, which by the mid-1950s had perhaps 500 or 600 employees, continued to go its own way. The company's initial semiconductor devices were made under license from Western Electric. But these first-generation commercial transistors were extremely limited in their frequency response. Sure, you could make radios with them, but the quality of the sound they produced left much to be desired. Improving the output performance required the addition to the incoming radio signal of a high-frequency component to aid in tuning and amplification.

Known as superheterodyne, this procedure was well understood, and vacuum tubes that could perform it were available. In the early 1950s, engineers at some companies talked of producing hybrid radios containing both tubes and transistors. But Ibuka Masaru and his researchers would have none of this compromise; instead, they would develop high-frequency transistors by improving the technology they had licensed.

The key to the frequency problem turned out to be the element used to "dope" the devices—which means, to add the extra electrons they needed in order to conduct electricity. An intriguing possibility was to substitute phosphorus for the conventional dopant, antimony. However, as the Sony scientists discovered to their dismay, long after they began their experiments, researchers at Bell Laboratories had already tried doping transistors with phosphorus—and it hadn't worked. The Americans had published their conclusion in the *Bell System Technical Journal*, which in those days was like the Bible to semiconductor scientists. Effectively, the voice of God had spoken and what it had said was: No.

But to be successful in science you have to be prepared to defy conventional wisdom, no matter how exalted its source. At an in-house meeting Tsukamoto Tetsuo, a determined young physicist in Sony's transistor manufacturing section, reported that he had managed, amid many failures, to persuade one phosphorus-doped device to work.

Tsukamoto was fortunate that the manager of transistor production at Sony, Iwama Kazuo, was wise enough to give him his head, despite the thumbs down from Bell Labs. "Well, if it looks to you as though you are getting interesting results," Iwama said, "why don't you just keep working and see what happens?"[19] Two or three days after this meeting, Tsukamoto was able to repeat his result. By increasing the impurity level even further, he went on to improve the high-frequency characteristics of the transistor by as much as fifty times.

For Sony, there was a multiple payoff. One was the improved device, which enabled them to produce a super new all-transistor radio that would take their competitors some time to match, a classic example of product differentiation on the basis of innovative componentry.[20]

Kikuchi Makoto reckons that Ibuka, Iwama, and Sony's top R&D managers had their sights set beyond improvements to the radio. "They were, I am very sure, thinking of the things coming next after the transistor radio—TV and other electronic products clearly demanded transistors with better high-frequency characteristics." Sony introduced the world's first all-transistor television in 1960.

The cream on the cake was that it was problems in producing this high-frequency transistor that led to Esaki's Nobel Prize–winning discovery of electron tunneling.

In addition, for Tsukamoto himself, there was an extra reward: an invitation to Murray Hill—the Mount Olympus of the semiconductor world—to explain to the great brains of Bell Labs how he, a lowly Japanese, had managed to do what they could not.

The name Sony looms large in any discussion of the early days of the Japanese semiconductor industry, and rightly so. The stories of Ibuka's visionary decision to license the transistor, his fight with MITI to obtain the foreign currency needed to pay for that license, Tsukamoto's re-engineering of Western Electric's transistor, and Esaki's tunnel diode—these are the stuff of legend.

But the fact remains that Sony was not the first Japanese company to import transistor technology, nor the first in Japan to produce the tiny devices. Those honors belong to Kobe Kogyo, a company now little remembered because it no longer exists. Sony went from strength to strength, bringing out one new transistorized product after another like rabbits from a hat. Kobe Kogyo, lacking visionary management, faltered and in effect went bankrupt. In 1968 the company was ignominiously folded into the corporate bosom of the telecom and computer equipment maker Fujitsu and never heard from again.

But at least one Kobe Kogyo alumnus was destined to play a major role in the history of the semiconductor industry. His real name was Sasaki Tadashi, but as they struggled vainly to keep up with him, his subordinates would give Sasaki a nickname. They called him "Doctor Rocket."

PART ONE

Calculators & Watches

I

Doctor Rocket
Goes to Disneyland

For a long time, the Japanese have been branded as imitators rather than creators. But I think it would be downright foolish to say that what Japanese industry has accomplished in the past forty years has been anything but creative . . .
—Morita Akio[1]

AMONG THE JAPANESE EXECUTIVES assembled in the Japan Airlines lounge at Los Angeles International Airport that smoggy morning in late 1968 was one who sat apart from his fellow travelers.

They were chatting eagerly amongst themselves, looking forward to going home, to rejoining their colleagues and families, to distributing their souvenirs—a bottle of duty-free Johnny Walker for the wife's father, a carton of Lucky Strikes for the office, a pair of Mickey Mouse ears for little Taro.

He alone sat silent, disconsolate, as if in shock.

His name was Sasaki Tadashi and he had seen the future of electronics. Sasaki's vision was of portable products. The first would be a calculator small enough to hold in your hand, yet cheap enough for anyone to afford. But for his dream to come true, he needed a new type of chip, one that would cut the umbilical cord that tethered electrical appliances to the wall socket. The sort of thing Sasaki had in mind would run on batteries only.

Back home in Japan, he had begged domestic chip makers to take on the challenge, but they turned him down. So Sasaki flew to America to try his luck there. He toured the country, pleading with semiconductor manufacturers on the East Coast, down in Texas, and over in what people would soon start calling Silicon Valley.[2] But to no avail: Wherever Sasaki went he was told, "We're too busy making chips for the Air Force, we don't have any spare capacity for you."

Until finally, on his way back home to Japan, Sasaki had driven down from L.A. to Anaheim, home of Disneyland and also, more prosaically, of Autonetics, electronics arm of the giant aerospace conglomerate North American Rockwell. Knowing this was his last chance, Sasaki stated his case with all the eloquence he could muster.

The order the feisty Japanese dangled in front of the Americans was huge. It would be worth tens of millions of dollars. But there was a catch: Though volume would be high, profit margins would be low. For a moment, Sasaki thought he detected a glimmer of interest in the eyes of the tall executive, Fred Eyestone, who headed Autonetics. But he was mistaken—once again the answer was a polite, "Sorry, we'd like to help you, but we're fully booked."

So here he was, at the end of the road, having failed in his quest, returning to Japan empty handed. Then, just as the flight was almost ready to board, a voice came crackling over the public address system: "Would Dr. Sasaki please come to the information desk?" There he found a message that a helicopter was waiting to fly him back to Autonetics. At the fifty-ninth minute of the eleventh hour, Sasaki's luck had changed.[3]

This last-minute change of fortune was merely the latest in a series of unforeseen twists and turns in an already remarkable career. Sasaki Tadashi was born in 1915 in Hamada, a small fishing port on Japan's western coast. Nearby was the home of Lafcadio Hearn, the nineteenth-century author whose romantic writings gave many Westerners their first glimpse of Japan. Sasaki grew up in Taiwan, then a Japanese colony, where his father, a former samurai from the garrison at Hamada castle, was a teacher.

Young Sasaki was expected to follow in his old man's footsteps. And it seemed he would. Sasaki studied electrical engineering at Kyoto University, one of Japan's top schools, where in recognition of his talent his professor had promised him a job. But the Pacific War intervened to upset this plan. Sasaki joined the Ministry of Communications, where he was assigned to an aircraft maker called Kawanishi. The outfit was based in the western Japanese port of Kobe. There Sasaki did research on vacuum tubes for use in telephones, wireless, and radar.

After the war ended Kawanishi, a minor-league *zaibatsu*, was broken up by the Occupation. Its vacuum tube manufacturing division was spun off to form a new company called Kobe Kogyo. Following the extensive bomb damage to most Japanese cities, it was an Allied priority to repair the nation's shattered telephone system, "bringing Japan's communications up to a standard which will meet the requirements of the Occupation forces and at the same time permit restoration of service sufficient to meet the reasonable needs of the Japanese people."[4]

A problem in achieving this goal was the very low quality of the domestically made vacuum tubes used in Japanese repeaters (amplifiers inserted at intervals along telephone lines to boost the signals). In fact, they could hardly handle long-distance calls. In 1947, at the expense of the Occupation's Civilian Communications Section, Sasaki was sent to the United States, where he studied modern methods of tube production at Western Electric's ultramodern factory in Allentown, Pennsylvania.

To make full use of what he learned, Sasaki also had to catch up with the latest in tube theory. When he didn't understand something, Sasaki was permitted to engage in discussions with one of the scientists at Western Electric's research arm, the Bell Telephone Laboratories in nearby Murray Hill. The scientist was a theorist named John Bardeen. Along with two colleagues, Walter Brattain and William Shockley, Bardeen was at this time developing a more reliable amplifier for use in repeaters and, more importantly, telephone exchanges. It was to be a solid-state substitute for the vacuum tube.

Shortly before Christmas 1947, just as he was about to return to Japan, Sasaki had a meeting with Bardeen. Normally the most mild-mannered, soft-spoken of men, Bardeen seemed uncharacteristically excited. He told his Japanese visitor that he and his coworkers had discovered a most interesting new phenomenon but he was not at liberty to say what it was. Months later, back in Japan, Sasaki would realize that what Bardeen had been talking about was none other than the first transistor, which he and his colleague Brattain had just made.[5]

For the first few years following the transistor's invention, the technology remained inaccessible because of Western Electric's patents. To an industrial researcher like Sasaki, semiconductors were thus of academic interest only. When Bell Labs decided to throw open the transistor patents to all comers in September 1951, by a happy chance Sasaki was once again in the U.S. His purpose on this occasion was to conclude a technical assistance agreement between Kobe Kogyo and RCA on subminiature receiving tubes, state-of-the-art, cigarette-filter-size components that were much in demand for the helmet radios then being used by tank crews in the Korean War.[6]

Sasaki and a colleague, Arizumi Tetsuya, heard about the transistor symposium Bell Labs had just held for its licensees. Eager to know what was going on, the pair hopped on a Pennsylvania Railroad train, which took them from Harrison, New Jersey, where the RCA facility was located, three stops up the line to Summit, the station for Murray Hill. At Bell Labs, they made a beeline for Bardeen, who obligingly told his Japanese visitors all about the transistor. He warned them that, because of their high cost, transistors might only be useful in special applications; they might not be competitive against the low-cost vacuum tube in mass markets. As a parting gift Bardeen gave the Japanese some single-crystal germanium to get them started. Arizumi was all fired up. As soon as they got back to Japan, he went straight to work together with some of his colleagues, including the young Esaki Leona. (Esaki worked at Kobe Kogyo for the first eight years of his career until a dispute with the management caused his departure for Sony, where, soon after, he discovered electron tunneling, for which he won the Nobel Prize.)

In early 1953, Kobe Kogyo became the first company in Japan to succeed in making a transistor—ahead of Sony and other, much larger Japanese firms. When Kobe Kogyo was ready to begin mass production, the company signed a licensing agreement with RCA. (The U.S. firm was able to offer transistor knowhow cut price by virtue of a cross-licensing deal with Western Electric.)

Kobe Kogyo's management evidently believed that they had acquired an exclusive license with RCA—in which case, it must have come as a nasty shock when RCA also issued transistor licenses to Hitachi (May 1953) and Toshiba (August 1953). Nonetheless, Kobe Kogyo was still able to beat its giant rivals to market. The company's first transistorized product was a car radio it supplied to Toyota, which in 1955 was just beginning to produce passenger cars in earnest.

At this point, Kobe Kogyo seemed poised for the kind of growth that would propel Japan's other pioneering transistor maker, Tokyo Tsushin Kogyo (subsequently known as Sony) into the ranks of the world's leading companies. But it was not to be. For Kobe Kogyo suffered from a fatal flaw—bad management.

The company president, Takao Shigezo, was a clever man, no one disputed that. Had not Emperor Hirohito himself given Takao a gold watch for excellent results at Kyoto University? But early success had made Takao arrogant. He believed that when his company needed money to invest in new technology, the banks would come running; he did not have to go to them. The result of this attitude was that, despite the excellence of its research department, Kobe Kogyo was perpetually short of cash.

Another problem was that, unlike Sony, which had no existing investment to protect, Kobe Kogyo was a manufacturer of vacuum tubes. Transistors threatened to cannibalize that business. And whereas Sony president Ibuka Masaru led his troops from the front, himself becoming an enthusiastic champion of transistor technology, Takao was a mechanical engineer. Despite all Sasaki's efforts to persuade him, he never became fully convinced of the transistor's potential.

Kobe Kogyo's initial success with Toyota soon attracted competition from Japan's largest consumer electronics firm, Matsushita. Sasaki claimed that since Matsushita held shares in Toyota, the car company felt obliged to accept the giant Osaka firm as a radio supplier. Matsushita soon brought its strength as a low-cost manufacturer to bear, elbowing little Kobe Kogyo out of the way. The experience was a salutary one for Sasaki: "Matsushita doesn't spend money on unimportant things," he commented, "whereas by comparison, Kobe Kogyo engineers indulged in technology. They didn't realize what was unnecessary."

Kobe Kogyo's financial condition slid from bad to worse, until finally in summer 1960 the banks stepped in. It was decided that the company would be merged with Fujitsu, a telecommunications equipment supplier that could make good use of Kobe Kogyo's semiconductor expertise.

What was Sasaki to do? There was no question of his joining Fujitsu, because he had been a director at Kobe Kogyo; that would always have counted against him. To acknowledge his share of the responsibility for Kobe Kogyo's woeful state, he resigned from the company's board. But he stayed on during the merger negotiations to look after his subordinates, and to weigh his options. By far the best of these was an invitation to return to Kyoto University to take up a professorship when the Japanese academic year began in April 1964.

Then, just as the groves of academe beckoned, fate intervened once again, sending Sasaki's career ricocheting off in a completely different direction. December 1963 found him flying back to Japan from yet another trip to the United States. The limited range of the propellor-engined aircraft used to make Pacific crossings in those days necessitated refueling stopovers at halfway houses like Hawaii and Wake Island. Disembarking at Honolulu, Sasaki encountered a familiar face.

This was the secretary of Saeki Akira, senior executive director of a consumer electrical appliance maker called Hayakawa Electric Industry. His boss was also stopping over in Hawaii, the secretary informed Sasaki: Would the *sensei* care to join Saeki-San for a meal? The two men already knew each other well. Kobe Kogyo supplied Hayakawa with components such as transistors for radios, picture tubes for televisions, and—most recently—tubes called magnetrons for use in microwave ovens.

Cooking magnetrons were a spinoff from radar, which is where Sasaki first came across them. During his wartime research he had worked on airborne radars for detecting Allied submarines. During the 1950s, Sasaki consulted for the military on a project to build a chain of early-warning radar installations around Japan to guard the archipelago against a Russian attack. The idea then was to transfer magnetron manufacturing technology to Kobe Kogyo so that if something went wrong with one of the radars—magnetron tubes were forever burning out—the installation would not have to wait for several days for a replacement part to be flown in from America. Once again Sasaki was sent to the U.S., this time to Litton Electronics, a leading defense contractor headquartered in Redwood City, California.

Around 1960, Litton came up with a redesigned magnetron intended for use in microwave ovens. This was a low-end component which

Kobe Kogyo would manufacture for export to the United States. But Litton remained first and foremost a military contractor, and never managed to produce an oven that was suitable for use in the average household. Compared to the technological challenges and fat margins of Pentagon procurement, the fierce competition and slim pickings of the consumer market made it an unattractive target for the U.S. firm.

Japanese companies, by contrast, were prohibited by Japan's war-renouncing constitution from the manufacture of military hardware. Microwave ovens, Sasaki figured, would be an ideal product for Japanese companies to make. The first firm he approached with the idea was Hayakawa, whose headquarters were located nearby Kobe's, in Osaka. Sasaki put together a demonstration unit. Over the next few months, he spent a lot of time explaining microwave cooking to Hayakawa executives, including Saeki.

Sasaki's arguments proved persuasive. In 1961 Hayakawa became the first Japanese company to develop a microwave oven. The following year, the firm put the cooker into mass production. This initial (restaurant-use) microwave oven enjoyed modest commercial success. But Saeki knew that Hayakawa would need to do better if the company was to avoid being dragged under by the harsh recession that was afflicting the electronics industry during the early 1960s. Aware that Sasaki's days at Kobe Kogyo were numbered, Saeki was also mindful of the key role the latter had played in the commercialization of the microwave oven. Over a meal on the terrace of his hotel at Waikiki Beach, Saeki invited Sasaki to join Hayakawa as head of the company's newly formed industrial equipment division. After due deliberation, Sasaki accepted.

It was an exceptionally brave decision. When he moved to Hayakawa's unassuming Osaka headquarters in April 1964, Sasaki was just one year short of his fiftieth birthday. He could have elected to take up his professorship at Kyoto University, a position of considerable status that would have assured him of a comfortable life until retirement.

Instead, he chose to jump from the frying pan into the fire—from a bankrupt firm to one that was in bad financial shape. So bad, in fact, a rumor was going round that Hayakawa was about to be acquired by Hitachi.

Why did he do it?

Sasaki couldn't resist the challenge. "Everybody wants to join an elite company," he said, "because they want to have it easy. But I'd rather try and rebuild a company that has collapsed." As for academe— Sasaki would soon have become bored with life in the ivory tower. His tremendous energy required a larger outlet. Very much a creature of the real world, Sasaki relished the wheeling and dealing of business.

Sasaki, according to those who know him, is a human dynamo. "He was a man who could be at this precise moment in twenty different places at once," said David Rubinfien, an American engineer who first met Sasaki in Japan during the latter's magnetron days at Kobe Kogyo. "He was just a marvelous person to be with," Rubinfien recalled, "exuberant, enthusiastic, wanted to do everything, wanted to conquer everywhere."

Takashi "Mits" Mitsutomi, a Hawaiian-born Japanese American who has known Sasaki for thirty years, said, "He has tremendous drive, and he's extremely interested in getting new technology applied in new product areas. . . . Dr. Sasaki loves to talk, he loves to give ideas, he loves to encourage people to get into new areas—he's a tremendous man."[7]

Relentless, too. No sooner would Mitsutomi pick Sasaki up at Los Angeles airport than "he would read the newspaper on the economic situation, and we'd be talking nothing but business, and never is there a relaxed moment with him."

Not even when appearances suggested otherwise. Fred Kahn, another U.S. engineer who knew Sasaki, recalled how during an investors' meeting in Silicon Valley, a jet-lagged Sasaki "fell asleep during the presentation—then he awoke and asked a germane question."

At Hayakawa Electric, his new company, Sasaki's unflagging energy soon won him a nickname from his subordinates. Unable to keep up with his cracking pace, they called him "Doctor Rocket." "Once he takes off, he's unstoppable," said Wada Tomio, a researcher who worked under Sasaki at Hayakawa for many years. "Everybody wonders where he's gone—he's a very active person, always zooming about all over the world, gathering information from here and there."[8]

As a manager, Wada recalled, Sasaki was authoritarian, chastising his people if they failed to perform up to expectations. Wary of his bark, subordinates would approach Sasaki with caution. On the other hand,

Sasaki Tadashi (Courtesy of Sharp)

as Wada remembered with evident affection, Sasaki would always protect them if they got into trouble: "In that sense, he was a real boss."

The firm that Sasaki had joined was founded in 1912 by a remarkable entrepreneur called Hayakawa Tokuji. Hayakawa was born in
central Tokyo on 3 November 1892. His life would have provided excellent source material for Horatio Alger and Samuel Smiles, both of
whom were still alive in 1892. Like Alger's (fictional) heroes,
Hayakawa led an exemplary existence, "struggling valiantly against
poverty and adversity to gain wealth and honor." Like Smiles's (actual)
subjects, he was an engineer. Indeed, so dramatic was Hayakawa's life
that it was actually turned into a stage play during his lifetime.[9]

Hayakawa Tokuji was the fifth son of a poor family of artisans. His mother, a seamstress, died when he was an infant, and Hayakawa was adopted by foster parents. Two years later, his foster mother also died, his foster father remarried, the family had more children, and money became tight. Hayakawa was treated very harshly, underfed and set to work—pasting together matchboxes—after only one year of elementary school.

When he was nine, Hayakawa was apprenticed to a metalworking shop. Aged 19, he made, and patented, his first invention—a belt buckle that required no fastening holes, using instead a row of metal teeth to grip the leather. The inspiration was apparently Hayakawa's irritation with a character in a movie who wore an ill-fitting belt. It was a remarkably prescient concept for a time when most Japanese men still wore kimono in preference to pants. Nonetheless, orders for the buckle came pouring in. On the proceeds, Hayakawa was able to set up his own metalworking shop.

His next important invention came in 1915. This was a mechanical pencil, dubbed in English, for export purposes, the Every-Ready Sharp Pencil. To this day, mechanical pencils (which are commonplace in Japan, unlike in the West, where they tend to be used only by specialists like draughtsmen) are invariably known, to the bemusement of nonnative students of Japanese, by the generic name *shya-pu penshiru*.

Initially, however, the newfangled writing instrument was not popular among conservative Japanese stationers. Then came a large export order from a Yokohama trading company. Once foreign approbation had been conferred on the product, domestic demand took off, an early instance of the peculiar "was invented here" (therefore can't be any good) phenomenon that is still characteristic of Japan today.

The company expanded on the strength of sales of mechanical pencils. By 1923, eleven years after he began in business, Hayakawa was the proprietor of a thriving concern that employed more than 200 people. Then on September 1 that year, disaster struck. The Great Kanto Earthquake and the subsequent fire killed 100,000 people, among whom were Hayakawa's wife and two infant sons. The catastrophe also flattened much of the city, including his factory, which was burned to the ground.

Nor were losing family and premises the end of Hayakawa's woes. He was left with debts to an Osaka stationery firm. The solution was humiliating: He and three of his former workers moved across to Osaka where they had to sign on as employees of the stationers, teaching them how to make Sharp pencils. Hayakawa was also forced to hand over all patent rights to his invention.

Undaunted, Hayakawa soon set up a new workshop in Osaka. He remained on the lookout for promising new products. Inspiration came from a local watch shop, in which he discovered a crystal radio set newly imported from the U.S. This was in 1924, the year before radio broadcasts were scheduled to begin in Japan. One mark of a true entrepreneur is a refusal to be put off by lack of knowledge. Despite an almost complete ignorance of the principles of radio—or of electricity for that matter—Hayakawa decided to make radio sets. In February 1925, he and his workers succeeded in building their first crystal set.

Since radio broadcasts did not begin in Osaka until June of that year, the pioneers had to make their own test transmissions, using a manual Morse code key as the signal source. A photograph survives of Hayakawa testing the crystal set. He is shown in profile, sitting at a laboratory bench covered in electrical equipment. In attendance opposite him stands a youthful acolyte. With his left hand, Hayakawa taps out a message on the Morse key. Poised between thumb and index finger of his right hand is a cat's whisker, the wire used to pick up the incoming signal from the crystal. He is using the whisker to monitor his own transmission. On his face is an expression as serene as that of a Zen monk captured in mid-*satori*.

Radio manufacturing was a good choice of business to enter. All it took was a design, some parts, and the workers to assemble them. Hayakawa Electrical Industries would be the first Japanese company to make radios, which they sold under the name Sharp, the old brand from mechanical pencil days. The sets were a huge hit with novelty-loving Japanese consumers. Monthly production quickly passed the 10,000 mark. Radios would remain the firm's mainstay for almost thirty years.

Then came television, a new technology which Hayakawa would again be quick to exploit. In 1951, the company was the first in Japan to develop a prototype (black-and-white) set; in 1952, first to license the basic TV patents from RCA; and in January 1953, first to get commercial production underway, one month before actual TV broadcasts

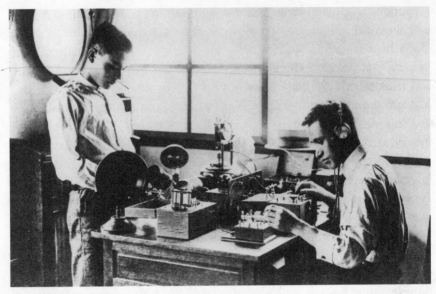

Hayakawa Tokuji receives his own signals on a crystal radio set. (© February 1925 Sharp)

began. By 1955, Hayakawa was the leading Japanese manufacturer of televisions, with nearly a quarter of the domestic market.

But despite this ability to innovate, Hayakawa Electric suffered from two chronic weaknesses, which allowed larger rivals to catch up and overtake. One was that the company remained primarily an assembler. Shortage of capital restricted its ability to invest in the facilities needed to produce key components like picture tubes. This left Hayakawa dependent for supplies on bigger, better-heeled rivals.

The other weakness was marketing. In Japan until very recently, most electrical appliances were sold through small "mom and pop"–style local stores. Many of these are exclusive outlets for a single brand. By 1960, Hayakawa's retail distribution network was just one seventh the size of that of Matsushita, its giant Osaka rival.

By 1960 Hayakawa himself was almost 70 years old. He was taking less interest in the day-to-day running of the company and more in philanthropic activities. These included a factory dedicated to training disabled people, especially those who had lost their sight, which he had established during World War II. The other, his pride and joy, was a nursery school he set up in 1954 to provide day care for children with working or disabled parents.

On his grand tour of Japan in 1960, RCA chairman David Sarnoff made a point of visiting this school. An RCA staffer recorded how "our old friend Hayakawa" met Sarnoff and party at Osaka station and brought them to his home for lunch. Then Hayakawa took the visitors to the kindergarten, "where 125 boys and girls, to whom we brought individual presents, were frolicking. All of us enjoyed this experience perhaps more than anything else in Japan, and Hayakawa-San was just beaming. He then showed us a small part of his plant where he employs blind people. It was refreshing as always to talk with him. He doesn't follow the subtle conventions of his country, is direct and open."[10]

There is a certain pathos in this meeting between the two great entrepreneurs, born just a year apart. Sarnoff was then at the height of his fame. Who could have guessed then that RCA, the company that had invented television, would decline after Sarnoff stepped down as chairman, and would eventually be sold and broken up? And who could have predicted that this second-tier Osaka assembler of television sets, whose continued existence when the two men met was by no means assured, would during the same period go from strength to strength? Not only that, but in large part by exploiting technologies invented at David Sarnoff's beloved RCA Laboratories?

But then "the secretive, autocratic Sarnoff had never been able to build a strong management team."[11] In 1965 he handed over the reins of the corporation to his son, Bobby. The younger Sarnoff, whose background was in network television, felt uncomfortable with technology. He promptly spent millions on modernizing RCA's image, changing the company logo—much to his father's displeasure. Before his ultimate, ignominious dismissal, Bobby spent many millions more on diversifying into unrelated businesses such as rental cars, rug manufacturing, and chicken farming.

Hayakawa, by contrast, was happy to delegate authority. He chose an able successor in Saeki Akira, a dynamic individual who was also a superb administrator. By the early 1960s Saeki had taken over day-to-day management of the firm. And it was Saeki in turn who brought Sasaki on board to provide technological vision.

The problem confronting Hayakawa Electric when Sasaki joined has long been the bugbear of consumer electronics: namely, the cyclical boom–bust nature of the industry. Most consumer electronics products are purchased during the Christmas–New Year holiday period. This means that even full-time assembly workers often work less than six months a year. Then, when a recession like that of the early 1960s hits, consumers don't buy, cash runs low, and, to cut costs, the company is forced to lay off workers.

But if you keep having to lop off branches, Sasaki argued, a tree will never grow. He had come up with a very different solution to the problem of seasonal variation. The industry was accustomed to adding bells and whistles to existing products in order to encourage consumers to replace their obsolete old models with new ones. Sasaki felt that it was better to try and develop entirely new products that people don't already own.

He had first put this philosophy into practice not in Japan, but in the United States. One of Kobe Kogyo's picture tube customers was a Los Angeles–based television assembler called Packard Bell.[12] This firm had entered Chapter 11 owing the Japanese firm a lot of money for parts already shipped. Sasaki went to L.A. as a representative of Kobe Kogyo to see what he could salvage.

"Ordinarily," he said, "in order to get your money back, you would seize some assets as collateral." To do so, of course, would be to deprive the ailing firm of its productive capacity. "But I thought, we shouldn't destroy them, we should keep them going. And that's what we did, and it proved to be very effective because they were able to pay us."

Sasaki began his rescue operation by pondering the problem of seasonal variation. "You can't sell TVs in the spring," he explained, "you have to sell them in the runup to Christmas. The reason is that during springtime and summer people don't spend much time indoors watching TV, they go out picnicking or vacationing. When it's cold, that's when things sell well.

"So I thought of things you could sell that could be used outside, but that don't require a lot of investment to make. And one of the things I suggested was a wireless remote-controlled garage door opener. It was easy to produce, and it became a big hit product."

When he joined Hayakawa, Sasaki recalled his experience with Packard Bell. He asked himself what sort of product would make a good locomotive to pull the ailing firm out of the recession? His conclusion: an electronic calculator.

This in itself was not an original idea. In the early 1960s, electronic calculators were a set of new technologies waiting for someone to assemble them, just as the transistor radio had been ten years earlier. It was a matter not so much of who would get there first, but of who would pursue the technologies to their logical conclusion. And this is where Sasaki's vision of portable products–and his determination to realize that vision–were to prove crucial.

The fuse that ignited what would later come to be known as the Calculator Wars was a compact desktop machine called the Amita Mark 8. This was introduced in 1962 by an obscure English company called Sumlock Computometer. The Amita was based on miniature tubes of the type that Kobe Kogyo manufactured. Which is why Sasaki, as a director of Kobe Kogyo, was well aware of calculators.

Conventional office calculators, like ones that the Kashio brothers had recently formed a company to manufacture, were based on electromechanical switches called relays. The Casio Computer Company was founded on 1 June 1957. The new firm's president, Tadao, the eldest of four brothers, came from origins every bit as humble as those of Hayakawa. Kashio (born 1917) was a near contemporary of Sasaki. His family were dirt-poor rice farmers. Tadao began his career at age 13, as a shop boy at a company that recycled oil cans. Though physically frail, Tadao had tremendous drive, and his brother Toshio turned out to be a talented inventor.

Their first product, the Casio 14–A, employed 342 relays. The 14–A's relays were housed in a cabinet on which the typewriter-size key-entry terminal sat. The calculator was 40 centimeters deep, 70 centimeters high, and 1 meter wide; weighed 125 kilograms; and cost ¥480,000 ($1,333).

When performing calculations, the relays made a loud "ka-ching, ka-ching, ka-ching" noise, rather like the cascading signboards that announce arrivals and departures at airports. Desire for quieter calculators was one of the stimuli that prompted Canon, which would ultimately become the third-largest Japanese calculator maker after Sharp and Casio. (Canon was a big user of calculators for designing camera lenses.)

Trading companies like Nissho Iwai and Itochu were importing the Amita for sale in Japan. The British machine's success with Japanese customers left would-be local manufacturers in no doubt that if you could make calculators, you could sell them. At the same time, the Amita's miniature tubes suffered from reliability problems. Like telephone exchanges in the 1940s, they were crying out for replacement with a more dependable switch—such as the transistor. But the companies that had transistor knowhow were not office equipment makers like Casio, they were consumer electronics firms like Hayakawa and Sony.[13]

In the early 1960s, an enthusiastic Sony engineer named Uemura Sanryo designed a prototype transistorized calculator. The company proudly displayed the machine at the 1964 New York World's Fair. Three years later Sony marketed a desktop calculator under the name SOBAX, a derivative of "solid-state abacus." But for once, Sony's visionary founder Ibuka Masaru seems to have had a blind spot. "Our products are for the consumer," he grumbled, "an electronic calculator just won't sell."[14]

Later on, as dozens of Japanese companies leapt into calculator production and a brutal price war ensued, Sony cofounder Morita Akio made the decision to pull out of the market. It was one he would later come to regret, criticizing himself for "lack of technical foresight." "[H]ad we stayed with calculators," he wrote, "we might have developed early expertise in digital technology, for use in later personal computers."[15]

In the early 1960s, Japanese companies across the industrial spectrum were looking for new opportunities to grow. Canon, for example, wanted to diversify out of the saturated camera market. Hayakawa, after a decade of continuous growth, was beginning to lose market share in televisions and radios. To both firms, the office equipment market—then exhibiting growth rates of 25 to 30 percent annually—looked extremely attractive. Canon would shoot for copiers and calculators. Hayakawa opted, among other things, to develop computers.[16]

But in its wisdom Japan's Ministry of International Trade & Industry had decided that in order to foster a strong domestic computer industry, competition in computers should be restricted to just six big firms—Fujitsu, Hitachi, Mitsubishi, NEC, Oki and Toshiba. All six were based in Tokyo, which made lobbying the government much easier. Lowly,

Osaka-based Hayakawa was cut off from government R&D subsidies, and shut out of a market that in large part still consisted of government procurement.

As an alternative to computers, Hayakawa chose a lesser, but still challenging target: calculators. Three young researchers were dispatched to Osaka University to learn about them from a professor who was deemed to be something of an expert on the subject by having translated a book about digital logic. They formed the nucleus of the team that Sasaki would lead.

Hayakawa launched its first calculator, the Sharp Compet CS-10A, on 30 June 1964, four months before the Tokyo Olympics, the event that celebrated Japan's coming of age as a global economic power. The Compet is described in Sharp's corporate literature as "the world's first all-transistor-diode calculator," presumably to differentiate it from Sony's all-transistor SOBAX, which preceded it by a few months. But Sony's machine was only a prototype, whereas Hayakawa's was put straight into mass production. Since 1984, the Compet has been on permanent display at the Science Museum in London. No calculators are displayed at the Science Museum in Tokyo.[17]

A desktop model resembling a cash register, the Compet weighed 25 kilograms and cost ¥535,000 ($1,486), about the same price as a contemporary Japanese family car. To the modern eye the Compet is a clumsy-looking machine, mounting more than 100 keys on its front panel. (Six months later, on its first calculator, Canon would introduce the familiar phone-type ten-key pad, which quickly became the industry standard.) But to makers of relay-based calculators like Kashio Tadao, the Compet's compact size and superior performance came as a nasty shock. Kashio described his reaction on seeing the new machine: "It felt like cold water had been thrown in my face."[18]

Bigger shocks were in store. Transistor-driven calculators soon became established—in 1965, one year after the machines hit the marketplace, Japanese manufacturers sold a respectable 4,355 units. To expand the market and improve reliability, the logical next step was to switch from discrete semiconductor components to the new integrated circuits.

Better known as "microchips," these were fingernail-size squares of silicon on which many transistors could be laid down and connected up. The Compet contained 2,830 individual transistors and diodes. By 1968, a calculator like the Canon 161S used only 160 discretes: Its 120 chips did the rest. But the 161S was still a desktop model, and it still cost over $1,000.

The next step in the calculator's evolution was not logical. It was, rather, the product of vision. Around 1965, two men as far apart geographically (and as similar in their strategic thinking) as Sarnoff and Hayakawa had independently come up with the idea of the calculator as something much bigger than a specialized office tool. One was Sasaki. The other was Patrick Haggerty, chairman of Texas Instruments, the company that made the first silicon transistors and that in 1958 invented the integrated circuit.

Haggerty's fundamental conviction was that microelectronics would become—to use his favorite word—pervasive, would eventually permeate every aspect of life. By the mid-1960s, however, the microchip was still largely confined to military applications, in particular, to aerospace, where its small size and light weight made the chip ideal for the likes of missile guidance systems. Such applications were, Haggerty felt, peanuts compared to the microchip's potential. He was forever trying to think up new ways in which integrated circuits could be used.

Often ideas came to him on airplane trips. The idea of a calculator small enough to fit into the palm of your hand occurred to him on one such trip in the fall of 1965. As it happened, sitting next to him was one of his brightest engineers, Jack Kilby, who during his first month at TI had invented the microchip. Before the plane landed, Haggerty had enlisted Kilby to build the device.

Haggerty's goal in developing the handheld calculator was not as a product, but as a demonstration to aid sales of TI's integrated circuits. Ten years previously, the same trick had succeeded brilliantly with the transistor. Haggerty had been determined to get into transistors despite the fact that, as he himself put it, "not one single hour of effort had gone into research and development on semiconductor devices at TI, nor was there anyone on the payroll, not anyone, who had any previous experience or background in the field." It was an attitude not unlike that of Hayakawa to radios.

Haggerty kept pestering Western Electric for a license to transistor technology. To show that he meant business he took night courses in physics. The Bell people doubted whether TI was up to the challenge, but eventually Haggerty's persistence paid off. When transistor licenses were first offered in September 1951, TI mailed Western Electric a check for $25,000 the next day.

Having mastered the intricacies of transistor production, it was clear to Haggerty that "a dramatic accomplishment by Texas Instruments in the field of semiconductors was needed to awaken potential users to the fact that the devices were usable now." To this end, he initiated a full-speed-ahead R&D program to build a pocket transistor radio.

When this was successful, Haggerty had his marketing director, Buddy Harris, contact "every major radio manufacturer in the United States by phone, telegram or letter," much as Sasaki would later importune every major chipmaker to get them to make what he wanted. And with similar—i.e., negative—result: "Their attitude was wait-and-see," Harris recalled.

Eventually, Haggerty and Harris found a small company that was prepared to manufacture transistor radios for them. The resultant product was a huge success. Texas Instruments sold millions of transistors to radio assemblers. And the little receivers drew the attention of Thomas Watson, Jr., whose company, IBM, would become one of TI's biggest customers.

Despite this triumph, Haggerty later regretted that TI had not managed to go one step further. Pricing the radios a little higher would have given the Texans extra cash to develop other consumer products themselves. Instead of being just a components supplier, Haggerty speculated in a 1980 speech, "I think the likelihood is very high that we would have been the Sony of consumer electronics."

Texas Instruments could conceivably also have been the Sharp of consumer electronics. In 1967, Kilby and his team delivered what Haggerty had ordered—the world's first handheld calculator. It was a magnificent technical accomplishment. They had boiled down a lab bench full of equipment into just four chips that fit into a box the size of a paperback book. Then, as Jerry Merryman, one of Kilby's collaborators on the project recalled, things started to go wrong:

"What they did was they assembled a marketing task force to try and evaluate the market for the thing. And since it was new, a revolutionary thing, they missed the major portion of the market. They went along the conventional line—the world has so many hand-crank adding machines, we'll get 12 percent of that market, so many motor-driven calculators, we'll get 25 percent of that market, etcetera, etcetera. And they far underscoped the market, because the thing created a market that couldn't have been visualized. Y'know, there's one in the kitchen cabinet that the housewife has—nobody foresaw that."

Nobody, that is, except Sasaki Tadashi. It would be 1970 before Kilby and Merryman's design saw the light of day, in the form of a commercial product called the Pocketronic. And even then the design would be manufactured by Canon, not TI. Not until 1971 would Texas Instruments enter the calculator market in its own right. By that time Japanese rivals like Sharp (as Hayakawa become known in 1970) and Casio were firmly entrenched. And, despite TI's best efforts to displace them, there they remain to this day.

When Sasaki arrived in Osaka in April 1964, he reported to Saeki for his first assignment. The executive director was blunt: He said, "Please increase sales and profit by one third as soon as possible!"

How to realize this daunting instruction? According to Sasaki, he spent his first three months at the company thinking through the implications of the microelectronic age.

In particular, Sasaki pondered the ability of tiny pieces of silicon to accommodate more and more transistors. In California that year, Gordon Moore, chief of engineering at Fairchild Semiconductor, was thinking along the same lines. He came up with his famous formulation, Moore's Law, which in its original form stated that the number of transistors on a chip would double each year.[19] The implication of this ever-increasing capacity was that any electronic product, no matter how complex, could be made portable. "The aim for the future was to have something small enough to carry around on you," Sasaki explained, "that was our priority."

Sasaki gathered his engineers together and told them what their target was. They had been trying to shrink the calculator so that it would fit on an office desktop. But Sasaki was way ahead of them. He told them the goal was to build a much smaller machine, one that could readily be used, not by a clerk, but by a greengrocer—or even a housewife.

The young researchers stared at him in disbelief. Had Sasaki taken leave of his senses? Using the technology they knew, his proposal was totally unrealistic. And even if they could make a portable calculator, who would buy such a thing?

Sharp's engineers were not the only ones who found a mass market for calculators hard to imagine. When some years later Casio's president Kashio Tadao asked his salesmen whether they thought ordinary consumers would purchase calculators, he discovered that "most people seemed to believe that we could not expect any sales in the United States, and more than half of them said that [they] probably wouldn't succeed in the [Japanese] market either."[20]

Sasaki, on the other hand, was confident that if the price was right, there would be a huge domestic market for portable calculators. After all, he reasoned, was there not already in every Japanese home, in every Japanese shop, on every Japanese desk, a manual calculator, otherwise known as an abacus? But abacus is a special skill. To become fluent in flicking the tiny beads up and down on their rods requires years of training, witness the special abacus schools which still flourish to this day in most Japanese neighborhoods (because Japanese parents believe that abacus helps develop manual dexterity and mental agility). What Sasaki was proposing was an electronic abacus that needed no special skills to operate. Now all he needed was the parts to make it.

To succeed as a developer of new products takes many things. First you have to have vision, then you need a supportive management to fund development, in addition to which you require clever people to carry out the development work. But you must also have good timing, otherwise all will come to naught. Sasaki's timing could hardly have been better. To build the kind of portable calculators he had in mind would take new technology. And as Sasaki knew, in the United States, a series of breakthroughs had recently occurred which would make that new technology feasible.

The world's first calculator to use integrated circuits was the CS-31A, introduced by Hayakawa Electric in 1966. In addition to over 2,000 discrete components, this machine featured 28 chips made by Mitsubishi Electric, each containing the equivalent of a few dozen transistors. These chips were bipolar integrated circuits, so called because they were made up of bipolar transistors.

Bipolar devices operate using current of two polarities: negatively charged electrons and positively charged holes. Your basic bipolar transistor consists of three layers of semiconductor material—a very thin filling of positively (or negatively) doped material sandwiched between two much thicker negatively (or positively) doped slices. Two types of current, three layers of material—you might think that this sounds like a complex sort of arrangement, and you would be absolutely right.

An alternative, much simpler, type of transistor had also been conceived back in the very earliest days of the semiconductor era. It had been the brainchild of the brilliant Bell Labs scientist Bill Shockley, the same man who had also invented the bipolar transistor. Since the alternative type operates using only one kind of current, Shockley might well have called it a unipolar transistor. Instead, the device takes its name from the phenomenon by which it works—the field effect—hence, field effect transistor, or FET.

An electrical field—that is, a voltage—applied to an insulated metal gate placed on top of the device opens a channel in the underlying silicon through which electrons can flow, thus switching the device from off to on or vice versa. The most common type of FET is a MOSFET (the initials standing for "metal oxide semiconductor," the three materials originally used in its construction).

Shockley came up with the idea for the field effect transistor as early as 1945. Fifteen years later, researchers at Bell Labs finally managed to make Shockley's idea work. But for all the FET's simplicity, in practice it proved impossible to build reliable devices. Thus, for the first twenty years of the semiconductor era, it was the inelegant but manufacturable bipolar transistor which held sway. Following the more or less simultaneous invention of the integrated circuit by TI's Jack Kilby and Fairchild's Bob Noyce at the end of the '50s, however, it was inevitable that sooner or later researchers would come to reconsider the balky FET.

The reason was that, in addition to being difficult to make, bipolar transistors also consumed far more power than FETs. As the level of integration on a single chip grew beyond a few dozen devices, it became more and more difficult to get rid of the byproduct of that power—the heat the circuits dissipated. Computer people came up with elaborate cooling schemes. They used air, then water, ultimately resorting in ultrafast machines (like Cray supercomputers) to liquefied inert gas. Consumer electronics companies constrained by size and cost could not afford to consider such exotic remedies.

MOS transistors were attractive because their simpler construction and mode of operation meant that they consumed far less power. They could in theory be pushed to far higher levels of integration—tens of thousand of transistors, hundreds of thousands, who knew? Maybe even millions.[21] But try as they might, researchers could not seem to produce MOS transistors that would function reliably. It drove them nuts.

In bipolar transistors, electrons and holes flow smoothly deep within the semiconductor crystal. In FETs, by contrast, all the action takes place on the surface of the device. Even the slightest impurity on that surface would cause the transistor's channel to open, sending the blasted thing drifting about all over the place. You'd start out with a device that came on at five volts, then you'd operate it a little, and the threshhold—the point at which it switched—would drift to 15 volts, making it totally useless.

In August 1962, a talented but painfully shy young physicist called Frank Wanlass came down to California from his native Utah to look for a job. He found one at the R&D division of Fairchild Semiconductor. It was, Wanlass recalled, "a marvelous place to go to work for a scientist type—they had all this fancy latest equipment and so on, and they had a policy then that new Ph.D.s could work on any project they wanted, till they could either fail or do something good with it."

As it happened, there was a project Wanlass wanted to work on. In his last year at the University of Utah, he had read about some work on thin-film transistors at RCA.[22] This intrigued him greatly, because the approach opened the way to laying down hundreds of transistors on a single substrate. The RCA researchers had been working with exotic compound materials like cadmium sulfide, which were very unstable. Would it not be possible, Wanlass wondered, to use a more reliable material like silicon instead? He told Gordon Moore, the man who had hired him, that he wanted to follow up on the RCA work. Moore gave Wanless his blessing.

Using end pieces left over from Fairchild's home-grown silicon ingots, Wanless proceeded to fabricate some MOS transistors. Much to his disappointment, these turned out to be every bit as unstable as RCA's thin-film devices. What could be the problem? Wanlass reasoned that rather than the silicon, which was nice and pure, maybe it was the aluminum gates that were to blame—the metal electrodes, that is, which sit on top of the channel controlling whether the transistor is on or off. To test his hypothesis, he decided to substitute other metals for aluminum as the electrode material.

Luck was with him. In the basement was one of Fairchild's fancy toys—a brand-new electron beam evaporation machine. You loaded your metal into a little carbon crucible, then zapped it with an electron beam. The crucible would turn white hot, and puff! the metal would evaporate off.

The first substitute Wanlass tried was platinum, one of the most stable metals known. The trouble was, having deposited a layer of the metal on the wafer, it proved impossible to get the damn stuff off again using the conventional chemicals that the semiconductor industry used for etching. Wanlass was forced to employ a sharp tungsten point to hand carve a transistor, scratching the gate and other portions of the device into the platinum under a microscope. The effort was worth it, however. When he tested the little dingus, it was stable as a rock, didn't drift at all. Encouraged by this result, Wanlass decided to run a complete scan of metals through the electron beam evaporator. He would start with aluminum and systematically work his way through the periodic table. So he made a device using aluminum and, by golly, "it was quite stable," Wanlass recalled with a chuckle, "it was as good as platinum!"

This unexpected result set Wanlass thinking about what was different about the aluminum that came out of the evaporator and the stuff that the semiconductor industry normally used. As luck would have it, in graduate school he had done research on contaminated materials. "You'd put a fingerprint on a perfectly clean crystal, get salt on there—that is, sodium—and that would totally ruin the electrical characteristics." Now, as he was driving along the road one day, Wanlass had a Eureka moment: "My gosh," he realized, "it's probably sodium that's getting into the devices in the normal way you evaporate aluminum!"

The normal way in those days was to take some tungsten wire, hang little pieces of aluminum on it, then run a current though the wire to heat it. The aluminum melts onto the wire, then vaporizes. Wanlass discovered that tungsten wire was made by drawing it through a die that was lubricated with sodium. Moreover, that sodium was the biggest single impurity in aluminum to begin with—"so what we had was a double whammy." But in the extremely high temperatures of the E-beam evaporator, all this cruddy stuff simply disappeared into thin air.

With this discovery, Wanlass had taken the first giant step towards the manufacture of reliable MOS devices. Support for his ideas came from Gordon Moore, who thought that "what I was working on had a great future, he really wanted me to push it hard." Moore got other people at Fairchild involved with sodium contamination, including a brilliant but hard-to-get-along-with young Hungarian called Andy Grove. By 1967, Grove and his colleagues would clear away all the remaining obstacles on the road to mass production of integrated circuits based on MOS field effect transistors.

But in 1964 Fairchild was doing very nicely thank you cranking out bipolar circuits. And while Moore was all for pushing MOS transistors through development, the prospect of commercializing anything still seemed a long way off. Wanlass wanted to see his ideas turned into practical products. Frustrated, he quit Fairchild in January 1964 to join a start-up company called General Microelectronics, lured away by the promise that he could pursue his ideas on MOS.

While at GMe, Wanlass made what he claimed were the first commercial MOS integrated circuits. The customer was NASA, which needed them for its satellites. These early chips contained maybe seven or eight transistors, no big deal. But Wanlass also designed and laid out a much larger chip, a basic digital storage circuit called a shift register. This mounted one hundred and twenty transistors, an awesome number for the time.

Wanlass showed off his pride and joy in a hotel suite at the 1964 Wescon conference in Los Angeles. He hooked the register up to an oscilloscope to show a test pattern looping through the device. "It just wowed people to see that much integration in one little package."

One of those wowed by Wanlass's demo was an exceptionally bright engineer called Bob Booher, who worked for Autonetics. Inspired, Booher went back to his company and designed a much bigger chip: "Under the microscope it looked like a battleship or something," laughed Wanlass. This huge MOS integrated circuit was the immediate precursor of the calculator chips that Autonetics would build for Sasaki. At first, however, Autonetics were not able to build MOS chips. They were forced to turn for assistance to General Instrument, where Wanlass was now working, having quit GMe after a year.

But as so often happens, just because a new technology had been developed did not mean that people were about to use it—not even the people who had originally developed it. As one former Fairchilder would bitterly recall: "Everybody knew that MOS was the wave of the future. It was obviously the technology for goddam calculators. Everybody could smell it. And yet we couldn't get anyone to work on it."[23]

Perhaps people were deterred by the fate that befell General Microelectronics. In 1964, the company won a contract to develop an MOS-based desktop calculator for Victor Comptometer, a specialist maker of hand-crank mechanical counters. The aim was to sell the machine to Victor for $2,000, but GMe couldn't get its costs down anywhere near that target. The company lost so much on the contract that it was unable to continue as an independent entity, and was sold to Philco-Ford.

MOS did not die along with GMe. By the late 1960s, a few other companies—notably General Instrument (where Wanlass went after leaving GMe), and custom-chip specialist AMI—were shipping MOS chips. But they were small beer: The rest of the industry was too busy to bother with this still largely unknown quantity.

In Japan, persuading people to produce MOS devices was, if anything, even more difficult. Sasaki had managed to wheedle some development cash out of MITI by telling the bureaucrats that handheld calculators would be a big export item for Japan. Hayakawa would use half the money to do the design and assembly. The other half was earmarked to pay for the manufacture of large-scale MOS integrated circuits.

At the time, the three biggest Japanese chip makers were NEC, Hitachi, and Mitsubishi Electric. At NEC and Hitachi, Sasaki couldn't get past the door: The answer was a straight, No. At Mitsubishi, management grumbled that they'd just started to make money from chips containing about 100 elements. Now, here was Sasaki asking them to leapfrog to a new generation of technology, "large-scale integration,"

LSI he called it, which meant thousands of elements on a chip—and to a new process technology (MOS) to boot.

(Levels of integration, at least according to one definition are as follows: small-scale integration, from 20 to 100 elements; medium-scale integration, from 200 to 500 elements; large-scale integration, 1,000-plus elements. After LSI comes V for very-large-scale integration, which means tens of thousands of elements.)

Sasaki persisted with his pitch. "You better watch out," he lectured the Mitsubishi executives, "when you're making money, you don't want to try something new. But when you're making money is the time when you *have* to do something new. That is the essence of good management."

Ultimately, he contacted an old friend at Mitsubishi Electric who was the general manager of one of the company's semiconductor plants. Stimulated by Sasaki's proposal, he agreed to take on the job. But the president of Mitsubishi Electric had his doubts. He consulted a professor who was a well-known authority on semiconductors about the wisdom of manufacturing MOS LSI chips. The sage opined that attempting to use such an untried technology was foolhardy and bound to fail, with the result that Mitsubishi would inevitably lose lots of money. And because the word of academics carries a lot of weight in Japan, the president pulled the plug on the project. Sasaki's friend was very apologetic, but there was nothing he could do about it.

Rebuffed at home, Sasaki flew to the U.S. to try his luck there. The obvious first stop on his itinerary was Fairchild, the company that had solved the MOS sodium contamination problem. There he saw Bob Noyce, the coinventor of the integrated circuit, who turned him down flat. It was the same story at other Silicon Valley firms like the newly formed National Semiconductor. And at East Coast outfits like General Instrument, Philco, RCA, and Westinghouse.

In all, Sasaki visited ten firms before he arrived at Autonetics. In every case, the answer was that making MOS LSIs was very difficult, the yields far too low. Plus everyone was too busy making chips for the military. And whereas the Air Force paid top dollar, the profit margins that Sasaki had in mind were very small.

Military meant mostly missiles, especially the Minuteman, America's first intercontinental ballistic missile. Which in turn made Autonetics, Sasaki's last stop, a very long shot indeed. For among U.S. chip makers, Autonetics, as prime contractor to the Minuteman program, had the strongest military ties of all.

In which case, why had Autonetics been on Sasaki's list at all? Charlie Kovac speculated that Sasaki "might have been impressed by the fact that we were the source for the largest volume of technical papers that were written for the various shows [i.e., conferences] ... Y'know, you have to keep the scientists happy, so you go out there, let them have the travel expenses and the hotel room to attend the show at a nice location, let them mouth off, because you certainly didn't have the opportunity to do that with the government. And because [the Japanese] are such prolific readers, I think this probably helped them see the impact of what we had going on here."

Autonetics—the name is an amalgam of "automatic" and "cybernetics"—was formed in 1955 as an offshoot of North American Aviation. During World War II, North American had built more aircraft for the military than any other company. They included the P–51 Mustang fighter and the B–25 Mitchell bombers flown by Jimmy Doolittle and his men in their surprise raid on Tokyo on 18 April 1942.

Since the end of the war NAA had built Chuck Yeager's X-15 rocket plane. In 1961, the company's space division won the contract to design and build the command module for the Apollo Lunar Landing program, while its Rocketdyne division made the engines for the program's Saturn rockets. In 1967, the year before Sasaki's visit, North American Aviation merged with an automotive parts manufacturer called Rockwell-Standard to become a conglomerate, North American Rockwell. In 1973, the company changed the name to its current form, Rockwell International.

Autonetics handled advanced technology projects such as the navigation systems of aircraft, submarines, and missiles. Such was its success—or at any rate, such was the Pentagon's largesse—that, by 1964, at the height of its work on the Minuteman program, Autonetics was North American's largest division, employing some 36,000 people.

Minuteman I, developed in the late 1950s, had been one of the first missile systems to use transistors. Semiconductors held several attractions for the military. First, they were small and lightweight, which was important in an era when the limited thrust of U.S. rockets restricted the load they could lift. The rule of thumb in a missile was that one extra pound of payload cost $100,000 worth of extra fuel.[24] Second, transistors were intrinsically more reliable than tubes. In 1960, "with generous funding from the Air Force, Autonetics established a program to improve the reliability of electronic components 'by a factor of 100,' awarding contracts of around $1 million to $2 million to at least thirteen electronics companies."[25]

The program was a resounding success.[26] Nonetheless, as the complexity of navigational guidance systems mounted, so the component count climbed, as did the likelihood that sooner or later one of those components would fail, with potentially devastating consequences. Thus to overcome "the tyranny of numbers," that is, to reduce the number of parts and increase the average time before one of those parts failed, in 1962 the designers of the second-generation Minuteman II decided to switch to chips. "With that decision, which led to $24 million in electronics contracts over the next three years, the integrated circuit took off."[27]

Once again, as prime contractor for the Minuteman guidance program, Autonetics had to show the rest of the industry the way. In effect, the Southern Californians were paid by the Air Force to teach existing semiconductor producers the most advanced technology. "Autonetics was really the source of technology for many of the U.S. companies, including TI and Motorola," said Charlie Kovac, the division's ebullient former marketing vice president. "It was not itself in the semiconductor business. We basically had a pilot line in our facility that allowed us to demonstrate that of which we spoke."

Significantly, however, the division had recently won approval from North American's management to build a manufacturing facility, although this was not in place when Sasaki arrived. On the plus side, what Autonetics did have as a result of its Minuteman work was a set of the most sophisticated chip design tools in the world. The rest of the industry was still designing chips the hard way, by laying huge sheets of plastic down on the floor, cutting and peeling the circuit patterns using razors and tweezers, then photographing the results. Meanwhile Autonetics was doing chip design the modern way, on computers.

But for all their technological excellence, there were areas of experience in which Autonetics was, to put it mildly, not well versed. Like consumer electronics, for instance: "At the time none of us knew what commercial meant," said Kovac, "or how to spell it, or the implications thereto . . . we were country bumpkins in the commercial marketplace."

So what was it, on that fateful day in 1968, that caused Fred Eyestone, Autonetics's president, to have second thoughts, and send the helicopter to bring Sasaki back for further talks?

Something the Japanese said had evidently stuck in Eyestone's mind. Perhaps Sasaki's crash course in the logic of consumer microelectronics did the trick. The essence of the consumer business was that mass production reduces costs dramatically, a basic rule of thumb that would soon become known as the experience (or learning) curve.

In the early days, went the theory, you don't make any profit. As time goes by, however, the more chips you make, the more experience you gain. This enables you to improve your yield. By the end of the cycle, high yields bring large profits, which more than make up for your initial losses.

This view of the world was news to Autonetics. In their business, the biggest production run was a couple of hundred avionics systems, each of which might consume all of ten chips.

They made an odd couple, Eyestone and Sasaki, as they met on the helipad on the roof of the Autonetics building after the latter's 30-minute flight from Los Angeles Airport. Eyestone was a taller-than-average American, Sasaki a shorter-than-average Japanese; the former had to stoop low to shake hands with the latter. The disparity in height reflected the huge difference in the size of their respective companies. In 1968, North American Rockwell would have revenues of around $2.5 billion, while Hayakawa would earn approximately $500 million.

And yet for all the differences between Eyestone and Sasaki, Kovac recalled (revealing his background as an electrical engineer) that "the impedance matching between them was just outstanding." The American was soft-spoken, sincere, and extremely polite—this last a big plus for the etiquette-conscious Japanese. By all accounts he was also, to use the old-fashioned term, a gentleman. In fact, his subordinates used to

wonder how such a decent man as Eyestone had made it to the top of
the greasy pole as president of Autonetics.

On the basis of their meeting, Sasaki awarded Autonetics a feasibility
study to see how far the Americans could boil down a calculator's electronics. By early 1969, the U.S. firm's designers were confident that
they could manage to cram everything needed for a four-function,
floating decimal point, 8-digit calculator into just four chips. Compared
with the 28 bipolar integrated circuits that powered Hayakawa's previous generation of calculators, this was a spectacular advance. Each
chip would mount almost 2,000 transistors, an enormous number in
those days. Autonetics sent samples of the chips to Japan.

In March 1969, Sasaki returned to Anaheim bringing with him
Saeki. This time, the Japanese were given the royal treatment. They
were shown around the facilities at Autonetics. At that time these included the command module of the Apollo II spacecraft which, some
four months later, would supervise the first lunar landing. Saeki had his
photograph taken with his hands on the module's controls, looking for
all the world like a kid in a candy store.[28]

The upshot of this visit was that Hayakawa awarded Autonetics a
$30 million contract, an order which the Autonetics in-house newslet-
ter described, accurately, as the "largest in history for advanced
MOS/LSI circuits." Now all the Americans had to do was produce
them.

This turned out to be more difficult than anticipated. "From April of
'69 through September of '69, we had zero yield in our factory—I mean,
zee-roh," Kovac recalled. Autonetics's marketing guru found himself
living in the factory that first year, spending all his time salving the
wounds caused by missed delivery dates.

Such production problems were unknown to Saeki in March 1969
when he unveiled, at an industry show in a New York hotel, the first
calculator to be equipped with MOS LSIs. Known as the Microcompet
QT–8D, the desktop calculator weighed just 1.4 kilograms and would
sell for $277. Autonetics fielded staff to provide technical support at the
show.

The rest of the industry was not convinced. Representatives from
Fairchild, the company that had made many of the key breakthroughs
on MOS devices, were particularly scathing: "Those aerospacers

Saeki Akira at the controls of the lunar mondule. (Courtesy of Sharp)

couldn't find their rear ends with both hands," Kovac recalled one Fairchilder commenting, "so why would you begin to believe them?"

A defiant Saeki fielded a barrage of inquiries about the new machine from the floor. Heretics who did not believe his claims were sent up to the hotel suite where the Autonetics staff waited. Onto the walls they had tacked the layouts for the devices showing how you could pack all those functions into just four chips (plus a clock generator). Hotshots from Silicon Valley would stop by the suite and leave shaking their heads, muttering "No way could you produce those."

But in September 1969 Autonetics proved the skeptics wrong, shipping its first batch of 25,000 good chips. By the following April, the division had demonstrated to Rockwell's management the ability to be profitable. The following year, the company's Japanese partner celebrated the production of its one millionth calculator, every one of them mounting Rockwell chips.

Success in making chips gave Rockwell the confidence to branch out and make calculators under its own name, as well as other brands such as Sears. "We made good money from 1970 to 1976," Charlie Kovac said. By then, the calculator market was more or less saturated, prices dived, and the business lost its attractiveness. In 1977, as part of a corporate restructuring, the company decided to exit the consumer electronics business.

But Rockwell continues to manufacture chips, and its relationship with Sharp remains strong to this day. For example, all Sharp faxes mount Rockwell modem chips. The friendship between Sasaki and Kovac endures. Fred Eyestone, Sasaki's greatest friend at Rockwell, was "retired" from the company in 1974. He subsequently moved north to Silicon Valley to join the equipment maker Varian. In 1979 Fred Eyestone died of cancer. For years afterwards, whenever he was in the Bay Area, Sasaki would visit Eyestone's grave, on which, as a token of his lasting gratitude, he would place Sharp's latest calculator.

Back in Japan, the Autonetics contract had landed Sasaki in hot water. When word got out that Hayakawa was buying chips from the United States, other Japanese calculator makers rushed to follow suit, applying to MITI for allocations of foreign currency. The Americans were quick to seize the opportunity. One Casio executive recalled that, as he emerged from customs and immigration at San Francisco Airport, there would be sales representatives from half a dozen chip makers waiting for him in the lobby. American chip makers in general did well out of the calculator boom—none more so than Texas Instruments, which moved from licensing designs and selling chips to Canon, to manufacturing calculators in its own right.

The company that had been the first to build a pocket calculator came bouncing back to dominate the U.S. market. "TI is the first major non-Japanese company . . . that understands and uses the learning curve," the firm's then president, Fred Bucy, would proudly tell his shareholders.[29]

Until Rockwell came along, Japanese semiconductor manufacturers had been the main suppliers of (bipolar) chips to the calculator makers. Upset at the prospect of their business disappearing overseas, they formed a deputation to complain to MITI. Japanese makers had been doing R&D and were confident they could make LSIs, too. So why was the ministry allowing calculator makers to use up precious foreign currency importing chips from the United States? It was unfair. The group's leader was a Hitachi general manager, the same one, ironically, who had turned Sasaki down flat when the latter was seeking a local supplier for MOS chips. He accused Sasaki of being a traitor to his country.

The result, Sasaki claimed, was that he had to go back to Rockwell to tell them that since LSIs could now be produced domestically in Japan, and since foreign currency was scarce, there would be no further orders for the U.S. firm.

Among Japanese domestic chip suppliers in 1970, Hitachi, Mitsubishi, and NEC were the most advanced. Lagging a long way behind came Toshiba. But Toshiba was keen to get into the calculator business. The company sent two of its engineers to ask Sasaki's advice. They met in the lobby of Tokyo's New Otani Hotel. Sasaki recommended that Toshiba concentrate on making chips using a new, extremely low-power process technology called complementary-MOS, or C-MOS (pronounced "see-moss") for short.

(The junior engineer was Kawanishi Tsuyoshi, who went on to become head of Toshiba's semiconductor division. Almost twenty years later, Kawanishi would again ask for advice from a Sharp executive, Tsuji Haruo, the company's president. Were liquid crystal displays a business worth getting into? Kawanishi wanted to know. In an answer worthy of Sasaki, Tsuji told him, Yes, but only if Toshiba was prepared to invest massively, over the long term. Once again, Toshiba took Sharp's advice and once again, the company has been successful in the endeavor.)

Sasaki knew that frugal C-MOS chips would enable the severing of the umbilical cord that still tied calculators to the wall socket. Powered only by a couple of flashlight-type batteries, C-MOS driven calculators would be truly portable. At Sasaki's urging, Toshiba focused all its energies on developing C-MOS technology. In the early days, manufacturing the chips was very tough, Toshiba's Kawanishi Tsuyoshi recalled, "because Sharp was always push, push, push, and the actual yield was very low."

But it was worth the effort. Early exposure gave Toshiba a head start in what would become the core technology for the entire semiconductor industry. And when around 1985 computer chips switched to C-MOS, Toshiba would become the leading manufacturer of the first generation of such circuits—the one megabit memory.

While pushing suppliers to produce what he wanted, Sasaki continued to think ahead. A profound change was taking place in the nature of the consumer electronics industry. In the past, it had been enough to buy components from outside suppliers and solder them together. In the future, however, as the scale of integration increased, the chip would itself become the system. And woe betide any company that did not have the capability to design and manufacture its own systems. Thus, Sasaki argued, if Hayakawa was to stay competitive, then the company had better learn how to make its own chips.

This realization coincided with a generational change in the company's top management. On 15 September 1970, after fifty-eight years as head of the firm he had founded, Hayakawa Tokuji stepped up to become chairman, and Saeki took over as president. To mark the transition, the company changed its name from from Hayakawa Electric to Sharp.

Saeki soon had the chance to demonstrate the nature of his leadership. Nineteen seventy was also the year of an international Expo in Osaka, Sharp's hometown. Bobby Sarnoff would no doubt have seen this event as an ideal opportunity to launch the new corporate logo. Instead, Saeki canceled Sharp's participation in the Osaka Expo, choosing rather to channel funds—at Sasaki's urging—into the construction of a semiconductor factory, in the hills of nearby Nara, in ancient times a Japanese capital city. Investment totaled ¥7.5 billion ($21 million), a massive sum in relation to the size of the firm, equal to about a quarter of its equity. It was a move worthy of Hayakawa Tokuji's entrepreneurial spirit, a real bet-the-company decision.

The engineer who led the chip manufacturing group at Sharp, Inoue Hiroshi, noted that in Japan from 1965 to 1970, "there was a raging debate, 'Make or buy'—whether it was better to make your own ICs or buy them [from outside suppliers]. Sharp chose to make; Casio [which had a very close relationship with chip maker NEC] to buy."

For Casio, the choice appears to have been a happy one. For Canon, which placed a distant third in the calculator race, dependence on outside suppliers for key components proved disastrous. "On some of the machines we sold," former Canon deputy chairman Yamaji Keizo recalled ruefully, "the LEDs had broken connections, so the displays couldn't be used and for the calculator business, that was fatal, I think.

It was because we didn't make any of the components that we had so many problems."

But despite this underlying logic, the building of Sharp's semiconductor factory, which was to be so crucial in the company's future success, was not at first a popular move within the company. The managers of other divisions couldn't understand the need to invest all that money. They complained bitterly that Sasaki was spending all the hard-earned profits they had made.

For its first five years, the factory bled red ink, losing between ¥400 and ¥600 million ($1 to $2 million) annually. Rather than transfer technology from Rockwell, as the agreement between the two companies allowed, Sharp elected to go its own way. For its next generation of calculators, the company needed C-MOS technology, a much more difficult process to manufacture. During this initial period, yields were low, and on occasion there was not enough demand to keep the factory fully occupied. Staff sometimes worked only half days, spending the rest of the time cutting the grass and doing other odd jobs.

Red ink gave his enemies at Sharp a stick to beat Sasaki with. Their attacks angered him, until at one point he considered resigning. Saeki, who had always backed him up, came to the rescue, encouraging everyone to look on the bright side. But the hemorrhaging continued, and finally Sasaki was forced to look for someone to buy the semiconductor factory. Motorola was keen, and Sasaki showed executives from the U.S. round the plant. Then, just as they were about to sign the purchase contract, the chip business turned profitable. Much to Sasaki's annoyance, the same directors who had been saying "Pull out," now insisted that the factory was too valuable an asset to sell.

When an evolutionary niche opens up, for example, when an erupting volcano creates a new island, incoming flora and fauna battle over the virgin territory in a struggle for domination. In much the same way, when a new market niche emerges, all sorts of companies rush in to try and take advantage of it.

During the early 1970s, a fierce war was waged over the calculator market. Nearly sixty firms slugged it out. It was a war in which almost all the best-known names in the electronics industry participated. When the smoke cleared, only a handful of firms would remain—Sharp and Casio among the Japanese; Texas Instruments and (at the high end of the market) Hewlett-Packard among the Americans. By 1980, annual production of calculators topped 120 million units, with the Japanese accounting for just under half the total. By 1993, a quarter of a century after the introduction of Sharp's first microchip-powered product, some 1.5 billion calculators had been produced. Today, you can buy one in a supermarket for about the same price as a tube of toothpaste.

When competition becomes that intense, new technologies get implemented fast. Innovation is key, because it gives firms the ability to differentiate themselves, enabling them to reduce price, or to add new functions, or both. Only the fittest survive.

When the struggle peaked during the early 1970s, calculators sucked in a whole slew of new technologies. All of these would later have much broader applications, especially in personal computers. The most famous example is the microprocessor, developed in 1971 by Intel for a Japanese startup called Nihon Keisanki ("Japan Calculator") better known by its brand name, Busicom. Like so many startups, Busicom was unable to convince banks to lend the fledgling firm enough money to get through a recession, in this case that of 1973–74, and it went belly up.[30]

But of all the calculator makers, Sharp was the most aggressive innovator. As we have seen, the company was first to introduce MOS LSI chips, and the first to shift to low-power C-MOS. In addition, Sharp pioneered a highly efficient technique for the automation of mass production. This delivers chips to the point of assembly encapsulated on a reel of tape, like the film on a movie projector.

As we shall see in chapters 3 and 4, Sharp was also a leader in display technologies. The company conjured vacuum fluorescent displays into being, then introduced some of the industry's first liquid crystal displays, whose extremely low power consumption matched that of C-MOS chips. In the quest for the ultimate in low power, Sharp was also one of the first to incorporate solar cells in calculators, thus eliminating the need for batteries altogether.

In just over a decade, from 1964 to 1976, the company cut the number of parts needed to make a calculator from three thousand to just three—a chip, a display, and a solar cell. By the time Sasaki retired in

1985, Sharp had reduced the price of a calculator by a factor of 100, its weight by a factor of 2,000, and its power consumption by a factor of 10 million.

More importantly for the future, the formerly fragile assembler had turned itself into a technological powerhouse, with all the skills needed to produce a continuous stream of innovative new products, such as the Wizard personal organizer and the ViewCam video camcorder.

Much of the credit for these achievements must go to Sasaki. "The like of Sasaki-San is seldom found among Japanese R&D managers," commented former Sony Research Center director Kikuchi Makoto, "Sharp owes Sasaki very much."

In late 1995, Dr. Rocket, over 80 years old, still maintained a punishing schedule, one that left men half his age shaking their heads in disbelief. His day typically began with an early morning breakfast meeting and continued until a late evening dinner. After retiring from Sharp, Sasaki remained active in the electronics industry. In particular, he served as booster and mentor to two of Japan's latest generation of entrepreneurs, ASCII's Kay Nishi and Softbank's Son Masayoshi.

But playing a background role was never Sasaki's style: He preferred to lead from the front. In 1995, he formed a new company, the International Center for Materials Research, a firm whose corporate structure featured many innovations. Asked why he kept up a such a hectic pace, he replied with a chuckle, "If a rocket stops, it falls—a rocket has got to keep going."

2

Blind Men Don't Fear Snakes

Technology has no intrinsic value—it takes on value only when manufacturers like us apply it to the products we make. No matter where technology comes from, from America or wherever, the most important thing is using it to make products.
—Nakamura Tsuneya, former president, Seiko Epson

ON DIAGONALLY OPPOSITE CORNERS of the main cross street of Ginza, Tokyo's posh downtown shopping district, on some of the most expensive real estate in the world, sit the flagships of two very different Japanese electronics companies.

The Sony Building, opened in 1966 to commemorate the brash upstart's twentieth anniversary, is an uncompromisingly modern edifice, a pocket skyscraper whose elongated front face at Christmastime becomes a giant electronic billboard. Its purpose is obvious—to be a showcase for Sony's latest products.

The message conveyed by the pile on the opposite corner is harder to construe. For one thing, although it is called the Wako Building, Wako is not the owner's name. The building was constructed in 1932, out of such strong stuff that it was one of the few in central Tokyo left standing after the devastating U.S. firebombing raids of March 1945. Today, to the casual observer, Wako appears to be simply an old-fashioned luxury department store.

Who owns this enigmatic edifice? The building's only distinctive feature, its clock tower, provides the clue. At noon the clock's chimes ring out, heralding the lunch hour. Turns out that Wako is owned by Seiko Corporation, Japan's leading maker of timepieces—and of some of the world's most advanced semiconductor chips. This combination of ultraconservatism and state-of-the-art technology may seem contradictory, but, in fact, the one leads to the other with a logic that is entirely scrutable.

It is impossible to say when the Japanese fascination with all things small and mechanical began. The earliest references to clocks in Japan's historical chronicles go back well over a thousand years. But the origins of the modern Japanese watch industry can be dated with precision. On 1 January 1873, Japan converted to the Western-style calendar and system of timekeeping.[1] The following year Hattori Kintaro, the 14-year-old son of a secondhand goods dealer, became apprenticed to a Tokyo clock and watch merchant. On reaching the age of 21, with entrepreneurial juices in full spate, young Hattori branched out on his own. He set up a shop—the primogenitor of Wako—to repair and sell imported timepieces.

In 1892, Hattori established a company to manufacture his own clocks and watches. He named it Seiko-sha—a happy choice, at least to Japanese ears. The name "Seiko" is compounded from two characters that mean "sophisticated manufacture," but written using different characters also happens to be the Japanese word for "success." (The name is now officially written using English letters or phonetic characters, making it impossible for anyone to tell the difference.)

Three years later an observer at the British Legion in Tokyo, a certain Mr. Gubbins, reported that in watchmaking, "so far as the Eastern market is concerned, no country can any longer compete with Japan." The Western market would come later. Exports of Japanese watches did not exceed imports until the 1920s; even then, the quality of Japanese manufactures remained well below that of the world's two other main watchmaking nations, Switzerland and the United States.

For hundreds of years, watch parts were made by hand, wrought by the kind of highly skilled craftsmen that Swiss watchmakers still boast about in their advertisements today. The United States became a power in watchmaking characteristically, through the introduction of new technology. In the mid-nineteenth century machine-made parts produced by American firms cut manufacturing costs and increased watch precision.

But until 1952, the watches themselves remained wholly mechanical. In that year, an American firm called Elgin produced a prototype electrical watch, in which a battery-powered motor replaced the traditional mainspring. Lacking commercially available batteries, that watch was never marketed. The first electrical watch to make it to the marketplace was introduced by the Hamilton Watch Company of Lancaster, Pennsylvania, in 1957. To generate its ticks and tocks, this watch still used a mechanical balance wheel. Then in 1960 a third U.S.–based firm, Bulova, introduced the Accutron, a watch that dispensed with the balance wheel altogether in favor of a tiny, electrically excited tuning fork.

(Bulova was, of course, Swiss in origin. But the Accutron was developed in the United States at the firm's headquarters in Jackson Heights, New York, by a Swiss, Max Hetzel, and an American, William Bennett, after the Swiss branch of the firm had turned up their noses at Hetzel's prototype electronic watches. The impetus behind the Accutron's development was an awareness that the U.S. Army needed a more precise time base. Thus it was entirely appropriate that the Accutron should have been announced, on 10 October 1960, by Bulova's new president, Omar Bradley, the general who had led the U.S. Army's Normandy landings in 1944.[2] By 1974, Bulova had sold over 4 million Accutrons, including one I bought in a watch shop near New York's Grand Central Station. The face of this watch face bears the legend "Railroad Approved," which–to me at least–seemed incontrovertible proof of its American origin.)

Driving this shift from the mechanical to the electrical was the watch industry's eternal pursuit of ever higher levels of precision. All watches operate on essentially the same principle. They all have an object that swings back and forth at regular intervals, a power source that drives the object, and a system for counting the swings. In a mechanical watch, the mainspring vibrates five times a second. In Bulova's Accutron, the tuning fork hummed away at 360 times a second. In practical terms, this translated into a watch that was accurate to within a minute a month, an order-of-magnitude higher precision than that of mechanical watches.

The announcement of Bulova's breakthrough took Nakamura Tsuneya, the engineer in charge of research and development at Seiko, completely by surprise. Clearly, as Japan's leading watch manufacturer, his company would have to respond with something similar. Then came a second shock. To protect its market, Bulova had erected a wall of patents around tuning fork technology. And the American firm had no intention of issuing licenses to its rivals.

But Nakamura was a tough competitor, and he kept his head. He knew that in technology it is a rare problem that has only a single solution. And though a considerable improvement, the Accutron was by no means the ultimate answer to the precision problem. It kept wonderful time humming away undisturbed on the lab bench. Strap an Accutron onto your wrist, however, and its precision soon fell victim to the jolts and buffets of the real world.

Wasn't there some other technology, Nakamura wondered, that would yield a more precise watch? To find an answer to this question, he formed a study group consisting of himself and nine young engineers, one of whom he assigned to search the technical literature.

It didn't take Seiko's man long to come up with a lead. In 1922 an RCA engineer named Walter Cady discovered that, when hooked up to a battery, quartz crystals would vibrate with amazing stability. Moreover—and this would be crucial to watchmaking—to sustain oscillation, the crystals required only minuscule amounts of energy. Armed with his stable crystals, Cady invented a frequency controller for the radio industry.

Five years later, Warren Marrison of the recently established Bell Telephone Laboratories applied Cady's quartz controller to drive a clock.[3] The primary purpose of this clock was to give the phone system an accurate standard of frequency. An improved version of Marrison's clock was subsequently employed to provide the telephone time-of-day service that subscribers could call to set their watches by. But perhaps the best known and certainly the most visible manifestation of quartz technology was the handsome display clock mounted in a window of AT&T's head office at 195 Broadway, New York City. This was sometimes called "the world's most accurate public clock."

The components needed to produce such accuracy occupied a cabinet the size of a wardrobe. The clock consumed about 10,000 watts of power—enough to run a dozen electric irons. More compact quartz chronometers were also built. In particular, Bell Labs made an instrument not much bigger than a milk crate that was taken by the U.S. submarine *Barracuda* on a gravity-measuring expedition in the West Indies.

But so long as vacuum tubes remained their basic component, it was hard to imagine quartz clocks finding applications beyond specialist areas such as astronomy, navigation, and the keeping of official standards. Certainly Marrison himself, in a paper he gave to the British Horological Institute in London in 1947, the year of the transistor's invention, saw no future possibilities for his invention beyond its continuing to be "a most useful instrument in all precision measurements of time."

Thirteen years later, quartz timepieces were still confined to scientific and official standards purposes. In Japan, Seiko had actually made one in 1958 for NHK, the national broadcaster, to regulate its hourly radio time signals. This clock was about the size of a small truck, and it ate electricity. In the interim, however, transistors had advanced in terms of price and reliability to the point where it was possible to contemplate their introduction into timepieces. Knowing this, Nakamura chose quartz as the most promising technology for watches of the future. On his initiative, Seiko began a project to develop a compact quartz clock.

Their timing was perfect: Tokyo was the venue for the 1964 Olympics, for which Seiko had been awarded timekeeping responsibilities—the first non-Swiss company to win the job. "There in front of our eyes was the prospect of the Olympics," Nakamura recalled, "so everybody got excited and said, Can't we make a portable quartz timepiece?"

The end product of this enthusiasm was a portable chronometer, the Model 951, developed in 1963. At the Tokyo Olympics the following year, the chronometer provided a dramatic demonstration of the advantages of quartz technology. It exhibited an accuracy that enabled world records to be measured for the first time in hundredths of a second.

Having succeeded in this initial goal, Seiko's engineers took another five years to reach their next milestone. This was the Astron, the world's first quartz watch, which went on sale in Japan in December 1969. Its tiny crystal oscillator beat at an astonishing 8,192 times a second, making it accurate to within one minute a year. The Astron was as much of an advance over the Accutron as the Accutron had been over mechanical watches.

But technical triumph though it undoubtedly was, the Astron was also what is known in engineering parlance as a kludge, that is, a poorly designed thing made of ill-fitting components. Its electronic heart, the part of the system that divided the crystal beats into hours, minutes, and seconds, was a hybrid integrated circuit; that is, it was not a single sliver of silicon but rather a piece of plastic onto which a hodgepodge consisting of 76 transistors, 29 capacitors, and 83 other components had somehow been wired together to form the oscillator and counter.

These intricate connections had to be painstakingly hand soldered by highly skilled craftsmen. In other words, though the underlying technology was completely different, the techniques of manufacture were much the same as those that had been employed for hundreds of years by the loupe-eyed master craftsmen of Geneva. The watch sold for ¥450,000 ($1,250), the price of a contemporary small car. Its motor was not terribly efficient. Only 200 Astrons were ever made. Seiko quickly withdrew the watch from the market.

At this point Nakamura made an important decision, one that illustrates the pragmatic nature of his thinking. During the 1960s, Seiko had entered quartz timepieces in the Neuchâtel Concours, an annual competition held in the heart of watchmaking country, at an observatory located in the Swiss Alps. The Japanese challengers did well in the Concours, eventually winning the top prize in 1969. Then their chief engineer decided to withdraw from participation in the competition.

Nakamura concluded that there was a contradiction between technical excellence and practical utility. "The timepieces that we entered in the Concours and the ones we actually commercialized were completely different," he explained. The Concours was conducted under ideal conditions: "There was no vibration there, in addition to which, they didn't perform a long-term test over the whole year, just over 45 days." The entrants could use as much electricity as they liked, "but so long as they didn't stop before the 45 days was up, that was OK. If they stopped the next day, that was irrelevant to the Concours.

"So what I realized is that we would try hard to make a timepiece that was good for the Concours, even though it would never go into actual use. But I always thought that technology should not be for its own sake; rather, we should apply it to make things for people. That is, unless we used this technology in the products that we made, it was meaningless. So we stopped participating in the Concours and channeled all the energy that we had put into the competition into research on useful themes.

"At that time, the most important thing was low-power consumption integrated circuits. If it had only been for 45 days, we wouldn't have needed such technology. But with watches, unless the battery lasts for a year or two, then it's no good. And because we had been making watches for a long time, we knew that."

The commercial failure of the Astron did nothing to diminish the attraction of quartz watches. To cut costs, Seiko's engineers would obviously have to replace hybrid technology with integrated circuitry that could be mass produced. Equally obviously, that circuitry would have to draw as little power as possible.

As he had done a decade earlier when seeking an alternative to tuning forks, Nakamura assigned a young engineer on his staff, Harigaya Hiroshi, to comb the technical literature for information, this time, on low-power integrated circuits. Harigaya came up with some intriguing papers on a new technology called "complementary metal oxide silicon," C-MOS for short. The papers said that with C-MOS, you should in principle be able to make integrated circuits whose power consumption would be very low. But as far as Harigaya could tell from his reading, there was as yet no such thing as an actual C-MOS chip.

Years later, Harigaya recalled that one of the papers was written by someone at RCA. The most likely author was Gerald Herzog, the engineer who championed the development of C-MOS at the U.S. firm. As one of his former colleagues said, "Gerry brought all the resources together, and he had the faith."

A graduate of the University of Minnesota, Herzog joined the RCA Laboratories at Princeton, New Jersey, in 1951. That year the facility was renamed the David Sarnoff Research Center to honor the commitment to R&D of the corporation's visionary chairman. C-MOS was just one of many innovative technologies developed at this "invention factory" during its golden age, an era that lasted from the early '50s through 1965, when the elder Sarnoff handed over the reins of RCA to his son, Bobby.

At this time, according to historian Margaret Graham, the Sarnoff Center was "one of the largest and most respected corporate research organizations in the United States," able to attract the pick of the nation's scientific and engineering crop.[4] The center, as described by former Sarnoff researcher George Heilmeier, "was a place of enormous intellectual stimulation, a place where some of the world's best scientists were found, a place that had a great deal of excitement associated with it." In the field of electronics, only Bell Laboratories had a better reputation, but Bell Labs lacked the focus on products that drove the Sarnoff Center. And products, as far as RCA was concerned, meant mostly television.

Herzog joined RCA just as Western Electric threw open its transistor patents to other companies. His initial assignment was to assist in the design and construction of the first transistorized television. In addition to the components from which it was built, this midget prototype—its screen was only five inches across—was also revolutionary in another respect. The TV incorporated a new concept in circuitry called complementary symmetry, in which two transistors of opposite (hence complementary) polarity, negative and positive, were harnessed together.

George Ziglei, the engineer who invented complementary symmetry, originally wanted to call it "inantiamorphic," which means "related like the left hand to the right hand." But Herzog and other colleagues managed to dissuade him. "We said, 'George, nobody'll ever be able to remember that, much less pronounce it.' So we came up with the name complementary symmetry, and that's how it got started."

The original idea behind complementarity had nothing to do with low power. Rather, the purpose had been to enhance the amplification of audio signals. Herzog and his colleagues implemented the first circuits using bipolar transistors. But this type of device was not well suited for television applications. The field effect transistor would be a much better match.

The reason was that the electrical characteristics of the FET were similar to those of vacuum tubes. "When the first discrete MOS devices were made, there was such joy in the TV operation," former RCA researcher Israel Kalish recalled. "They said, 'Hey, this thing operates like a vacuum tube, I can use my old vacuum tube schematics!' And they plugged it in, they were overjoyed with it, it was wonderful."

The first practical MOS transistor was fabricated by John Atalla at Bell Labs in 1960. RCA's researchers were quick to follow the phone company's lead. The trouble was that, as we saw in the previous chapter, until Frank Wanlass cracked the sodium contamination problem at Fairchild, it was impossible to make MOS transistors stable. You'd have the bare devices working perfectly on the lab bench, then somebody would breathe on them, and they'd go haywire.

The Sarnoff Center is a brick and steel frame complex located in a leafy suburb of Princeton, not far from from the ivory towers that once housed Albert Einstein and John von Neumann. The idea of putting the RCA labs in Princeton was to lure top scientific talent with the promise that life in industry would not be so different from life in academe. Part of the package in those faroff days was that corporate researchers at elite labs were allowed to take sabbaticals, just like their university counterparts.

In 1960, Herzog took off for Cambridge University on one such sabbatical. His mission was to learn about computers, in order to assist with RCA's ill-fated attempt to take on IBM. While in England, Herzog began thinking about using semiconductors for computer memory. In 1960, this was a radical idea. The microchip was less than two years old, and it would be another decade before Intel introduced today's computer industry workhorse, the dynamic random access memory.

Back then computer memory was typically constructed out of cores, tiny donuts made from a ceramic material called ferrite, strung on grids of fine wire. Unfortunately for Herzog, one of the coinventors of core memory happened to be a senior researcher at the Sarnoff Center. He, predictably, "couldn't see how a semiconductor memory could *ever* compete economically, because cores are nothing but mud with a hole in it. So, semiconductor memories? Forget it!"

But few people are more resourceful than an engineer in possession of a good idea. On his return to Princeton, itching to try out his hunch, Herzog managed to drum up some military funding. Fortuitously, the circuit technology with which he was most familiar, complementary symmetry, seemed to map nicely onto memory applications. The two opposite polarity transistors could be coupled together to form a flipflop (on–off switch), the basic digital memory circuit.

Complementary-symmetry MOS structures thus looked ideal for computer memory, Herzog reckoned, "if only we knew how to make them." Unfortunately, it was hard to make individual positive-type MOS transistors, harder still to make negative-type ones, and the idea of combining both types on the same chip seemed like pure folly.

Down the corridor at the Sarnoff Center, Paul Weimer had recently invented a device that for a while seemed like it might rival the MOSFET. One of RCA's most creative scientists, Weimer was aiming to build a "tubeless" television camera. He was making thin-film transistors by evaporating onto glass compound semiconductor materials like cadmium sulfide.[5] To be sure, "most of the early TFT devices were so unstable they made MOS transistors look like Bureau of Standards references by comparison."[6] Nonetheless, thin-film transistors had the great virtue of being easy to make in large, integrated arrays and could be made in negative as well as positive type. Herzog assigned a designer from his group to work with Weimer.

Thus the first complementary integrated circuits were actually thin-film transistors rather than FETs, and they were implemented in compound semiconductors, not silicon. As we saw in the previous chapter, Weimer's work inspired Wanlass at Fairchild. After solving the showstopper problem of sodium contamination, Wanlass went on to repay the favor. In the semiconductor business, everyone stands on everyone else's shoulders.

Sometime in late 1962, Wanlass had a brainstorm. He envisaged a digital logic circuit that would be made up of negative and positive type transistors on the same chip. That year Wanlass filed a basic patent on his idea. In the 1970s, several years after he left Fairchild, Wanlass went back to his old outfit and happened to bump into some people from the Silicon Valley firm's patent department. "Boy, you guys must really have made a lot of money on my C-MOS patent," he said. To which he claims they replied, "Nah, we're so big, we just use our patents for defensive purposes around here—we could never license them for anything." RCA's licensing people knew better.

In February 1963, at the International Solid State Circuits Conference, the semiconductor industry's premier bash, Wanlass gave a paper

Frank Wanlass, C-MOS pioneer, at Hakone Gardens, Saratoga.

outlining the complementary logic concept, in which he indicated the feasibility of producing such circuits.

This was of course exactly what Herzog and his people had in mind. Wanlass had beaten them to the patent office, and into print: "We were rather miffed," Herzog recalled, "because we really felt that we'd done more, but we just didn't bother taking the time to write a paper on it. On the other hand, I feel sorry for him, because he didn't get the support on the technology from Fairchild that he should have."

But unlike Wanlass, Herzog was able to take the initiative himself. Using corporate funds, he commissioned a group of engineers at RCA's Electronic Components semiconductor products group, a few miles up the highway from Princeton in Somerville, New Jersey, to take a crack at making actual C-MOS devices. "Initially very few people in the product group believed useful complementary devices could be built on a common substrate," Herzog said, "and almost all agreed that it wasn't worth the effort."

One engineer who thought it might be worth a try was Israel Kalish, a New Yorker whose thick beard and jovial manner belied a keen mind and a deft hand. Kalish led the group at Somerville. "When we went over there and said, What we want to do is C-MOS," Herzog recalled, "everybody went, Too complex—can't do it. But I said, 'If it can be done, we can do it.' "

Compared with positive or negative MOS, C-MOS required many more manufacturing steps. Doping silicon wafers with minute quantities of impurities to make chips behave in the desired fashion is an extremely complex process. Herzog explained: "To make a p [for positive]-MOS device, you start with an n [for negative] substrate, and you put down p-MOS islands, so you've got these piles of p on n. Well, if you want to make an n-type device over here, you have to have an island of p on which you put down n-MOS piles. Now, how are you going to have an island of p here and an island of n there? So you got a problem, and what you do is you make a well.

"You start with one type of material, let's say p-type, and then you push a lot of n-material in here, until you've got this sump of n-type material, and now you can put n-type piles on top of the p here, and you put p-type piles on top of this sump of material here, so now you've got two types of devices. Well, when you do that, when you drive one type of impurity through another, you do a lot of damage to the silicon, so that you tend not to get good characteristics in these devices.

"And that's only the simplest of the problems. I mean, you've got all the oxide contamination problems, and you've got all the hills going up and down because nothing is level anymore, and you drive this sump in and you etch back things . . . there are a lot of steps that go into it."

Later on, in the early 1970s, the introduction of ion implantation, a spinoff from the giant accelerators used in particle physics, would enable silicon to be doped with impurities of either polarity quickly and with pinpoint accuracy. This in turn would make it possible for any company to produce complementary circuits. But in those early days, researchers had to rely on brute force, using a long and extremely tedious process called diffusion. To make wells in the silicon, you had to put the wafers in a long glass tube, then you sealed the tube and baked them for at least twelve hours.

Not only did diffusion lack accuracy, heating for such a long time also allowed defects to enter the wafers. Achieving control under such circumstances required much ingenuity. By 1964, however, Kalish and his team had managed to produce the first working C-MOS devices. RCA's management remained unconvinced. Especially since C-MOS turned out not to be—for the moment, at any rate—a good technology for memory, the application Herzog had originally targeted.

RCA's C-MOS project would undoubtedly have been axed had Herzog not managed in 1965 to win more government funding. This time it was a three-year contract from the Air Force to build large-scale integrated circuits—"large-scale" in those days meant more than 100 elements on a chip—for airborne computers.

Two years later, Herzog made a presentation to the manager of the integrated circuit product line at Somerville, trying to convince him to bring out a range of C-MOS chips. "His response was typical of RCA management." Herzog recalled: "He said, Well, how big is the market? And I said, There *is* no market—we haven't done it yet! If there's no device, there's no market. And he said, Well, y'know, we don't need it."

To the rescue came further government contracts, this time from NASA. From the space agency's point of view, C-MOS had two great advantages. One was that it was "radiation-hard"; that is, C-MOS devices were much less sensitive than their bipolar equivalents to radiation bombardment from ambient sources in space such as the Van Allen belt or, God forbid, an exploding nuclear weapon. The other advantage was that C-MOS chips consume much less power—up to 100,000 times less power—than bipolar or other types of MOS circuitry.

The secret of the incredibly low-power consumption of C-MOS integrated circuits is that, unlike n- or p-type devices, they use no standby power. Current flows in C-MOS circuits only when they switch from on to off and vice versa. As a helpful analogy to explain this energy efficiency, Richard Turton suggests the funicular railway.[7] Used to transport people up and down steep hills, funiculars consist of two cars connected by a cable. As one car goes down, it helps to pull the other one up. Operating cars in pairs uses far less energy than operating them individually. In the same way, with C-MOS, as one transistor goes off, the other comes on.

Lower power consumption in turn meant that a satellite's on-board computer configured out of C-MOS chips could get by with smaller batteries and solar panels, a significant advantage at a time when most U.S. satellites were not much bigger than a basketball.

Herzog used the NASA contracts to demonstrate to RCA's marketing people that there was indeed demand for C-MOS. Eventually, his persistence paid off. By the end of 1967 the company began selling sample C-MOS devices. To extend the market beyond its niche with NASA and the space agency's contractors, Herzog hit the conference trail, extolling the virtues of C-MOS technology.

But the U.S. semiconductor industry was not interested in the virtues of C-MOS. So what if it was low power? It was also, as detractors were quick to point out, painfully slow, perhaps a thousand times slower than competing bipolar and MOS technologies. "Nobody in [Silicon] Valley really recognized C-MOS as a viable future product until the late '70s, early '80s," said Bernie Vonderschmitt, who took over as general manager of RCA's Solid-State Division in 1972, "and that's an astounding statement to make, given the fact that Silicon Valley is supposed to be where the action is."

To be fair, there were some who did recognize the merits of C-MOS, but were otherwise constrained. Herzog remembered talking in the early 1970s to Gordon Moore of Intel, which would subsequently be roundly criticized for not getting into C-MOS earlier. Moore told Herzog that he really wished that Intel could get into C-MOS, but that they had their hands full with conventional MOS memories, and couldn't afford to invest the necessary resources in developing the new process.

RCA was left to soldier on as the most visible champion of C-MOS. But the corporation was in no shape to fight the good fight. RCA launched its new range of C-MOS devices around 1970. The following year the company slunk out of the computer business, taking a write-off of close to half a billion dollars, one of the largest ever recorded. From then on, RCA management resolved to stick to their knitting–the consumer electronics business. And, as Vonderschmitt pointed out, "consumer electronics saw no need for digital electronics at all, and therefore really had no interest in C-MOS."

"RCA was a TV company," Kalish reflected, "and anything that stood in the way of TV would get screwed at some point. Within the solid-state division in those years, we had a lot of times where we were ahead of everybody, and it required the follow-through and the guts. If [RCA] had had the same guts in our area that they had in the TV area, we would have owned the world ten times over."

"But we still did a lot of things, and as you think back you say, Hey, we made a difference and good things happened. . . . [T]here was a certain dynamism then, you could do simple things and the world could be changed because people respected RCA, so you could make them sit up and take notice."

Prominent among those sitting up and taking notice were Nakamura's young engineers at Seiko. Or to be more accurate, at Suwa Seiko, one of the four companies that made up the byzantine and still largely family-owned Hattori empire. Of these, the first two—Hattori Seiko, the original (marketing) company, and the only publicly traded concern, and Seiko-sha (its manufacturing arm)—we have already encountered. In 1937, three years after the founder's death, a third company, known as Dai-ni Seikosha ("number two Seiko company") was formed to manufacture precision instruments.

During the war, this company's Tokyo factory was destroyed by bombing. The firm reestablished itself in four separate locations, one of which was a former *miso* (fermented bean paste) factory in Suwa, about 150 miles northwest of the capital. The other three factories subsequently regrouped as Dai-ni Seikosha, the company today known as Seiko Instruments. Formally established in 1959, Suwa Seiko would eventually merge with Epson, the empire's youngest offshoot, to become Seiko Epson.

Epson—the name is compounded from "*son* of *e*lectronic *p*rinter"— was originally the brand name for Seiko's miniature dot matrix printers. These were developed to produce printouts from the chronometers used at the Tokyo Olympics. The printers, which the company began selling in 1969 (slightly before Seiko's first quartz watches), became very popular with makers of desktop calculators, winning an overwhelming share of this market. As a result of this experience, Epson was perfectly positioned to catch the personal computer boom of the mid-1980s. The printer factory was eventually spun off as a separate company with Nakamura as president. Epson merged with Suwa Seiko in 1985. Today, printers account for some 40 percent of Seiko Epson's sales.

Suwa is a lakeside town in Nagano Prefecture, a mountainous region of central Japan and the site of the 1998 Winter Olympics. A region, in short, that is geographically quite like Switzerland, making it not inappropriate that a watchmaker should choose to locate there. Rather than any desire to emulate Geneva, however, expedience was more likely responsible for the choice of location. The Hattori clan had connections in the area. And with the collapse of silk making, formerly the region's principal industry, there was plenty of labor available.

Once Nakamura had determined that C-MOS was needed to make low-powered quartz watches, he set about finding a source of C-MOS chips. Much as Sharp's Sasaki had done, he and a couple of his fellow directors made the rounds of domestic chip makers like NEC.

They quickly discovered that, other than some small-scale research activity, there was no C-MOS work going on in Japan. Would chip makers be interested in tooling up to make special C-MOS integrated circuits for watches? Not really, came the reply—it would take a lot of engineering effort. And even if we succeed, will there really be a market for such chips in the future?

Since no-one would make C-MOS integrated circuits for them, Nakamura decided that it couldn't be helped—they would have to do it themselves. Depending on how you looked at it, this was either a decision that took a lot of guts, or one that was completely nuts. After all, Suwa Seiko was a company that did not have a single semiconductor specialist on their payroll. Yet here they were, proposing to make chips from scratch. Not only that, but to make those chips, they had elected to use a highly complex and commercially unproven manufacturing process. It was an extremely risky thing to attempt, but as an old Japanese proverb says, "blind men don't fear snakes."

An American firm would have brought in an expert from another company. But hiring from the outside was (and remains) rare in Japan. Besides, few people at other firms had the requisite skills.

On the positive side, top management—including, crucially, Hattori Kintaro's eldest son, Kentaro—understood what was at stake and were supportive. "There may have been some people who felt it was risky," Nakamura recalled, "but nobody came out and said, This is dangerous, we shouldn't do it—everyone was aware of the commercial promise of quartz watches. Everyone knew that quartz was important for the future, so the decision was made quite naturally." To be sure, it would be an expensive undertaking, in terms of investment in semiconductor production equipment and clean-room facilities. But in those days, Seiko's Marvel brand mechanical watches were very profitable, so there was cash available to underwrite such an investment.

The situation was the same regarding the motors needed to move the hands of the electronic watch. No one was prepared to supply the special kind of motor that Seiko required. "If it takes two seconds to complete a rotation, then it is too slow to be called a motor," scoffed one Japanese manufacturer that Seiko approached. So the company designed and made their own motors, and the electromagnets that drove them. "One important innovation they introduced," according to John Goodall of *International Watch* magazine, "was the use of a seconds hand that moved in steps, thus using current for only a few hundredths of a second, in order to reduce power consumption." The company also developed their own ultraslim watch batteries. Some years later, when Seiko Epson decided to automate their watch production line, the company would build—and subsequently sell—its own assembly robots, too. In November 1968, Nakamura approached Harigaya Hiroshi, the energetic young materials specialist he had assigned to investigate low-power technologies. He asked him to head a research team whose task would be to develop C-MOS integrated circuits. The team consisted of thirteen members, mostly mechanical engineers in their late twenties. Harigaya, at thirty, was the oldest.

Harigaya remembered that at the outset, there were fears among the team (understandably, given that none of them knew the first thing about integrated circuits) that what they were being asked to do was unrealistic. They sought reassurance from two experts who advised Seiko's researchers that rather than wasting time worrying, they had better get cracking. Other Japanese semiconductor makers were already ten years ahead of them. The last bus was leaving, and they were in danger of missing it.

One of these experts was Tarui Yasuo, a researcher at the Japanese government's Electro-Technical Laboratory in Tokyo, where transistor technology had first been developed in Japan back in the early '50s.[8]

When big companies like Hitachi or Toshiba wanted to learn a new technology, they would send one of their bright young employees off on study leave to an elite U.S. university like MIT or Stanford. For smaller, less sophisticated companies such as Seiko and Sharp, overseas study was not an option. Instead, they would send their people to ETL.

Tarui's then boss Kikuchi Makoto recalled that "there would always be five or six executives from smaller companies [there], waiting in my office. After talking to one, it would be 'Next, please,' it was like a doctor's waiting room! I hated it, I wanted to get on with my research, but I couldn't do that—because I was a government employee, I had to see them. . . . The worst case was the president of a small company who demanded: What are semiconductors, and how can we make money from them?"

On the other hand, there were also cases like Suwa Seiko, who were genuinely interested in learning. The watchmaker sent three engineers to the laboratory for a year's technical training. "So we started," Harigaya said, "and while we were learning things from our teachers, we began doing experiments, working until late at night, with no Sundays or holidays off. But [despite all that], it was really good fun, because we were creating things that didn't exist."

Harigaya's counterpart at Sharp, Inoue Hiroshi, attended ETL at the same time as the Seiko engineers. "I was sent on study leave to Dr. Tarui's group at the Electro-Technical Laboratory just when he was doing work on the physical phenomena of silicon surfaces, research that was aimed at what we would now call a MOS transistor, and I worked there for about a year." Inoue returned to Sharp to head up a team of engineers in their mid–twenties. "We made C-MOS by ourselves and kept on developing it. We hadn't mass-produced transistors, or bipolar ICs, and we hardly made any p-MOS, we just jumped straight to C-MOS, which we could do because the theory was out in the world for anybody to study. So from that we were able to develop an industrial base from which to make products. . . .

"It was a risky thing to do, but nonetheless we did it. As we say in Japanese, we were burning—we felt, 'Let's do it,' let's make new things under our own steam; really, it was all that can-do type spirit. But though we suffered setbacks, the young engineers who suffered them grew up to be the key people who support Sharp's IC group."[9]

Bootstrapping was a strategy that would take time to pay off. The Suwa people reckoned that to make C-MOS chips would take them at least six years and cost $10 million. Then, unexpectedly, a dramatic development occurred. *Deus ex machina* descended upon Tokyo in the shape of a Swiss-born physicist and entrepreneur named Jean Hoerni.

In semiconductor Valhalla, pride of place goes to Bill Shockley, the inventor of both bipolar and MOS transistors. On either side of Shockley stand his collaborators, John Bardeen the theorist and Walter Brattain the experimentalist. At Shockley's feet sit Jack Kilby and Bob Noyce, the coinventors of the chip. Behind Noyce hovers Hoerni, who played a role analogous to that of John the Baptist.

Hoerni was one of the eight prodigiously gifted young men whom Shockley summoned to Mountain View, California, in 1955 to form Shockley Laboratories, the very first semiconductor start-up. Two years later, Hoerni and his seven peers defected from Shockley to found Fairchild Semiconductor, the firm that put the "silicon" in Silicon Valley.

At Fairchild Hoerni invented the planar transistor, a momentous development that began as a radical improvement in production technology and ended up as the *sine qua non* for Noyce's integrated circuit. Prior to Hoerni's work, transistors had been produced in the form of little lumps called mesas. Connecting up the mesas—as Kilby proposed—would have been a labor-intensive process (hence expensive and intrinsically unreliable). As the name "planar" suggests, Hoerni's new transistors were essentially flat, two-dimensional structures. It was a relatively simple process to deposit metal connections between them.

Bitten by the entrepreneurial bug, Hoerni left Fairchild to found a succession of startups. The most notable of these was Intersil, a Cupertino, California, -based firm which he formed in 1967 to produce, among other things, MOS devices. Given that Hoerni was himself from Switzerland, it was hardly surprising that he should have tapped some Swiss firms for funding. His backers included the company that made Omega watches, and Portescap, a manufacturer of watch movements. Equally, given such shareholders, it was only natural when contemplating what kind of applications would be worthwhile for a pioneering chip maker to work on, that Hoerni and his colleagues should think of watch chips.

In 1969 Hoerni flew to Switzerland hoping to convince his Swiss backers to give Intersil a development contract for $75,000. They listened politely to his proposal. Then, over an excellent dinner, they told him that they were not interested. The Swiss had been working with an American technology development consultancy that had a branch in Geneva.[10] The consultants advised them that what Hoerni was proposing was impossible. Which left him "wondering why they had invested in my company if they didn't believe it would work."

As an insurance policy against such an outcome, Hoerni had bought himself a round-the-world ticket. He flew on from Switzerland to Japan, where he had heard that there was interest in electronic watches. Through contacts in Tokyo, he gained an introduction to Hattori Shoji.

The chairman of Suwa Seiko and Dai-ni Seikosha was then in his sixty-ninth year. But age had done nothing to diminish Shoji's ability to make a quick decision. "He gave me the contract on the spot," Hoerni recalled, "he didn't even bother to check it."

The youngest of Seiko founder Kintaro's three sons, Shoji was also the most dynamic. He is credited with having made Seiko an international force in watchmaking. He also, according to Nakamura, "had a good understanding of new things."

It was Shoji who made the decision to participate in the Tokyo Olympics, the publicity from which really put Seiko on the map. It was also Shoji who had instituted competition within the Seiko group. "Competition brings out the best in products and the worst in men," a favorite maxim of David Sarnoff, is one that Shoji would have heartily endorsed.

Competition between members of the same corporate group or *keiretsu* is by no means uncommon in Japan. For example, two members of the Mitsu *keiretsu*, Mitsui Toatsu Chemicals and Mitsui Petrochemical Industries, have remarkably similar product lines, yet have resisted efforts at consolidation for decades. Another famous example is the three different companies within the Matsushita conglomerate that make bicycles. Individual divisions within companies also compete with each other. Such rivalries are often overlooked in the literature on Japan because they are at odds with the stereotype of Japan, Inc., the monolithic entity.

The competition between Suwa Seiko and Dai-ni Seikosha was particularly intense. Not to put too fine a point on it, the two siblings loathed each other, much more than they did outside rivals like Citizen Watch. A former Japanese trading company executive remembers driving four Seiko engineers from New York to visit RCA's Solid-State Division in Somerville, New Jersey. A stony silence prevailed throughout the journey. Afterwards, the executive discovered that two of the engineers were from Suwa Seiko, the other two from Dai-ni Seikosha. Each side had been concerned lest any information should leak to the other.

One of the fruits of this rivalry had been the quartz chronometer developed for the Tokyo Olympics. This sprang from a technology contest between the two rival branches, with Suwa Seiko emerging as the winner.[11]

Now, with Suwa newly committed to in-house development of C-MOS, the crafty old Shoji no doubt saw Intersil's development contract as a handy prod to stoke the competitive embers into flame again. And that is exactly what happened. Six months after Hattori and Hoerni signed the contract, much to Suwa's fury, Intersil delivered its first chips.

The U.S. company would continue to ship watch chips to Japan for the next two or three years. In December 1970 John Hall, Intersil's process specialist, came to Tokyo where he spent six months teaching the chip-making art to engineers at Dai-ni Seikosha. This work was successful, and Dai-ni was the first to make a producible watch. Stung by their hated rival's prowess, Suwa Seiko redoubled their efforts. Try as they might, though, Nakamura's young troops could not manufacture their designs.

In desperation, they turned to RCA for help. But the RCA chips used too much current. Comparatively low power though they were, RCA's first generation C-MOS devices operated at 15 volts. What Seiko needed were chips that would operate off 1.5 volts, ten times less, so that a watch could run for a year on a single button battery. Unwilling to undertake further development, RCA told the Japanese that the chips were already close to the theoretical minimum current consumption. But this was not in fact true.

Eventually, the Suwa people were forced to swallow their pride, and ask Hall for assistance. This time they were successful: The company shipped its first C-MOS integrated circuits in November 1971, four years ahead of the original projection. Old Shoji must have been delighted: Now he had two separate IC production lines up and running.

Seiko filed hundreds of patents on its quartz watch technology. Unlike Bulova, which had attempted to use its patents to block rivals from entering the market, the Japanese firm encouraged other firms to license from them. In 1974 Seiko also began selling chips to other watchmakers. By 1980, the bulk of Japanese watch production had switched from mechanical to quartz. In classic experience-curve fashion, as production quantities soared, chip prices plummeted. The first batch of C-MOS frequency dividers from Intersil cost ¥10,000 ($28) each; today, an equivalent circuit costs just ¥20 (20¢).

Mass production of millions of inexpensive yet highly precise watches established Japanese manufacturers as the dominant force in the industry. In the late 1970s, worldwide demand for watches doubled. C-MOS–powered quartz watches almost blew away Switzerland's hitherto stable, well-organized, and highly profitable cottage industry.

It was of course highly ironic that a Swiss should have played such an important role in its demise. Hoerni's Swiss backers later accused him of being, in effect, a traitor. The entrepreneur was unrepentant; he simply shrugged his shoulders and asked them, "What did you expect me to do? I gave you the right of first refusal. Besides, you are shareholders, and I have to work for the good of the shareholders." To which one of his backers memorably replied, "If we had known that you were so serious about getting this contract, we would have given you the money so that you wouldn't have gone to the Japanese."

Long after Intersil ceased to exist, Hoerni would draw satisfaction from the fact that his prophecy had come to pass: "One of the things which motivated Intersil was that I thought that [electronic watches] would be a product which eventually everyone in the world would have. And you know, it's true—in India, in Bangla Desh, in very poor countries, everyone has an electronic watch, and they all use a process that we really developed."

Watch and calculator chips were the first high-volume C-MOS products. By the mid-1970s, following the lead of Seiko and Sharp, the rest of the Japanese semiconductor industry piled into C-MOS production.

They were soon cranking out millions of 1.5-volt C-MOS devices a month.

Meanwhile, among makers of computer chips—which, during this period, means almost exclusively U.S. companies—n-MOS had supplanted p-MOS as the process technology of choice because it was faster. Silicon Valley engineers were puzzled by the emphasis Japanese companies were putting on C-MOS technology. In their view, C-MOS still appeared to switch far too slowly for application to computers.

Indeed, according to one contemporary Japanese view, C-MOS and n-MOS could be characterized as bride and groom. Prompt at decision-making, quick to act, and with a good head for detail—these were the manly attributes of n-MOS that in this outstandingly sexist view corresponded to high speed and high integration. Meekness and obedience were the female virtues of C-MOS that equated to low power. The flaw of macho n-MOS was short-temperedness = high power consumption; that of ladylike C-MOS, a fondness for leisure = slow speed and low level of integration.

(Yasui Tokumasa was a bachelor in his twenties when he drew up this playful description. Twenty-something years later, as a married man and deputy general manager of Hitachi's memory business, he allowed that "recently, my feeling is that the truth is the opposite.")

In 1970 Intel introduced the first dynamic random access memory, the chip that would become the workhorse of the computer industry. Five years earlier, while still at Fairchild, Intel cofounder Gordon Moore had come up with his now-famous law, which in its original form stated that the number of transistors that could be accommodated on one chip doubles every year.

Study leave at the University of California at Berkeley in 1974 gave a young Hitachi researcher named Masuhara Toshiaki time to ponder the implications of Moore's Law for the future of semiconductor memories. As devices became more densely integrated, he reckoned, eventually—at the million transistor mark, perhaps—the high power consumption of n-MOS would preclude further integration. In other words, the heat generated by all those transistors would cause the chips to fry.

On his return to Hitachi's Central Research Laboratories in Tokyo, Masuhara began working on a high-speed C-MOS memory. Together with Yasui, an old school friend now assigned to the production side of the company, he came up with a workable design. The pair announced their results at an industry conference in February 1978. This was the trigger for a massive shift that within ten years would see virtually all chip designs migrating to C-MOS—with Japanese companies leading the way. Somewhat ironically under the circumstances, in the vanguard would be, not Hitachi, but the company's archrival, Toshiba.

For RCA, whose licensing people had signed up the Japanese to its C-MOS patents with their usual efficiency, there was a much greater irony. As Israel Kalish, the engineer who had built the first C-MOS circuits, recalled, "I used to travel to Japan . . . and we would go and tell them all we knew about C-MOS, and they were happy. Then, by the end of the cycle, we were paying money to Toshiba to learn how they designed their 4K[ilobit] memory."

Seeing Japanese chip manufacturing at first hand was a revelation to Kalish: "Here we were, making memories and getting 10, 15, 20 percent yield on good days, and they were getting 70, 80 percent yield on the wafer, and I said, 'What are they doing right?' Well, they were following the specs that we gave them—they took the numbers seriously. They said, You want it clean? Then let it be clean . . . they're used to following rules very precisely, and that's a major difference in culture."

C-MOS champion Gerry Herzog was similarly surprised by Japanese prowess. "When I left RCA to join Texas Instruments in 1979," he recalled, "my first task was to go over to Japan to negotiate with some of the Japanese manufacturers to make C-MOS watch and calculator chips for TI. And what I found was that they were just so superior in making perfect [circuit pattern] masks, and in handling their wafers so that they had low defect density, and that their yield on wafers was so much higher than anything I had experienced before. There's just no question that they knew how to do things right."

(The ultimate triumph of C-MOS over all other types of chip—bipolar, gallium arsenide and cryogenically cooled exotics like Josephson junctions—came on 31 May 1995. On that day, Fujitsu announced a new series of supercomputers, configured entirely out of C-MOS chips.)

But perhaps most impressed of all was Bernie Vonderschmitt, chief of semiconductor manufacturing at RCA, who toured the corporation's Japanese licensees with Kalish in 1973. As a World War II U.S. Navy veteran, Vonderschmitt had no reason to be well disposed towards the Japanese. But on his first trip to Suwa Seiko, he was simply knocked out by what he saw.

"It became clear to me," he recalled, "that here was a company that was almost peerless in its commitment to cost-effective manufacturing. I remember going and seeing a small area where they were turning out mechanical pieces for watches, which was just a work of art.

"They had I don't know how many machines running, and there were two or three people that walked around and monitored [them], to make sure that if something went down, they recognized it, and there was somebody there to get that piece of equipment up and running again—it was untouched by human hands, they would just sit there and run 24 hours a day, and it made a *hell* of an impression on me.

"And of course, when I saw that meticulous and heavy commitment to detail in manufacturing, I knew that eventually, when these people became a force in semiconductor manufacturing, they were going to be among the best."

Ten years later Vonderschmitt quit RCA. The last straw had been the management's decision to buy a consumer finance company rather than invest in key areas like solid-state components. After a spell at microprocessor maker Zilog, Vonderschmitt was looking for backing for a new start-up. Christened Xilinx, the outfit would specialize in a new and extremely flexible category of chip known, somewhat ponderously, as a field programmable gate array. Key to the venture's success would be access to manufacturing that was both state-of-the-art and cost-effective. With semiconductor plants costing hundreds of millions of dollars to build, it was clear from the outset that Xilinx could not afford to do its own fabrication.

Meanwhile, having expanded so aggressively that it had chip production capacity to spare, Suwa Seiko was looking for partners.[12] In February 1984 a meeting was arranged between the two sides. At this point, Xilinx was "just barely alive," Vonderschmitt recalled. "There were only three of us, and since we didn't have a place yet, we met at [San Francisco–based venture capitalist] Hambrecht & Quist and made a presentation to Mr. Yamamura," one of Seiko's top managers.

Two weeks later, Yamamura wrote back saying he had considered their proposal and presented it to Seiko's management. He concluded by inviting Vonderschmitt and Co. to come to Japan and meet his company's top brass. Such a prompt response, Vonderschmitt reckoned, indicated that "here's a fellow who doesn't have to have every i dotted and every t crossed before proceeding . . . a risk taker, somebody who's willing to gamble on something new."

From this auspicious beginning, the relationship between the two firms, so very different in scale and culture, flourished during the late 1980s. Ironically, this was a time when the U.S. and Japanese semiconductor industries were perceived by politicians and media alike as locked in mortal combat. Xilinx went on to become one of the most successful start-ups in the history of Silicon Valley. By all accounts, the relationship between Xilinx and Seiko continues to go from strength to strength.

Seiko Epson, as it was now known (after the 1985 merger between Suwa Seiko and Epson), would later produce chips for other successful U.S. design houses, such as Lattice Semiconductor, Cirrus Logic, Catalyst Semiconductor, Integrated Information Technology, and Rockwell spinoff Brooktree. For its part, Sharp provides leading-edge foundry services for Xilinx archrival Altera. There are now over two hundred "factory-less" semiconductor firms, four-fifths of them American. The majority use Japanese manufacturing partners to make their most advanced designs.

In 1994, silicon foundry business accounted for about 20 percent of Seiko Epson's semiconductor sales. Chips are now the company's second-largest business, after printers, accounting for almost 20 percent of revenues. These days, according to Harigaya, just 3 percent of the chips go into watches.

Watches themselves represent only 13 percent of Seiko Epson's sales (of about ¥480 billion [about $4 billion] in 1994). But the pursuit of the watchmaker's twin grails—higher precision and lower power—continues regardless. In both areas, Seiko's latest efforts seem to be approaching the ultimate.

On the low-power front, the company recently introduced a new range of batteryless automatic watches. Of course, automatic watches have been around for many years. My father had one, an Omega, which—to the considerable annoyance of my mother—he would wear even when in bed. The reason was that old-style automatics require al-most constant motion, otherwise they stop.

Seiko's range of Kinetic brand watches contain a capacitor which, when fully charged, can store enough energy to run the watch for five days. Meanwhile, the company has also built prototype pager watches that automatically adjust themselves according to an FM radio signal transmitted every half an hour.

For all its advanced mechatronics, the Kinetic watch remains recog-nizably a representative of the analog style of timekeeping; that is to say, it contains all the ingredients of a traditional watch—power source, oscillator, motor, gears, dial, and hands.

The pager watch, by contrast, descends from an entirely different type of timepiece, one that contains no mechanical parts whatsoever. The characteristic feature of this all-electronic–style watch is the way it displays time, in the form of digits.

Digital displays were key to the success of both calculators and watches. Having succeeded in developing a low-power form of cir-cuitry, it was now imperative to come up with a correspondingly low-power form of display to match. Here, too, Seiko and Sharp would show the rest of the world the way.

3

The Race Is Not
to the Swift

*I returned, and saw under the sun, that the race is not to the swift,
nor the battle to the strong, neither yet bread to the wise, nor yet
riches to men of understanding, nor yet favor to men of skill; but
time and chance happeneth to them all.*
—Ecclesiastes 9:11; quoted by George Heilmeier in
his acceptance speech on receiving an award for
pioneering work in LCDs, Tokyo, 5 November 1990

WHEN RCA ANNOUNCED, the world listened. The corporation
was famous for its great leaps forward. There had been television
itself, unveiled by David Sarnoff at the 1939 World's Fair in New York.
Fifteen years later came color TV, launched in 1953 with a media blitz
that included enormous print advertisements and lavish special broadcasts on RCA's own network, NBC. Now, fifteen years on from color
TV, came the announcement of the corporation's latest leap.

On 28 May 1968 some fifty reporters, photographers, and network
camera crews crowded into a conference room in the RCA Building at
30 Rockefeller Plaza, New York City. They had been summoned to the
headquarters of consumer electronics to behold the unveiling of the
television of the future.

RCA promised that tomorrow's TV would be a vast improvement on
the boob tube, a clumsy funnel of evacuated glass. The new television

would be flat as a pancake and light enough to hang on your wall like a picture. And it would consume almost no power.

When would this modern marvel hit the shops, the media people wanted to know? It seemed that some research and development still remained to be done on the revolutionary new technology—liquid crystal was its oxymoronic-sounding name—that was the basis for the new TV. But the RCA presenters were confident that these finishing touches would not take all that long.

In addition to the flat-screen television (which at the time of the press conference was a mockup capable only of displaying static, monochrome images), on show that day were several other prototype liquid crystal applications. They included numeric instrument readouts and electronic clocks with digital displays, the fruits of four years of energetic effort by a team at the David Sarnoff Center led by the tall young engineer who was one of the presenters. His name was George Heilmeier.

RCA's promotional gambit worked beyond the corporation's wildest dreams. The unveiling of the liquid crystal display sparked off an explosion of press coverage. Heilmeier and his team spent the next few weeks doing little but talking to journalists. The LCD story was picked up all over the world. Nowhere more so than in Japan where NHK, the national broadcasting company, ran the story repeatedly on its evening news bulletins. The mass-circulation *Asahi* newspaper also published a report on the technology, accompanied by a picture of the electronic clock.

An island people, the Japanese have always been intensely curious about new developments from the outside world. But for two individuals in particular, Yamazaki Yoshio of Suwa Seiko and Wada Tomio of Hayakawa Electric, the news about liquid crystals and their display applications was of especial interest.

For Yamazaki, liquid crystals were exciting because they represented the answer to a question that had been bugging him ever since he joined Suwa Seiko in 1965: namely, What on earth did a watchmaker like Seiko want with a chemical engineer like himself?

This in turn prompted a second question: Why on earth had Yamazaki, a chemical engineer, chosen to sign on with a watchmaker in the first place? The answer is simple. Yamazaki was typical of many, if not most, Japanese university graduates, then and now. Lacking any clear idea of where to make a career, he asked his professor for a recommendation. The *sensei* suggested Suwa Seiko.

Yamazaki was born in Niigata, a region in central Japan known for its deep winter snowfalls. His birthplace was a small town called Tsubama, where the principal occupation was the production of tableware for export. Yamazaki had gone only to a local university, but he was fortunate enough to have graduated in the mid-sixties, just at the beginning of Japan's boom years. It was a period when even an engineer with such humble credentials as his could have got a job almost anywhere, even with a blue-chip firm like Hitachi.

For a chemical engineer, the obvious place to apply would have been a chemical company. But having asked his professor's advice, Yamazaki felt obliged to follow through on it, even though he'd never even heard of Suwa Seiko. All he knew was that Seiko made watches, and that Suwa was somewhere up in the mountains. But the *sensei* said that Suwa Seiko was a good company with a promising future, and recommended that Yamazaki should go and see them. So off the young man went.

After changing trains many times, Yamazaki arrived in Suwa which, as he expected, was *way* out in the sticks. There, after being shown around, he was interviewed by the company's top managers, including the chief engineer, Nakamura Tsuneya. They asked him if he would join, and he replied: I will, I guess. And that was that.

Yamazaki's professor had predicted—presciently, as it turned out—that chemicals would become an important component in the watches of the future. When that happened, the young chemist would be able to make good use of his specialty. But several years had passed without anything coming up, and Yamazaki was beginning to think that he would have to quit and look for another job soon.

During this period, the focus of Seiko's research and development effort was the quartz watch. After hundreds of years of mechanical movements, watches were on the verge of going electronic. And yet, when the first quartz watches came out, not everyone was impressed. If the new-style timepieces were really electronic, the objectors wanted to know, how come they still needed mechanical hands just like ordinary watches? This problem of perception prompted Yamazaki to speculate that electronic displays might be a research theme worth looking into.

Then the picture of RCA's liquid crystal clock in the *Asahi* newspaper caught his eye. "I thought, What's that?" he recalled. After reading the article he was not much wiser, because Yamazaki had never heard of liquid crystals before. But when he looked them up, it turned out that liquid crystals were–glory be!–chemicals. At long last, Yamazaki had found his *raison d'être*.

Hayakawa Electric's Wada was also a chemist by training. But Wada had none of Yamazaki's why-am-I-here? angst. Wada knew exactly why Hayakawa had hired him. His problem was that, no matter how hard he tried, he just could not produce what his company wanted.

Since joining Hayakawa in 1960, Wada had worked on a display technology called electroluminescence–the emission, that is, of light by crystalline powders called phosphors. Television tubes work using phosphors, too. The difference is that in a TV, the phosphors–coated on the inside of the screen–are excited by electrons that come whizzing out of guns mounted in the neck of the tube. In an electroluminescent display, by contrast, the light emitted by the phosphors is due to the application of an electric field. No need for that big glass tube.

EL research began at the U.S. light-bulb manufacturer Sylvania in the late 1940s. Initially, work concentrated on making flat lamps. But in 1953, a Sylvania researcher called W. W. Piper proposed that by combining flat lamps into a segmented font, you could make an alphanumeric display. Piper's proposition launched the electronics industry on its first crusade in pursuit of what would prove to be an elusive grail, the TV-on-a-wall.

Wada was a belated entrant in this campaign. Like his peers elsewhere, he discovered that there were several apparently insoluble technical problems that prevented the production of a commercially viable EL screen. In particular, it seemed impossible to make the display sufficiently bright. You could boost the brightness by cranking up the voltage. But that reduced the display's life expectancy. Not that EL displays had much life expectancy to begin with: They tended to dim with age. According to electronics industry chronicler George Rotsky, "Engineers coped with this situation by ... surrounding the display with a cardboard light shield, then turning down the lights in the lab."[1]

Hayakawa's development people couldn't turn Wada's research into a product, and he was reassigned to other tasks. This was a bitter pill for the young engineer to swallow. But though hard to bear, Wada's failure also had two positive outcomes. One was that it left him with a highly developed awareness of what attributes were required for a commercial flat-panel display. The other was a burning determination that, next chance he got, he would succeed. Hence Wada's excitement when he saw on NHK news something that he immediately recognized as an entirely new type of display.

Hayakawa's need for a numeric display technology was urgent. Displays were key to the realization of Rocket Sasaki's vision of a hand-held, battery-driven calculator. After all, what was the point of having low-power chips if the displays gobbled electricity? But in the mid-1960s, power-hungry displays were all there was.

(In their prototype pocket calculator, Jack Kilby and his colleagues at Texas Instruments had sidestepped the display issue entirely. The Pocketronic printed the results of its calculations on a thin strip of thermal paper. Since the roll that held this paper had to be replaced at regular intervals, this solution, though ingenious, was obviously not ideal.)

To display the digits on their first, desktop, calculators, Hayakawa's designers employed what was then far and away the most common type of display, the Nixie tube. Invented in 1954, the Nixie was a kind of vacuum tube. Lined up inside its transparent glass bulb were ten wire filaments, each shaped like a digit from 0 to 9. When a filament was selected, it would glow bright orange.[2] But the further back in the tube the lit digit, the more it was obscured by the unlit filaments in front of it.

Despite their inelegant structure, Nixies did have a certain esthetic appeal. On a larger scale, the tube would have made wonderful sculpture. But to light one of its digits took 170 volts, a far cry from the 1.5 volts that was Seiko's target for watch displays.

From Sasaki's point of view, in addition to excessive power consumption, there was a second reason for not using Nixies in calcula-

tors: The basic patent on the displays was owned by an American computer company, Burroughs, which used the tubes as output devices in
its mainframes. In order to manufacture Nixies, Hayakawa had first to
obtain a license from Burroughs. Sasaki set off for New Jersey, where
Burroughs was based, to negotiate one.

Sasaki wanted to pay the U.S. firm a sliding-scale percentage of the
sales price of the devices. That way, although the percentage would
drop as the volume of production rose, the total amount of royalties
would increase. Burroughs insisted on charging a fixed royalty of more
than 10 cents per Nixie. Computer makers could live with this, because
the cost of displays was only a tiny fraction of the overall price of their
machines. But in a consumer product of the type that Sasaki had in
mind, where the goal for displays was less than a dollar a digit, there
was no room for inflexible margins.

But no matter how strongly Sasaki argued, Burroughs wouldn't
budge. Eventually, Sasaki lost patience; he resolved that Hayakawa
would do without the Nixie. His people would invent a substitute, he
told the Americans. And remarkably enough, that is exactly what happened. Sasaki assembled a team consisting of some of his former un-
derlings from Kobe Kogyo and a university professor he knew. In 1966
they rented a laboratory and began kicking ideas around. Out of that
creative interaction came an all-Japanese tube technology called the
vacuum fluorescent display.

Today, long after the last Nixie tube fizzled out, the low-current vacuum fluorescent display shines on in all sorts of different applications.[3]
Its distinctive bright blue-green digits can be seen glowing on most car
dashboards, in the form of clocks and numerical gauges. Sound-level
meters on stereos are another common VFD application, along with that
universal irritant, the blinking digital clock on the video cassette
recorder.

The eye is particularly sensitive to green, making it an excellent color
for a display. Nixies were orange, and for the first couple of years,
Sasaki said, it was very difficult to persuade the market to accept a display of any other hue. But fickle customers were eventually persuaded.
"After another two years," he claimed, "when people had realized that
green was easy on the eye and that you could use green for data, then
displays had to be green or else they were no good."

Sasaki was instrumental in setting up a company, Ise Electronics, to manufacture the new type of display. When Ise subsequently tried to shut other companies out of the market by denying them a license to its patent, Sasaki foiled the attempt. In his view, competition was essential because it reduced prices and improved quality. Having a sole source of supply for such a key component would have been almost as bad as having to pay Burroughs a fixed royalty. He warned Ise's management that if they didn't let other companies use the VFD patent, he'd conjure up yet another type of display and use that instead.

Ise capitulated, licensing NEC and a component maker called Futaba, which today is the leading manufacturer of VFDs. Sasaki had secured his multiple sources of supply. But at the same time he realized that vacuum fluorescents were only a temporary solution to the calculator display problem. They were after all still tubes, albeit tiny ones. As such they drew too much power ever to become a viable battery-driven technology, so VFDs were not suitable for use in portable products. Always thinking at least one generation ahead, Sasaki knew that the time had come to prepare for the next step, a truly low-power numerical readout, one that would need only a tiny fraction of the power the VFD used—the liquid crystal display.

Sharp's VFD calculators consumed 10 watts of power. The first LCD calculators drew just 10 milliwatts, one thousand times less; within ten years, the company's engineers had reduced LCD power consumption a further thousand times, to under 10 microwatts. The reason for the extremely low power requirements of liquid crystals by comparison with EL, plasma, and other types of flat-panel display technology is that unlike the latter, liquid crystals do not themselves emit light—they merely block light or allow it to pass.

Sasaki's threat to Ise had gained particular force from the fact that when he made it, he was already aware of RCA's liquid crystal display announcement. Wada had informed his boss about this promising new technology, and Sasaki assigned the young engineer to work on it. But in-house development would take time. To bridge the gap, in 1971 Sasaki approached RCA—much as three years earlier he had approached Rockwell—to ask them whether they would make LCDs for Sharp's calculators.

Liquid crystals were discovered in 1888 by an Austrian botanist called Friedrich Reinitzer. Upon heating cholesteryl benzoate, a compound which he had extracted from a plant, Reinitzer was surprised to note that it had two distinct melting points. At 145°C the solid turned into a cloudy liquid, and at 179°, the liquid became clear. Shortly afterwards a German physicist, O. Lehmann, showed that the cloudy intermediate phase appeared to have a crystallike molecular structure. He suggested that while in this phase the compounds should be called "liquid crystals."

As the name implies, liquid crystals are a class of organic compounds that behave like liquids (pour them into a container, for example, and they assume its shape) but whose molecules exhibit the regular crystalline arrangement characteristic of a solid.

The compounds appear naturally in many forms, from cell membranes to soap bubbles. "The most important category of liquid crystals are the nematic, or threadlike, compounds. Their rod-shaped molecules are free to move with respect to one another, yet subtle intermolecular forces tend to keep their long axes aligned. The effect somewhat resembles the schooling of fish."[4]

These strange, betwixt-and-between materials intrigued theoretical chemists, who were curious to know what caused them to behave in such an unusual fashion. Research on liquid crystals was fashionable in Europe during the 1920s and 1930s. Then, when no one could find anything useful to do with them, the molecules lapsed back into obscurity.

The first book in English describing liquid crystals was not published until 1962.[5] "Before its publication," wrote Joe Castellano, the senior chemist on Heilmeier's team at RCA, "students of organic chemistry at most U.S. universities did not know what a liquid crystal was!"

One of the few who did know about liquid crystals was Richard Williams. A soft-spoken, diffident man, Williams had been an instructor at Harvard for several years before joining RCA's Sarnoff Center in 1958. The center, he soon discovered, was in essence "a large laboratory for investigating displays." And as for televisions on the wall, "the idea that there should be a flat display and that that would be a good idea was not a discovery, it was something obvious to anyone working at Sarnoff. But the question was, could anyone make one?"

Though tightly focused on television, research at the center nonetheless ranged over a wide spectrum of topics. Thanks to the easy availability of military funding in those days, scientists like Williams were allowed considerable freedom to satisfy their intellectual curiosity. Sometime around 1960, it occurred to him that it might be possible to construct a flat display that would work using optical switches and reflected light—that is, a screen whose components could be alternated from reflective to nonreflective in order to display information and pictures.

To test his hunch, Williams assembled a sandwich consisting of two plates of glass coated with transparent conducting electrodes. Into the millimeter-wide gap between them, he spread some liquid crystal gunk. When heated up to about 120°C, the gunk would melt (in those days, there were no liquid crystals that were liquid at room temperature). Then, by applying a low voltage of between 5 and 10 volts to the electrodes, Williams discovered that, where they crossed, he could make the crystals change from transparent to opaque. "And this was quite remarkable," he recalled, "because this [effect] wasn't known."

Williams had invented the basic liquid crystal display. His results, he said, "created a fair amount of excitement around the labs, because people immediately thought of flat reflective television . . . and would it be possible to do something like that?" Williams performed some further experiments which confirmed that, yes, it would indeed be possible. Having done that, like the good scientist he was, he wrote up his results and filed a patent application.[6] Then in 1963 he packed his bags and took off for a year's sabbatical at RCA's labs in Zurich, Switzerland. There, Williams would be invited to give a talk on liquid crystals to the Swiss watch institute in Geneva.

With Williams out of the way, the stage was now set for the entrance of a very different sort of character. George Heilmeier had joined the Sarnoff Center's technical staff in 1962 at the age of 26. The scion of a working-class German family from Philadelphia, Heilmeier had won an RCA fellowship to Princeton, where he did his doctorate as an engineer.

An ambitious young man, Heilmeier was on the lookout for some way of making his presence felt. His supervisor advised him that the best way to achieve this end was to eschew the conventional semiconductors on which the fledgling scientist had been working up until that point. Instead, Heilmeier should aim for a field that was new, where there would be more potential for making breakthroughs.

Heilmeier hit on the idea of investigating organic transistors. Though it won him his academic spurs, this investigation didn't pan out in practical terms. But Heilmeier continued to pursue applications for organic materials. His interest ultimately led him to review Williams's work on liquid crystals.

Heilmeier and his coworkers began by replicating Williams's experiment with the glass plate sandwich, adding a strong red dye to the liquid crystal material to amplify the switching effect. In the following passage, written twelve years after the fact, Heilmeier described what happened next.

> A DC voltage of several volts was applied and we watched the cell change color from red to colorless as a function of the applied field. It was found almost immediately that the effect was more dramatic with a polarizer in place. The device was drawing less than a microwatt of power per square centimeter and we were switching color with voltages of less than ten volts in some cases! It was Fall 1964. The wall-sized flat panel color TV was just around the corner—all you had to do was ask us![7]

Like Williams before him, Heilmeier was well aware of the potential significance of the discovery: "It wasn't a question of stumbling on something and saying, Gee, what's this good for?" he said. "It was a case of right from the start knowing what one was trying to do." But unlike Williams, who was something of a loner, Heilmeier was out to make a name for himself beyond scientific circles. He rushed off down the corridors of the Sarnoff Center, cornering senior managers, dragging them back to his lab to show them what he and his group had done. His enthusiasm did the trick: The center's top brass rallied round with support. Liquid crystal displays were on their way.

A great deal still remained to be done, however. One of the earliest problems was finding suitable materials. The liquid crystals used in the first experiments were obviously impracticable; in addition to requiring that they be heated, the crystals and dyes were not stable over long periods.

In their search for promising candidates, the RCA researchers noticed that under an applied field certain types of materials would become markedly turbulent. In the process, these liquid crystals would turn from transparent to milky white. Heilmeier and his colleagues had discovered, as he put it, "how to electronically control the reflection of light in a most striking and dramatic way. We had to think of a sexy name for this effect, and the term 'dynamic scattering' was coined. Nineteen sixty-four was a very exciting year."

Exciting though it may have been, RCA's patent lawyers kept the young researchers from divulging the most exciting aspects of their work. In particular, the dramatic display effects that they had observed remained closely guarded company secrets until the 1968 press conference.

Pride in their achievements, together with the prohibition on discussing them, did not make the RCA researchers particularly popular with their peers. At the first conference on liquid crystals, held at Kent State University in the summer of 1965, the peacocks from New Jersey strutted around with a superior air, not saying much and making jokes about the work of other researchers. "We were all about the same age, I was like 28," recalled Castellano the chemist, "and we thought we were hotshots, y'know how it is, the young scientists, so to speak."

"They were ill-mannered and rude," remembered another attendee at the conference, James Fergason. Among other things, he recalled Heilmeier and the RCA people poking fun at him for a paper he gave. But Fergason would have the last laugh. When LCDs hit the big time, it would be his invention, not Heilmeier's, that would predominate.

In the hierarchy of the great East Coast industrial research laboratories, Bell Labs was undisputedly top of the ladder. One rung down came RCA's Sarnoff, which was a more product-oriented institution. Sarnoff ranked about equal with the laboratories of the two pioneers of electric power generation, General Electric and Westinghouse.

GE's laboratory is located in a wooded bluff near Schenectady, New York; Westinghouse's, in grimy Pittsburgh, Pennsylvania. During the golden years of the 1950s and 1960s, both labs did very good basic research. Just as good as, if not better than, their researchers liked to think, that of any university.

James Fergason joined the Westinghouse Research Laboratories in 1956. He began work on liquid crystals the following year. His initial target was thermal sensors, the kind of thing you could use to check the temperature of water in a pipe—which might be carrying waste water from cooling the reactor in one of the nuclear power plants that Westinghouse was building during this period—without actually having to break open the pipe. The liquid crystals would change color depending on how hot the pipe was.

This work found an extremely popular—and entirely accidental—outlet in the shape of that psychedelic fashion accessory so beloved of 1960s hippies: the mood ring. Today, this type of material, known as cholesteric liquid crystal, is routinely sold in the form of battery checkers.

Fergason was thus responsible for the first practical applications of liquid crystals. In 1961, not long after Williams at RCA, he turned his attention to displays. But Westinghouse decided that such applications were outside their corporate purview.[8] The company made most of its money from heavy electrical equipment like transformers and generators. In 1966 Fergason left to start a program on liquid crystal research at Ohio's Kent State University.

Kent State turned out to be an unfortunate choice of location for doing research that had industrial applications. On the highly politicized campuses of the late 1960s, "industrial applications" were dirty words. The atmosphere at Kent State went from bad to worse, culminating in the fateful anti–Vietnam War demonstration of 1970, in which U.S. National Guardsmen shot four students dead and wounded eleven others. This incident was the last straw for Fergason, who left the university that year to form his own company, International Liquid Xtal. The previous year (1969), while nominally still at the university, the prolific inventor had come up with what would be his most important discovery: the twisted nematic liquid crystal display.

In this type of LCD, the long, thin (nematic) molecules line up horizontally—"as if they were a precision marching band"—between two sheets of glass to which polarizers are attached. Orientation of the crystals is achieved simply by rubbing the glass in the desired direction with a velvetlike cloth. The twist comes from rotating one of the sheets through 90 degrees with respect to the other, so that the molecules form a helix.

Light enters through one polarizer, twists around the helix, and exits through the other. In this state, the display appears dull gray.

Applying an electric field causes the molecules to stand up perpendicular to the glass, disrupting the helix. The light is not rotated, hence cannot pass through the rear polarizer, with the result that the display turns black. The pattern on the display comes from the shape of the transparent electrodes, the most familiar being the seven-segment italic numerals used in calculators, watches, and a hundred thousand other applications besides. A cursory check on artifacts in my office turns up ten LCDs. In addition to those on my digital watch and calculator, there are liquid crystal displays built into my telephone, tape recorder, CD player, camera, flashgun, and camcorder.

For a while RCA's milky-white, dynamic scattering LCDs competed with Fergason's matt-black twisted nematics. The battle between the two types of display raged for several years during the early 1970s, ending in rout for the RCA style. The reason was simple: Though customers tended to prefer the white color, dynamic scattering displays not only used more power than twisted nematics, they were also intrinsically unreliable.

Among the first producers of dynamic scattering LCDs was Optel, an RCA spinoff founded in 1969 with $700,000 backing from Swiss watchmakers by a flamboyant Hungarian named Zoltan Kiss. Fred Kahn, the then chief of LCD development at Hewlett Packard, recalled buying some state-of-the-art four-digit watch displays from Optel for about $20 each. He put them in a desk drawer for safekeeping. On opening the drawer two weeks later, he discovered that the seals had all ruptured and the displays had big bubbles in them. Larry Tannas, Kahn's counterpart at Rockwell, remembered that when he tested his Optel displays, they failed within about five hours.[9]

Alerted to the enormous potential of the calculator market through their role as supplier of chips to Sharp, Rockwell had decided to enter the calculator business in their own right. The problem was that there were no commercially available displays that could be incorporated in handheld calculators. A frantic search for a solution ensued. Tannas, an electrical engineer who had been working on electronic displays for the Apollo space vehicles that Rockwell was building for NASA, was drafted to come up with the goods in house.

In those days, Tannas recalled, you could not buy liquid crystals. LCD pioneers had to make most of their own materials themselves. Not that you needed much of the stuff—a jugful of liquid crystals was enough to run a factory for a week.

A big problem back then was contamination with moisture, which would rapidly render displays useless. The basic compounds from which liquid crystals could be synthesized were sold by pharmaceutical suppliers. To avoid moisture contamination, display makers ordered "electronic grade material" from these suppliers. According to Tannas, "the pharmaceutical people said, 'This is better than electronic grade material, this is "medically pure"'—suitable for going in the human body.'

"Well, we were convinced," Tannas recalled. "Boy, you couldn't be more pure than that, and it was interesting because the communication between electrical engineers and chemists was like, zero. We'd never talked to each other in the past, and here all of a sudden, we're talking about applying electrical fields across this material, and why it was going through hydrolysis" [reacting with water to form other compounds].

"And we found out that 'medically pure' meant that it could have 0.7 percent water in it, because water is no contaminant to the human body. But when you put that material into a display, it hydrolyzed right away, and so you had oxygen and hydrogen in there raising all kinds of chemical hell."

Tannas made a prototype liquid crystal display in 1969, a few months before Wada produced his first LCD at Sharp. Rockwell entered the calculator business the following year. The U.S. firm continued to ship calculators until 1975, when price competition reached its fiercest, and Rockwell decided to exit the consumer business.

The end came suddenly. Display production "was just killed," Tannas recalled. "I mean, there was an opportunity to sell the display activity we had there to somebody else that was interested in it, but Rockwell just quit, cold turkey. It ended very abruptly, very nonprofessionally and certainly noneconomically . . . the facilities were just torn apart."

At least Rockwell had had a proper crack at LCD production. That was more than could be said of RCA, where the technology had originated. After the euphoria of the 1968 press conference wore off, RCA's man-

First liquid crystal display calculator made by Sharp (© June 1973). (Photo courtesy of Sharp)

agement dithered about what to do with LCDs. In their efforts to get their liquid crystal prototypes translated into products, Heilmeier and his people ran into a brick wall.

Top management was reluctant to back the development of the TV-on-a-wall. This, it soon became clear, would take many years of further research. The perception that liquid crystals were not going to be the next big thing discouraged engineers, who generally like to work on things that will be winners in the next year or so. At the same time, the product division was unhappy about the long-term threat that LCDs might pose to its current cash cow, television picture tubes.

For its part, RCA's electronic components division viewed the prospect of manufacturing LCDs with distaste. "After all," Heilmeier recalled them sniffing, " 'it wasn't silicon', the materials were 'dirty' by semiconductor standards and it was too easy for 'garage operators' to get into the business. When customers began clamoring for more information, attempts were made to discourage them . . . "

How different things might have been had David Sarnoff himself still been at the helm of the corporation. The TV-on-a-wall had long been a dream of RCA's visionary chairman. And Sarnoff was the kind of ruthless individual who would stop at nothing to make his dreams come true, as he had demonstrated with television, developed by RCA during the Great Depression of the 1930s at a cost of over $50 million, and again with color TV, which RCA laboratories perfected in the early 1950s for an investment of $130 million.

The General (as Sarnoff liked to be styled) had come to see the liquid crystal prototypes the day before the 1968 press conference. But he was then 77 years old, just weeks away from a debilitating attack of shingles that would leave his balance unsteady and his speech slurred. David Sarnoff died on 12 December 1971, aged 80.

It is not hard to imagine the great man turning in his grave as RCA's management proceeded to squander the fruits of their technological heritage. Sarnoff's precious laboratories were responsible for many if not most of the inventions that went into the pocket calculator, the digital watch, and their myriad progeny. The C-MOS chips, the LCD display, the thin-film transistors that would turn the LCD into a TV, the amorphous silicon material from which the transistors are made, all were pioneered by RCA scientists. The corporation's failure to follow up on these breakthroughs—which between them today represent markets that are worth hundreds of billions of dollars—can be seen as an industrial tragedy of unprecedented magnitude.

For a while Heilmeier's group continued to build liquid crystal prototypes—calculators, clocks, all sorts of instrument displays—that they believed, rightly as it turned out, would be popular in the future. But RCA's management appeared indifferent to the potential of these newly emerging mass markets. The corporation would eventually dip its toe into LCDs, but targeting a mere niche: point-of-purchase displays, moving advertisement panels intended for use on supermarket shelves.

Faced with such indifference from on high, the LCD group began to fall apart. Some of the first defectors went off down the road to form the ill-starred Optel. This was the first of many U.S. 'garage operators,' small outfits that sprang up to make displays for the nascent watch and calculator markets. Others included Princeton Materials Science (like Optel, an RCA spinoff, led by Joe Castellano), Microma (an Intel division based in Cupertino, California), and Micro Display Systems (a TI spinoff of Dallas, Texas). Heilmeier himself was soon to follow, leaving

RCA in 1970 to become a White House Fellow. By that time, it must have been quite clear to him that LCDs were not going to be his ticket to a career in upper management. After his departure, liquid crystal work at the Sarnoff Center was cut way back.

Heilmeier went on to a distinguished career, moving from the White House to the Defense Department. There he headed the Defense Advanced Research Project Agency, initiating development projects that included stealth aircraft. In 1977, he returned to private industry to become chief technology officer at Texas Instruments. After his departure from RCA, Heilmeier appears to have lost all enthusiasm for liquid crystal displays. It is striking, in conversations with American LCD pioneers, how often the subject comes up of Heilmeier's apparently negative attitude to the technology he helped pioneer. Fred Kahn, the researcher who initiated LCD work at Bell Labs and Hewlett Packard, summed up the paradox as follows: "[Heilmeier] did more to stimulate liquid crystal work than anyone I can think of, and he did more to retard liquid crystal work in the United States than anyone I can think of—he has both those distinctions."

The main bone of contention seemed to be that, while director of DARPA, Heilmeier declined to fund liquid crystal display research. Heilmeier mounted a brisk counterattack to such charges: "If you had the choice of putting money into stealth aircraft, which would essentially provide the United States with a new level of defence capability ... would you put your money into that, or into [advanced] liquid crystal displays? It's pretty clear what you would do."

What is not so convincing, however, is Heilmeier's defence of Texas Instruments' decision to use light-emitting diodes in their calculators in preference to LCDs, a choice which dramatically reduced the battery life of their machines. (In LED calculators, to save power, the numerical readout was only displayed for a few seconds before the display switched to a single dot ticker-taping across the decimal points of the digits.) He justified the choice on esthetic grounds, arguing that in this respect, there was no contest—LEDs were brighter, sharper, and easier to read than LCDs.

One might have expected someone as closely identified with LCDs as Heilmeier to be more supportive of his own technology's merits. But not so: Larry Tannas recalled being taken aback while giving an invited talk in about 1986 on the exciting prospects for a new type of liquid crystal television to a group of Texas Instruments researchers, when he was subjected to a withering broadside from Heilmeier as to why this would never happen.

Following the exit of the leading player from RCA in 1970, there was still a final act to come before the corporation brought down the curtain on LCDs. At the beginning of 1972, the corporation belatedly announced that it would be in full-scale production of LCDs by the end of that year.

The announcement must have come after Sharp's Sasaki visited Somerville, where RCA's electronic components division was located. He went there to ask Bernie Vonderschmitt, who had recently become the division's general manager, whether RCA would make LCDs for Sharp calculators. Vonderschmitt told Sasaki that RCA was not ready to make such a commitment—the technology was still too immature.

Sasaki returned to Japan with no more than a patent license from RCA—and a determination to go it alone. Sharp paid RCA about $3 million for the LCD license. Ever eager to oblige licensees, especially Hayakawa/Sharp, with whom relations had always been especially cordial, the RCA licensing people subsequently arranged for a team of four researchers from Sharp to visit the laboratories and talk to Heilmeier. Denied permission to take photographs, the Japanese made voluminous drawings of the equipment there. Though Wada recalled visiting Princeton several times, he said that it was after Heilmeier left, and after he himself had made his first calculator displays.[10]

During the 1970s, the Japanese firm would invest $200 million—an enormous sum for a company its size—in LCD manufacturing facilities.

RCA did build an LCD factory in Somerville. But the facility only ran for a few months before it was shut down, and its contents were sold off to the watchmaker Timex.

Watchmakers like Timex had recently become aware of the importance of electronic displays. In 1970 the Hamilton Watch Company introduced the Pulsar, the world's first digital wristwatch. The revolution that had begun with the introduction of electronic parts was now complete: The Pulsar dispensed with moving parts entirely. It came encased in a sleek stainless-steel case and featured a dial made of dark plastic. To see the time, you pressed a button located below the dial, and—lo and behold!—four red digits lit up.

The digits were made up of light-emitting diodes, a display device invented at General Electric in 1962.[11] Two enterprising Texans—George Theiss and Willy Crabtree—at a small Dallas-based company called Electro-Data were the first to spot the significance of LEDs for watch applications. Knowing nothing about watches themselves, they brought their prototype timepiece to the attention of John Bergey, an engineer at Hamilton who was also developing digital electronic watches. The two companies joined forces, with Electro-Data providing the electronic guts of the watch—the chip and display—and Hamilton the case and the marketing.

At $1,500, the Pulsar was expensive and unreliable. "The watch did suffer from at least one limitation," George Rotsky remarked dryly, "it didn't work. It couldn't. Packed with a multitude of discrete components, it was a manufacturing nightmare." In an article he wrote at the time, Rotsky mentioned that Hamilton had found bugs in six watches. He added that the company had thus far manufactured six watches.[12]

For all its faults, the Pulsar nonetheless caught the public's imagination. Especially after the widespread exposure the watch received on Roger Moore's wrist in the 1973 James Bond movie *Live and Let Die*. In the scene immediately following the opening credits, Bond is seen checking the time on the watch. (Ironically, the Pulsar is merely a replacement for Bond's regular watch, a mechanical Rolex loaded with high-tech gadgetry.)

LED watches enjoyed a vogue for two or three years. Then, novelty value exhausted, they disappeared.[13] People got tired of having to push the button every time the wanted to know what time it was. Also, of having to squint in order to read the dim displays in sunlight. And most of all, of having to replace the batteries every two or three months. Battery life depended on how often you pressed the button to read the time. You had a total of just under four hours of power at your disposal. LED watchmakers reckoned—overoptimistically, as it turned out—that customers would learn not to check the time too often; they predicted that the third set of batteries would last customers a year.

The demise of the LED watch came as no surprise to Suwa Seiko's management, which had long since concluded that the technology was impractical. If you wanted to do an electronic display, they figured, liquid crystals were the only way to go. The company had also decided against using RCA-style dynamic scattering displays because they needed too much power—two batteries to the twisted nematic's one.

The Japanese were quick to pick up on Fergason's gray-and-black digital displays. He remembered that soon after announcing his discovery, "almost every Japanese company you can name" visited the International Liquid Xtal plant in Ohio. "They came through, talked to us, talked about a deal, had us make some parts for them."[14] Twenty-five years on, Fergason was hard put to remember all the names of his visitors. But he was sure which of the Japanese had been first—Seiko.

At this point, the plot thickens. Hattori Shoji and his advisors at Seiko wanted to make a deal but, sensing that Fergason's company was in trouble financially, the Japanese held back. They were right: Strapped for cash and with serious debts to pay, Fergason was shortly afterwards forced to sell his patent rights to the Swiss pharmaceutical company Hoffman LaRoche.

In the history of technology, it is not unusual for the same invention to be made simultaneously, or nearly simultaneously, in different places. In the case of twisted nematic LCDs, a chemist called Wolfgang Helfrich had independently come up with the same idea as Fergason while working in Heilmeier's group at RCA. Shortly afterwards, Helfrich decamped for Basel, Switzerland, the headquarters of the pharmaceutical firm Hoffman LaRoche.

There in 1971 he and Martin Schadt, a Hoffman LaRoche researcher, published a paper on twisted nematics and applied for a patent on the effect. This was more than a year after Fergason's invention, but technical problems over disclosure delayed a patent being issued to the American. A legal battle ensued which ended up in an out-of-court settlement, with the Swiss buying Fergason out.

According to Fergason, Hoffman LaRoche's motives in acquiring his patent went beyond mere commercial considerations. Since each display uses only a tiny amount of the material, the market for liquid crystals, though lucrative, was (and is) relatively small. In addition to which, during this period, thanks to the enormous success of Librium and Valium, its antidepressant drugs, Hoffman LaRoche was awash with cash. So the financial incentive to manufacture liquid crystals was slight.

The main reason Hoffman LaRoche wanted Fergason's LCD patents was apparently a patriotic one–to prevent them being used to block Swiss watchmakers from entering the digital watch market. Having acquired the patents, Hoffman LaRoche proceeded to license them to all comers. The irony is, as Fergason pointed out, that the drugmaker "wanted to save [the market] for the Swiss, but what they really did was save it for the Japanese!"

Fergason's technology was transferred at Seiko's behest to Micro Display Systems in Dallas. This company made twisted nematic LCDs for Dai-ni Seikosha. As with C-MOS chips, there was fierce competition within the Seiko group: Suwa made its own twisted nematic LCDs based on technology licensed from Hoffman LaRoche. This time, Suwa seems to have won the race. Seiko's first LCD watch, introduced in October 1973, featured displays made by Suwa. Two months later, Seiko marketed the same watch with displays from Dai-ni Seikosha. Asked whether there was any contact between the two rival Seiko groups Yamazaki replied, "almost none."

Seiko introduced its first digital LCD watch, model 06LC, in October 1973. It cost ¥138,000 ($500). That LCDs should have come to market in such short order seemed in retrospect to Yamazaki, Suwa Seiko's chemist, little short of miraculous. "After all," he said, "it wasn't a case of taking something then making it. We were taking something that had been completely unknown and turning it into a consumer product–and that's fantastic! When I look back at how quickly it happened," he laughed, "I feel that we really did well, didn't we?"

Yamazaki was entitled to feel proud of his efforts. He had stuck with liquid crystals through thick and thin for five long years, beginning with dynamic scattering displays then subsequently switching to twisted nematics. He had done most of the work himself, up to and including synthesizing his own liquid crystals.

Suwa's management had not been especially supportive. To them, LCDs lost points on esthetic grounds: compared to analog watches, digital displays looked dull. There was also the question of reliability:

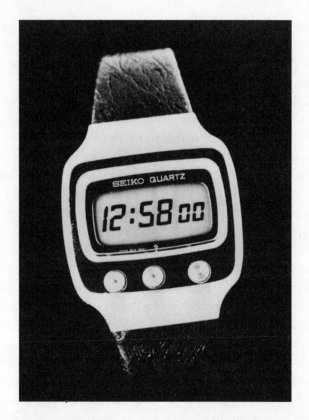

First liquid crystal display watch made by Seiko
(© October 1973). (Photo courtesy of Seiko)

Would Yamazaki's liquid crystal materials be able to withstand the rigors of the real world?

The director in charge of the watch business at Suwa approached Yamazaki. "If we market LCD watches and they all fail," this director wanted to know, "how much do we stand to lose from customer claims?" "About 100 to 200 million yen" [approximately $250,000 to $500,000], Yamazaki replied. "And he said, 'Oh, that's all right, then.'"

The director had reason to be nonchalant. At the time, Seiko was making such huge profits selling quartz watches that the company could afford to drop a half million dollars without batting an eyelid. For the young chemist, however, the prospect of watches being returned with faulty LCDs was unbearable: He would never be able to live it down. So in the months before the digital watch was introduced, Yamazaki threw himself into a frantic round of experiments. He performed all sorts of accelerated aging tests to make sure that his liquid crystals came up to snuff.

Yamazaki's efforts paid off. Watchmakers typically offer a one-year guarantee with their products. After a year was up, he was gratified to learn that not a single watch had been returned with a defective display.

Seiko never really expected LCD watches to be big sellers. Rather, according to Yamazaki, the company's policy was: "We are watchmakers, and if it's a watch, then no matter what type, we'll make it." The Japanese were thus unprepared for the digital boom that was about to explode.

The shift from analog to digital had revolutionary implications for watchmakers, even greater than the switch from mechanical to electronic movements a few years earlier. So long as watches had hands, you still needed tiny gears and special process technology, machinery and know-how to build them. Only watchmakers possessed such skills and equipment. With the elimination of hands, however, suddenly *any* company with an assembly line could make watches. All you had to do was find someone to supply the components and you were in business.

The prospect of being able to buy highly accurate digital watches for next to nothing was an extremely worrying one for watchmakers. Yamazaki recalled Hattori Kentaro, the then-patriarch of Seiko's owning family, confessing at a company New Year party in the mid 1970s that the thought kept him awake at night. Hattori feared that the digital watch might bring crashing down the Japanese watch industry, this proud edifice which had been built up over nine decades with Seiko as its keystone.

For a while, it looked as if Hattori's dire prophesy would come true. The digital boom began in earnest around 1975. Dozens of companies piled into the market. The first wave was LED watches, which were made by at least forty companies, including Fairchild, Hughes Aircraft and Texas Instruments. Then, after the LED fad receded, came a second wave of LCD watches. These were made by some twenty firms, including American Microsystems, Fairchild again (which brought Joe Castellano out to the West Coast to set up its display operation), and Intel subsidiary Microma.

By 1975, annual production of digital watches had reached 3 million at an average price of about $150. By 1977, in the wake of vicious price competition, the price of a digital watch had plummeted to less than $10. Profits evaporated, and the business collapsed. At this point, much to watchmakers' relief, customers began buying analog watches again. The novelty value of having a watch with numbers that disappeared then reappeared had worn off. "People tend to fly at anything new," Yamazaki reflected, "but after a while they cool down and come back. So the watch industry didn't go digital after all."

To remind him of the consequences of excessive price competition, Intel chairman Gordon Moore still wears his twenty-year-old Microma timepiece. He calls it his $30 million watch.[15] Yamazaki recalled hearing about the sort of problems Microma had with its (dynamic scattering) LCD watches: "There was something wrong with the material, it was vulnerable to sunshine, so air bubbles appeared in all of them, worst case within a week, best case within a month, but without exception, they were all no good. That sort of 100 per cent failure is unusual, isn't it? And the result was that, in America, there was bad publicity for LCD watches, people thought that they were absolutely useless. So for awhile in America, LEDs were very popular, in America digital watches only used LEDs. So when I went to America around that time, people would ask me, Why do you use liquid crystals in Japan, they aren't any good are they? That was the reputation that liquid crystals had in America."

In Japan, although the reliability of liquid crystal displays had ceased to be an issue, the question of esthetics remained. This was one to which even Yamazaki, ardent LCD pioneer though he was, could relate. "To be quite frank," he says, "even while I was working on liquid crystals, I never really liked those digital numerals—personally, I prefer analog watches with proper numbers and hands."

After all, a watch is more than just a timekeeping tool: It is also a personal accessory, a status symbol, and, in many cases, a piece of jewelry. For all their functional merits, LCDs didn't look much like jewelry. Long after they ceased to be fashionable, digital watches found it hard to shake their image of being cheap.

Twenty years after the introduction of the LCD watch, in his current position of general manager of patents and licensing at Seiko Epson,

Yamazaki would run a database search on LCD patents granted to
Japanese companies. He was gratified to discover that Seiko had won
far more patents than any of its Japanese rivals. In particular, more
than Hitachi, which was the first company in Japan to do liquid crystal
research, and also more than Sharp, the company that is today most
closely associated in people's minds with LCDs and by far the largest
producer of the devices.

Suwa Seiko's initial entry into liquid crystal displays was motivated
by one engineer's need to find a role for himself, and on his company's
policy of staying up with the latest trends in watch technology. But as
we shall see in the next chapter, the company's true moment of glory in
LCDs was yet to come. Building on the base that Yamazaki established,
another young Seiko engineer would go on to produce what RCA had
promised, but failed to deliver: a liquid crystal color television.

"Despite their early difficulties [in producing LCDs]," wrote Charles
Burck in the October 1973 issue of *Fortune* magazine, in a perfect if un-
witting illustration of why journalists should refrain from making predictions, "big companies like Rockwell, Motorola, and RCA will no
doubt become major forces in the market."

None of the three firms that Burck listed became major forces in the
LCD market. Nor did any of the other elite U.S. firms that dabbled in
liquid crystal displays during the 1970s.[16] They included AT&T, General
Electric, and Xerox. But in the could've-beens category perhaps the
saddest story of all is that of Hewlett-Packard.

Silicon Valley's oldest and most respected firm got into LCDs by hiring Fred Kahn, a researcher with a most unusual resumé. On graduating from Harvard with a doctor's degree in solid-state physics in 1968,
Kahn decided that before settling down with a job at a large U.S. company, it might be fun to rack up a bit of work experience somewhere
that was technologically advanced but culturally different. Kahn concluded that the one country that fit this description was Japan. At the
time, he had never been west of Ithaca, New York.

Kahn went to the university library. There, in the proceedings of a recent electrical engineering conference, he found papers from a session
called "Closing the Technology Gap" (i.e., with the United States). The
Japanese speaker had been Kobayashi Koji, president of the Nippon

Electric Company, Tokyo, Japan. Armed with this minimal address, Kahn wrote off to Kobayashi, enclosing his resumé and asking for a job.

Two weeks later, he received a reply: Dr. Kobayashi had read his letter with great interest, and would be happy to offer Kahn a position at NEC's central research and development laboratories in Kawasaki. Starting salary would be ¥100,000 ($275) a month, about a fifth what U.S. firms were offering him. Much to the consternation of his research advisor, Kahn accepted the offer. He thus became probably the first American scientist ever to work as a regular employee of a Japanese company.

While doing the rounds of job interviews, Kahn had come across a group of researchers at the Xerox laboratories in Rochester, New York, who were working on liquid crystals. When he first met with the NEC people at their office in the Pan Am Building in Manhattan, he suggested that liquid crystals might be a good topic to investigate. The Japanese thought that the idea sounded interesting, but told Kahn that since there were no liquid crystal materials in Japan, could he possibly bring some with him?

By the time Kahn arrived in Tokyo in December 1968, RCA had made its momentous announcement. The day after Kahn arrived in Kawasaki, the head of NEC's laboratories—Uenohara Michiyuki, a researcher who had recently returned to Japan after a distinguished career at Bell Labs—called the young American into his office and suggested that he work on liquid crystal displays. Several hectic months of research later, Kahn was given the honor of demonstrating what may well have been the first made-in-Japan liquid crystal display to NEC's dynamic president, Dr. Kobayashi. Kahn recalled that Kobayashi took one look at his crude device and sniffed, "I've seen better at RCA."

It would be many years before NEC became a major player in LCDs. Meanwhile, frustrated by the lack of infrastructure in Japan, Kahn returned to the United States in January 1970 to join Bell Laboratories, in Murray Hill, New Jersey. At the Labs, he worked in Area 20, where device development was done.

The early 1970s were the heyday of the phone company's labs, when young researchers had the freedom to do more or less what they liked.

It was a heady time in liquid crystal research: "I felt like an eighteenth century biologist," Kahn recalled, "because every time I looked under my microscope, or applied [an electric] field to anything, I would discover some extraordinary new phenomena."

The golden age could not last. A major rationale for the development of liquid crystal displays at Bell was the potential of the device for incorporation in a new version of Picturephone, on which AT&T was pinning hopes of future revenue growth.[17] But Picturephone turned out to be a commercial disaster. Almost overnight, all related research projects were cancelled. Kahn began looking around for other companies that might be interested in liquid crystal displays. After the rigors of New Jersey winters, the prospect of relocating to California was particularly appealing. He signed on with Hewlett-Packard in October 1973.

At that time, the Palo Alto–based firm was on a roll. The HP-35, the first handheld scientific calculator, introduced in early 1972, had become one of the most commercially successful products in the company's history. It had blown away the slide rule, the engineer's traditional reckoning tool.

Key to the HP-35's success had been its red LED readout, the result of a major commitment by Hewlett-Packard to develop display technology. And therein, from Kahn's point of view, lay the problem. A rival technology was already entrenched at the firm.

By April 1974, just six months after his arrival, Kahn demonstrated a prototype LCD calculator display that was probably the most advanced of its time. The obvious place to apply this display was in a calculator watch that Hewlett-Packard was developing. The requirement was for the watch's power consumption to be ten thousand times less than that of the HP-35 calculator. This should have made the LCD, which drew almost no power, a shoo-in for the job.

But the division that made LEDs protested that LCDs were unreliable. Why bet on a new and unproven technology, they argued, when we already have what you need? And HP's calculator division decided to stick to what they knew and go with LEDs.

As it turned out, however, the component division did not have a small enough display in hand. Developing one delayed the introduction of the watch by about a year. The watch itself was a rare commercial flop for HP. This might have been because of the display, which suffered from all the usual LED drawbacks: You had to press a button to view them, you couldn't see them outdoors, and battery life was only a few weeks. Equally, at $600-plus, the watch was overpriced and so big that users had to have the buttons on their shirt-cuff altered in order to accommodate it.

Despite this setback, Hewlett-Packard remained wedded to LED displays for its calculators for another five years, until 1979, when it proved impracticable to shrink the red-colored numerals any further. In that year, HP built an LCD manufacturing facility in Corvallis, Oregon, to which the technology was transferred from Hewlett-Packard's labs in Palo Alto.

But Kahn's triumph was short lived; within a year, HP decided to shut down the LCD facility. Former HP labs executive Bob Burmeister was at the meeting where the decision was made. "The manager who was responsible for running that production division announced that they were going to close down that facility and get out of the liquid crystal business." Burmeister recalled that he was stunned, "because I saw this as a growing area, the company was certainly going to use more [LCDs], and we were an early leader—so why on earth would you shut it down?

"Well the answer, of course, was Japanese competition: 'The Japanese are making these and we can't compete with the Japanese'—the words ring in my ears to this day." And with this self-fulfilling prophesy, Hewlett-Packard exited the LCD business and thenceforth bought displays from Hitachi. These were judged to be equal in quality to HP's own screens, the difference being that Hitachi could provide them at a lower cost.

Some fifteen years later, Kahn was inclined to be philosophical about Hewlett-Packard's decision to pull out of LCDs. "I think HP made the right decisions in general," he said. "Virtually 50% of HP's R&D budget went into developing the next-generation computer system based on RISC technology, and it was more important for HP to develop the computer system than virtually any other R&D activity. So the major funding for R&D activities at HP in the 1980s was to perfect the ink-jet printer and to develop the RISC system of computers, and that together with good fiscal management has made them a $30 billion company."

The departure of HP left Japanese firms in sole possession of the LCD field. Liquid crystal displays of the sort that are now commonplace in portable computers and–increasingly–above train doors and in back of airplane seats would take longer to develop and require more investment than anyone expected. But the development efforts did eventually bear fruit. In 1995, according to figures compiled by Stanford Resources, the market research consultancy run by Joe Castellano, George Heilmeier's old RCA sidekick, the LCD market was worth about $10 billion. By the year 2001, the company predicted, it would be worth more than $20 billion.

The winners in this market are the strategic players–companies like Sharp, which have consistently taken a long-term view. The losers are the tactical players, which includes all U.S. companies that have participated in liquid crystal display activities over the past 25 years.

Japan's victory in the LCD industry was achieved entirely through the efforts of entrepreneurial firms, without any help whatsoever from the Japanese government. How ironic, then, that the Clinton Administration should have targeted this industry for the application of what it perceived to be Japanese-style industrial policy.

In May 1994, the White House announced plans to spend up to $1 billion to subsidize the creation of a domestic U.S. flat panel display capabability. The centerpiece of the initiative is the U.S. Display Consortium, based in San Jose, California. The consortium has ten corporate members, led by AT&T and Xerox. It is funded via the Department of Defense's Advanced Research Projects Agency (ARPA, formerly known as DARPA). By mid-1996, Larry Tannas estimated, total U.S. government outlays on displays amounted to some $1.3 billion.

This may sound like a lot. For James Fergason, however, it was "too little, too late. This issue was decided almost 20 years ago," he said, adding that "the time to have made those decisions was when the field was really beginning to bop." Just when George Heilmeier was director of DARPA, in other words. "It would have cost a lot less then than it's going to cost now," Fergason laughed.

With hindsight, Fergason reckoned that "we could have done everything that [the Japanese] did, but they saw the need to do it, and understood the importance of low-power displays long before we did." Asked whether he felt bitter about the success of the Japanese, Fergason replied, "not really–I'm more bitter about the attitude we had in this country in the '70s." But then he added that he was not really bitter at all.

Today, Fergason runs a small Menlo Park, California–based company called Optical Shields. Among other things, the firm makes ultrafast liquid crystal cells that go from clear to opaque in a fraction of a second, to protect the eyes from flashes of light from the likes of industrial lasers. Nearly forty years on from when he began working on liquid crystals at Westinghouse, and almost uniquely among American LCD pioneers, Fergason is, as he put it, "still around, still doing my thing."

4

The Lunatics Have Taken Over the Asylum

Because of the unusual properties and the low energy requirements of ... liquid crystals, the flat screen TV is a possibility. Also, because of the high resolution and low power ... even the wristwatch TV of Dick Tracy is not impossible.
                                        —James Fergason[1]

"Did you see it?"
"Yes, I saw it—did *you* see it?"
"Yes, I saw it too!"

Morozumi Shinji and his friend and former classmate Oguchi Koichi could hardly believe their eyes. For months now, the two young Suwa Seiko researchers had been working together on the development of a new application for liquid crystals: television.

Outside activities had long since ceased to interest them. Weekdays they worked until midnight and sometimes beyond. Saturdays and Sundays, too, the pair would come in to the lab in the lakeside town of Suwa and toil all day, attempting to persuade their tiny two-inch TV screen to perform.

On this particular morning in 1982—Morozumi recalled it was a Sunday and the eve of a national holiday—he and Oguchi came in as usual, and there was nobody else about. They flicked the switches and saw, for the first time, the screen light up with moving TV pictures.

Then, after a few seconds the tantalizing images disappeared, leaving the pair staring at each other incredulously, wondering whether in their tiredness they had been imagining things.

After the holiday, Morozumi and Oguchi told their colleagues what they had seen. But the screen was no longer working, and nobody believed them. "It was like a kind of ghost panel," Morozumi laughed. Over the next few days they took the screen apart, found out what was wrong and fixed it. This time, when they hit the switches, their miniature television lit up with crystal-clear pictures—and stayed lit up. And this time, there could be no doubting what they had done.

But impressive though it was, their little masterpiece was a long way from being ready for the market. For one thing, it could only show TV pictures in black and white. Seiko's marketing people insisted that if LCD television was going to be commercially successful, it would have to be capable of color. So the next challenge for Morozumi and his friend was to incorporate color into their display. Casting around for a solution, they found inspiration in the tiny red, green, and blue color filters coated on the surface of the vidicon tubes that conventional TV cameras use to pick up images. Then they persuaded a reluctant printing company to make them some scaled-up vidicon color filters to fit their screen.

Switching on the prototype panel they built that incorporated the new color filters was much more exciting, Morozumi recalled, even than their experience with the monochrome screen. It was, after all, the first time that anyone had ever seen color TV pictures on a liquid crystal display. This time, after Morozumi had dragged Suwa Seiko managing director Nakamura Tsuneya down to his lab for a demonstration, the conversation quickly turned to the business prospects for pocket-sized LCD TVs.

Nakamura gave his approval to go ahead with commercialization. But Morozumi was still not satisfied. He wanted to tell the world what he and his friend had achieved—before anybody else jumped in ahead of them with a similar claim. Nakamura opposed making an early announcement. He argued that it should be made just before the introduction of the product, still at least a year away.

The youngsters would have none of this caution: "We were excited with our technologies, we wanted to announce as soon as possible,"

Morozumi said. "That was the feeling of our research and engineering people. So I begged [Nakamura] to allow us to make the announcement the next month, and finally he agreed."

In May 1983 Suwa Seiko announced their tiny TV simultaneously at a press conference in Tokyo and in Philadelphia at the annual meeting of the Society for Information Display, the industry's premier forum. When the slide showing Suwa's color liquid crystal display was screened at this meeting, the audience burst into a spontaneous round of applause.

Back home, the announcement of the miniature television triggered an avalanche of publicity. In particular, Morozumi remembered one re-markable piece of coverage: "In Japan," he said, "everyone watches the NHK news at seven o'clock. A camera crew came to our press conference and videotaped me holding the TV, and they used it in their report on the seven o'clock news—it was really amazing!"

It was also eerily reminiscent of RCA's ill-fated LCD press conference of exactly fifteen years earlier. Ironically, the similarity would extend to what happened at Seiko in the years following the dramatic announcement.

Thanks to Morozumi's achievement, Seiko would make much of the early running in the market for color LCD televisions and, more importantly in the short run, laptop computer screens. But like RCA, Seiko would ultimately falter, fail to capitalize on their lead, and be eclipsed by more aggressive rivals, most notably Sharp.

Why had Morozumi's peers in the display business accorded him an ovation in Philadelphia? The reason was that in the great flat-panel derby, he had rescued liquid crystals from also-ran status. Until Suwa Seiko's epoch-making (as they like to say in Japan) announcement, it seemed that liquid crystals would never go beyond simple, slow-switch-ing applications like the four- and eight-digit numeric displays on cal-culators and watches. Conventional wisdom said that the materials simply could not cope with the huge volumes of rapidly changing infor-mation that constitute television pictures.

A TV picture is made up of thousands of dots arranged in hundreds of horizontal rows. Each dot is updated with new information—as one picture frame succeeds another—every sixtieth of a second. In a cath-ode ray (boob) tube, the dots consist of red, blue, and green phosphors coated on the inside of the screen. They light up when struck by electrons fired by guns at the neck of the tube.

Liquid crystals produce no light of their own. Illumination in an LCD comes from a backlight located behind the liquid crystal cells. Each cell acts as a tiny shutter, either blocking the light or allowing it to pass. The shutters are controlled by a matrix made up of rows and columns of transparent electrodes. These are deposited on either side of the glass plates used to contain the liquid crystals. A dot is defined as a point at which the horizontal and vertical electrodes cross.

To produce a picture, you begin by applying a voltage (horizontally) across the top row. To this you add voltages (vertically) to the columns in which the dots you wish to select are located. The combined voltage is sufficient to open (or close) the shutter. Then you repeat the process for the next row, then the next, and so on, scanning down until you reach the bottom.

The trouble with this method is that in each row, the dots that are not selected also receive some fraction of the applied voltage. This causes shutters that are supposed to be closed to open a little. The result is reduced contrast (between selected and unselected dots).

The more rows you add, the worse the problem becomes. Since the period required to display a complete picture–i.e., a sixtieth of a second–remains constant, you keep having to divide it into smaller and smaller chunks. This gives the sluggish liquid crystals less and less time to react. You end up with shutters that are sort of open and sort of closed–a dim picture, in other words.

A radical solution to the contrast problem is to isolate the dots by giving each one a switch of its own. Using this approach, only dots whose switches are on can be selected. Unlike an electrode, which is a merely passive component, a switch is an active device. Hence the term "active matrix" to describe this type of display.

The active matrix concept emerged early on in flat-panel display research; the switch used to build it, the thin-film transistor, earlier still. Both were American inventions. As we saw in chapter 1, the bipolar transistor, the semiconductor industry's mainstay for its first two decades, was not suited to high levels of integration, forcing researchers to hunt for alternatives.

One possibility was the MOS device; another was the thin-film transistor. The rivals resembled each other in that both were variants on the field effect theme. The principal difference was that, by definition, you have to build MOS transistors on a semiconductor–typically silicon–whereas you could deposit thin-film transistors on an insulator, notably glass.

Most big U.S. electronics companies investigated both approaches. By the mid-1960s, however, the contest was over, with MOS having won the day. Only two laboratories continued thin-film transistor research–the same two that pioneered liquid crystal displays–RCA and Westinghouse.

At RCA Paul Weimer, one of the Sarnoff Center's most creative scientists, led the way. Weimer was primarily interested in developing thin-film image sensors that might eventually be used to replace the vidicon in "tubeless" color TV cameras, a key area of interest to RCA.

Weimer worked with exotic compound semiconductors such as cadmium selenide and cadmium sulfide. These materials had their merits–notably that, unlike silicon at this time, the films could be made in both positive and negative types–but they were far too unstable for commercial consideration. RCA axed the TFT program in 1971, the year of the corporation's ignominious exit from the computer business and of the death of its founding father, David Sarnoff.

That left Westinghouse, in the words of Peter Brody, the leader of the Westinghouse thin-film transistor group, "alone in possession of a deserted field." The tale of woe Brody tells of TFT development at Westinghouse gives a good idea of how hard it is–and how much resourcefulness it takes–to keep a research program in a new area going in the face of indifference and, on occasion, downright hostility from corporate management.[2]

Stimulated by Weimer's work at RCA, Brody set up a small TFT research program at Westinghouse in 1963. Having just killed an MOS program, Westinghouse's integrated circuit division was "not overly enthusiastic" about TFTs, either. "Indeed," Brody wrote, "we were told that if TFTs did not make it in 1963, then we might as well forget about them." But 1963 came and went, and a couple of small research contracts plus some interest from the corporation's defense divisions kept the TFT effort–just barely–alive.

Brody's group continued to come up with ideas that demonstrated the potential of their technology. In 1967, for example, one of its members had the idea of trying to deposit a TFT on a strip of paper, "just for a lark." The paper transistor worked "amazingly well," and within a few months, the group had a range of paper and other flexible circuits working.

But "[t]he IC Division (by that time in serious trouble themselves) did not appreciate our little fun and games at all, and continued to insist that TFTs were of no use to them—or indeed to anyone else. We received an ultimatum from management: if we could not come up with support from some other operating divisions within three months, then all work on TFTs and flexible circuits was to stop."

Brody made a quick round of Westinghouse's manufacturing divisions to drum up some support. From them he managed to scrounge enough funding to continue. Shortly afterwards, the IC Division went out of business, relieving the pressure on the group, "since—for the time being—no-one was actively agitating to 'stop this waste of corporate funds.'"

Funding from the operating divisions enabled Brody and Co. to broaden their horizons to include displays. This was not a popular area at the company. "Westinghouse had just gotten out of the TV business, they were not in the computer or terminal business, the Defense Divisions were not interested, and anyhow, our idea of building an integrated TFT circuit the size of a TV screen was clearly absurd."

There were also lingering memories at Westinghouse of previous failures to build a flat-panel display screen. Prime among them was an early 1960s attempt by the company to build an electroluminescent screen that had had a switch behind every picture element.

"To us looking at the problem of flat-panel displays from a TFT-oriented point of view, this did not seem such an absurd idea at all, but rather a logical one. . . . We were looking for a good application for our TFT technology that did not run afoul of the all-conquering silicon chip. On the other side of the coin, the construction of a solid-state analog of the cathode ray tube was a clear-cut challenge."

The RCA group that built the first TFTs had also been interested in the potential of the device for application to large areas. They had gone so far as to obtain some patents on this idea but never actually got round to putting the idea into practice before running out of time and support.

For several years Brody peddled the display concept to anyone who would listen. Finally, in 1971, he managed to win two small development contracts, one from the U.S. Army for a six-inch electroluminescent display, the other from the Air Force for an LCD of the same size.

By this time, the Westinghouse TFT group was beginning to build up quite a bit of momentum. Worryingly, however, the rest of the world paid no attention to TFTs. "We felt that we were doing all the right things, but the isolation was uncomfortable, if not downright dangerous."

The military contracts exposed the group to review by the unfortunately acronymed Advisory Group on Electron Devices, or AGED. This elderly-sounding governmental committee, staffed by semiconductor industry worthies, was "horrified to discover that, several years after the official demise of TFT technology, some agency scientists still had the temerity to recommend and support programs involving the proscribed device."

In response to criticism from this committee, the Air Force canceled its contract, something normally only done in cases of complete failure to deliver. "In this case," Brody claimed, "although the contract was only $60,000, so far from a failure, the work was completely successful and resulted in the first operating active matrix liquid crystal display."

Brody is justified in claiming priority for this work. However, "completely successful" may be something of an overstatement to describe his group's TFT-LCD. According to one witness who saw it, this first device "was only of interest to other technologists, no one else would have been able to see that it had any merit."

Following this Air Force setback, "the internal struggle within Westinghouse again intensified ('See, even your contracts are now being canceled') and we were subjected to a six-month-long 'un-Westinghouse activities' committee investigation, which we survived, though not unscathed. Luckily, our work for the Army was progressing well, and by 1973 we were able to demonstrate a rudimentary performance of our active matrix EL panel . . .

"[B]y late 1974 we had demonstrated an electroluminescent video panel, and at this time we began to receive a good deal of recognition and even some company support. Liquid crystal displays were dead as far as Westinghouse was concerned—losing our one contract was clear evidence of a false trail—but electroluminescence was going strong." Indeed, the Westinghouse Electron Tube Division even began to provide funding for TFT-EL panels.

Two years later, however, the group was in trouble again, with the closure of most of the tube division, by then Brody's principal sponsor. "This resulted in a significant cut in our funding, and once again a very uncertain future was facing us." Making matters worse were changes to top management at Westinghouse, "then going through a difficult period due to its debacle with its uranium supply deals with the utilities."

Brody began looking for alternative means of support for the display work outside the company. "These moves," he noted, "were not appreciated." Further corporate reorganization brought in even less sympathetic managers, "and our days at Westinghouse were numbered." As their swan song, Brody's group gave the first public showing of video on a TFT-EL screen early in 1978. The following year, Westinghouse decided to stop all work on active matrix displays, and Brody resigned to form his own firm.

But he quickly discovered that "raising the necessary funds wasn't as easy as I had imagined, mainly because at this time there were still no other credible practitioners of the TFT art." It took him two years to raise the cash to start up his company, Panelvision.

Alas, poor Brody! Though Pittsburgh-based Panelvision may have been the first to commercialize active matrix displays, the initial market for them was tiny, and the company's venture capital backers soon got cold feet. In 1985 the firm was sold to the defense contractor Litton.

Panelvision's first product was to be the Minigraphic, a small (2.5 × 4-inch) panel capable of displaying twelve rows of 32 characters each, priced at $200. Target markets, according to the May 1984 issue of *High Technology* magazine, included portable computers, scientific and medical instruments, "dataphones," process control units, aircraft and automobile panels, and electronic cash registers. Engineering prototypes of the Minigraphic were due to be delivered in 1984; whether commercialization had actually occurred by the time of the Litton takeover the following year is unclear.

Today, like so many other American LCD pioneers, Brody is a consultant, "selling my brains instead of my products."[3] The embittering experience of the American researcher drew a sympathetic response from his counterpart at Sharp, Wada Tomio. "Brody-San was unlucky, wasn't he?" Wada reflected. "If your company doesn't give you proper support," he added, "then your research can't be successful—it'll run out of steam along the way. In our case at Sharp, everyone supported us: we had a dream, and we were able to do our research."

At Suwa Seiko, too, in stark contrast to the relentlessly negative attitude that prevailed at Westinghouse, researchers were also able to carry out their research with the full support of management. As we have seen in the previous two chapters, Seiko was led by pragmatic engineers like Nakamura Tsuneya, whose initial motivation in getting into displays had been to stay abreast of the leading edge of watchmaking technology.

As time went by, however, the company became increasingly driven by the creative urges of its younger researchers. "At Suwa Seiko [in the 1970s]," said Yamazaki Yoshio, the chemist who initiated LCD research at the company, "if there was something you wanted to do, there were hardly any restrictions."

Yamazaki elaborated: "The company's culture is that, unless there is a good reason not to, top management usually approves what the lower levels decide is the best way to go. It's not our style for top management to say, Do this. Rather, [the direction] comes from the bottom up, like, that way looks good, why don't we do that? And though there have been some cases where top management said, 'No, not that way, stop that,' the usual way, if there are no problems, is 'OK, go ahead and do it.'"

Morozumi, who would build on the base that Yamazaki established at Seiko, agreed: "It was always bottom up. At that time [during the early 1980s, when Brody was hustling for funds to start his company], Seiko was a very nice company—almost everything we proposed, top management accepted."

In those heady days, it was a simple matter for Seiko's researchers to get approval to purchase expensive equipment. "To be honest," Morozumi laughed, "I spent a lot of money! I'd make a proposal saying that we'd like to develop something, we need equipment and it costs 500 million yen [approximately $2 million]. I'd send the proposal to top management, and they'd be like, Oh yes, do it, and they'd sign it easily."

Later on, when LCD televisions moved from development to production, and much larger sums–Morozumi guessed on the order of $30 to $50 million dollars–would be involved, it was just the same. The decision to proceed was made almost casually.

Cash from the sale of quartz watches (and subsequently of dot-matrix printers) was pouring into Seiko, supporting all sorts of diversification activities. An American visitor to the company recalled wandering around and being overwhelmed by the number of projects that were simultaneously on the go: "Every place you'd turn there would be somebody doing something interesting."[4] In addition to watches, a profile of the Seiko Epson group, compiled in 1993, lists seventeen other business areas in which the company was involved. Most are spin-offs from watch technology. They include quartz devices, semiconductors, magnets and motors, printers (mini and computer), personal computers, engineering plastics, optical products (plastic lenses), liquid crystal displays, small instruments, disk drives (floppy and optical), and factory automation (robots).

Seiko's young engineers were in control, doing more or less exactly as they pleased. In effect, the lunatics had taken over the asylum. There was little that Seiko's owners, the Hattori family, could do to stop this corporate anarchy. Under the lifelong employment system that obtains at large Japanese companies, it is virtually impossible to fire anyone. The most dynamic of the Hattoris was Shoji's son Ichiro, who took over as chairman of the company on his father's death in 1974. Ichiro tried hard to regain command. But in doing so, he encountered considerable resistance. "Japanese managers are harder to control than Americans," he would grumble, "because their self-motivation is stronger and their tenures more secure."[5]

Few at Seiko had stronger self-motivation than Morozumi Shinji, the LCD TV pioneer. An electronic engineer by training, Morozumi graduated from Tohoku University, one of Japan's top schools in that field. Most of his fellow-graduates signed up with the big electronics firms based in Tokyo and Osaka. But Morozumi was never one to follow the pack; besides, he didn't fancy living in a big, overcrowded city. Looking around for jobs elsewhere, he encountered recruiters from Suwa Seiko, who were in the process of hiring their first batch of electronic specialists. By coincidence, Suwa just happened to be Morozumi's hometown. His father had been a trader in silk, formerly Suwa's main industry. Young Morozumi was glad to find a job so close to where he grew up.

Morozumi joined Seiko in 1971, aged 22. His first job was designing C-MOS integrated circuits for watches. With the company just gearing up to produce its initial chips, he was able to gain valuable experience in semiconductor process technology and device development as well as design.

Throughout the 1970s, Morozumi worked on ICs. In the room next door to his at Seiko's R&D labs another group was developing a wristwatch TV. This was a natural outgrowth of Seiko's success in making LCDs for watches. The company was seeking other applications to absorb available production capacity.

At the same time, the idea of making a tiny television came more naturally to watchmakers, who were accustomed to thinking of the world in terms of what would fit on the wrist. Electrical appliance makers, by contrast, had a very different view of what a television should be. "They probably thought that the idea of a tiny TV was odd," Yamazaki laughed, "because television is meant to be seen, and if it's too small, you can't see it. But our logic was that we were a watchmaker, and to a watchmaker, small is beautiful."

Meanwhile, Seiko's rivals were also working on wristwatch televisions. For their TVs Casio and Citizen were concentrating on conventional, passive matrix displays. Though novel, these would never be capable of producing high-contrast pictures. In their approach to liquid crystal televisions, Seiko's irrepressible engineers took the technological high road. That meant shooting for active matrix displays.

Active matrix displays needed switches. At this time, however, thin-film transistors were not ready for production; all known materials—including Brody's exotic compounds—were extremely unstable. In the United States, a group at Hughes Aircraft had tried to solve the materials problem. Instead of TFTs on glass panels, they substituted C-MOS transistors on silicon wafers.

Seiko decided to adopt a similar approach. But opting for silicon as the material for the base also meant having to forgo twisted nematic liquid crystals. These were ideal for picture quality, but they required a transparent base material like glass or quartz. Instead, Seiko chose a reflective type of display.

This approach did enable them to make a TV, but at a price. Polishing up the surface of the wafers to a mirror finish to make them reflective required some fancy processing footwork. Even then, viewability was poor. Making this television became a production nightmare, but nonetheless Seiko somehow succeeded. In December 1982 the company announced the world's first wristwatch TV. Fifty years on from the first Dick Tracy comic strip, reality had finally caught up with the imagination of Chester Gould, the hawk-nosed gumshoe's creator.

Reaction to the announcement was enormous. Yamazaki recalled that Seiko got inquiries from all over the world, including one from NASA. The American space agency was intrigued with the possibilities for compact, lightweight information displays that the tiny screen promised.

Domestically, the announcement of the wristwatch TV also brought a second, unexpected windfall. Up to that point Suwa was regarded as being too far out in the sticks. As a result graduates from top schools—other than the odd maverick like Morozumi—would turn their noses up at signing on with Seiko.

After the wristwatch TV announcement, however, applications from graduates who wanted to join Seiko—including some from Tokyo University, the nation's number one school—poured in. "It was unbelievable how many of them we got," Yamazaki laughed, "we'd never had such an effective way of publicizing the company's name before!"

(Generating publicity about the high-tech nature of their research and development has since become a commonplace recruiting tool for Japanese companies, especially those in traditional industries. A good instance of this phenomenon is the enthusiasm shown by Japanese construction firms for building space stations and lunar bases.)

Seiko's Dick Tracy television generated publicity out of all proportion to its commercial significance. The little monochrome screen had never really been intended as a product. Like the Astron, Seiko's first quartz watch introduced thirteen years earlier, it was a kludge. And like the Astron, it was quietly discontinued after only one batch was produced.

Morozumi was drafted by Seiko's top management to join the wrist-watch television development group midway through the project. The idea was that he would be able to bring his experience in producing integrated circuits to bear on the problems the TV group were having with their C-MOS wafers. But after working with this group for some time, Morozumi came to realize that silicon wafers were never going to be a realistic approach for the mass production of liquid crystal TVs. He recommended that they discontinue this line of development. Meanwhile he looked around for a more practical approach. His conclusion: "We would have to challenge thin-film transistors."

Having made this decision, the next choice was which material to use for the transistors. Several possibilities had been proposed. There was, for instance, cadmium selenide, which Brody's (by now defunct) group at Westinghouse had worked on. But Morozumi quickly rejected this material, partly because of its reputation for being highly prone to defects, but also because cadmium is toxic. As such it must be handled with great caution, to avoid poisoning workers and polluting the environment.

Two other promising possibilities were different varieties of silicon material. Depending on how it is processed, silicon can take various forms. The most common type—the one predominantly used by the semiconductor industry—is single-crystal silicon. This form of the material is grown by dipping a rotating seed crystal into a vat of molten silicon, then withdrawing it slowly. The resultant ingot, which resembles a sausage, is subsequently sliced—like salami—into thin, silver-colored wafers.

In complete contrast to the regularly oriented structure of single-crystal silicon is amorphous silicon, a metallic brown-colored material which—as the name suggests—has no definite form or structure. Somewhere in between the two extremes comes polycrystalline silicon, a mottled, blue-colored material that is not as well organized as single crystal, but more coherent than amorphous. It is in fact made up of randomly oriented single crystals. Polysilicon is made by recrystallization, a process in which a film of material is heated by scanning a powerful laser beam across it.

In 1980, when Morozumi began to work on displays, not much was known about either poly- or amorphous silicon. Amorphous silicon, which was discovered in 1975, was originally used to make solar cells. In 1979, experiments showed that transistors could be made from the material. Amorphous would go on to become in the 1990s the workhorse thin-film transistor of the liquid crystal display industry.[6]

Morozumi chose to work on polysilicon. As an integrated circuit specialist he knew a good deal about this material. He had been experimenting with polysilicon as a substitute for metal on the gates on MOS transistors. But despite his experience, Morizumi's first polysilicon thin-film transistors performed very poorly. He tried all sorts of techniques to optimize the quality of the thin film. Finally he was able to make transistors good enough to apply to liquid crystal cells. Then he and his buddy Oguchi went to work on developing their tiny TV screen.

Suwa Seiko's 1983 announcement of LCD television took the electronics industry completely by surprise. Until that time, few believed that TFT-LCD was a feasible approach to making flat-screen displays. Morozumi's breakthrough changed people's minds. Alerted to the fact that it was possible to build an attractive liquid crystal display television out of thin-film transistors, giant firms like Matsushita, Hitachi, and Toshiba swung into action with crash development programs of their own.

To capitalize on their head start, Suwa had to get LCD televisions into production, quick. The decision to invest in a TFT factory had been made before the announcement. But before any products could be shipped, the factory had to be started up, equipment installed, and production processes established. The tiny screens were made out of quartz, an insulating material that behaves very differently from a semiconductor such as silicon, necessary because glass could not withstand the heat of high-temperature laser processing. Until Seiko's workers understood these differences and were able to adjust for them, production yields remained very low.

For a whole year after the announcement, Morozumi was incredibly busy. "From equipment installation to getting a good yield, I came home at midnight, or 1:00 or 2:00 A.M., then returned to my office at eight o'clock in the morning," he recalled. For him, problems at work were compounded by inconveniences at home. "At the time, I was rebuilding my house, so I had to move to my wife's parents' house close by. So I was coming back, not to my own house, but to my wife's parents' house at midnight, when everyone was sleeping," he laughed. "They didn't care, but a big problem for me at that time was that it was hard to get meals!"

Seiko marketed the world's first commercial flat-screen color television in 1984 under the name "My Channel." With its tuning dial, speaker, and pull-out antenna, the TV resembled a portable radio, the tiny two-inch screen taking up perhaps one sixth of its front panel. Priced at around ¥75,000 ($315), the television was little more than an expensive toy. Certainly, Seiko's marketing arm did not expect to sell many of them. "There's no way that this color TV will become a substantial item," said Hattori Kentaro, the parent company's then chairman.[7]

If active matrix LCDs were to become a consumer product, then production volumes would have to go up in order to bring the price down. That in turn meant looking for new markets. Morozumi met this challenge by developing LCDs for use as components to sell to other manufacturers for incorporation in their products.

He identified three new niche markets. One was "light valves" for video projection displays. These exploit the shutter function of liquid crystal cells to project large—up to several hundred inches in diagonal—pictures onto a movie screen or a white wall. Brody's group had demonstrated this application in 1977, but Seiko was the first to commercialize it in 1985. Ten years later, the Japanese firm was still the largest maker of LCD components for this application.

The second niche was to apply active matrix LCDs as electronic viewfinders in video cameras. Makers had previously used tiny picture tubes. But these could only handle monochrome images, whereas LCDs were capable of color, making them more attractive. Seiko sold viewfinders to leading video camera makers—including Sony—until the makers began to produce their own components. Recently these tiny screens have found a new market in the shape of virtual reality goggles.

The third market that Morozumi found for active matrix LCDs was as image-reading sensors in facsimile machines. These components convert into electronic form whatever is printed on paper fed into the fax. For a few years, this was a good business until the LCD was supplanted in this application by the charge-coupled device.[8]

Morozumi's success in developing these components led to his being promoted during the mid-1980s to a high-level management position in Seiko Epson's R&D division. In his new job, he was responsible for managing a whole range of development projects, including computer software, optical disks, and printing technologies.

But these responsibilities were not to Morozumi's liking. They left him little time for LCDs, which had become his passion in life. So he asked Seiko's top management to transfer him to the LCD business division. It was a move that would ultimately lead to his leaving the company.

By the late 1980s Seiko was no longer the happy ship it had been during the previous decade. In 1987, the company had suffered a tragic loss in the early death at age 55 of its charismatic chairman, Hattori Ichiro.

In a rare and insightful profile of the Seiko Group published in the 12 November 1984 issue of *Fortune* magazine, Edward Boyer described the founder's grandson as "handsome, worldly, assertive, impatient and sharp. After graduating from the University of Tokyo, Japan's best, he did graduate work at the University of Zurich and Yale. He plays tennis, golf and bridge, and reads Somerset Maugham. James Hodgson, former U.S. ambassador to Japan, sees him as 'one of maybe three upcoming young businessmen who'll someday take the economic leadership of Japan.' "

In pursuit of his goal, diversification into new business, Ichiro was not afraid to spend big. In 1984, for example, he authorized the investment of more than $100 million—equivalent to about 10 percent of Seiko Epson's sales that year—in new semiconductor production facilities. At the same time printers, which by the mid-1980s had become the company's largest business, also demanded further huge investments.

As a private company, the only way for Seiko Epson to finance such expansions was through bank loans. These were easy to obtain so long as the bubble economy continued to froth. But in 1989, Japan's stock market crashed, bursting the bubble and souring the Japanese economy. The crash left Seiko seriously overextended, struggling to make massive repayments to its bankers.

With sales of laptop personal computers soaring, liquid crystal displays obviously had a golden future. Morozumi tried desperately to convince Seiko's top management to invest in new LCD production facilities. If they did not, he argued, then the company would lose a business opportunity that it was uniquely positioned to exploit. But to no avail–he was told that there was no money available for investment.

"When I joined Suwa Seiko, it was only a small company with maybe $500 million sales," Morozumi said. "But within the next ten years, sales grew to like $5 billion. And I think the reason why the company had such big growth was that we had a lot of freedom to do everything, and top management said, Yes, go ahead. But after the mid-1980s, it changed, the freedom disappeared, and now their sales are flat."

Morozumi was so disappointed, he decided to quit Seiko. In his frustration, he had no idea of what he would do next; all he knew was that he wanted out. In Japan, it is very rare for employees of large companies to quit their jobs in mid-career. Salaried workers normally stay with the same company all the way from graduation until retirement. To resign at the age of 42, as Morozumi did, was an extremely risky thing to do.

Everybody tried to persuade him to reconsider, but Morozumi was determined. Even so, it took a year of delicate negotiations with top management in order to win their agreement to his departure. His next move was equally unexpected: In 1991 he moved to California and a job at one of the world's most famous corporate laboratories: the Xerox Palo Alto Research Center, or PARC.

Morozumi's motivation in moving to the United States was twofold. On the one hand, he wanted to keep up with the latest in LCD manufacturing. He had heard that Xerox was planning to build a state-of-the-art facility. On the other, he was keen to sample the famous California lifestyle.

Morozumi stayed 18 months at PARC waiting for Xerox to make up their minds about LCD production. But the U.S. firm hesitated, and the opportunity was lost. It was the same old Xerox story of excellent research and poor business judgment that had caused the company to invent, then ignore most of the key personal computer technologies. Morozumi knew that Japanese firms were already tooling up to build second-generation LCD manufacturing facilities. An ambitious man, he was itching for a share of the action.

In 1992, he returned to Japan to a job that could have been tailor-made for him. He became deputy general manager of the active-matrix LCD business division of Hosiden, an entrepreneurial firm that, more than any other company in the world, had staked its future on liquid crystal displays.

A glance at the company's logo tells insiders how committed Hosiden is to displays. The middle three letters of the logo are rendered in bold, HO**SID**EN. "SID" just happens to stand for the Society for Information Display, which includes among its members all the industry's leading practitioners.

What had transformed Osaka-based Hosiden from a small, family-owned maker of humble electromechanical bits and pieces into a purveyor of thin-film transistor liquid crystal displays, some of the most high-tech components in the world? Components such as the cockpit displays in Boeing's most advanced passenger aircraft, the 777, of which Hosiden is the sole supplier?

The short answer was Morozumi's good friend Aoki Shigeo, the firm's tough-minded, hard-charging executive vice-president. LCD work at Hosiden had begun at his urging in 1970, just two years after the original RCA announcement. The company was also early into active matrix displays, initiating research as early as 1978.

Unlike all other Japanese makers of advanced LCDs, Hosiden is not a huge, vertically integrated company. In 1991, when Morozumi joined, the firm had sales of less than $500 million. In other words, Hosiden was about the same size as Seiko had been when Morozumi began there, twenty years previously. To overcome the problem of limited resources, the company adopted a unique approach to development: teaming up with U.S. partners.

One such partner is the instrument maker Honeywell. The U.S. firm provides technical support for Hosiden in the area of advanced cockpit systems for Boeing. Honeywell supplies the overall systems; Hosiden, the displays.

Another important partner is Apple Computer. Hosiden provided the solution to a serious problem that bedeviled the computer maker in the late 1980s. Rival makers were able to launch laptop computers ahead of Apple, because their machines could get away with displaying text only.

Apple needed a display that could handle its famous graphical user interface. Since ordinary displays could not react fast enough, that meant active matrix. Executives from the U.S. company toured Japan begging display makers to produce monochrome screens for them. All the big firms turned them down. Hosiden said: We'll do it. And sure enough, they did, producing in 1989 the screen for the Macintosh Portable, "the first major computer product . . . employing an active matrix LCD."

Ironically, the relationship with Apple led in 1990 to Hosiden being cited, along with eleven other Japanese manufacturers, in a flat-panel dumping suit brought by the U.S. International Trade Administration. As a result of this suit, a punitive tariff of 62.67 percent was levied on panels imported into the United States. Hosiden loudly proclaimed its innocence: "The ITA's ruling says that we sold products at 60 percent lower than our costs," a Hosiden executive told a reporter from *Electronic Engineering Times*. "How in the world could a company like Hosiden survive if we had been dumping products?" the exasperated exec wanted to know. He added that he and his colleagues were "still in a state of shock to learn how much it costs to hire an attorney [to fight the ITA ruling] in the United States."[9]

A Department of Commerce study subsequently found that Hosiden had made no sales at less than fair value. Pressure from U.S. computer makers–including Apple, which like other U.S. companies had promptly shifted production offshore (in Apple's case, to its plant in Ireland) to avoid paying the tariff–led to the tariff being revoked in July 1993.

On a summer afternoon in 1995, Morozumi discussed his plans for the future in a meeting room at Hosiden's second-generation LCD manufacturing plant in Kobe. Next door, just nearing completion was Morozumi's baby, a massive, third-generation LCD factory.

"In the first phase, we started with small panels for TV screens," he said, "then we challenged personal computer screens like the 10-inch size. The next target is 15- to 20-inch monitors for PCs. Then we'll challenge 40 inches for TV screens."

As he has already demonstrated, Morozumi's ambition to build ever bigger displays comes before company loyalty. Asked what he would do

Morozumi Shinji outside the R&D Center, Hosiden, Kobe.

if Hosiden were to be sidelined by bigger players in the race to build wall-hanging TVs, Morozumi replied, "Frankly speaking, my goal is not to make a business in Hosiden—it could be any company that would give me a chance to make a business out of displays to fulfill my dreams. So if Hosiden has a problem in the future, of course I would try and resolve the problem, but if it prevented me continuing my efforts here, then I would have to change my company."

If any company could knock Hosiden off course, it would be Sharp. Sharp is by far the world's largest manufacturer of LCDs, with a market share in the mid-1990s that verged on 40 percent. As we saw in the previous chapter, Sharp was one of the first Japanese companies to mass-produce (passive matrix) liquid crystal displays.

It would be logical to assume that the company simply went from strength to strength, from early presence to later predominance. But that is not what in fact happened. Along the way, Sharp was distracted by a rival technology. It was only by virtue of brave—and extremely risky–decisions that the company subsequently got back on track, caught up, and took the lead.

Sharp commercialized a calculator with a liquid crystal display in April 1973, six months before Seiko marketed their first LCD watch. This calculator was yet another technological triumph/manufacturing disaster. The display was an RCA-style dynamic scattering type. The LCD, the chips, and all the other components were mounted on the same piece of glass, a packaging technique that was way ahead of its time.

Not surprisingly, yields on this first LCD calculator were very low. But Sharp was undaunted. On a trip to Japan around this time Bob Burmeister, then a senior manager at the laboratories of Hewlett-Packard, recalls having dinner with Rocket Sasaki at a restaurant in Osaka: "We sat on the *tatami* [mats] and talked about the future–calculators and mobile computers. I mean, [HP] envisioned this in '73, and I realized that Sharp–Sasaki in particular–was thinking pretty far out, too.

"It was a very nice dinner, but I particularly remember the nature of the discussion: Where was liquid crystal technology going, could you multiplex them [i.e., use one signal source to drive several display segments, a key technological issue], and how large might they be? These were all very strong indicators of the future, and it was clear to me that he was personally quite committed to liquid crystals, and saw a future for them."

In the early 1970s, remember, almost nobody thought that sluggish liquid crystals would be suitable for anything other than slow-changing numerical digits. Television, which requires a fast response time, was unthinkable. Yet still the idea of the TV-on-the-wall remained beguiling. Especially to a company like Sharp, which, unlike most other major Japanese electronic appliance makers, did not make its own television picture tubes.

Sharp's LCD pioneer Wada Tomio had begun his career working on electroluminescent flat-panel displays. With their relatively low brightness and short lifetimes, these had proved to be a technological dead end. By the mid-1960s, most researchers had written EL panels off. Then a group of researchers based in Santa Barbara, California, came up with a new approach. This was called thin-film EL, to distinguish it from the older approach, known as powder EL.

The difference between the two lies in the thickness of the layer of phosphors, the chemicals that emit the light. In powder EL, the phosphors are formed by grinding them into grains, mixing them with a binder, then painting the mixture onto the panel. Thin-film EL phosphors are heated until they evaporate, then deposited onto the panel in a vacuum chamber. In this form, they are just a few molecules thick.

The Southern Californians formed a company, Sigmatron, to commercialize their displays. In 1965, they unveiled their work at an industry conference in New York. "The demonstration was most impressive," wrote Larry Tannas.[10] "It made true believers of all who ever saw it. The display was the most functionally pleasing of any numeric display ever made up to that time."

Particularly impressive was that the display was readable even in sunlight. By 1972, the company had demonstrated panels with a lifetime of several thousand hours. Unfortunately, however, Sigmatron could not manufacture the damn thing, and the company went bankrupt the following year.

Sharp picked up the thin-film baton that Sigmatron dropped, and ran with it. The company's head of research, Mito Sanai,[11] was convinced that EL was the way to get to the TV onto the wall. Led by Mito, a former professor from Osaka Municipal University, Sharp's researchers mounted a large-scale effort to develop thin-film EL displays. They took a fresh look at the problems and eventually, through perseverance and financial commitment, managed to solve most of them.

Their finest hour came in September 1978, at the Consumer Electronics Show in Chicago, when they demonstrated a panel that was bright, long-lasting, and capable of displaying television pictures. To be sure, the screen was only a few inches in diagonal and the pictures it displayed were only black and white. But the main thing about the "glowing wall" as Sharp's EL screen was dubbed, was that it was just 1.2 inches (3 centimeters) thick—plus, of course, that it actually worked.

Mito's breakthrough sparked a resurgence of interest in EL technology, inspiring several U.S. firms to enter (in some cases, reenter) the field—in particular, Tektronix, whose spin-off Planar would become the leading manufacturer in this field. In a commemorative issue celebrating its twenty-fifth anniversary, *Playboy* magazine featured Sharp's prototype panel, dubbing it the technology of 1978.

In 1983, Sharp became the first company to succeed in mass-producing EL panels. The same year, the company scored a PR triumph when NASA announced that the company's flat screens would be used in the Space Shuttle's orbital navigation system to display maps of the Earth. Another early customer for Sharp's EL displays was a U.S. company, Grid, which produced the first laptop computer.

But although Sharp would continue to tout its success in commercializing EL in public, behind the scenes it was a very different story. In 1983, Morozumi announced his LCD television, taking everybody by surprise. Suddenly EL had a rival that not only consumed far less power but also displayed full color.

Color was an area of particular weakness for electroluminescent displays. Most EL panels are monochrome, displaying text and figures in a characteristic manganese orange or yellow color on a black background. As time went by, researchers persuaded the displays to emit red and green light, too. But a phosphor capable of emitting blue has continued to elude them, with the result that, to this day, EL cannot be used to produce full-color TV pictures.

Sharp now had to scramble to catch up with Suwa Seiko. Within the company the R&D chief, Mito, was severely criticized for putting too much emphasis on a single technology. In fact, however, Sharp had not quite put all its eggs into one basket. In 1981 the company's researchers learned that thin-film transistors could be made from amorphous silicon, a material they were familiar with from having used it for the solar cells that powered the company's latest calculators. Sharp initiated a small project to apply thin-film transistors to flat panels.

In the early days, it was an uphill struggle. Larry Tannas visited Sharp's R&D facility at Tenri in 1985, two years after Morozumi's announcement. At that time, he reported, they did not have a single TFT liquid crystal cell working. Meanwhile, several other companies, including Sharp's big Osaka rivals, Matsushita and Sanyo, had already begun small-scale commercial production of active matrix liquid crystal displays.

This crucial period also saw a generational change in Sharp's top management. In 1985 Rocket Sasaki, the dynamic visionary who for over twenty years had played a leading role in transforming Sharp from a minor player into one of Japan's most innovative electronics firms, retired at age 70. Two years later, Saeki Akira, the powerful administrator without whom Sasaki claimed that he would not have been able to accomplish anything, stepped down as chairman.

The LCD would be the first test of the new management's mettle. In 1987, Sharp finally managed to put into production a 3-inch liquid crystal television. Production yields were low, however, and the most that Sharp's engineers dared hope for were incremental increases in scale, from 3-inch screens to 4 inches, and then 5, improving the yield bit by bit.

But the leader of the LCD development team, Washizuka Isamu, had other ideas. Twenty years before, Washizuka had been one of the four young engineers who did the initial development of the calculator at the company. He remembered Sasaki setting them what seemed an impossible goal—a handheld calculator.

Now Washizuka in his turn would set his young engineers an apparently unachievable target. In early 1988 he summoned Sharp's LCD researchers to a meeting at the factory and told them, "Let's try and build the biggest screen we can." He challenged them to build a display that would be not 5, not even 10, but an enormous 14 inches in diagonal. Such a panel would require the deposition of more than a million thin-film transistors, an order of magnitude higher than anything anyone had previously attempted.

A 14-inch screen required all sorts of design and process innovations. To build it, Sharp's engineers had to push the state of the art to the limit, using what were then the biggest glass panels available. But somehow they managed to pull it off. Visitors to the Japan Electronics Show that October marveled at the size of the screen and the brightness of the pictures it displayed.

More significant than the effect on the general public was the impact that the 14-inch panel had within the company itself. Hijikigawa Masaya, a member of the team that built the panel, recalls that "it was a very emotional thing for us, that 14-inch screen.[12] We were really inspired, because it was the first time that any of us had seen anything like it. And we thought that if we can build something as big as that, then maybe the LCD will be able to rival the CRT. So because we had built and been impressed by that 14-inch display, we were able to dream about future prospects—that was the most important thing."

For his inspirational leadership, Washizuka would win the 1992 Consumer Electronics Award from the Institute of Electrical and Electronic Engineers. But far more important than the approbation of his peers was the fact that Washizuka had the total support of his fellow managers at Sharp, Sasaki's protege Asada Atsushi, and Saeki's successor Tsuji Haruo. In 1991, they decided to pour a massive, extremely high-risk investment—$640 million over three years—into the construction of new facilities for the production of liquid crystal displays.

TFT displays are often compared to large-scale integrated circuits. There are indeed many similarities in the ways the devices are produced. For example, both are made using photolithography. But as Joe Castellano pointed out, there are also significant differences that make producing displays a much more formidable challenge than producing chips. "The main difference," he wrote, "is the need to obtain a 99.9% yield of good devices on a single display [glass] substrate. This, compounded by the problem of a selling price constrained by the value of a similar CRT, makes the economical manufacturing of TFT LCDs a risky venture." [13]

Of the two Japanese firms that pioneered LCDs, Sharp won and Seiko lost.[14] Looking back, Seiko's Yamazaki thought he could see why: "The reason we did poorly in business had nothing to do with R&D, it was a problem with the business divisions, I think. How [a technology] progresses from invention to research and development to commercialization depends on motivation.

"The concept begins with an individual, because he's interested or whatever: there are all sorts of interesting ideas, contributed by all sorts of people, and that's true all over the world (although America may be particularly good at it, and Japan relatively weak—there are various opinions about that). But the basic thing is that, in the first place, ideas come from individuals.

"Once the idea has emerged, whether it gets adopted or not varies depending on the stage—whether it's early-stage or close to actual use. The early stages are close to actual research, where the role of the individual is big. But after that, it depends more and more on the company—on company policy, on where in the company the research occurs, after it becomes clear what the theme means to the company, and how it reflects company policy.

"So finally, when it comes to mass production, assuming that that takes a huge amount of money, what you decide depends on company policy. With Sharp, it became a point of honor for the company, they said, 'We're going to do this at all costs, and give it the highest priority in terms of people and money.' With Seiko Epson, we didn't go that far. The reason was that with LCDs, as with semiconductors, you have to keep investing huge amounts of money, and you have to decide whether that is good for the company. And with Seiko Epson, there were other things that we felt we should invest in."

Sharp won the race to commercialize active matrix LCDs. The first panels were naturally very expensive. Wastage was very high, and it was rumored that "mountains of glass"—i.e., panels that had to be trashed due to defects—were hidden behind the company's LCD plants. To drive down production costs, Washizuka followed Morozumi's policy of developing new markets.

Today, some twenty years after Brody et al. developed the first active matrix LCDs at Westinghouse, the screens are found in an ever-increasing variety of new products. Most notably, as far as Sharp is concerned, in what one observer described as "the only two bona fide hit products produced by Japan's electronics makers in the 1990s."[15] These were Sharp's ViewCam video camcorder, which uses an easy-to-see 4-inch active matrix color LCD in place of the traditional viewfinder, and the company's Zaurus, a personal digital assistant whose touch-screen LCD boasts accurate recognition of handwritten characters.

To these could be added a third product, the digital still camera. Like the ViewCam, these cameras typically employ a color LCD in place of a viewfinder to provide an instant playback. But by far the biggest application for color active matrix displays in the mid-1990s—accounting for some 80 percent of the market—was as screens for notebook computers.

All of this success has come in markets that the CRT cannot reach. But on the desktop, big, bulky, power-hungry tubes of evacuated glass in the form of personal computer monitors still dominate. And as for the living room—the LCD has barely begun to make a dent. There, the cathode ray tube—or the Braun tube, as it is still known in Japan, after its inventor, Karl Braun—continues to reign unchallenged. In 1997, the boob tube celebrated its centenary. Along with Edison's light bulb, Braun's invention has proved itself to be one of the most enduring electronic technologies of all.

Estimates vary enormously on the extent to which the LCD will eat into the CRT market. In the mid-1990s, predictions ranged from 5 percent of PC monitors by 2001, to about half of all TVs eventually. However, everyone agrees that the LCD still has a long way to go before it can match the CRT on price.

And what about the wall-hanging television? Will thin-film-transistor, active matrix, liquid crystal displays finally provide this much discussed and apparently much desired appliance?[16] As Peter Brody wrote in response to his own question back in 1984: "One is always much safer with positive than with negative predictions."

5

Under-the-Table Research

The winner is the first to market a product.
—Japanese business maxim, quoted by Kuwano Yukinori

[*The year is 1976; the scene, the University of Dundee, Scotland, where Walter Spear, a professor in the Department of Applied Physics and Electronic & Mechanical Engineering, is in his office awaiting visitors. There is a knock at the door.*

Enter the U.K. representative of Sanyo, the Japanese consumer electronics firm. He is followed by Yamano Masaru, director of Sanyo's research center, and Kuwano Yukinori, a scientist at the center.]

SANYO REPRESENTATIVE: Professor Spear?

[*Sanyo's U.K. representative has been assigned to step forward and make the introductions.*]

PROFESSOR SPEAR: Dr. Kuwano!

[*Mistaking representative for scientist, the professor leaps up from behind his desk and rushes forward to shake hands. Aghast at the prospect of taking precedence over his superiors—an embarrassing breach of Japanese etiquette—the young man backpedals away from the professor's outstretched arm, and dodges behind a nearby table.*]

This wonderful moment of near farce marks the first encounter between two of the protagonists in a drama of science and technology. The action takes place over thirty years and across three continents. Its subject is the almost alchemical transformation of an apparently worthless glassy material into the bedrock of a multibillion-dollar industry. Dundee provides an unexpected backdrop to the drama's first act. The drab little Scottish seaport had no prior record of scientific excellence. Indeed, aside from its famous fruitcake, Dundee was best known for an engineering disaster. On the night of 28 December 1879, during a storm, the railroad bridge across the River Tay collapsed under the weight of a train, causing the loss of some ninety lives.

Dundee formerly prided itself on three industries: jute, jam, and journalism.[1] By far the largest was jute. But by 1960, synthetic fibers had largely overtaken jute as the material of choice for the manufacture of sackcloth and rope, forcing many of the city's mills out of business.

During the 1960s, developers ripped the heart out of the city, depriving Dundee of much of what character it possessed. One of the few positive developments around this time occurred in 1967, when Dundee University became independent from the nearby University of St. Andrews, of which it had long been an adjunct (as it was when my father attended courses there). Now it could hire professors of its own. Among the first was Walter Spear.

Spear was a Jewish refugee who had managed to escape from the Nazis, getting out of Germany in the nick of time. He arrived in Britain with just the clothes he was wearing. After the war Spear did his Ph.D. in physics at the University of London, then got a job as a lecturer at Leicester.

Following the advent of the transistor in 1947, most solid-state physicists focused on crystalline semiconductors like germanium and silicon. Spear chose to work on unfashionable materials like sulfur and selenium. The crystals that others were studying exhibit a pleasingly regular structure. Spear's materials, by comparison, were a disorderly mess.

Spear brought with him to Dundee the brightest of his postdoctoral students, Peter LeComber, the son of a Ford assembly line worker from Dagenham, Essex. The pair turned out to possess complementary talents. Spear was the pure scientist, interested primarily in fundamental research. LeComber led work on the applied side.

While the aim of the rest of the physics community was to urge electrons to whiz through solids at ever-increasing speeds, the concern of

Spear and LeComber was on the contrary to slow electrons down. A more sedate pace enabled the pair to get a better picture on their oscilloscopes of how the minuscule particles proceeded from A to B.

In 1969, researchers at Standard Telecommunications Laboratories in England were working on a low-cost, low-temperature process for the production of crystalline silicon via the deposition of silane gas. They noticed that in addition to their target substance, they were also getting unexpected deposits of a glassy, brown-colored material. This turned out to be amorphous silicon.

In place of the crystal's regular honeycomblike shape, the amorphous (literally: "formless") material possesses an atomic structure that resembles a jumbled-up pile of matches that have been tipped out of their box. Or, to use an anthropomorphic analogy, crystalline silicon atoms are like schoolkids in class, sitting in neatly arranged rows of desks. Amorphous atoms, by contrast, are like kids during playtime, running around freely.

Not surprisingly, electrons took considerably longer to travel through this dog's-breakfast amorphous stuff than through the well-ordered pathways of the crystalline material. Knowing that Spear was the U.K.'s leading expert on low-mobility solids, STL sent some samples up to Scotland for him to examine.

Amorphous silicon turned out to be an ideal material for the Dundee group's experiments. Compared to the conventional low-mobility solids, it was wonderfully easy to analyze. However, amorphous silicon was not at all what the STL people were looking for. Shortly afterwards the company discontinued the production of the material.

STL's withdrawal meant that in order to continue their work, Spear and LeComber were obliged to construct their own reactor. Built on a shoestring and required to handle extremely dangerous gases, the thing was a safety nightmare. Somehow, miraculously, the reactor never blew up. In it, the Dundee researchers were able to produce thin films of amorphous silicon on which to experiment. In 1974, during the course of one such experiment they noticed something completely unexpected.

To make crystalline silicon electronically useful, you have to "dope" it; that is, you have to add tiny quantities of phosphorus, boron, or some such element to the material. This donates to the silicon the extra electrons or holes that turn it into negative- or positive-type material that can then be used to make semiconductor devices such as transistors.

Theory said that amorphous materials couldn't be doped. It was thought that all those randomly distributed atoms would simply rearrange themselves to mop up any leftover electrons or holes. But Spear and LeComber discovered that amorphous silicon *was* in fact amenable to doping. As well as being unexpected, this was scientifically significant.

The period following this discovery was a time of enormous excitement for the Dundee group. The scientists worked day and night churning out results, systematically varying the amounts of phosphorus and boron they added, until finally they had plotted a classic conductivity curve. The graph clearly showed that the more you doped amorphous silicon, the more conductive it became.

An important implication of these results was that everything that had been done with crystalline silicon could now also be done with amorphous silicon. For example, you could use it to make simple semiconductor devices like p–n junctions. But only if you wanted to, and who on earth would want to substitute this sluggish stuff for the swift-flowing crystalline material?

The idea that what they were doing might have useful applications seems at this point to have been far from the Dundee group's minds. Like the good scientists they were, Spear and LeComber were motivated purely by the desire to learn more about the physics of amorphous materials.

In 1975, the Dundee group published a paper detailing their results. At the end, in a throwaway line, they mentioned that they had observed photovoltaic activity–i.e., the conversion of light to electricity–in one of their devices. In other words, amorphous silicon could be used to make solar cells.

The cat was out of the bag.

Several weeks later, in a laboratory on the other side of the world, Kuwano Yukinori read with mounting excitement the Dundee group's paper. When he came to the part about photovoltaic activity, his heart leapt. Kuwano had spent the past decade working fruitlessly on amorphous materials. Here, at long last, was vindication of his prophesy that his precious stuff would play a key role in electronics.

Kuwano was born in 1941 in a rural part of Fukuoka Prefecture on Kyushu, the southernmost of the four main islands that make up the Japanese archipelago. After high school, he went on to nearby Kumamoto University, where he was supposed to study chemistry. In fact, like the vast majority of Japanese undergraduates then and now, Kuwano was not a diligent student. In Japan, college is viewed as a brief respite between entrance exam hell and a lifetime of *sarariman* drudgery. It is, in other words, the last chance to have a little fun.

Kuwano would often skip lectures to indulge in his passion for rock climbing. Kumamoto was a great place to go climbing: The prefecture is famous for its mountains. Kuwano's favorite spot was the slopes of Kumamoto's highest peak, Mount Aso. As he clambered up from one ledge to another, the hot sun beat down on him unmercifully, burning his exposed head.

Kuwano could afford to goof off. The 1960s were Japan's income-doubling decade. With the economy booming, an engineering graduate like himself was never going to have much trouble finding a job. But what sort of company to join? Though his major was chemistry, Kuwano had always been interested in electronics. At school he had manifested the classic gearhead symptoms: building and taking apart radios. He decided he would send his resume to an electronics company. Now the question was, to which of Japan's many electronics companies should he apply?

It pleases us to believe that we make choices on the basis of hard logic. Fact is, though, that we sometimes make decisions—even really important ones that profoundly affect the course of our lives—for the most whimsical of reasons. Kuwano selected Sanyo Electric Works, a second-tier Osaka-based maker of consumer electrical appliances, not because it was the biggest or the most profitable company of its kind, but because it was the sponsor of a popular American TV program, *Ben Casey*.

Older readers will remember Ben Casey as the first in a long line of altruistic TV doctors. "When I was young, I wanted to do such philanthropic social work, too," Kuwano laughed, "and because Sanyo sponsored *Ben Casey* [on Japanese television], I thought that maybe they had that kind of philosophy; that is, that they were not just a mass producer, but that their products had some good effect on society. I'm not sure if that was true, but that's what I felt."

A less high-minded reason for his choice was that Kuwano had been impressed by a fully automatic washing machine that Sanyo had recently marketed. As late as the 1980s, many Japanese housewives believed that washing clothes manually was a way of demonstrating their resolve to work hard in the service of the family. (Or perhaps it was their husbands and mothers-in-law who believed this.) An automatic washing machine with built-in spin-dryer and heater was thus a revolutionary product. Its existence made Kuwano feel that "Sanyo was a company which was able to challenge new technology and new products."

Sanyo was far from being an innovative outfit like Sharp or Sony. In actual fact the company's origins were bizarre. The individual most responsible for Sanyo's foundation was not a Japanese entrepreneur, but rather an American general. As Supreme Commander Allied Powers, General Douglas MacArthur presided over one of the key democratic reforms attempted during the Occupation—the breakup of the *zaibatsu*.

These were the giant family-owned industrial and financial combines that formerly dominated Japan. It is estimated that by the end of World War II, the four biggest *zaibatsu*—Mitsui, Mitsubishi, Sumitomo, and Yasuda—between them controlled a quarter of the Japanese economy.

About a dozen other, smaller conglomerates were also designated *zaibatsu* by the Occupation. For a while the blacklist also included the Osaka based electrical goods maker, Matsushita. There was considerable irony in this. The other firms thus designated were mostly long-established, blue-blooded companies that owed their prominence in large part to government favors. Matsushita by contrast was the creation of a remarkable Japanese entrepreneur by the name of Matsushita Konosuke.[2]

In 1917, while working as a lowly inspector at the Osaka Electric Light Company, in his spare time Matsushita had come up with a useful device—a Y-shaped adapter that plugged into a light socket to allow other appliances to be connected. When his employer showed no interest in his invention, Matsushita, pausing only to pawn his wife's kimonos in order to raise capital, struck out on his own. He set up a company to manufacture the adapter. Later, Matsushita would also make the appliances that plugged into it—every last one of them.

The wherewithal to enlarge the firm came from his first big success—a battery-powered bicycle lamp, introduced in 1923. By the time World War II broke out, Matsushita had grown into a large company. Some of the firm's plants were commandeered by the military. Among other things, they built planes and boats for the Japanese Imperial Navy. When the war ended, the Occupation ordered all factories that had been involved in military production to shut down. The company's assets were frozen and in June 1946, Matsushita Electric was designated a *zaibatsu*.

In November that year Matsushita Konosuke was purged. Under the terms of the order, Matsushita could no longer hold a position as a company executive. He was instructed to resign and to sever all ties with the company he had founded. He was not even allowed to set foot in his old office. Faced with the same situation, presidents of other firms designated *zaibatsu* stepped down. Matsushita characteristically decided to stay on, loudly protesting his innocence, determined to fight what he saw as a grievous miscarriage of justice.

His battle to get back into business took many forms. One was to offer up a scapegoat in the person of Iue Toshio, Matsushita Electric's executive managing director. Iue resigned from the company to take responsibility for Matsushita's contributions to the Japanese war effort.

Whether it was this sacrifice or some other scheme that did the trick is not clear. But the fact is that in May 1947, the order that Matsushita resign from his company was lifted. That same year, Iue founded his own firm, Sanyo ("Three Oceans") Electric Works. To get Iue started in business, a grateful Matsushita gave him a product to make. This was a generator for bicycle lamps, which the fledgling firm manufactured under Matsushita's National brand.

The bicycle generator was a big hit commercially. As a portable source of electric power, it was also in a sense a precursor of what would become virtually the only product that differentiates Sanyo from other Japanese consumer electronics firms—the amorphous silicon solar cell.

Kuwano was fortunate to sign on with Sanyo at an auspicious time. In 1961, flush with cash from exports of transistor radios, the company splashed out on the establishment of that corporate status symbol par excellence—an R&D center. Kuwano was one of the initial batch of young scientists hired to man the center. Its director was Yamano Masaru, a physicist from Kyoto University. He gave his young staff the freedom to do their own research, instructing them to use their originality.

In Japan, as elsewhere, most researchers chose to work on crystalline semiconductors. But Kuwano came from Kyushu, where people have a reputation for contrariness. He took one look at the crystalline field and decided that it was too crowded for him. If he was going to use his originality, the young chemist decided, then he would have to look elsewhere.

A category of amorphous materials known collectively as the chalcogenites seemed like a promising area to investigate. The best known of them, selenium, had recently risen to prominence. It was used as the photoreceptive material on the drums of Xerox's first copiers. These made their debut in 1961, just as the Sanyo research center was tooling up. Selenium's photosensitive properties had also found another useful niche as the material for the built-in light meters on cameras. Kuwano reasoned that chalcogenites might well have practical applications in other electronic products, too. He began basic research on amorphous materials.

The first thing Kuwano came up with was a chalcogenite switch. He intended this as a replacement for the glow tube, a device formerly used to jump-start fluorescent lamps. A glow-tube–triggered lamp took a few seconds to light up; using Kuwano's invention, the lamp would come on instantaneously. An excited Kuwano set off to see the manager of Sanyo's lamp factory.

But after the young researcher had explained the merits of his invention, the factory manager looked at him and asked, "Kuwano-San, how much does your switch cost?" And of course at the time, because not commercialized, Kuwano's device was very expensive. In addition, its reliability was only half that of the conventional switching element.

"Then the manager said to me, 'Please go back to the research center,'" Kuwano said, laughing loudly as he recalled this early setback. "So I returned to the research center, which was located at the top of a hill. It was a very hot summer's day, and I had to walk because I did not have a car. I was *so* disappointed."

Kuwano subsequently came up with a string of other chalcogenite devices, but in every case the answer was the same. None was accepted for commercialization. This was a difficult period for the young researcher. "Others in the company were succeeding," he said. "For example, the nickel-cadmium [battery] group succeeded, the semiconductor device group succeeded, so scientist-engineers the same age as me were getting promoted to higher positions, and I was bringing up the rear."

Then, on 17 October 1973, the Organization of Petroleum Exporting Countries unexpectedly announced a 21-percent hike in the price of crude oil. The recession that followed hit Japan—which of all industrialized nations is the most dependent on imported oil—particularly hard. Sanyo's business performance sagged. This in turn meant that the company had to cut back its spending on R&D. Kuwano was hauled before his boss at the R&D center, Dr. Yamano, who demanded, "Why do you persist in continuing with such unpromising research?"

At this point, Kuwano and two coworkers had been working on amorphous materials for more than ten years. But in terms of commercial results they had nothing to show for all their effort. Kuwano himself was beginning to think that perhaps they were barking up the wrong tree. He told his boss that they would stop work on amorphous devices and move on to other, more practical themes.

But Kuwano did not abandon his research on amorphous materials entirely. In his spare time, he continued his work "under the table," as they say in Japan. He collected the equipment he needed for this research by surreptitiously tacking on "extras" to orders for equipment intended for other purposes. And, as his boss had instructed, he used his originality. For example, a surplus metal locker became the deposition chamber in which he made his first amorphous silicon devices.

Devastating economic blow though it was, the oil shock did have some positive effects. For one thing, it provided a huge incentive for inventors to come up with alternate sources of energy. Having previously considered only electronic device applications for his amorphous materials, Kuwano now turned his thoughts to energy conversion.

That is why he was so excited to discover Spear and LeComber's 1975 paper, with its throwaway reference to photovoltaic activity. Kuwano remembered the burns his head had suffered while he was climbing Mount Aso. The sun could indeed be a powerful source of energy.

Kuwano convinced Dr. Yamano to let him try to develop amorphous silicon solar cells. But his budget was tiny—too small to build a proper vacuum chamber in which to deposit the silicon. Despite all their efforts, Sanyo's researchers were unable to produce devices that converted light into electricity. Then came exciting news from America. A group at RCA's David Sarnoff Research Center in Princeton had succeeded in making an amorphous silicon solar cell that worked.

Kuwano was not the only one who had been stimulated by the Arab oil embargo. In 1972 David Carlson, a 30-year-old physicist from Rutgers just back from a six-month tour of duty in Vietnam, joined the RCA laboratories. He had been hired to do exploratory work on glasses because RCA were planning to make their own television picture tubes.

In fact, however, Carlson had gone off on a tangent. He was working on the deposition of thin films of metal oxide on glass for use as the electrodes in liquid crystal displays. When the oil embargo was imposed, Carlson immediately became interested in the possibility of adapting this technique to the production of low-cost solar cells.

In 1974 the technology of silicon solar cells was already twenty years old. The photoelectric effect, the phenomenon on which solar cells are based, was first noticed in 1839. The effect was explained in 1905 by Albert Einstein, an achievement which won him his Nobel Prize (apparently the awards committee found this explanation easier to understand than Einstein's special theory of relativity). But it was not until many years later that improved crystal growth techniques enabled the production of the purer materials needed for practical applications of the effect.

One morning in February 1940, a Bell Labs chemist named Russell Ohl was making current measurements on his oscilloscope of some specially grown samples of silicon that he was hoping to use in shortwave radio detectors. As the morning wore on, Ohl noticed something peculiar: Placing the sample near other objects on his bench affected the shape of the curve on the scope. A hot soldering iron would do the trick; so would the 40-watt desk lamp on his bench. Finally, Ohl placed an electric fan in front of the light, so that it interrupted the light as it spun.

"As the choppy light shone on Ohl's silicon, something very queer began to show up on the oscilloscope. The voltage seemed to follow the chop of the light." By accident the sample had been prepared in such a way that when light fell on it, an electrical current was produced. "Ohl had hit upon the essential ingredient for producing photovoltaic solar electricity."[3]

"Until that time, photocells had operated on the electrical effect produced by the interaction of the surfaces of two different metals exposed to light. Ohl's cell, by contrast, generated current in a [piece of single crystal]—and the current was ten times stronger than usual."[4]

But World War II intervened and it was not until April 1954 that three Bell Labs scientists, Gerald Pearson, Calvin Fuller, and Daryl Chapin—respectively a physicist, a chemist, and an electrical engineer—were able to follow up on Ohl's discovery. "With an amazingly simple-looking apparatus made of wafer-thin strips of silicon," read the press release issued by the labs, "they showed how the sun's rays could be used to power the transmission of voices over telephone wires."

Powering voice transmission over wire would not in fact be the solar battery's first application. In 1954, the year the solar cell was invented, another Bell Labs scientist, J. R. Pierce (the man who had named the transistor), was asked to give a talk on space to the Princeton chapter of the Institute of Radio Engineers. The invitation had been issued because, among his many talents, Pierce was also a writer of science fiction. As such he was used to giving highly speculative lectures on how technology would be applied in the future. But that was to lay audiences. This time, his listeners would be a group of highly skeptical peers.

"I thought, my God, isn't space good for something?" Pierce recalled, "and I decided that it would be good for communications satellites." He did some back-of-envelope calculations and was astounded to discover that his idea was not so crazy after all. It led to a development program at Bell Labs which culminated in 1962 with the launch of Telstar, the world's first communications satellite.

Telstar and all of its successors have been powered by solar cells. But though ideal for price-no-object items like satellites, cells made from single-crystal or polycrystalline silicon were far too expensive for terrestrial power generation other than remote applications such as buoys and lighthouses. In Japan, Sharp began producing conventional solar cells for these applications during the 1960s. Examples of solar cell installations include buoys in Yokohama Port and the Strait of Malacca (1963) and a lighthouse at Nagasaki (1966), which the company claims was at the time the largest solar cell system in the world.

Solar cells made from single- and polycrystalline silicon are easy to recognize because of their characteristic round shape. This derives from the fact that the cells are sliced from salami-like ingots of bulk silicon. But as former Royal Society President Sir George Porter once commented, "making solar cells from polysilicon is like making newspapers by chopping slices off logs."

RCA's Carlson had been depositing thin films of metal on glass. Wouldn't it be possible, Carlson wondered, to substitute silicon for metal? If so, you could produce solar cells like making newspapers the proper way—by printing them on rolls of paper several feet wide and hundreds of yards long.

"I started making films around October '74," Carlson recalled, "and I actually tried to make some solar cell devices right off the bat, not knowing what I had, but just seeing if I could get anything that would work. To my surprise, I saw a photovoltaic effect very soon, from one of the first few devices I made."

But it was not until a couple of months after those first experiments, when he got an analysis of the films back, that Carlson found out what he had been working with. This was not the polysilicon that he had been trying to produce, but amorphous silicon, a material which he knew was supposed to be electronically useless.

Carlson was unable to drum up any support from the management of RCA's laboratories to pursue his remarkable discovery. For the next eighteen months, Carlson's work—like that of Kuwano—had to be done under the table, or "bootlegged" in other words.

Happily, because his job description called for him to perform exploratory research into glassy materials, Carlson had a cover for what he was doing. He was able to interest a group of other scientists at the labs in his work. In December 1974, they started an informal crash program to try and improve the material.

Encouraged by their progress, late the following year Carlson made another pitch to RCA management, to expand the effort. This too was turned down. As it happened, Paul Rappaport, the director of Carlson's lab, knew a lot about solar cells because some years previously he himself had been involved in a vigorous development program on single-crystal devices for RCA satellites.

Rappaport was well aware that conventional cells were capable of converting sunlight to electricity with an efficiency of 6 percent or more. The best that Carlson's early cells could manage was a measly 2 percent. You could get such piddling results with almost any semiconductor material, he told the young researcher. Rappaport also felt that solar cells were a distraction from RCA's principle preoccupation during the mid-seventies. This was the ill-fated VideoDisc program, which in 1975 was at a critical phase of its development.

Carlson was transferred to another laboratory. He begged his new boss, Jim Tietjen, to allow him to continue working on amorphous silicon solar cells. Initially Tietjen was skeptical. After all, Rappaport had said that he didn't see much point in what Carlson was proposing, and he was the Sarnoff Center's expert on photovoltaics.

Carlson told Tietjen that he thought Rappaport was wrong. Let him work half time for another year, and Carlson promised that he would push the efficiency of the cells over 5 percent. Tietjen gave the young researcher his head, told him to go ahead and work on it full time. Within a few months, Carlson made good on his promise.

At this point things really started to happen. Carlson had been encouraged to apply for funding from the government's Energy Research & Development Agency. When his application was granted, RCA management sat up and took notice of his work. Amorphous silicon was given an authorized project number, and from that point on, the effort had the company's official support.

In 1976, having duly applied for a patent on their cells, Carlson and his colleague Chris Wronski published a paper in *Applied Physics Letters*. The result was an enormous surge of interest in amorphous silicon solar cells. Because the group had a government contract, RCA was obliged to maintain an open-door policy, whereby people could come in and tour their laboratory. As usual, it was the Japanese who were most curious about the new development.

"In 1977, the year after we published, we had literally hundreds of Japanese visitors coming through," Carlson recalled. RCA's licensing people had a field day, issuing licenses for about a 2 percent royalty to most of Japan's big electronics firms. Including, naturally, Sanyo.

Kuwano was one of the first to make the pilgrimage to Princeton. For him, the RCA announcement had been crucial in two ways. First, it confirmed that it was indeed possible to make solar cells out of amorphous silicon. Second, he could now go to his boss, Dr. Yamano, and tell him that "the fact that RCA, one of the largest companies in the world, is so interested proves that amorphous silicon is a major technology." Kuwano had made his point. Yamano gave him the money he needed, and his group quickly added new members.

Fate had presented him with an opportunity, and Kuwano was determined to use it to make up for his previous failures. "We decided that although RCA was the first to publish a report, we would be the first to market," he recalled, adding, "for a private company, mass production is the most important thing."

Now, there was no stopping him. For four years, Kuwano and his group at the Sanyo lab toiled on the development of solar cells until late every night and most weekends, too. They came up with a series of important innovations. For example, though practical application to electronic equipment would require a supply of 3 volts, the best a single amorphous silicon solar cell could manage was just half a volt.

Obviously, to produce the desired output, several cells would have to be hooked up. You could do that using wires to make the connection, but wires would increase cost and reduce reliability. And as Kuwano knew all too well from his painful conversation with the manager of the lamp factory all those years ago, cost and reliability were the two key considerations for mass production. To get around the problem, he and his team developed a technique for integrating solar cells in series. Using a pattern mask like the ones employed by microchip producers to transfer circuit designs onto silicon, they deposited a layer of connections all at once.

Mass production was further enhanced by a second Sanyo innovation. This was to use separate reaction chambers to deposit each of the layers of p- and n-type material involved in the construction of solar cells. (At the time, everyone else was using a single-chamber system. This meant that the chamber had to be cleaned after each deposition, which in turn led to all sorts of contamination problems.) From such seemingly simple ideas, high yields derive.

But to be successful in commercialization, efficient manufacturing is just one of the elements required. You also need good timing—and good luck. Kuwano had both. Happily for him and his amorphous silicon cells, a golden opportunity was ready and waiting.

As we saw in earlier chapters, the crucial factor in portable products like calculators was to reduce the amount of power they consumed. By 1980, the demand for power had been lowered to the point where it could be satisfied by two flashlight batteries. Now the advent of cheap and lightweight solar cells raised the possibility that calculators would be able to dispense with batteries altogether.

For the conventional, outdoor applications of solar batteries, amorphous silicon cells left a good deal to be desired. Their conversion efficiency still lagged well behind that of single- and polycrystalline cells. Worse, after a few months of exposure to sunlight the early amorphous silicon cells degraded, losing up to half of their already modest efficiency.

Indoors, however, it was an entirely different story. On his desk at the research center, Kuwano ran a little experiment, checking the performance of his amorphous cells against that of single-crystal devices. During the day, when sunlight streamed in through the window, crystalline beat amorphous hands down.

But when Kuwano made the comparison at night, he was surprised to discover that amorphous outperformed crystalline. How to explain this unexpected result? When Kuwano measured the characteristics of both materials, he discovered that amorphous is more sensitive than conventional silicon to the wavelength of light output by fluorescent lamps. Since calculators are much more likely to be used under fluorescent lights, in offices and classrooms for example, than under sunlight (where stability was an issue), this was good news indeed.

Sanyo launched the world's first commercial amorphous silicon solar cells in 1980. The initial product that incorporated them was the calculator. Carlson remembered meeting Kuwano shortly afterwards at an international photovoltaics conference in Cannes, France. "He gave me one of the first solar-powered calculators they had made," Carlson said, "and I was really impressed by it, because they had a pretty good-sized cell in it. But it was quite good-looking and it worked very well, and I thought it was an excellent application."

Indeed it was. Many other applications for amorphous silicon solar cells would emerge during the next few years (most of them dreamed up by Kuwano and his team at Sanyo). During the 1980s, I interviewed Kuwano several times. On each occasion he was full of enthusiasm for some new usage of Amorton, Sanyo's brand name for amorphous silicon solar cells. Most memorable was a blanket made of Amorton, which was undergoing trials by a team of eye surgeons practicing in remote parts of Nepal. But the solar-powered calculator remained by far the dominant application, racking up sales on the order of 100 million units a year by the late 1980s. Sanyo remained the largest supplier of such cells, with a monthly production of some 5 million units.

If the reason for Sanyo's early lead was fortune favoring Kuwano's prepared mind, then the secret of the company's success in commercialization was his drive and ambition. "Kuwano is an excellent motivator," Carlson said. "He's pretty unique among the Japanese I've known . . . . He has a style that works very well for him, and I think he was able to make things happen a lot faster than some of his counterparts at other companies."

Carlson and his colleagues had also considered calculators as a possible application. At RCA, however, "there just didn't seem to be a mechanism to do that," Carlson sighed. RCA's management thought that calculators were a diversion—the proper target should be power generation, working with the utilities, that sort of thing. This of course was a good idea, but one that was way ahead of where the technology was at the time.

As we have seen, RCA had a terrible track record in getting new technologies out of the lab. Carlson's group also did some pioneering work on amorphous silicon thin-film transistors. But here, too, support

Kuwano Yukinori (Photo courtesy of Sanyo)

from RCA's management was lacking. "We made some I thought fairly good transistor devices," Carlson recalled, "but [management] felt they were too slow, and the project was squelched ... they basically killed the project in a year and a half, and unfortunately, none of the work in that area was ever published."

It was very difficult for the company to commercialize something that was not actually sponsored by one of its operating divisions. So in order to try and get amorphous silicon off the ground, RCA's management initially decided that they needed to form some sort of venture partnership.

But just as talks with potential partners were making progress, a change in management occurred. RCA's new executive vice president saw no connection between solar cells and the company's core consumer electronics business and promptly pulled the plug on the negotiations. In September 1983 RCA sold their thin-film amorphous silicon solar cell technology lock, stock, and barrel to the oil company Amoco. At the same time, to provide a home for their newly acquired amorphous silicon, Amoco took over Solarex, an existing manufacturer of photovoltaic cells.

Carlson went with his technology and joined Solarex as head of the thin-film division. He convinced his new bosses to set up an operation in Newtown, Pennsylvania, near enough to Princeton to enable him to recruit key people from RCA labs. He managed to persuade about ten people, including a team of five of the most crucial scientists plus support staff, to make the transition. It was a timely move: Two years later RCA was acquired by GE, which sold off the Sarnoff Center for a song.

Solar cells were the main thrust of amorphous silicon research during the '70s because of the commercial potential of this application. Most of the development work in this area was done in the United States and Japan. In the U.K., where the material had originated and been characterized, there was little commercially oriented activity.

British industry seemed to have neither the vision nor the money to invest in solar cells. In addition, Britain suffered from what one observer described, in the determinedly obfuscatory language of scientific journals, as "the intermittency of the solar resource."[5] Rotten weather, in other words.

In few places was the solar resource more intermittent than Dundee. But the dynamic duo of Spear and LeComber and their team of postdoctoral researchers continued to set the pace, at least as far as the science of amorphous silicon was concerned.

In addition to their work on solar cells, the group also pioneered the development of thin-film transistors made from amorphous silicon. These became famous when applied to drive liquid crystal displays. But LCDs did not come first. According to Rod Gibson, a member of the Dundee team, the original application for the devices was rather more prosaic.

To measure what was happening in their pet material, the group had been fabricating amorphous silicon field effect transistors on quartz disks. At about 180 microns (millionths of an inch), these were rather thick devices by the standards of the day. To get the transistors to perform you had to zap them with over a thousand volts.

Experimenting using such high voltages could be an exciting business—every so often, the current would arc over, there would be a blue flash, and bang would go the input of the electrometer the researchers were using to do their measurements. Each time that happened, it would cost some horrendous sum like $150 to replace—a lot of money for a university group in those days.

A thin-film transistor made of amorphous silicon just 1 micron thick was no match in performance for a regular FET. But as far as Spear, LeComber, and Co. were concerned, it meant that they could get away with using low voltages to make their measurements. There would be no more broken electrometers.

At a U.K. solar cell conference in 1977, the pair were approached by some researchers from the Royal Signals & Research Establishment, Britain's top government electronics lab. The latter were looking for a suitable transistor to drive the liquid crystal displays they were working on for avionic (read: fighter cockpit) applications. They proposed a joint program to investigate the feasibility of amorphous silicon.

The Dundee group put together a little prototype array. This did not drive any actual liquid crystals, just some capacitors simulating liquid crystals, but it proved that the idea was sound in principle. The group went on to demonstrate that amorphous silicon thin-film transistors could be used in 1,000-line displays, more than enough for regular television.

In 1979, Spear and LeComber published a paper setting out their results—and reaped a second whirlwind of interest. Celebrities on the scientific conference circuit since the publication of their first paper in 1975, the pair now found themselves inundated with invitations to give talks here, there, and everywhere. In the light of subsequent developments, perhaps the most important of these was to a 1980 conference held in the ancient Japanese capital of Kyoto.

Before the conference, Spear and LeComber visited the laboratories of several companies, including those of Sanyo in nearby Osaka. There, Kuwano showed them around Sanyo's newly established solar cell production line, and in return they gave a seminar on their latest TFT work. Then everybody went off to the conference in Kyoto.

A week or so later, as part of another tour of Japanese corporate labs, the pair returned to Sanyo. They were astonished to discover that their seminar had had an immediate impact. In the interim, a group consisting of some fifteen scientists and engineers had been hastily assembled to work on amorphous silicon thin-film transistors.

Sanyo's speed off the mark paid dividends. At the Japan Electronics Show in October 1983 the company demonstrated the world's first active matrix LCD television driven by amorphous silicon thin-film transistors. But as so often happens, the company failed to follow through on this early lead. Matsushita, the old block off which Sanyo was a chip, would be the first to commercialize amorphous silicon–driven displays. Then it was Matsushita's turn to be elbowed aside, this time by the most aggressive display maker of them all–Sharp.

At Sharp, Rocket Sasaki had been quick to understand the significance of amorphous silicon. The company had been producing solar cells since 1963, the year before he joined. These of course were the conventional, crystalline variety. But as Sasaki knew better than anybody, "for something to be used in consumer products, you have to be able to make it cheaply, so [crystalline cells] were only good for military or industrial uses like satellites, and the price would not come down."

In 1976, Sharp announced a solar-powered calculator. This, however, was only a prototype driven by conventional cells. Then the dramatic news from Dundee and Princeton arrived. Not long afterwards, a call came through to Sasaki's office from the trading company Mitsui. They were looking after an American entrepreneur who had recently arrived in Tokyo. His name was Stanford Ovshinsky. Mitsui was making introductions on his behalf and that of his company, Energy Conversion Devices, of Troy, Michigan. The American claimed to have invented a new kind of solar cell made from some sort of amorphous material and a process for manufacturing it–would Dr. Sasaki be interested in meeting him? Sasaki said he would.

Ovshinsky is larger than life, a self-taught inventor who has spent a lifetime doggedly pursuing commercial applications for amorphous materials. Ovshinsky is much beloved of journalists because he tells such wonderful stories. With investors, however, Ovshinsky's reputation is not so high, because in raising funds for his various ventures over the years, he has on occasion promised somewhat more than he could deliver.

Forever in search of new ways to keep the cash flow positive, Ovshinsky (like many another entrepreneur) had developed a very persuasive line in presentations. Sasaki had heard that amorphous silicon solar cells were unstable. Was this true? he asked Ovshinsky. In reply, the ebullient inventor dropped a sample cell onto the floor of the meeting room and stamped on it with his foot. Then he picked up the cell, measured its output, and showed that it was completely unaffected by the ill treatment he had given it.

Sasaki was impressed with Ovshinsky's performance. At his urging Sharp set up a joint venture with Energy Conversion Devices and Standard Oil of Ohio. Under the terms of the agreement, the Japanese firm purchased a machine from Ovshinsky's company with which to do mass production in Japan.

Unlike Sanyo and RCA, whose approach was to deposit solar cells on glass panels, this equipment was designed to print amorphous silicon devices on rolls of stainless steel foil. Unfortunately, however, Sharp had nothing but problems with the machine: It never worked properly, and the joint venture eventually foundered. (The irrepressible Ovshinsky has since formed another joint venture, United Solar Systems Corporation, with Canon.)

But though Sharp failed to put amorphous silicon solar cells into production, the experience gained by many of the company's scientists and engineers in handling the material would prove invaluable when it came to making thin-film transistors. In 1981 Walter Spear gave a presentation on the technology at Sharp's Central Research Laboratory. From then on, the company dropped other approaches and concentrated on amorphous silicon as the material of choice to drive active matrix displays. Sharp has never looked back since.

By the early 1990s Japanese companies were investing tens of billions of dollars a year in production facilities for liquid crystal displays backed by amorphous silicon thin-film transistors. At the same time, however, it was widely recognized that amorphous silicon's dominance in displays would not last forever.

Electrons had always moved through the material much more slowly than through crystalline silicon. That was why Spear and LeComber had been interested in amorphous silicon in the first place. But the material's sluggishness meant that it was not suitable for handling other functions. So the controller circuits surrounding the display had to be fabricated out of regular crystalline silicon.

Obviously, the ideal would be to make both display transistors and controllers out of the same material. Integrating the circuitry would reduce display production costs by up to 50 percent. But so long as depositing polysilicon remained a high-temperature (= 1000° C plus) process, that was out of the question. At such temperatures, ordinary display glass simply melts. For the first polysilicon displays, Seiko's Morozumi had used heat-resistant quartz glass. This was an effective solution, but prohibitively expensive.

October 1995 marked the announcement of what was claimed to be the world's first liquid crystal display in which all the circuits–display and control–were fabricated in polysilicon on glass. Lending particular credence to the announcement was the fact that it was made by none other than the new director of Sanyo's R&D center, Kuwano Yukinori.

While polysilicon threatened to become a replacement in displays, amorphous silicon was also under attack in its original application, solar cells.[6] During the 1980s, sales of amorphous photovoltaics grew rapidly. By the end of the decade, they accounted for some 30 percent of the world market for solar cells. In the early '90s, however, production of amorphous devices leveled off. Market share actually declined, to about 20 percent in 1993.

There were two reasons for the drop. On the one hand, the market for indoor consumer applications such as calculators had matured. On the other, outdoors, amorphous silicon solar cells have yet to find their place in the sun.

As David Carlson wrote, "Most remote [outdoor] applications require high performance photovoltaic modules with a proven track record of long-term reliability. . . . Amorphous silicon solar cells exhibit stabilized conversion efficiencies of only about 5%, and thus use in remote applications is limited."[7]

Nonetheless, Carlson remained optimistic. "In the photovoltaics business," he said, "amorphous silicon has a very real advantage over other technologies in that it's very easy to deposit over large areas. And photovoltaics is a real macro-electronic application–you've got to be able to crank out very large areas, with very uniform properties, at high yields."

The technology continues to advance, with new and more complex devices–called multijunction cells–having been demonstrated to be capable of delivering a stabilized conversion efficiency of over 10 percent.

The most common structure used in the production of amorphous silicon photovoltaics is the so-called single-junction cell. This is made up of three layers of material—a sandwich consisting of a positively-doped layer and a negatively doped layer separated by an undoped layer. By combining several single-junction devices, it is possible to raise the overall conversion efficiency of the cell.

"Amorphous silicon photovoltaic technology seems to be in the midst of a paradigm shift," Carlson observed, "that should lead to the appearance of a new generation of low-cost, high performance thin-film photovoltaic modules in the next few years."

Evidence for this paradigm shift was the fact that in early 1997 Carlson's own firm, Solarex, now America's largest manufacturer of photovoltaic cells, started up a new, large-scale automated production plant in Virginia. "And we're looking toward even bigger plants if the one in Virginia works right," he said. Several other companies, including Canon, Sanyo, and Sharp were also commercializing amorphous cell technology. As production volumes increase and prices fall, Carlson predicted, the market for amorphous silicon solar cells would show "explosive growth over the next few years."

Today, more than twenty years down the track, Carlson is still with the technology that he originally invented. That makes him a rare exception among former researchers from the David Sarnoff Research Center. "In my case, I sort of felt that it was my baby," he said, "and I wanted to see it happen more than anything else." He added with a laugh, "I didn't think it was going to take this long, though."

Kuwano Yukinori also reckons that amorphous silicon is his baby.[8] Like Carlson, he too has an upbeat long-term view of the future for the technology. In the mid-1990s, having used consumer electronics to gain experience with mass production and to bring down the price of cells, Kuwano is aiming for a much larger market—providing electric power for private houses.

The idea is to use solar-generated power to run your household appliances. Any excess electricity you sell to the local power company. In Japan, the laws governing electric power generation were formerly very restrictive. They forbade the connection of solar-powered houses to the utility grid. Japanese power companies were keen to keep it that way.

Kuwano fought tenaciously to get the law changed, arguing that solar cell technology was now up to the challenge. In 1992, he won his case: Japanese law was changed, forcing power companies to accept reverse-flow solar-cell–generated electricity from private residences.

In July that year, Kuwano set up Japan's first domestic power station–on the rooftop of his own house in Osaka. "I got very nice data," he reported happily. His system generates 2 kilowatts of power, enough to run all the electrical equipment in the house, including his refrigerator, television, and lighting system.

"In the daytime," Kuwano said, "I have excess electricity which I can sell to the power company. Without the solar system on my house, the sunshine would be wasted. Instead, it's converted to heat, so it's a very good system. Peak energy demand in the daytime is a very serious situation for Japan. So if domestic solar power stations generate electricity during the peak energy demand, it's very good for society–clean energy, generated at peak time."

Kuwano passed on the results of his experiment to government officials. Since Japan has to import over 90 percent of its fuel, supporting initiatives to lessen this dependence has long been government policy. In 1994, the Japanese government introduced a 50 percent subsidy to encourage people to install solar systems in their homes. The plan envisages that by the turn of the century some 60,000 homeowners will take up the offer.[9]

Demand on this scale ought to do wonders for production costs. In 1995, Kuwano reckoned that electricity generated by solar cells was still between three and six times more expensive than that supplied over the grid. Reducing the cost of production and increasing the efficiency of conversion were his two priorities.

Kuwano looked forward to the day when the price of solar energy would be equal to that of the grid. He speculated that this could come as early as the year 2000. Thenceforth all new houses in Japan would be built with solar cells on their roofs.

But Kuwano's vision of a solar-powered future extends well beyond individual residences. In a plan he calls the Genesis Project, Kuwano envisages a global energy network of interconnected solar generating systems.[10] The idea is to overcome the main disadvantage of solar cells:

What to do when the solar resource is unavailable. In other words, when the sky is overcast or it is nighttime.

Based on a calculation of world energy demands in the year 2000, Kuwano reckoned that to meet this requirement 800 square kilometers of solar cells located at sites around the world would be needed. "This plan is quite feasible," he said, "because barely four percent of the world's desert area would suffice." Hooking them up would be an international grid consisting of superconducting cables.

This plan might sound grandiose, but Kuwano proposes that the system should be built step by step. It would begin by plugging homes and factories into individual national grids, then connecting together the national grids of adjacent countries, ultimately forming a truly global network.

The Genesis Project is, in David Carlson's opinion, "a fascinating conceptual view of what could happen long term." In proposing the deliverance of clean, low-cost energy for all humankind, Kuwano's vision is also a profoundly philanthropic one. Ben Casey would have been proud of him.

Gathering dust on top of a filing cabinet in Rod Gibson's office at the University of Dundee sits a cardboard box labeled "FTVG 5MHz Data." It contains the results of the group's pioneering work on amorphous silicon thin-film transistors.

The initials, Gibson explained, stand for Flat TV Group. "We called them that as a joke, thinking that it would never ever see the light of day. Even the people who worked in the group never thought that it would actually come off, that it would become a commercial product. But it shows how wrong you can be really—it was well-named."

Almost certainly, the work never would have become a commercial product if it had been left up to British companies to do the commercializing. Attempting to get joint efforts going with local firms was, in Gibson's view, "embarrassing."

He recalled collaborating with one well-known U.K. outfit on the development of solar cells. For their research his counterpart at the company had to buy an electrometer to measure current. To authorize the expenditure, the unfortunate scientist was forced to collect the signatures from all fifteen of the company's directors. Then, once the equipment arrived, he had to go back to the same fifteen directors to get them to sign again to say that the purchase had been made.

Gibson couldn't help contrasting the stifling petty-mindedness of the British firm with the unbridled enthusiasm shown by the Sanyo researchers when they visited Dundee back in 1976. At the U.K. company, he had rarely seen anyone more senior than a section manager (and even then it was usually an accountant).

Now here was this very senior executive, the director of research from Sanyo—a company whose name was familiar to anyone who'd ever been to an electrical appliances store—and this other guy, Kuwano, who was raving on about amorphous materials as being the way of the future. These were the first Japanese Gibson had ever met—and their attitude made a lasting impression on him.

The Dundee group never patented any of their discoveries. For them, the incentive was to beat the competition—rival scientists—by being the first to publish their results. They little thought that these results might have commercial significance—and never in their wildest dreams would they have imagined that their discoveries might engender applications worth many billions of dollars.

In addition to the solar cell and thin-film transistor, amorphous silicon also found several other major commercial applications. They included the drums of photocopiers. In a 1987 paper, "Amorphous Silicon—Electronics into the 21st Century," LeComber wrote, "It has been estimated that Canon will sell one million machines containing amorphous silicon photoreceptor drums and each of these drums represents approximately $100 of business." He went on to mention another important use of amorphous silicon: as the linear image sensors of fax machines. In scaled-up form, these sensors are also used in electronic whiteboards that produce a copy of what is written on them at the touch of a button.

"The gist of it," Gibson summed up, "was that it was a time of otherworldly British physics. People had enough money to run their labs and to do what interested them. They weren't reliant on patents and sponsorship (as they would be today)—a nice little consultancy to top up their academic salary was the most that people might hope for.[11] It would have been regarded as infra-dig to be involved in wealth creation as such."

Walter Spear retired from the University of Dundee in 1990. Two years later Peter LeComber, his colleague of almost three decades, died of a heart attack at the tragically young age of 55. After LeComber's death, the mantle of leadership passed to Rod Gibson. As one of the group's junior members, he had previously been somewhat isolated from seeing the impact their work had had on the real world.

Now, as he started to travel the world himself, Gibson realized that "we did all this first, and it wasn't just fun, like it seemed at the time—it was quite significant, it actually led somewhere, which is quite exciting in solid-state—y'know, lots of people work all their lives and make refinements, but they never go to the shops and see what they've done. But you can go out and look at any solar-powered calculator and think, well, yeah, I worked on the first half-dozen of these things in the world."

Their work has not gone entirely unnoticed at home. Today, as you drive north across the road bridge over the River Tay, there are signs that say, "Welcome to Dundee—City of Amorphous Silicon."

PART TWO

Camcorders & Synthesizers

6

The Man Who
Loved Gossip

I believe that the process of technological development is as creative as basic research.
— Ibuka Masaru, Honorary Chairman, Sony

IN A PEACEFUL VALLEY JUST OUTSIDE the ancient Japanese capital of Kamakura, on the terraced slope of a huge cemetery, stands a black granite headstone. The grave differs in one significant respect from the thousands of others that surround it. The casual visitor would never notice, but glued to the top righthand corner of the back of this particular slab is a tiny microchip.

The monolith marks the last resting place of Iwama Kazuo, third president of Sony. But Iwama's real monument is not the stone. Rather, it is the chip, a type of semiconductor known as a charge-coupled device.

Charge-coupled devices are electronic eyes, tiny cameras small enough to go almost anywhere: behind the driver's head on racing cars, for example; level with the bar as pole vaulters heave into view; at the front door scrutinizing visitors; or—more sinisterly—on the business end of cruise missiles heading down the ventilation shafts of Baghdad.

CCDs are also the secret of the incredible shrinking camcorder. They reduced the video camera/tape recorder from a hulking great pack that could only be toted on a strong man's shoulder to a neat little box that a child can hold comfortably in one hand. Charge-coupled devices transformed the camcorder from a pricey piece of professional broadcasting equipment into a consumer product that has allowed tens of millions of doting parents to capture on video their toddler's first faltering steps and other such magic moments.

Without Iwama's vision, without his driving the development of the CCD over a decade, at enormous cost and against the wishes of his colleagues, this microelectronic metamorphosis would never have happened.

The origin of the charge-coupled device was unusual. It was not, like so many other breakthroughs, a happy accident. The device was invented deliberately, in response to a threat.

The threat was made by Jack Morton, the hard-driving vice president who headed device development at Bell Laboratories. At the time, Morton was arguably the most important person in the entire electronics industry. He directed the world's largest research effort in this field.

The Bell Telephone Laboratories were established in 1925. Their task was to do (a) research and engineering for AT&T, which owned half the stock in the labs, and (b) product development for Western Electric, the Bell System's manufacturing arm, which owned the other half. Though the organization would ultimately muster twenty-one laboratories located in eight states and employing 17,000 staff, the name "Bell Labs" almost invariably refers to the site at Murray Hill, New Jersey, where most of the basic research was (and is) done. Murray Hill's original mission: to provide technology that would be useful in the telephone system in twenty years.

The Murray Hill labs opened in 1941. They are housed in a barracks-like brick complex in a clearing of a scrub forest. The most notable feature of the laboratories is the main entrance (a later addition), a huge pyramid-shaped structure that local wags have dubbed "Darth Vader's helmet." The sheer scale of the facility is impressive. In its prime during the '60s and '70s, Murray Hill was home to an army of researchers some four thousand strong.

Miles of dark, extravagantly piped and ducted corridors connect the various wings of the four-story complex. The corridors form arteries linking offices with labs. The architecture had a built-in serendipity. Researchers on their way to lunch in the cafeteria or to look something up in the library would bump into colleagues. Such accidental meetings provided opportunities to get progress reports of the latest developments in other fields. People would tell each other about what they were doing, and how they were doing it. On occasion, cooperative projects would spring up as a result.

In its heyday, Murray Hill was the pinnacle of research in the United States. It offered much better pay than a university position, but with just as much freedom to pursue individual ideas. If you had a good offer, it made sense to go there.

During Murray Hill's golden years, the labs were divided into areas where different sorts of activities took place. Area 10 was where pure research was done; Area 20, which Morton headed, was where exploratory device development took place.

By all accounts Morton was an effective driver. But he could also be a difficult person to work with. For one thing the vice president was extremely opinionated. He loved to debate, and when he did, "there were no holds barred—he just pulled out all the stops."

When Morton had got it into his crew-cut head that some idea was the way to go, there was no arguing with him. It had been like that with the corrosion-resistant contacts on transistors—they had to be gold and no other material. The result was that when researchers working on different metals heard that Morton was coming by to inspect their results, they would hastily fit yellow filters on their microscopes to make it look like they were using gold.

In 1966, acting on an idea dreamed up by transistor pioneer Bill Shockley, a researcher in Area 20 called Andy Bobeck invented a technology called magnetic bubbles. This was an exciting development. "Memory turns out to be a major technical and economic barrier to progress," Morton wrote.[1] Now here were bubbles, promising to provide a low-cost, solid-state replacement for large-capacity computer memories.

In the mid-sixties, memory meant ferrite cores, tiny ceramic donuts strung along wire grids. This was an expensive arrangement that severely constrained the amount of information a computer could store. Hence the attraction of bubbles, minuscule magnetized circles, millions of which could be squeezed into a square inch of garnet crystal thin film, each bubble corresponding to a bit of digital data. In addition to being stored in large numbers, bubbles could also be shunted around by applying a voltage. Through the microscope you could actually see this happening: "These very ingenious patterns of moving the bubbles around were extremely appealing to everybody, both the technical side and just the casual observer–it looked like great stuff," according to a Bell Lab researcher. The people working on magnetic bubbles were very imaginative; it seemed like they were coming up with a new idea every week, and the number of patents they generated was tremendous.

Morton was pushing hard on bubbles. This was not good news for the folks working on semiconductors down the corridor in Area 20. They regarded the advances in magnetic bubbles with some awe. The then director of the semiconductor division was a soft-spoken, 45-year-old Canadian called Willard Boyle, known to his friends as Bill.

One day in the fall of 1969, Morton took the director aside and told him in no uncertain terms: "Look, Boyle, if you guys in the semiconductor division can't come up with something better, then we're going to have to cut your budget next year and put all our money into bubbles."

The irony of it! In the very spot where the transistor had been invented, here was the man who had been largely responsible for turning the transistor from a laboratory curiosity into the basis for a whole new industry, threatening to cut further funding on semiconductor research.

There would be more gnashing of teeth at Murray Hill the following year, 1970, when a little upstart company out in California called Intel came up with a 500-bit semiconductor memory–"dynamic RAM" they called it–leaving Bell Labs, with all its extraordinary resources, behind. Though magnetic bubbles did eventually go into regular use–in the form of a recorded message system ("The number you have dialed is not in service"), introduced by the phone company in 1978–they were too slow to compete with D-RAM and eventually fell by the wayside.

Boyle's response to Morton's threat was to call George Elwood Smith into his office. The two men knew each other well. Boyle, who during World War II had been a Spitfire fighter pilot in the Royal Navy, was the older of the two. In fact, ten years earlier he had actually hired Smith, and had been the young New Yorker's supervisor in Area 10, where both men had previously worked.

During this period, Boyle and Smith had become close personal friends. They shared a love of sailing–the two of them liked nothing better than to go out on a boat and bat things around, talk about new ideas. A Mutt-and-Jeff pair of inventor types is how they saw themselves. Prior to the CCD, they already had several joint patents under their belts.

So when Boyle called Smith into his office on that day (Boyle thought it was a morning, Smith insisted it was an afternoon) and said, "C'mon George, we've got to invent something here," it was natural that the two should immediately start "batting ideas around." Within an hour, they had come up not only with the structure of the charge-coupled device, but also with some applications for it. It was, Smith would later recall, "like a light bulb coming on," an invention made in classic comic-book style.

An important aspect of the invention, Boyle felt, was that neither he nor Smith was "heavily schooled in the intricacies of the semiconductor device field." Boyle himself had just returned from two years away from the labs, working down in Washington for Bellcomm, "worrying about the science aspects of the Apollo mission—solar flares, cosmic dust, and all that sort of thing, and not thinking very much about physics or devices of any kind. Then I came back [to Murray Hill] and my first job was head of the semiconductor exploratory device division, not knowing a hell of a lot about semiconductor devices."

Blissfully unaware of the minutiae of designing digital logical circuits, Boyle and Smith were thus free to take a fresh approach. What they invented was a completely new class of integrated circuits.

The pair proceeded by analogy. Morton wanted a semiconductor device that would outperform magnetic bubbles, so why not take a leaf out of the rival technology's book? Smith explained the train of thought that led to the invention: "First, the semiconductor analogy of the magnetic bubble . . . is a packet of [electrical] charge. The next problem is how to store this charge in a confined region. The method which came to mind was the metal-oxide-semiconductor (MOS) capacitor . . . The last problem was to find a way to shift the charge from one site to the next, thereby allowing manipulation of the information. This is solved by placing the MOS capacitors very close together in order to easily pass the charge from one to the next, by applying a more attractive voltage to the receiver."[2]

The business of passing electrical charge from one capacitor to another inspired Boyle to dub the thing a charge-coupled device, which seemed to him a nice, descriptive sort of term. From a layman's point of view, however, a more evocative name was the one coined by researchers at the Philips Eindhoven Laboratory in Holland to describe a similar technology that, unbeknownst to Boyle and Smith, the Dutch company was working on at around the same time. The Philips people called their invention a bucket-brigade device.

Encouraged by the blackboard sketches and the preliminary calculations they had made, Boyle and Smith discussed their idea with various colleagues around the labs. Strangely enough, though, there didn't seem to be much enthusiasm for it. In particular, Boyle recalled, "the dyed-in-the-wool integrated circuit types" were unimpressed, wanting to know what the device would be good for, or why it was better than existing chips. Other colleagues reeled off lengthy lists of reasons why the idea would not work.

The pair themselves were by no means entirely convinced that they were onto a winner. "It seemed almost too easy and straightforward," Smith wrote, "so, having had past experience in seemingly brilliant ideas which subsequently fizzle, we allowed the idea to remain just that for some weeks."

But Boyle and Smith had also experienced the frustration of dropping a good idea only to see someone else independently propose the same idea and have it succeed. One of their first joint inventions had been a sort of field effect device that they had never done anything about. Then a couple of years later, a similar proposal made by another group had won rave reviews.

"It was like 'Oh wow! This is great stuff,' " Boyle recalled, "and we both looked at each other and said, 'Gee, we thought about that.' But I guess we tried it out on some other people and they didn't think it was such a great idea . . . but there you go, we had no claim to have originated anything, we didn't write it up, we didn't patent anything, we didn't write a paper on it, we were just playing around with various structures, understanding the physics of semiconductor devices a little bit, and we showed, 'Oh that's another way of doing it, that's sort of interesting . . . well, let's get on with something else.' "

With the CCD, it would be different. "[A] certain amount of arrogance is essential in carrying forward an idea," Smith wrote. "Our frame of mind at this time was such that we had confidence that our idea was sound and important regardless of how negative a few of the comments from out colleagues might be." Or, as Boyle put it bluntly, "We said, 'Goddammit, this is a good idea, and we're going to push it.' "

To demonstrate the feasibility of the CCD, Boyle and Smith had a model made. Consisting of just six elements, it worked beautifully. The demonstration took place on 20 October 1969. During the next few weeks, according to Smith, Area 20 became "a beehive of activity and intellectual excitement."

One reason for the excitement was the importance of the potential applications for the device. Memory had been the pair's starting point. But it so happened that for about two years prior to the invention of CCD, Smith's main job had been working on silicon diode arrays. These were a type of imaging device that his department was developing for the front end of the camera tube. The tube was intended for use in what was then AT&T's most important development project—Picturephone.

The idea of being able to see as well as hear the person you were calling had long been the phone company's dream. The first public demonstration of visual telephony took place in April 1927, when Herbert Hoover, the Stanford-trained engineer who was then Secretary of Commerce, spoke face to face with Walter Gifford, AT&T's then president. This was way ahead of its time: It took thirty years for the technology to catch up with the concept.

Advancing the state of the art was not the sole consideration. In the late 1950s, the phone company's management realized that demand for their regular service was approaching saturation—almost everyone who wanted a phone now had one. Growth in the future would have to come from new traffic, and TV telephones—which would require two extra lines for each set in order to carry the two-way video signal—seemed like a good way of generating it. In 1969, the year of the CCD's invention, AT&T's annual report optimistically predicted: "With perhaps one million sets in use, Picturephone may be a billion-dollar business by 1980."

Final plans to develop a video telephone set for trial use had been made back in 1959. Picturephone got its first public exposure at the 1964 New York World's Fair. The exhibit consisted of six individual booths and one group booth. In each was installed a special telephone and a display unit containing a cathode-ray picture tube, a vidicon camera tube, and a loudspeaker. Visitors selected at random were asked to try the video telephone for about ten minutes each. At the conclusion of the trial the guinea pigs were interviewed.

During a one-month test period, some seven hundred visitors were asked for their views on the demonstration system. One half of the respondents felt that it was important to see the other person during a telephone conversation. But as Michael Noll wrote in a perceptive postmortem on Picturephone, "perhaps more importantly, one-half felt that it was *not* important to see the other person; this negative finding was ignored."[3]

"Picturephone had become a reality in 1964," Noll concluded, "and nothing could halt its progress. It seems that once a top management commitment has been made to a new product or service, market research will be distorted to represent only positive findings. The whole project, no matter how doomed, will continue headlong on its course to the very end." In early 1967 an AT&T committee initiated plans targeting market introduction of Picturephone service for 1970.

One of the technologies that Bell Labs developed for Picturephone was a new camera tube. This had to be so sensitive that no special, studio-style lighting would be required to produce clear pictures. The insectlike eye of the new camera was smaller than a nickel. Behind the lens sat a square array consisting of more than a quarter of a million silicon photodiodes, devices for converting light to electrical energy. This silicon vidicon was the technology that George Smith had been intimately involved with. And that is why imaging was one of the first applications for the CCD that he wrote down in his notebook.

Sticking silicon diodes on the front of the camera tube solved some of the problems that the plain old vidicon suffered from. The new device was not susceptible to burn-in (damage caused by bright light) and it was more stable. But it was still a tube, a fragile cylinder of glass some 9 inches long. And, like all tubes, it took time to warm up, ate electricity once it got going, and sooner or later would burn out.

The CCD by contrast was a solid-state device, which meant long life, low power consumption, and remarkably small size. In addition, the CCD was more sensitive than tube cameras—a critical advantage in

Bill Boyle (left) and George Smith demonstrate the CCD camera at Bell Labs, December 1974. (Photo courtesy of Bell Labs)

low-light conditions. "From the beginning, the most widely heralded application of the CCD has been its use as an image sensor in a solid-state TV camera."[4]

In 1971, Smith and his team at Bell Labs built the world's first black-and-white CCD camera. (Boyle's larger management responsibilities prevented him from involvement with much of the hands-on development work.) The following year, the team also built the first solid-state color TV camera. But even as the research went rolling merrily along, dark clouds were forming on the horizon around its only possible destination—Picturephone.

"Contrary to predictions and expectations, the market response to Picturephone service was very limited and disappointing. Market research performed in 1971 showed that strict face-to-face applications had limited appeal."[5] In April 1972, due to lack of demand, Western Electric discontinued production of Picturephone sets.

"The failure of Picturephone came as a complete surprise to AT&T," Noll wrote. "Up to then the technological accomplishments of Bell Labs usually resulted in market success ... the Picturephone was the first major market failure for the Bell System."

The development of Picturephone is estimated to have cost AT&T $500 million—about as much, and for as little return, as RCA's disastrous foray into the computer business, which ended around the same time. In the early 1970s, the phone company came under fire for wasting money on futuristic technology that nobody wanted at a time when it seemed like nine out of ten public phone booths in places like New York City were not working. There were times in Manhattan when you had to wait several minutes even to get a dial tone. AT&T was advised to stick to its knitting.

The demise of Picturephone together with the more or less simultaneous rise of the dynamic random access memory (D-RAM) for computer applications meant that there was no further reason to continue work on CCDs at Bell Labs. As Smith explained, "We could only do [development] for internal things like Picturephone—the Bell System at the time was not even allowed to put any commercial products on the market, it was against the law for us to do that."[6]

It must have been hard for Smith to stop work on the CCD and accept assignment to other tasks. But knowing that the interests of the company came first, he took the decision philosophically. "It's not a matter of desire on one's part," he said later. "It's a matter of what is going to make the company money." Wasn't he disappointed about having to drop what was, after all, his baby? "O-o-o," he laughed, "one is mature enough in this life that that was no big deal."

But working under George Smith at Murray Hill was an ambitious young Italian-American who could not bring himself to share the scientific detachment of his boss. He had been, to use his words, "captivated" by the CCD, he had "got the bug," and he was not about to throw in the towel without a struggle. His name was Gil Amelio.[7]

The rest of the world got to hear about the CCD quite soon after its invention. At the New York IEEE Convention held in March 1970, Bill Boyle was a member of a panel discussing the future of integrated circuits. (Another member of the panel was Bob Noyce, who would no doubt have been explaining the workings of the CCD's nemesis in memory applications, the D-RAM.) Boyle had brought with him a single viewgraph showing the basic operation of the CCD. He spent less than five minutes explaining the device, but many people in the audience immediately understood the significance of what he was saying. They included RCA researcher Walter Kosonocky, who rushed back to Princeton and told his boss, "I want to work on this!"

A lively discussion followed Boyle's presentation. When he got back to Murray Hill, "the phone rang off the hook from everybody around the country," he recalled. "They all thought, Boy, this is really something great! The TI people and the IBM people were calling for more information. And at that point," Boyle added with a chuckle, "the Bell Labs people also felt, 'This is pretty good, we'd better start pursuing it a little bit.' " Nothing like a bit of outside interest to kindle some appreciation for what you have at home.

The invention was further disseminated in a technical paper that Boyle and Smith wrote for the April 1970 issue of the *Bell System Journal*. This discussed the structure and possible applications of the device. A companion paper coauthored by Amelio reported the team's first experimental results.

One of the most avid readers of these papers was Ochi Shigeyuki, a 31-year-old researcher at Sony's Research Center in Yokohama. Ochi had been in charge of developing MOS chips for use in the next generation of Sony's calculators.

As we saw in chapter 1, Sony had unveiled a prototype desktop calculator, the SOBAX, at the same 1964 New York World's Fair, where the equally ill-fated Picturephone was first demonstrated. Three years later, the Japanese firm introduced a commercial version. But despite this early lead, Sony never became a force in calculators. Founder Ibuka Masaru did not see the calculator as consistent with his philosophy of making products that would benefit the general public. For his part, Morita Akio had thought that calculators would be a good addition to Sony's product line. But he shrank from participating in the kind of brutal price war that broke out between Casio, Sharp, and dozens of other, smaller players. Competing on price, Morita believed, was not Sony's style.

That, at any rate, is the official version of the story. However, according to Kawana Yoshiyuki, a Sony semiconductor specialist who in 1975 would be called in to manage the CCD project, the real reason Sony pulled out was that it simply couldn't compete. "We planned to make MOS integrated circuits ourselves," he said, "and we started, but we were too late for the MOS era . . . we had problems with yield and profitability, so we stopped. We didn't stop because calculators were not our kind of product, it was from the viewpoint of competitiveness."

For Ochi, the decision to pull out of the calculator market was like having the horse shot from between his legs. The company no longer had any use for the MOS integrated circuits he was developing. Casting around for something else to work on, Ochi's eyes fell upon the CCD papers in the *Bell System Journal*. Like Amelio before him, he too was immediately captivated by the device. But reasoning that "the development of technology is pointless unless it meets actual needs," Ochi began his campaign cautiously. He circulated a memo around the Sony labs, describing the American invention and asking whether anyone else was interested in pursuing the subject. He received several positive replies.

In December 1970, Ochi began research on CCDs. Initially, the team consisted of just himself and one process specialist. But as time went by, two or three others joined in. "At the time," he recalled, everyone was relatively free to do their own thing—we didn't have to worry about budget like you do nowadays. In those days, Sony just sort of let it go: a few people doing research freely, playing around with the CCD."

The first that Jim Early heard of the CCD was at the Device Research Conference held in Seattle that June, where Smith presented the first regular technical paper on the invention. Early was a former Bell Labs researcher who had left Murray Hill the previous September—right around the time when Boyle and Smith began batting ideas around—to manage R&D at the seminal Silicon Valley firm Fairchild Semiconductor.

But it was not until the following March that he got around to calling his ex-colleague at Bell Labs, Gene Gordon, who at that time was George Smith's boss. In passing, Early asked about CCDs, and Gordon told him "one thing of vital importance—that the CCD had the lowest input capacitance of any photoconductor known. And he didn't need to say any more than that, [because] that item has enormous implications."

Early knew very well that the higher the capacitance a device has, the more the electrical noise in the system. Noise tends to swamp the signal. On the other hand, the lower the capacitance, the greater the dynamic range–the signal-to-noise ratio–which in practical terms means a clearer picture.

Early immediately started making preparations for CCD research at Fairchild. As a preliminary, in April 1971 he visited Murray Hill, where Smith and his colleagues "showed me what they had, what they were doing–they were not totally open, they never are–even if I was an alumnus, and a beloved alumnus [Early had played an important role in transistor development at Bell Labs, and had also managed the production of solar cells for Telstar], never mind–I was with the competition, but they showed me as much as they showed other people."

By this time Early had fallen in love with the CCD and its possibilities. Though at this time around 50 years old, he plunged cheerfully into the research, contributing several ideas for which he later won patents. At the same time, Early enthusiastically promoted the device within the Fairchild group, in particular, to the company's federal systems division, in Syosset, Long Island, which produced electronic cameras for aerial reconnaissance applications.

Sherman Fairchild's company, which he founded in 1920, was originally known as Fairchild Aerial Camera, because most of his inventions were designed for that market. Fairchild Camera & Instrument, the parent of Fairchild Semiconductor, was founded in 1936. The CCD's ability to operate in low-light conditions was particularly attractive for reconnaissance purposes. Together, Early and the Long Island people put together a pitch for Pentagon funding. He recalled spending a lot of the summer and fall of 1971 on airplanes; in the worst case, Early made the long coast-to-coast trip from San Francisco to Washington twice in the same week.

Around this period, Early heard that Gil Amelio had let it be known he was restless at Bell Labs. While at Murray Hill, Early had met Amelio casually a few times, but didn't really know him. Now, he arranged to meet the young man at New York's J. F. Kennedy Airport in the coffee shop on the second floor of one of the buildings, Early thought it might have been the TWA terminal. The two physicists chatted there for about an hour. That was long enough for the older man "to reveal some of our hand, to make it clear that I understood [the CCD] and loved the possibility" of developing it. Long enough, also, to determine that "Gil was raring to go."

Amelio joined Fairchild in late 1971. Now the young engineer had a vehicle for the commercialization of the CCD and he proceeded to go at it with a will. The U.S. Navy came through with a contract worth several million dollars to develop low-light image sensors. Early's frequent flier miles had paid off.[8]

Over the next five years, Amelio led a highly successful development program which grew from himself and a couple of colleagues to a 150-man operation. During 1972, Fairchild manufactured a working prototype of a basic image sensor. The following year, Fairchild's systems people took the devices that Amelio and his team had made and applied them to practical cameras that got designed into military systems.

The applications were all related to sensing in extreme situations. Night vision was one, looking out onto the horizon though a hazy sky was another, a long-range sensing system that Amelio claimed "worked spectacularly well, better than any of us thought it would." There were also some devices that were specially designed to take the place of film in aerial (and subsequently satellite) reconnaissance photography. There was even a CCD camera that was mounted in a 150mm round. Shot from a howitzer, this was deployed by means of a parachute to give the generals live TV pictures of the battleground beneath.

But though lucrative in a small way, such applications were never going to be anything other than niche markets. Amelio's ambitions extended well beyond niches. "I was really heavily committed to driving this thing and to being a high-volume manufacturer of the device," he recalled. Where would such volumes come from? "We all knew that someday doing something like a camcorder was a possibility," Amelio said, "but we also knew that we would have to go through a lot more development to get the price down, and to solve problems like how do you do color imaging and things that were not of terribly much interest to the Navy."

There was also one other possibility that was easier to imagine being commercially successful in the short term. Instead of the full-scale, hundreds-of-lines TV camera, there was a stripped-down version, a single-line sensor that could be used in facsimile machines to scan images.

"The only hope for commercialization," Amelio came to realize, "was linear sensors for fax machines."

Facsimile machines had been around since the 1920s. Newspapers in particular used them to transmit photographs. These were huge, special-purpose machines costing tens of thousands of dollars. Then in 1966, Xerox introduced the "telecopier," the first general-purpose business fax. This was able to transmit a standard-size A4 page in 6 minutes. But the telecopier was still very expensive, and as a result the market for fax machines remained minuscule.

Following the recent dramatic success of the calculator, however, designers of business machines recognized that you could apply the same principles to the fax to make it smaller and cheaper. Key to this process was the system by which the image was scanned from the paper into electrical signals that could then be transmitted over the phone. The conventional method was a mechanical scanner that worked by shining a bright light through two pinholes punched at opposite ends of a rapidly rotating disk. A solid-state linear scanner seemed like an ideal replacement for this cumbersome contraption.

As the maker of the telecopier, Xerox was the obvious partner for Amelio and his team at Fairchild. And indeed, the two firms did work together on a development program. "But for some strange reason, Xerox ultimately dropped the CCD as not being the technology of choice," Amelio recalled. That left two smaller makers of facsimile machines—Graphic Sciences, now long since defunct, and Rapifax, which around this time ran out of funds and was acquired by its manufacturer, the Japanese copier maker, Ricoh.

Ricoh was founded in 1936—the same year as Fairchild Camera and Instrument—as a manufacturer of light-sensitive coated paper. During the '50s, the company parlayed this expertise into positions in both the camera and copier businesses. By 1965, as a result of the huge success of Xerox's plain-paper copiers, the company was teetering on the verge of bankruptcy. A decade later, Ricoh came bouncing back with a new range of copiers and fax machines, both of which were developed in conjunction with an assortment of small U.S. firms.

Thus it came to pass that the first commercial application of the CCD was in a Japanese-made machine, the Rifax 600S, introduced in late 1973. Billed as the world's first office facsimile, it was able to transmit an A4 page from Tokyo to New York in under a minute. The 600S did win some prestigious customers, most notably Boeing, which in 1974 took delivery of the first fax to be exported by a Japanese manufacturer. But though a breakthrough in technology, the Rifax was not a big seller.[9] Unlike the calculator, which was a stand-alone device, the fax had to wait for the establishment of international standards. And it was not until after 1980, when the G-3 standard was adopted, that the fax market really took off.

Without volume, Fairchild could not reduce the price of its linear CCD scanner. In sample quantities, the chip cost ¥20,000 ($70), an enormous amount for a single component. But at least it was a start. The next step should have been to make improvements to the device. But then disaster struck in the form of the recession that followed the 1974–75 oil crisis.

"Within Fairchild, this was a devastating recession, probably the worst in the history of the industry," Amelio recalled, "and we were cutting back people and programs left and right. So when it came to the CCD program, we were still an infant child, just barely off the ground. And the decision was, if you can't find a way to get this program completely funded, we're going to have kill it."

Amelio was forced to fall back on his only real customers—Fairchild's space and defense systems division. "I basically sold my soul to them," he said. "I told them we'll focus all our energy on what you want if you'll fund us. And we agreed on a funding level and so forth, and that's what we did. They had no interest in the commercial sector, and they were our money.

"So, the bottom line is that, by the time we get into the mid-seventies, the only people who were willing to put their money up were the defense people. The commercial side of the semiconductor business couldn't afford it because they'd been in a deep, deep recession ... they saw it as too far into the future to want to gamble on it. ... [It was a case of] tell me where I can invest my R&D dollars so that I'll get a payback in nine months, don't tell me about a few years in the future."

So perished Amelio's dream of developing CCDs for commercial applications. But the ambitious young manager was not quite ready to give up yet. Research on commercial applications for the CCD continued on a moonlight basis, and the Fairchild researchers went on publishing technical papers about their work. In 1975, in the hope of drumming up some fresh funding for their research, Amelio embarked on a round-the-world road show.

Over several months, he gave a series of talks at conferences and other venues. In Europe, the audiences Amelio spoke to were tiny. But in Japan, it was a very different story. "I went to both Tokyo and Osaka," he recalled, "and I was there for like two weeks, giving one or two talks a day . . . and it literally was standing-room-only audiences. They had read about all this work, and they were fascinated by the potential for it."

In 1991, for his efforts in turning the CCD into a manufacturable product, Amelio would win the Masaru Ibuka Award, the IEEE's top prize for contributions to consumer electronics. What Amelio did not know back in 1975 was that Ibuka's company, Sony, had already embarked upon a secret, large-scale project to develop CCDs.

Amelio continued to run the CCD group at Fairchild for another few years. But he was no longer able to devote his full attention to device development. Fairchild needed his abilities elsewhere, to fix the company's MOS engineering organization, which at that time was experiencing all sorts of problems. It was the beginning of his career as a turnaround specialist that took Amelio to Rockwell's semiconductor division, National Semiconductor, and eventually to Apple Computer.

At Rockwell, looking for an area where the firm had an edge, Amelio chose fax modem chips, which he built up into an extremely successful product. Here the connections that he had formed through supplying CCDs to Ricoh were invaluable. The office equipment maker managed to maintain its early lead in the fax market, with the result that, as Amelio recalled, "for a long time, Ricoh was Rockwell's biggest customer." But Amelio's rise in the world also marked the end of significant CCD developments at Fairchild.

Following the breakup and sale of Fairchild in the mid 1980s, the company's CCD patents were acquired by the defense systems maker Loral. In 1992, Loral sued twenty-five Japanese and Korean firms for infringing these patents, claiming that the value of products that use CCDs exceeded $5 billion.

By the mid 1970s, the CCD was no longer taken seriously at other U.S. firms, either. In 1977, Texas Instruments introduced the first commercial CCD memory, a 64-kilobit chip that was no match for the much faster D-RAM. RCA's tube division in Lancaster, Pennsylvania, was interested in the CCD as a replacement for the vidicon tubes in the cameras used by television broadcasters like its NBC subsidiary. This division invested heavily in CCD research, but they did not manage to make a commercial product until 1984, by which time it was too late.

In the face of indifference from its operating divisions and lack of financial resources, RCA never mounted an attempt to develop CCD-based consumer products like camcorders. Former RCA researcher Paul Weimer thought that the fault was lack of vision: "RCA failed to have enough people who knew enough about the potentiality of the kind of products we could have made. For example, there was no interest whatsoever in the amateur type of cameras, although RCA as a whole had been interested in the vidicon for use in industry, and its possible use in reconnaissance and surveillance, and that sort of thing."

The corporation did, however, push one of the CCD's more prosaic applications—as the delay line in comb filters. This type of device is used to clean up signals by eliminating noise from them. Such filters were attractive as a way of improving picture quality in RCA's stock-in-trade—television receivers. By 1976, Walter Kosonocky and his team at the David Sarnoff Research Center had developed comb filters incorporating CCD delay lines to the point where they were ready for production. The question was, Who would be able to manufacture the device for less than $5? Any more than that would make the component too expensive for use in such a price-sensitive product as a TV.

RCA could have made the comb filters itself, by adapting an existing process that the company was using to make memories. Another possibility was to have Amelio's people at Fairchild produce the part for them. But Fairchild wanted too much money. So RCA began negotiations with Japanese manufacturers, finally picking Toshiba because they were willing to do the job for much less than anyone else. As a result, Kosonocky spent a couple of weeks in Japan transferring the technology to fabricate these devices. Using technology licensed from RCA, Toshiba would subsequently corner the lion's share of the linear sensors for facsimiles market that Fairchild had pioneered. The company is not, however, a major player in the much more challenging CCD camera market.

While in Japan Kosonocky also visited several other Japanese firms, including Sony, whom he realized were "very serious about this whole thing."

Avid readers of the *Bell Technical Journal* that they were, the Japanese had picked up on the CCD as soon as the invention was announced. Many made a beeline for Murray Hill to see it for themselves. George Smith noticed that "right after the CCD, the number of Japanese visitors increased substantially." They were given demonstrations, because "Bell Labs were completely open about everything, as they were essentially required to be by government." Smith himself helped spread the good word when shortly afterwards he went to Japan for a conference. While there, he gave some talks on the CCD at Japanese companies.

Boyle also remembered that there were "tons of Japanese visitors" eager to find out about the CCD from the horse's mouth. He participated in many of these visits himself. "We'd trot out some of the goodies we were working on," he recalled, "and there wasn't very much feeling of proprietary information. On the contrary, I guess we had a feeling that it was important to disseminate technology, and that way people in Japan or in other companies would share information with us. We were more interested in being sure that we had access to the very latest technology, and we felt that by being open, other people would be open with us."

But as so often with Japanese visiting U.S. labs, the visitors tended to blend into a composite in the minds of their hosts. It was hard to remember any individual visitor, even a thin, aristocratic-looking one who may have been especially interested in the goodies on display. This was the then president of Sony of America, Iwama Kazuo, who apparently made the pilgrimage to Murray Hill soon after the CCD's invention.[10]

This was not Iwama's first visit to Bell Labs. The first time had been almost two decades previously, back in January 1954. It came hard on the heels of MITI's decision to allow Tokyo Tsushin Kogyo—as Sony was then known—the foreign exchange to license the transistor.

In late 1953 Morita Akio had returned from the United States brandishing the license agreement with Western Electric. In his luggage was

Transistor Technology, a two-volume work the U.S. firm had prepared for its licensees. Long the only reference available on the subject, "Mother Bell's Cookbook," was the bible for early semiconductor researchers. It achieved a wide circulation in Japan, largely via pirated editions. But while enlightening on the subject of what transistors *were* and how they worked, the books contained relatively little about how to actually *make* the devices. Iwama's mission was thus to learn as much as possible about transistor production, then to relay that knowledge back to his colleagues waiting eagerly in Tokyo.

That Iwama should have been chosen to perform such a crucial task was not unexpected. Ever since the company's earliest days, it had usually been Iwama who took charge of developing the unconventional.

Tokyo Tsushin Kogyo was founded on 7 May 1946. As with all start-ups, one of the company's first priorities was to recruit good people. Morita tapped the obvious source: "I found many people from among my [former] classmates at school ... I even called on people with whom I had gone to elementary school because I knew them and their families."[11]

Iwama was one of Morita's neighbors in Shirakabe-cho, Nagoya, a bustling industrial city where Japan's famous Zero fighter had been built. "All of our neighbors were the richest people in Nagoya when I was growing up," Morita recalled. "We had tennis courts ... maids and butlers and private cars with chauffeurs." Morita's father went to work in a chauffeur-driven Buick. "At home, we had a General Electric washing machine and a Westinghouse refrigerator. ... When the new phonographs arrived, he spent a lot of money to buy one of the first in Japan."[12]

Iwama Kazuo also came from a wealthy family. "He was a real gentleman, very well-bred," recalled Ochi Shigeyuki, who would become Iwama's unofficial secretary at Sony's research center. One of Iwama's uncles owned a building in central Tokyo, which he loaned to his nephew's fledgling firm after they had been evicted from their original premises, a bombed-out department store. The connection that bound the Moritas and the Iwamas was an intimate one. During the war, Iwama became engaged to marry Morita's sister, Kikuko. But the marriage had to be postponed because of the confusion and dislocation of wartime. The wedding eventually took place soon after the company was established, with Sony cofounder Ibuka Masaru acting as the go-between. (At a Japanese wedding, the go-between or *nakodo*—who is often, as in this case, the bridegroom's superior at work—presides over the ceremony and makes a speech wishing the newlyweds a long and happy marriage.)

Iwama had not originally planned a career in commerce. On graduating from Tokyo University as a geophysicist, he had joined the university's Earthquake Research Institute. It was a prestigious position. His young friend—Iwama was born in 1919, two years before Morita—must have drawn upon all his considerable powers of persuasion to talk his future brother-in-law into giving it up in favor of a new and untried venture. But Iwama took the plunge, joining on 1 June 1946, just three weeks after the firm incorporated. He was then 27 years old.

The following January, Tokyo Tsushin Kogyo—known as Totsuko for short—relocated to Gotenyama in southwestern Tokyo (where it remains to this day). They took over a shabby building formerly used as a carburetor warehouse. A photograph taken that year shows Iwama with Ibuka and Morita standing outside their new headquarters. To an outsider's eye the building appears more like one of old man Morita's sake breweries than a high-tech facility. Nattily dressed all in white, with a straw boater tilted back on his head, Iwama looks for all the world like a varsity man out on a spree.

In those early days, Totsuko had yet to hit upon the tape recorder, which would be the company's first successful product. In the meantime, they were experimenting with all sorts of ideas. First attempts included a rice cooker, which never worked, and an electrically heated cushion. When folded, the latter gave off sparks that could ruin the pants of an unwary owner.

Iwama's contribution to product innovation was a monstrous power megaphone which used a carbon microphone instead of a vacuum tube. "As Iwama enthusiastically worked on the prototype, the small workshop resounded with his loud voice for days on end."[13] In product form, the megaphone found eager buyers among Japanese politicians, who used it at street rallies during election campaigns.

During this search for a promising consumer product, it was often suggested to Ibuka that Totsuko should make radios, for which in postwar Japan there was much demand. But Ibuka adamantly refused, reasoning that there was no way a tiny company like theirs could compete against the likes of Hitachi and Toshiba, giant firms that manufactured their own components.

Radios made from conventional parts were thus out of the question. But a radio made from an unconventional part like the transistor was a different story. Remember that, at this time, as yet no transistors were available for radio use. When Morita signed the license agreement, the Western Electric people told him that the only thing the Japanese could expect to make with transistors was a hearing aid. The transistor was thus "the embodiment of the goal that had led Ibuka to found his company in the first place: making high technology available to the general consumer."[14]

At the same time, uppermost in Ibuka's mind was the question of how to keep the company's most precious asset—their staff of young engineers—occupied. Out of some 120 employees, graduate physicists and chemical, electrical, mechanical, and metallurgical engineers made up about one third of the total. Producing transistors seemed like a challenge that such bright young men might relish. The more Ibuka thought about the idea the more excited he became.

His enthusiasm proved contagious. While MITI officials dragged their feet, sulking over Totsuko's failure to inform them before signing the contract with Western Electric, Ibuka formed a task force to study transistor technology. The team would consist of his most capable people. Iwama, who was then in charge of tape recorder production, volunteered to lead it. This, despite the fact that as he himself would later confess, "I had no knowledge of semiconductor devices whatsoever . . . I was very, very young."

Iwama was in fact 35 years old, reckoned to be a researcher's creative peak. He threw himself into his task with tremendous energy. No sooner had MITI given the green light than he and Ibuka headed off to Haneda Airport and boarded a Stratocruiser bound for New York. For the next three months the pair were whirlwinds of activity, bouncing from place to place, gleaning every last scrap of information about semiconductor manufacture they could lay their hands on.

"During the day, they visited factories, plants, production facilities of all kinds, laboratories; Western Electric was particularly helpful. They went to Bell [Labs] . . . to Westinghouse, to see a high-frequency generator, out to the Midwest, to Milwaukee, where a heavy-duty furnace was being used . . . ."[15]

"On these tours Iwama would stop in front of each item that seemed of particular interest and ask questions to the best of his (none too perfect) English ability."[16] Back in the hotel room at night, he would write a report on what he had seen, racking his memory for every last detail.

The first of these reports, dispatched in mid-February 1954, ran to nine foolscap pages. Each was crammed with handwritten descriptions and diagrams that stretched from the very top of the page to the very bottom, no margins, both sides of the paper. Eight more pages followed on February 19, nine more on February 21, and so it continued. Though Iwama did not write every day, his output was prodigious—by the time he got back to Tokyo in late April, his letters filled four fat folders.

Awaiting Iwama when he returned was a surprise. A week before he was due back, the team at Totsuko produced their first transistor. They hooked it up to an oscillator, switched the device on, and the needle on the oscillator's dial twitched. This was greeted with shouts of joy: no one, least of all Iwama, had expected to see a transistor working so soon.

It was to be the first of many triumphs. As head of the transistor development team, and subsequently manager of transistor production, Iwama was intimately involved with all of them. It was he who encouraged his colleague Tsukamoto Tetsu to challenge conventional wisdom. Tsukamoto reengineered Western Electric's transistor into a device capable of handling high frequencies.[17] This enabled the production of radios with a performance far superior to that of rival makers. It was also Iwama who recruited the brilliant young physicist Esaki Leona, who went on to win the Nobel Prize for discovering tunneling electrons in Tsukamoto's transistor.

(Esaki joined Totsuko from Kobe Kogyo, where he had become, as he put it, "embroiled in some trouble" with an unsympathetic management. Word of his discontent somehow reached Iwama, who promptly invited Esaki to join Totsuko. Kobe Kogyo's management were infuriated by this attempt to poach one of their best people, and punished Esaki by "giving him cold rice," as the Japanese say, assigning him to a business office, a most unsatisfactory posting for the brilliant young researcher. Eventually, senior government scientists intervened to rescue Esaki. But face required that he not move directly from Kobe Kogyo to Totsuko, so Esaki was forced to spend some time at a halfway house, a small maker of power supplies called Origin Electric.)

A photograph taken around 1957, just after these triumphs, shows Iwama in the lab on the second story of Totsuko's wooden headquarters building in Gotenyama. Behind him can be seen benches crammed with electronic measuring instruments. He stands holding open a box in which are stuffed hundreds of transistors, like pins in a pincushion. As always, the pencil-thin Iwama is immaculately dressed, in rolled-up shirt sleeves and a natty bow tie. His forehead is high, his face intelligent, the expression on it reserved. Iwama was not a boastful person—in fact, he was shy, a quiet man of few words—and yet he must have been extremely proud of his team's remarkable achievements.

Totsuko adopted the name Sony in January 1958. That same month Iwama told Tsukamoto to begin research on a high-frequency silicon transistor for television use. Transistorized TV sets went on sale in 1960; the famous Trinitron made its first appearance eight years later. During the income-doubling years of the 1960s, Sony's sales took off like a rocket.

The company began the decade with less than 4,500 employees and ended it with more than 16,500. Within this burgeoning organization, Iwama moved from one senior management position to another. In May 1971, he was made president of Sony of America. And it was then, while living in New York, that he heard about the charge-coupled device, and headed off to meet its inventors.

Iwama was a man who liked to stay well informed. He told his senior managers at Sony not to spend time in the office. In Iwama's view, "a manager of a research section shouldn't be lounging around with his colleagues or subordinates. [He should] go outside and eat with outside people."[18] By chatting over lunch or dinner, his managers could find out what their counterparts were up to and, if they discovered anything interesting, let him know. He told his people: "I don't want reports, I don't want to have to read difficult research papers—what I want is the latest gossip."

Iwama was always eager for news. His favorite ploy was to invite people to dine with him at Maxim de Paris, a branch of the famous

Iwama Kazuo shows off a box of transistors, Tokyo, © 1957–58. (Photo courtesy of Sony).

French restaurant which had been established in the basement of the Sony Building in Ginza, central Tokyo, when the latter opened in 1966. When, for instance, Esaki–who had left Sony in 1960 to join IBM's Yorktown Heights laboratory–came back to Japan for a few days, Iwama would call him and say, Let's have dinner at Maxim's. There, over the *hors d'oeuvres*, he would pepper his guest with a barrage of short questions like, How is so-and-so at IBM? What's he up to these days?

Once Iwama heard some news, he liked to check it using several different channels. For example, he would call Sony research director Kikuchi Makoto and say, Last night I saw Esaki, and he said such-and-such. I was extremely interested–what do you think?

Iwama's was not an idle curiosity: He was quick to act upon what he had learned. Kikuchi recalls having dinner with Iwama on Kikuchi's return from a fact-finding trip to the United States. Iwama asked how his visit had been, and Kikuchi told him that researchers at leading universities like MIT and Stanford had just begun using computers to simulate devices. On hearing this, Iwama immediately became very serious: "How about starting this kind of thing at Sony?" he asked Kikuchi.

In late 1972, Iwama returned from the United States to become Sony's deputy president. Within the company, it was widely understood that this posting was a preliminary to his taking over from Morita as Sony's next president.[19] The following year, 1973, the position of director of the company's research center fell vacant. Top management was at a loss, because there was no obvious candidate available for this key job. Despite an already heavy workload, Iwama agreed to fill in as director until a replacement could be found.

His first step was to review the state of R&D at Sony. Over the next few months, Iwama would lunch with many of the center's 300-odd researchers, asking them about their work, listening to their opinions. Himself a scientist, Iwama well understood the workings of the scientific mind. Not surprisingly, he was very popular with the people at the center.

What Iwama learned was extremely disturbing. Sony's withdrawal from the calculator business had left the company without a rationale for continuing research on MOS chips, much as AT&T's decision to axe Picturephone removed the justification for continuing CCD work at Bell Labs. Absence from mainstream microchip technology effectively meant that, as Ochi Shigeyuki bluntly put it, "at Sony, semiconductors were dead."

To Iwama, the man who had begun semiconductor work at the company, who had overseen initial production of transistors and their subsequent incorporation in transistor radios, televisions, and a host of other successful products, this must have come as a shock. To see his beloved semiconductors in such dire straits, to know that rival companies had left Sony—the company that had after all pioneered the technology in Japan—eating their dust—must have been mortifying to him. It was an intolerable situation, and Iwama resolved to do something about it.

Among the demonstrations Iwama had seen at the Yokohama research center was one that stuck in his mind. Ochi and his colleagues had built a primitive charge-coupled device. Capable of a resolution of only eight lines, it was a crude effort. So crude, in fact, that the display the device produced, which was supposed to be the letter "S" for Sony, actually looked more like the number "5." It was, however, a start and it reminded Iwama of the (much more sophisticated) demo he had seen at Bell Labs not long before. "Oh, so we're working on CCDs, too?" Ochi recalled him remarking.

The CCD, Iwama quickly grasped, could serve as the vehicle for re-suscitating semiconductors at Sony. Such a complex device would give the company much-needed experience in making big chips. Moreover, just as Ibuka had decided to license the transistor to give his young engineers something they could get their teeth into, so Iwama was also looking for a grand theme to challenge his people. Something that, if successful, would produce big results, which would in turn bolster their confidence.

In November 1973, Iwama announced a complete reorganization of the center. Researchers would henceforth focus on four new large-scale projects. Of these, the CCD would have top priority. A team of forty scientists and engineers was assigned to this project, with a budget to match.

Revitalizing semiconductor research was of course not the ultimate goal. As the company's next president, Iwama knew perfectly well that it was his responsibility to come up with a vision of a successful product for the future. And so he did: Just as Sony had developed the transistor in order to make an entirely new type of radio, so the company would develop the CCD in order to make an entirely new type of camera.

Like RCA, Sony had a long history of developing vidicon imaging tubes for television cameras. In 1971 the research center had come up with the Trinicon, a camera tube intended as the name suggests to complement the Trinitron receiver. In 1974, this was transferred from lab to factory.

Though an improvement over conventional tubes, the Trinicon still suffered from problems like lag (afterimage), lack of image clarity, and poor reliability. In response to these deficiencies, the research center had also attempted to develop a silicon vidicon much like the one that George Smith had produced for Picturephone. But this project ran into so many problems that in 1971 the research was curtailed. Now, many of the same people who had participated in the Trinicon and silicon vidicon projects were drafted to work on the CCD.

Their target this time would not be professional equipment, but a compact camera for the consumer market. The competition, too, would be different. Instead of other electronics companies like Matsushita, NEC, or Toshiba, Iwama declared that "our main rival is Kodak. We will compete with film, and it will be a new business for us." He set an extremely ambitious target: to develop in five years a color video camera that cost ¥100,000 ($370).

The notion that Kodak was the competition suggests that what Iwama had in mind was a still as opposed to a video camera. And indeed Sony did work on such a camera, the Mavica, which was trialed by the *Asahi* newspaper at the 1984 Olympic Games in Los Angeles. Opinions of Sony managers and researchers involved in the CCD project differ as to which type of camera Iwama originally conceived. However, given on the one hand the fact that Sony had just (1971) introduced the U-matic, the world's first video cassette recorder, which a video camera would serve to complement, and on the other the extremely competitive nature of the 35mm camera business, it seems plausible that uppermost in Iwama's mind would have been the new product category represented by the video camera, and that the still camera was an afterthought.

His researchers were taken aback: This was a formidable task. Indeed, one senior company official would later describe the development of the device as "Sony's greatest technical challenge."[20] When research on CCDs began, Sony was way behind other Japanese semiconductor makers. At the time, there were no clean rooms at the Yokohama research center, a prerequisite for serious microchip work. Nor was there much in the way of process equipment—mask makers, aligners, deposition chambers, diffusion furnaces and that sort of thing. Worst of all, apart from Ochi and one or two others, Sony mustered precious little hands-on experience in modern chip-making methods.

Not surprisingly, in its early days the project didn't go well at all. In fact, during the first year, virtually no progress was made. Burdened with his other responsibilities, Iwama was keen to hire a full-time director for the research center. An ideal candidate was transistor pioneer Kikuchi Makoto, who was about to retire from the government's

Electro-Technical Laboratory, where he headed semiconductor re-search.[21] Initially Kikuchi was reluctant, but Iwama would not take no for an answer. Kikuchi finally gave in after Iwama called him at 1:30 in the morning.

When Kikuchi reported for duty in August 1974, Iwama briefed him about the CCD. Kikuchi was fascinated to learn about this project, which Sony had been working on in secret. But when he visited the lab where the work was going on, he got a nasty shock. "I found a *terrible* situation," he recalled, "the picture coming out of the experimental CCD camera was awful—full of black dots and white scratches." Kikuchi could hardly believe his eyes. The images on the screen looked as if they had been captured during an exceptionally severe snowstorm. It was impossi-ble to tell what they depicted. Aghast, Kikuchi asked, "What *is* this?"

Things were in fact so bad that Kikuchi couldn't imagine the project ever being successful. "I had to pretend that I was optimistic," he said, "but in fact when I got home that night, I was extremely pessimistic." Iwama had given Kikuchi permission to kill the project if he judged it not worth continuing. After careful consideration, however, Kikuchi decided to go on with CCD research.

What was causing all these flaws in the picture? Kikuchi took a long hard look at the data. Suddenly he remembered some research he had done almost twenty years before. It was very academic stuff about a mysterious class of substances "which somehow crept into semicon-ductors and acted as traps for holes, gobbling them up and further shortening their already-too-brief lifetimes."[22] At Bell Labs, Bill Shock-ley had dubbed these substances "deathnium." Now Kikuchi wondered whether deathnium might be relevant to the problems that Sony's CCD's researchers were encountering with streaks and dots? He dis-cussed the matter with the physicists at the center, telling them to focus on how defects formed in the crystal lattice.

For the next fourteen months, the lights burned late in the Yoko-hama labs. It turned out that particles of heavy metals like iron and copper (introduced in particular from photoresist, a chemical used to transfer circuit patterns onto silicon wafers) were indeed playing merry hell with the picture. Excess electrons came pouring out of the ionized metal particles, causing the white lines that blotted almost everything else out on the screen.

Having understood the nature of the defect, the next step was to find ways of dealing with it. Improving the purity of the silicon crystal was clearly crucial. At one stage Iwama wanted to go the whole hog and buy a crystal manufacturer, but in the end Sony settled for doing joint research with a firm called Toyo Silicon.[23] A main source of defects in the wafers was the swirling of the molten silicon out of which the ingots were pulled. To eliminate this, Sony's researchers stilled the melt by applying a very strong magnetic field, a technique borrowed from Harry Gatos's lab at MIT. Step by step, they built up a wealth of process knowhow.

This progress did not immediately translate into improved devices. With many other duties to perform, Iwama was only able to visit the center once a month. But he continued to oversee CCD research from a distance. By 1976 Iwama was seriously concerned about the lack of progress. Looking for a way to improve the situation, he came up with a highly unusual proposal. Maybe Sony had bitten off more than they could chew, especially since they had so little chip-making experience. Perhaps it would be better to spread the risk by teaming up with a partner who knew more about that sort of thing. He asked Kikuchi to run the idea of cooperation by some of the research director's friends at other companies.

Kikuchi suggested that NEC and Hitachi would be the best bets. He went to see his old friend Uenohara Michiyuki, a former Bell Labs researcher who was then director of R&D at NEC. Their conclusion: No go. Next he visited another old friend, Watanabe Hiroshi, director of Hitachi's Central Laboratories. Hitachi's researchers had also been working on imaging chips. As early as 1973, they had built the first really large-size solid-state image sensor. This, however, was a MOS chip, not a CCD.

"MOS imagers came first," Ochi said. "MOS technology already existed, and it was relatively simple to produce pictures with it. However, [because of the noise problem] they couldn't produce good pictures. Whereas with the CCD, although it was difficult to produce pictures, from the beginning the theory predicted that the pictures would be good."

Watanabe and Kikuchi agreed that researchers from the two companies should get together to compare the merits of their respective approaches and to discuss the possibility of working together. The first meeting took place, in great secrecy, at Sony's research center in Yokohama; the second, at Hitachi's labs in Tokyo. Evidently the two sides could not find much to agree on; there was no third meeting.

Now, three years into the CCD project and with precious little to show for it, Iwama began to come under fire within Sony. According to Kawana Yoshiyuki, the project manager, "Iwama-San was really worried, because he'd spent so much on it. All over Sony, you'd hear critical voices—What's he doing, spending all that money? Will it ever become a business? And even if it does, will there be a return on the investment? But because Iwama was president, no matter how much criticism there was, no one could confront him directly and say, Stop it. So people just discussed it behind his back."

In fact, Iwama was actually confronted by other top managers within the company. Sony's board of directors used to lunch together every Tuesday. On one such occasion Kikuchi recalls Morita, then Sony's CEO, teasing Iwama. "How's the CCD coming along?" Morita asked, "Still sucking up lots of cash?" Iwama smiled and acknowledged that it was. "When will we recoup our investment?" Morita wanted to know. "After I die, maybe," came what would prove to be an unwittingly prophetic response.

A more persistent critic was Iwama's designated successor, Ohga Norio. The company's deputy president was particularly concerned about financial matters. Kawana recalls Ohga telling Iwama, "This CCD stuff is all very well, but it's costing too much money, and will anything ever come of it?" [24]

Such negative comments took their toll on Iwama. Though still outwardly optimistic, he was beginning to have second thoughts about the CCD. On one occasion, Iwama called Kikuchi and told him that perhaps the time had come to quit. Nonplused, Kikuchi in turn called Kawana to tell him what Iwama had said. But Kawana shot back, "Just when we're almost there, there's absolutely no need to talk about giving up—we'll just have to try harder, that's all."

In early 1977, when it seemed that "the sword was broken and there were no arrows left," as they say in Japanese, the tide finally turned. The enormous effort that the researchers had poured into understanding and eliminating defects in the crystal began to pay dividends. In

March 1978, Sony succeeded in making its first practical CCD camera. The company held a press conference at which Iwama explained the merits of the new camera to reporters and talked about how he had first encountered the device at Bell Labs. Inspired by Sony's example, other Japanese companies initiated crash CCD development programs.

Meanwhile, researchers at the center continued whittling away at the faults in the image the device produced until they had reduced the number to about a dozen—a drastic improvement. What happened next, according to Kikuchi, was that one day in May 1978, "Iwama-San came to the research center—sometimes he visited us without warning— and I guided him to the place where we were doing the CCD research. Then, when we came back to my room ... Iwama-San told me, Kikuchi-San, the time has come to move this project to Atsugi," where Sony's semiconductor production plant was located.

Kikuchi was taken aback. After all, his people had made numerous improvements to the technology, and they were proud of their achievements—surely they should be allowed to go on and finish the job? To Kikuchi, a bureaucrat's son who had spent most of his life working in a government institution, Iwama's reply was highly instructive. "He said, 'We have experts in doing research here at the center, but we have experts in *making* things at the Atsugi plant. If you keep this project here any longer, you'll end up damaging it.'"

And after a brief discussion lasting ten minutes or so, Kikuchi agreed that he would try to transfer the project as soon as possible. "I made up my mind and told Iwama-San, Yes, and we came downstairs; then, just as he was leaving the research center, getting into his car, he looked over his shoulder and said, 'In two weeks, please!'"

Kikuchi was flabbergasted. "I had spent twenty-six years in a government lab where there was *no* movement of people, and *no* movement of projects," he recalled, laughing. "So that was very good training for me, having to make the move in two weeks." Next day, Kikuchi called members of the CCD team into his office one by one. He told them the situation, and asked whether they would be prepared to move to the Atsugi plant. This was located in the western suburbs of Tokyo, about 20 miles from the Yokohama research center. Out of forty-five researchers, only one said no. (It turned out that the reason for this researcher's reluctance was that he'd just bought a house near the center.)

Kikuchi ended up picking about thirty-five of the team to make the transition, including Ochi and his group of engineers. And sure enough, just as Iwama had predicted, once the technology was transferred to the factory, the number of defects dropped to just a few. At long last, by the end of 1978–five years after research at Sony began–it was possible to make plans for putting the CCD into production.

But Sony was not out of the woods yet. The first commercial application of the CCD camera was on board jumbo jets flown by All Nippon Airways. The electronic eyes were (and are) used to give passengers on Japan's second-largest airline a pilot's eye view of takeoffs and landings.

This most reassuring service had already been installed, using conventional, vidicon-based cameras, on ANA's fleet of Lockheed Tristars. However, following the Lockheed scandal of 1976, which led to the prosecution on bribery charges of seventeen high-ranking individuals (including former prime minister Tanaka Kakuei), the airline decided to switch its procurement to Boeing 747s. Naturally, ANA wanted to offer the same service on these airliners, too. But though overall the jumbo was bigger than the Tristar, it had a much smaller cockpit–too small to accommodate a conventional-image tube camera. In short, the application was tailor-made for the more compact cameras that could be configured using CCDs.

Because the resolution of an individual chip was not yet sufficient to produce a decent picture, each camera carried two chips, the images they produced being combined using a prism. Again, because the quality of the pictures taken through the cockpit glass was not terribly clear, a second camera was installed in the landing gear, above the 747's front wheel. Thus, since ANA had bought thirteen jumbos, the requirement for CCDs was $2 \times 2 \times 13 = 52$.

Not, you would have thought, a particularly tall order. But making those fifty-two chips took Sony a whole year. "Production yields were so low, you couldn't count them," Ochi laughed. To get a single good CCD, they had to produce several thousand chips. Each chip cost around ¥370,000 ($1,630), a far cry from the ¥100,000 camera that had been Sony's original target.

Iwama had been right in thinking that the CCD would challenge his engineers. In fact, CCDs turned out to be an even greater challenge than the MOS memories that other semiconductor firms were cranking out at this time. "If a speck of dust lands on the surface of a MOS chip," Ochi explained, "it's OK, so long as it doesn't cause any reliability problems. But on a CCD, you can actually *see* a speck of dust as a black spot on the screen. Even if it only covers 10 percent of an individual cell, then that part will look 10 percent darker ... and the human eye is extremely sensitive to that sort of thing. So unless you can remove [dust] it's no good."

In spite of all these problems, in early 1982 Sony went ahead and built a line for the mass production of CCDs. This commitment would ultimately drive total R&D expenditure on the device over ten years at the company to $200 million–a huge amount for a single component.

On 24 August 1982, just before shipments of the chips began, Iwama Kazuo died of cancer, aged 63.

Thus Iwama did not live to see the fulfillment of his vision–the consumer video camera. In January 1985, Sony introduced the first 8mm-format camcorder to feature a CCD. Rival firms were still using imaging tubes. For about a year, Sony had the market to themselves, then JVC launched a VHS-C camcorder incorporating a chip made by NEC. The resolution on both chips was 250,000 picture elements, approximately equivalent to the 256 kilobit D-RAM. In 1987, attempting to up the ante to 380,000 elements, both firms came unstuck. Production of CCDs ground to a halt. The culprit, it turned out, was dust. Japanese newspapers had a field day: "Electronic Eye Beaten by Speck of Dust" ran the headline in one.

NEC withdrew from CCD competition to concentrate on D-RAMs. Matsushita, which along with its affiliate JVC had been NEC's principal customer, were forced to initiate development of their own chips. Most recently, Sharp has also begun making CCDs. Between them the three firms dominate the markets for both components and camcorders.

In 1994 Sony's share of the camcorder market was just over 40 percent. The same year, the company produced around 10 million CCDs. But perhaps Sony's greatest moment of glory came in June 1989, with the introduction of a lightweight passport-sized "handycam." This hugely successful product bore the model number TR55. Few realized that this was a symbolic gesture: thirty-four years earlier this had also been the number of Sony's first transistor radio—whose production Iwama had overseen.

Camcorders became one of the most profitable products in Sony's history. In recognition, the CCD won an in-company prize awarded annually to the product that has contributed most to the company's needs over the past few years. On the day of the award ceremony, Ohga—who had stepped into Iwama's shoes as president—noticed that his late predecessor's name was not listed among the prizewinners. He asked for it to be added.

In his speech Ohga apologized for not having acknowledged the merits of CCD technology earlier. He gave instructions that a chip should be attached to the back of Iwama's tomb, so that the late president could continue to watch over them all from beyond the grave. In May 1990, when cumulative production of CCDs reached 10 million units, Sony staff working on CCD production visited Iwama's grave to report the achievement of this milestone to their late boss.

By the mid 1990s, camcorders still accounted for 85 percent of all CCDs produced. Some 6 million camcorders are sold every year. But Ochi Shigeyuki, now general manager of Sony's semiconductor division, dreamed of a new and potentially much larger market for the device that he had begun working on over twenty years before. That was CCDs used to connect personal computers together, a market otherwise known as desktop videoconferencing. This latter-day version of Picturephone was what Ochi was really looking forward to: "The technology's all lined up and ready," he said.

His counterpart at Sharp, Inoue Hiroshi, had similar dreams. "At the moment, CCDs are mainly used in video cameras," he said, "and that's a very small market, not of much interest to semiconductor makers, because CCDs are difficult to do and you can't make any money out of them, you only do them because you need them for the sets.

CCD chip on the back of Iwama's gravestone.

"But as we move into the multimedia era, CCDs will be used to capture all sorts of images and send them down phone lines, and all personal computers will have CCDs built into them. And not just multimedia either, but in the home, too, for all sorts of automation—wherever there's a need for something to play the role of the human eye, if it's electronic, it'll be the CCD. So in that sort of age, it's going to become an extremely important device."

In late 1997 it seemed that, in vindication of Iwama's original vision, digital cameras rather than desktop video would be the next big application for the CCD. The first company to leap into this market was not Sony, but the irrepressible Casio. Many bought the company's $500

QV-10 "filmless" digital camera to post images on the Internet. At least a dozen other companies have subsequently entered this market.

In retirement in Palo Alto, Jim Early, too, still had dreams for the CCD that remained to be fulfilled. "For example," he said, "to a degree that has not yet been realized in practice, the CCD is capable of measuring in the same image, a wider range of light level than any other photosensor we know. Add to this enormous range of photosensitivity the possibilities that have already been shown for electronic shuttering and the like, and you have an incredible affair, just gorgeous. And if you think I'm a technology lover," he laughed, "you're right."

Bill Boyle retired from Bell Labs in 1979. These days, he divides his time between the tiny fishing village in Nova Scotia where he was born, and milder climes. George Smith retired in 1986, intending to do a three-year circumnavigation of the globe in his 9.5-meter yacht *Apogee*. Ten years later, he was about halfway.

In 1993, the two old friends got together for some sailing in the South Pacific around New Caledonia. Of all the ideas that they used to bat around, the CCD has proven the most durable. For his part, Boyle took greatest satisfaction from the scientific uses their device has been put to, especially in astronomy, where the CDD's tremendous sensitivity to light has revolutionized the field.

Since 1976, when a CCD was first used to record images of planets, the use of CCDs by astronomers has grown enormously, allowing them to peer deeply into space, revealing faint light sources such as quasars.

And now and then, there are gratifications closer to hand. For example, when a Nova Scotian neighbor of Boyle's had her gall bladder removed, she told him "Bill, I was so glad they're using your CCD in there. It made the operation so much better."

7

The Sound of One Chip Clapping

People who enter a business solely in pursuit of profit are destined to fail.

—Kawakami Gen'ichi, former president, Yamaha

IF YOU WERE TO BUMP INTO JOHN CHOWNING at a commencement, say, or a Palo Alto cocktail party, you might conceivably guess what he does for a living. The broad forehead, the serious demeanor, the slightly owlish features—all the physiognomic clues point to an artist of some sort. The French and German words that pepper his conversation—properly pronounced, mind you—suggest time spent abroad. But no telltale flecks on his clothes and not a whiff of turpentine, so not a painter. A poet, perhaps, or . . . a composer? Got it in two.

But never in a month of Sundays would you guess this modest Stanford University professor of music's other claim to fame. Which is that John Chowning also has an invention to his name.

And what an invention!

An invention that by the mid-1990s had enabled Stanford to rake in more than $20 million dollars in patent license fees—second only in terms of revenue generated to the university's basic biotechnology patents. Second, moreover, at *Stanford*, whose licensing income far outstrips that of any other U.S. school.

It was an invention that earned the computer music center Chowning founded pride of place on the Stanford campus, in what was once the university president's residence, and ensured the center's permanence through endowment. The invention also made Chowning himself a rich man—rich at least by the modest standards of composers—witness his 44-foot yacht *Paradise,* moored at Sausalito marina.

Chowning's invention was FM synthesis, a simple way of generating complex sounds. In the form of a microchip, FM synthesis became the sound source first for the most successful music synthesizer ever made, then for a whole range of keyboard instruments. Latterly, it has become the key component on sound boards, personal computer accessories that in 1994 became multimedia's first billion-dollar market. The supply of FM chips is monopolized by one firm, the Japanese musical instrument maker Yamaha.

When John Chowning arrived at Stanford's music school in 1962 as a 29-year-old graduate student, he had never so much as seen a computer. Chowning was fresh back from three years studying composition in Paris with Nadia Boulanger. In Europe, technology had begun to manifest itself in music. Chowning had sat enraptured at concerts of electronic music where pieces by Pierre Boulez, Karlheinz Stockhausen, and Luciano Berio had premiered. "The idea of speakers as musical instruments was very much in the air," Chowning recalled. The young American was eager to try composing for these new instruments himself.

In the early 1960s, a major barrier to would-be electronic music composers was the almost unbelievably primitive means of sound creation at their disposal. Back then, the most familiar technique for producing new sounds was *music concrete.* Composers like Stockhausen would record onto quarter-inch magnetic tape the bleeps and bloops made by audio oscillators (the sort of equipment that radio stations use to test their broadcasting equipment). Then they would use razor blades to chop up the tapes into short strips, splicing them back together in whatever order sounded best and looping the result. Creating a few minutes of concrete music could take weeks or even months of painstaking work.

There had to be a better way—and, sure enough, there was. Chowning found out about it quite by chance. In his second year at graduate school, Chowning played percussion in the Stanford orchestra. Knowing his interest in electronic music, an orchestra colleague passed him a copy of an article from the 1 November 1963 issue of *Science* magazine.

The article was by Max Mathews, a researcher at Bell Laboratories. It was the first publication of his work outside the labs' technical journal. Mathews described how computers could be programmed to play music. Intrigued by the possibility, Chowning headed back to his native New Jersey, where Bell Labs was located, to find out how it was done.[1]

Mathews worked in the acoustic and behavioral research department of the laboratories at Murray Hill. This was a group consisting of around eighty researchers. It included computer scientists, mathematicians, experimental psychologists, as well as electrical engineers like Mathews himself. To simulate the behavior of new telephones, the Bell Labs scientists had figured out how to digitize speech, squirt it into the computer, run their experiments, then turn the bits back into sound waves.

A keen amateur musician, Mathews immediately realized that it would be relatively straightforward for him to adapt this process to the writing and reproduction of music. In 1957, to make the computer accessible to nonspecialists, he wrote a program called MUSIC I. Then he invited some composers to come by the labs nights and weekends to try it out.

Though less primitive than cut-and-splice, composing music on the computer was anything but straightforward. "We had decks of punch cards," Mathews recalled, "on which the computer scores were produced, which we would carry around in boxes." They would load the boxes into a car, then drive over into Manhattan to the IBM Building on Madison Avenue and 57th Street.

There, in the basement, was a mainframe computer on which time could be rented, at the astronomical rate of $600 an hour. "We would line up," Mathews explained, "then, when it was our turn, we would run down the stairs, stick our cards in the machine, and press the button." The result would be a tape full of digital sound samples, which they would squirrel off to Bell Laboratories for playback through a specially built digital-to-analog converter.

Despite the expense and the inconvenience of all this toing and fro-ing, the composers immediately fell head over heels in love with the computer. It offered a solution to one of the thorniest problems they faced: How to get their music performed? Finding an orchestra willing to play one's latest piece was a perennial headache for the profession, especially for its more avant-garde practitioners. ("The reason I keep these expensive gentlemen with me," Duke Ellington said, referring to his orchestra, "is that unlike most composers, I can immediately hear what I've written.") One composer became so enamored of the com-puter that he began spending all night, every night, at the labs. Eventu-ally, Mathews recalled, the man's wife left him.

A second attraction of computers was that they didn't screw up—they would play your score exactly as written. Plus, they offered composers the chance to go back and make as many changes as they liked. But for all their joy at having found a new and flexible way to organize and perform sounds, composers of electronic music could not help but be aware that there was still something lacking.

As anyone who has ever heard a radio test tone knows, the sine waves that your garden-variety oscillator puts out are not exactly fun listening. The human ear craves richness: overtones, stray harmonics, distortions. Anything, in short, rather than the unwavering monotony of the oscillator's pure electronic tones.

Chowning returned to California for the fall 1964 semester clutching the box of punch cards that Mathews had given him. Now all he needed was a computer to run them on. He went hunting around cam-pus and discovered SAIL, Stanford's newly established artificial intelli-gence laboratory.

John McCarthy, the AI pioneer who set up the lab, allowed Chown-ing to freeload time on the university's DEC and IBM machines nights and weekends, just like the composers at Bell Labs. This was doubly fortunate. At a time when large computers typically processed jobs in batches, McCarthy had perceived the need for users to process interac-tively, and had configured the machines to allow this. So Chowning could immediately hear his work played, and make changes to it as he went along.

In addition to possessing a state-of-the-art computer system, SAIL was a wonderfully stimulating place for the young composer to work.

At the lab, Chowning recalled, "you had engineers, you had scientists, mathematicians, philosophers, psychologists, people using computers. So it was a very rich intellectual environment, on which I depended—I could cycle through these people until I got an answer that connected, and that was a technique of learning that I often used, because I had no technical background. I had a lot to learn, but it was probably the most exciting learning experience I've ever had."

Chowning was now 30 years old, a long way from his last high-school math class. But with the help of an undergraduate he got Mathews's program up and running in short order. Other than a single course he took in FORTRAN programming, Chowning picked up everything through osmosis and his own hands-on experience. He soon realized that "with a modicum of programming skills, one can accomplish some truly astonishing things."

One night in 1967, the young composer was experimenting with wildly exaggerated vibratos (fluctuations in pitch often added to electronic sounds to give them a more realistic quality). While fooling around with a couple of oscillators, feeding back the output of one to control the other, half fearing that he'd break the computer if he went too far, Chowning heard something remarkable.

At about 20 Hertz, down around the lowest frequencies that the human ear can hear, he noticed that instead of an instantaneous change in pitch from one pure tone to another, the machine was emitting a rough sort of *whoo-ch-ch-ch-ch-ch* sound. Chowning had made what he would later call "an ear discovery."

"I kept pushing the rates and I noticed that at 50 Hertz and 100 Hertz what I was hearing was no longer a pure tone, but one that was rich in harmonics." He also discovered that if he kept the frequency of the vibrato constant while altering the depth of the waveform output by the other oscillator, what happened was that the pitch stayed the same, but the richness of the sound changed. As the sound got deeper and deeper, more and more harmonics appeared.

It was a discovery that an engineer would have been unlikely to make. What Chowning had stumbled upon, he later discovered, was frequency modulation—a technique that radio and television broadcasters had long used to transmit noise-free signals, only transposed down into the audio domain. Of this, the composer was blissfully ignorant:

All he wanted to do was to make colorful sounds. Chowning began tweaking his algorithm and pretty soon, as he recalled, "using only two oscillators, I was making bell tones and clarinetlike tones and bassoonlike tones, and I thought, you know, *this* is interesting."

But not interesting enough to go dashing out yelling Eureka. Chowning put his discovery to one side and got on with other things. He had yet, he later confessed, to connect his ear to the theory. This conjunction would not occur until 1971, when Chowning remembered some synthetic trumpet tones that a Bell Labs researcher had played for him and wondered whether he could achieve a similar effect using FM synthesis.

It turned out that he could indeed produce some quite realistic brass tones. And it was at this point that Chowning realized that his technique was a lot more powerful than he had at first thought. Being a composer, the first thing he did was to write some pieces of music for FM synthesis. One of these was *Turenas,* written in 1972.

Turenas—the name is an anagram of "Natures"—gives a good idea of FM synthesis's versatility as an aural palette from which to mix new sounds. It is a lively piece in which sounds are constantly whizzing from one speaker to the other (reflecting another of Chowning's preoccupations, the use of sound to create a sensation of space).

The sounds the piece employs fall into three distinct categories: First, there are those that resemble the sounds of regular instruments, like organ, horn and bassoon, and chimes, bells, and gongs. Then there are sounds that are more or less familiar, like water dripping onto a canvas awning, or the teeth of a comb being twanged. Finally, there are some sounds that are like nothing you have ever heard before. For Chowning, these previously unimagined sounds were "the wonderful part of art making contact with technology, of connecting your art with another domain."

One of the first people to whom Chowning demonstrated his discovery was J. R. Pierce, Max Mathews's boss at Bell Labs. In the annals of twentieth-century technology, Pierce cuts a formidable figure. Among a string of other achievements, Pierce was responsible for naming the transistor, for pioneering the communications satellite, and was himself a sometime composer of computer music. As soon as Pierce heard the tape of FM samples, he looked Chowning right in the eye and barked in his commanding manner, "Patent it!"

By this time it was clear that FM synthesis had interesting potential applications, so Chowning took his tape over to Niels Reimers, who ran Stanford's Office of Technology Licensing, and played it to him. Reimers agreed that Chowning's idea had commercial potential. He contacted the U.S. companies that were most likely to be interested, the makers of electric organs.

Among them, the obvious target was the company that had invented the electric organ, that had created the market to go with it, and whose name had as a result become so famous that it had become a household word, listed in dictionaries, encyclopedias, and textbooks: a company called Hammond Organ.

There are thousands of different electric keyboard instruments out there. But with the possible exception of the Fender Rhodes electric piano, only one of them has a truly distinctive sound—the rich, fat, shimmering, swelling roar of the Hammond Model B-3. Introduced in 1953, the B-3 went on to become the most popular electric organ ever made. It is a sound that is instantly recognizable to anyone who grew up in the 1950s and 1960s, the sound that first jazz organist Jimmy Smith, then later Booker T. Jones—remember *Green Onions*?—made famous. And it is a sound that even today merits a special mention on album credits and in live introductions—"On the *Hammond* organ, ladies and gentlemen . . . "

The funny thing is that Laurens Hammond, the inventor of this illustrious instrument, could not himself play a note, could not even hold a tune.[2] Born in 1895 in Evanston, a suburb of Chicago, Hammond was a latter-day member of that elite band of individual American inventors that includes Thomas Edison, Alexander Graham Bell, and Edwin Armstrong (the man responsible, among other things, for the original FM).

From an early age, Hammond was an inveterate tinkerer, winning the first of his 110 U.S. patents—for an improved barometer—when he was just 16 years old. By education, Hammond was a mechanical engineer. After fighting with the U.S. forces in France during World War I, he returned to take up a position as chief engineer with a small Detroit firm of marine engine makers.

But Hammond was not cut out to be a company man—at least, not unless it was his own company. In 1920, annoyed by the noise made by the spring mechanism of a clock, he invented a "tickless" clock enclosed in a soundproof box. Selling this idea enabled him to set himself up with his own laboratory in New York City. It was there, the following year, that Hammond came up with his core invention—a synchronous motor that would run in phase with the 60-cycles-a-second alternating current power supply that was then becoming standard. The significance of stable power was that it made Hammond's motor run very efficiently—even in miniature form.

Hammond investigated several applications for his invention, including a projector for the first 3-D movies. But it was not until years later that he would tie his two inventions together to create a tickless electric clock driven by the synchronous motor. In 1928, he moved back to Evanston to establish the Hammond Electric Clock Company in premises above a local grocery store.

For a few years the company prospered, but by the early 1930s the clock market was saturated and the Depression was at hand. Clearly, if he was to remain in business, Hammond would have to come up with a new product. And come up with one he did, unveiling in 1932 ... an automated bridge table, equipped with a synchronous-motor-driven mechanism that would shuffle a pack of cards, then deal out four hands. Though the table was a success, selling some 14,000 units at $25 each in the runup to Christmas that year, it was obviously just a stopgap.

Once again Hammond went back to his workbench. Employees soon began to hear strange noises emanating from his laboratory, some of them loud enough to shake the building to its foundations. Then one day, passersby heard the sound of a flute floating out the laboratory window.

The source of this wonder was an invention that came to be known as a tone wheel. This was an iron disk about the size of a silver dollar, from the edge of which protruded coglike bumps. Spinning the wheel in front of a coil-wound magnet would induce an electric current in the coil which, amplified and sent to a loudspeaker, could be translated into sound. Hammond and his researchers discovered that by lining up 91 tone wheels on shafts driven by his magic motor, and using precision gears to change the speed of rotation, they could reproduce all the sounds made by a conventional pipe organ—and then some.

On the organ that they built, each key was connected to a bunch of switches. The switches, in turn, were connected to each other by a system of metal strips called drawbars. The organ contained 1,500 switches equipped with long-lasting platinum contacts. The switches were hooked up via some eight and a half *miles* of wire. When a key was pressed, a combination of switches would close, forming a sound-generating circuit in much the same way as the electromechanical relays of contemporary telephone exchanges would connect to complete a call.

In January 1934, Hammond packed his prototype into a box and shipped it to the U.S. Patent Office in Washington D.C., where it was set up in the basement of the building. On 24 August that year, in almost record time, the office granted Hammond a patent on his organ.

The Hammond organ was an overnight success. Among the company's first customers were George Gershwin and Henry Ford. But priced at $1,250, the Hammond was cheap enough for regular folk to afford, too. One organ nut who just had to have a Hammond in his living room was a young man from Pasadena, California, called Don Leslie. Leslie didn't buy a speaker to go with his purchase, figuring that it would be cheaper to build one himself, which he proceeded to do.

To his great disappointment, the result didn't sound nearly as good as what he'd heard in the music shop. But then the shop had a long, high-ceilinged showroom, ideal for producing the reverberations that are crucial for sonic richness. How to compensate for the lack of reverb in his living room? Leslie came up with the idea of revolving the speaker inside its cabinet. He built a prototype: It sounded great! In the first flush of his enthusiasm, Leslie figured that the organ maker ought to be interested in his idea, so he arranged for a demo and invited the Hammond brass over to hear it.

Leslie's hopes were dashed: The Hammond people turned up their noses at his invention. Worse, when Leslie went into business making speaker cabinets on his own, Hammond declared war. Leslie speakers were not to be used with Hammond organs in stores; Hammond dealers were prohibited from handling Leslie products. (So they sold them on the sly; organ buyers were asked if they would like to step into the back room, where salesmen would demo the speakers.)

Hammond's feud with Leslie reveals much about the firm's attitude toward innovation. If it was not invented by Hammond, then Hammond didn't want to know, even to the extent of cutting off his nose to spite his face. Hammond the company would eventually acquire Leslie, but not until 1980, long after Hammond the man's death in 1973. They thus missed out on several decades' worth of speaker cabinet revenues.

In 1960 Laurens Hammond retired as chairman of his company and went to live in Cornwall, Connecticut. The official story is that in his retirement, Hammond devoted himself to research. In fact, according to Doug Jackson, a veteran Wisconsin-based Hammond dealer, the old man acted as "a puppeteer from afar—he was a very strong character, and anything he didn't want done didn't get done." So it is not unreasonable to assume that Hammond's negative attitude toward innovation from the outside would have continued to prevail at the firm even after his retirement.

By 1971, when Niels Reimers of Stanford's licensing office got in touch, Hammond was, in Jackson's words, "a very stodgy company—they were very set in their ways, they were resting on their laurels and had been for years." The trouble was that by the early 1970s tone wheel technology was almost obsolete. The company could not afford to go on much longer producing such an archaic system, with all its miles of wire and thousands of switches. At the same time, Hammond's engineers were undoubtedly aware that the emerging microchip technology had the potential to create new sounds in less space and for lower cost.[3]

Perhaps it was a sense of urgency that caused Hammond to dispatch almost their entire engineering staff to Palo Alto for a look-see. Reimers recalls that they also brought along a virtuoso organist with them. When this musician heard Chowning's FM tapes, he became enthusiastic about the technique's potential. The engineers, however, just didn't get it.

Chowning recalled that the Hammond people "kept asking me things like, how many pins will it need? Well, I didn't know anything about pins, chips, or analog circuitry at all, so I couldn't answer them. I said, 'Look, it's an algorithm, and here's the code.' " By this time, he had confirmed that the technique was indeed frequency modulation, so he was able to explain the principle to the Hammond people. But they couldn't see how it connected with what they did. Chowning concluded that "it was simply not part of their world."

Other U.S. organ and piano manufacturers that Stanford contacted—including Allen, Baldwin, and Lowrie—were likewise unable to make the connection. But rather than give up, the resourceful Reimers assigned a graduate at the university's business school to look into electric instrument makers, to see if there was anyone else who might conceivably be interested in FM. It did not take long for the grad to come up with the name of Yamaha. Although at that time virtually unknown in the United States, the Japanese company turned out to be the largest maker of electric organs and pianos in the world.

Yamaha had an office in Los Angeles. In January 1972, Reimers called to tell them that there was an interesting new technology available for license. A 34-year-old engineer called Ishimura Kazukiyo happened to be visiting from Japan, and he flew up to San Francisco, rented a car, and drove down to Palo Alto to meet Chowning at the AI lab.

Chowning played Ishimura a few examples of FM sounds and explained what was going on. It took Ishimura all of ten minutes to grasp the concept. Why was he so quick? Two reasons: One was that as a student Ishimura had majored in communications technology at Tokyo's prestigious Waseda University, so he knew all about frequency modulation. The other was that, for the past five years, Yamaha had been working on the development of digital musical instruments.

Yamaha, this huge company of which no one seemed to have heard, owes its origins to a chance encounter between Yamaha Torakatsu, a 36-year-old medical equipment repairman, and a bellows-driven Mason & Hamlin reed organ.[4] The encounter took place in 1887 in the Pacific coast port of Hamamatsu, a small post station on the old highway that linked Tokyo with Osaka. In those days the town was known mainly, if it was known at all, for its local delicacy—broiled eels.

But Hamamatsu evidently did not see itself as a backwater, or at least the town had ambitions of upward mobility. Witness the purchase of an expensive imported American organ—a symbol of modernity—for the local school. Then the blasted thing went wrong, and Yamaha—who fixed equipment at the local hospital—was sent for to put it right.

When Yamaha Torakatsu was born in 1851, the third son of a prominent samurai, there were no Western instruments in Japan, nor Western music, nor Western anything for that matter. At that time, the country was closed to foreigners and all things foreign, and had been for the best part of 250 years. Two years later, when Commodore Matthew Perry and his fleet of black ships sailed into Tokyo Bay, the American brought with him a naval brass band. For Japan, the modern age begins with Perry stepping ashore to the accompaniment of martial fanfares and oompahs.

At the age of 20, Yamaha left home for the southern city of Nagasaki, where for several years he was apprenticed to a British watchmaker. Then, after attempting to make watches on his own account, a venture which foundered due to lack of funds and commercial experience, Yamaha turned to repairing medical equipment, landing a job with an Osaka-based firm of suppliers. He was assigned Hamamatsu as part of his territory.

Yamaha was evidently fascinated by the organ. After fixing it, he went over the instrument with a fine toothcomb, drawing elaborate diagrams and taking copious notes. By the time he had completed this early instance of what would later come to be known as reverse engineering, Yamaha was confident he could build one himself. Which he proceeded to do, improvising with local materials like tortoiseshell for the key coverings in place of unobtainable ivory. Though crude, his prototype organ worked persuasively enough for him to recruit a workforce of seven and ¥30,000 (about $10,000) in capital from local Hamamatsu investors. The year was 1888 and Yamaha was in business.

Others would soon follow Torakatsu's example, as Western-style music became part of Japan's national school curriculum and the market for instruments blossomed. By 1895, the year of Laurens Hammond's birth, a dozen Japanese manufacturers were producing approximately 10,000 reed organs a year.

Yamaha, with an annual production of 2,000 units, was unquestionably the leading maker.[5] The company continued to flourish, making a timely transition around the turn of the century to the new upright pianos, which from then on would be the keyboard instrument of choice for the home market, in place of the more expensive organ.

In 1916, Yamaha Torakatsu died suddenly at the age of 64. The next decade was not a happy period for the company he had founded. Beset by a series of disasters—fires, earthquakes, and strikes—Yamaha lurched to the brink of bankruptcy. The firm was eventually saved by a most remarkable man.

Kawakami Kaichi was Hamamatsu born but destined, or so it seemed, for great things elsewhere. He graduated top of his class in physics at Tokyo University, then joined Sumitomo Wire, the electric cable-making wing of one of Japan's biggest *zaibatsu* conglomerates. The company put Kawakami onto the fast track, sending him abroad for two years on a study tour of the United States, England, and Germany.

In May 1927, when Yamaha's harried board of directors offered him the chief executive's job, Kawakami was 42 years old. Much to the horror of his family and friends, he accepted their offer. Perhaps rescuing a moribund musical instrument maker was more of a challenge for him than playing corporate politics at Sumitomo.

Kawakami made three invaluable contributions to Yamaha. One was his knowledge of modern management techniques, which he immediately set about applying. The second was some desperately needed investment, which came from Sumitomo. Over the next half century and beyond, the Sumitomo connection would continue to provide Yamaha with financial backing, underwriting some of the company's subsequent forays into new businesses. (In the early 1990s, group companies including Sumitomo Bank, Sumitomo Marine & Fire Insurance, and Sumitomo Life Insurance would between them own almost 14 percent of Yamaha's stock, the single largest block of shares.)

But Kaichi's third and most important contribution to Yamaha was his son, Gen'ichi, who took over the presidency of the company in 1950, when a stroke incapacitated his father.

In 1956, the year before computer music was born at Bell Laboratories, a most unusual job interview took place in Hamamatsu. The interviewee was a 29-year-old twinkle-eyed electrical engineer called Mochida Yasunori; the interviewer, Kawakami Gen'ichi, fourth president of Yamaha. What made the interview unusual was that it took place in Kawakami's bedroom, with the chief executive lying flat on his back.

Kawakami was laid up because he had recently broken his leg falling off a "Red Dragon," one of the 125cc motorcycles that Yamaha had recently started making. What was Yamaha, a manufacturer of musical instruments, a company whose stock in trade was organs and pianos, doing in the motorbike business? The answer is that Kawakami Gen'ichi liked to try his hand at new things. And once he got started, there was seldom any stopping him.

During World War II, Hamamatsu had been razed to the ground by American firebombs. Some of these were no doubt intended for Yamaha's factories, which had been converted for the duration to the production of airplane parts such as propellers—including all the wooden propellers installed on Japanese Imperial Army aircraft—and fuel tanks. By 1950, however, Yamaha was back at its usual business, cranking out pianos and organs.

It would have been easy for Kawakami, like so many second-generation chief executives, to coast along on the momentum that his father had generated. But Kawakami was not the sort of man to coast. The way he saw it, the role of a manager was not just to look after current business but also to go out and look for new opportunities.

Strongly held convictions were one thing that set Kawakami apart from his fellow countrymen. Another was an intense dislike of wearing ties—polo shirts would become his trademark. A third differentiating factor was that, unlike all but a few Japanese in the 1950s, Kawakami had seen the world and been inspired by it.

On a three-month round-the-world trip in 1953 (the year in which Sony's Morita Akio would make a similar journey), he had visited the United States. There, Kawakami was astonished by the range and variety of products on offer, and by the sophistication of the techniques Americans used to manufacture them. After visiting modern U.S. facilities like the Baldwin piano factory in Cincinnati, Kawakami realized how primitive Yamaha's were by comparison. For the moment, his dreams of exporting was shattered.

Kawakami returned to Japan determined to modernize every facet of Yamaha's operations. He plowed company profits into upgrading manufacturing processes, installing newfangled equipment like conveyor belts and woodworking machinery. But his biggest investment came in 1956, in a huge automated kiln used to dry wood for making pianos.

It was characteristic of Kawakami to think on a grand scale. At a time when Yamaha's annual production was just 15,000 pianos, the

kiln could hold enough wood for 50,000. Kawakami was widely criticized for this apparent extravagance. But as status-hungry, culture-
starved Japanese consumers began buying pianos in record numbers,
Kawakami's vision of future markets turned out to be right on the
money. Within ten years Yamaha's output increased to 100,000 units a
year, making the company the largest producer of pianos in the world.

In addition to thinking big, Kawakami was also by nature intensely
competitive. By the early 1950s, Hamamatsu had become Motorbike
City Japan, serving as headquarters for both Suzuki and a new outfit
called Honda. Kawakami was determined to get into the motorbike
business too, and the metalworking tools that Yamaha had used to
make airplane parts during the war gave him an effective means of entry. In 1955, he spun off the bike division as an independent firm,
Yamaha Motor.

Another spur was the knowledge that entirely new markets were
opening up. In 1954, a brash new start-up, Tokyo Tsushin Kogyo, a
firm that would shortly change its name to Sony, had approached
Kawakami to ask whether Yamaha would agree to become a distributor
for their new tape recorders. They wanted access to Yamaha's nationwide network of dealers through which the firm sold its pianos and
other musical instruments to schools. Ordinarily, Yamaha's policy was
to handle only products which they themselves manufactured. But
Kawakami must have been intrigued by the tape recorder, because in
this case he made an exception.[6]

As a distributor, Yamaha turned out to be a disaster: ". . . they had no
knowledge of electronics or electrical engineering; they could not answer questions about the machine and thus could not sell it; when they
did, they could not service it properly."[7]

But at least the experience left Kawakami well positioned to appreciate Sony's success in introducing new electronic products. As with motorbikes, such products represented a challenge for a man like
Kawakami. And one he felt more than qualified to meet. "Ibuka-San
[Sony's first president] is a talented person," Kawakami commented at
the time, "but *I* am a genius."

This time, however, unlike the motorbike business, Kawakami had
no existing resources to throw at the problem. There was not even a
single electrical engineer on Yamaha's payroll. Which explains why on

that momentous day in 1956, broken-legged and swell-headed, Kawakami summoned young Mochida to his bedroom for an interview.

Mochida Yasunori was born in the provincial northwestern Japanese city of Kanazawa in 1927. His father was a professional soldier, but more important, a man with an inquisitive mind who loved new toys like radios and single lens reflex cameras. Mochida junior was very much a chip off the old block.

Young Yasunori grew up in a household surrounded by gadgets that his father had bought. He was evidently one those insatiably curious kids who just have to know how things work, taking them apart then putting them back together again. Aged 14 or 15, Mochida built himself a radio out of vacuum tubes. Above all, the youngster loved finding new things to do.

Though obviously bright—math and physics were his favorite subjects—Mochida hated the rote learning that was (and is) such a dominant feature of the Japanese education system. To their credit, his parents put no pressure on him to cram to get into a good school. The end of the war found Mochida old enough to go to university, but he opted instead to enter a local technical college, where he thought he would be able to pick up more practical skills.

After graduating, the 20-year-old Mochida came to Tokyo to work for Denon, a subsidiary of Nihon Columbia, which made phonograph records and recording equipment. His boss there was a former classmate of Sony's Ibuka, and the two friends used to meet regularly and discuss tape recorders. As a result of these conversations, Mochida was assigned to develop a tape recorder, his specific responsibility being the electronics of the machine.

The project was successful, but late. Sony had already captured the lion's share of the market for audio tape recorders, forcing Denon's management to look elsewhere for customers. They found a niche selling their products as data recorders to power companies for monitoring lightning strikes on their high-voltage transmission lines and to seismologists for tracking earthquakes.

This early exposure to both audio and data processing would later stand Mochida in good stead when it came to developing digital musical instruments at Yamaha. For the moment, however, his practical experience in developing tape recorders was the reason for Kawakami's interest in him.

What did Mochida and Kawakami make of each other on this first meeting? Mochida recalled little about it other than the fact that Kawakami was testing him, finding out what the younger man was made of, what his attitude was. One thing, however, stuck in his mind: Kawakami revealed a burning ambition to make his mark in the world, to do something that no one else was doing, something completely new and different.

Mochida was (and is) a man whose passion is doing new things. The two men were thus immediately on the same wavelength: The one would become the instrument for fulfilling the dreams of the other. While working at Yamaha, Mochida would be conscious of a curious resonance between himself and Kawakami, a sort of kindred spirithood that for him would develop into close personal identification. "My feeling was that I myself was president," he said, laughing at the recollection, "and that there was another Kawakami-San who was the real president."

Mochida joined the company with a brief to open up new business areas for the company to exploit. During his first few years at Yamaha, the young engineer developed a range of magnetic metal alloys for use as the record and playback heads of tape recorders. Having succeeded in metals, Mochida characteristically lost interest and started looking around for something else to do. Evidently pleased with his progress, Kawakami assigned him the most important job in the company—coming up with an electric organ that could compete against organs made by the U.S. firm, Hammond, that by the late 1950s were just beginning to penetrate the Japanese market.

Yamaha's first attempts to build an electric organ were based on vacuum tubes. But by the time Mochida took up his new assignment, transistors were just beginning to replace tubes. Transistors were attractive because they were smaller and, in theory at least, more reliable. But the methods used to produce transistors in those days were crude by modern standards, and the devices caused Yamaha no end of trouble.

Nonetheless, Mochida succeeded in his task. In 1959, he and his staff of two assistants unveiled Yamaha's first electronic product, the

D-1. It was launched onto the Japanese market under the prosaic brand name of Electone. Like many first-generation products, the D-1 was expensive, and it was not a great success commercially. Kawakami, however, was delighted: He had seen the future and it worked. He increased Mochida's staff and built an electronics R&D center for them to work in. Yamaha's next step was to switch from using individual transistors to chips that integrated lots of transistors on the same tiny piece of silicon.

The logic of the integrated circuit was inexorable, as the American Apollo space program would clearly demonstrate. The more features you wanted to include, the more transistors you needed. But the more individual transistors you used, the more likely you were to have a dud one. By integrating 100 transistors onto a chip, you could increase reliability by 100 times.

For a company like Yamaha that had been plagued by consistency problems, chips were a godsend. They placed orders with domestic makers like NEC. This was in the late 1960s, around the time when chips were also starting to be used in calculators. But these early devices were merely miniaturized versions of circuits that had formerly been made out of transistors. The next step would be to use the unique potential of chips to create something entirely new—just as Kawakami had hoped.

Around 1962, while Yamaha was still wrestling with the reliability problems that plagued its first electric organs, before John Chowning had even begun to mess about with algorithms, a radical change was taking place in the design of keyboard instruments. It would have huge consequences for the musical instrument industry.

In San Francisco, a young composer called Don Buchla had gotten fed up with the rigmarole of recording tones, then chopping and splicing the tapes. Instead of having to borrow tone generators from broadcasting studios, he reasoned, wouldn't it be neat if you could have an inexpensive instrument in your home that you could use to compose on?[8]

Meanwhile, over on the East Coast, Bob Moog was finishing up his Ph.D. at Cornell, building and selling theremins in his spare time. (Theremins produce the eerie wailing sound familiar to most of us via old horror movie soundtracks and the Beach Boys' classic *Good Vibrations*.)[9] Moog's hobby led to contacts with composers of electronic music. This in turn stimulated him to start building audio oscillators and amplifiers whose output could be controlled, by varying a voltage, to produce complex tones.

It was Buchla who came up with a name for this new category of instrument: He called it the synthesizer.[10] "The reason was because we started with elements of sound," Buchla explained, "building sound from basic elements like pitch, timbre, amplitude, and a few other things." But it would be Moog whose name would stick in the public mind as the father of the synthesizer. One main reason was the huge success in 1968 of *Switched-On Bach* by Walter (now Wendy) Carlos, a million-selling record that made the sound of the Moog synthesizer world famous.

For about ten years, from roughly the mid-sixties to the mid-seventies, the small but rapidly growing market for synthesizers was dominated by tiny U.S. start-ups, most notably Moog and ARP (a Massachusetts-based firm best remembered as the maker of the synthesizer used to communicate with the aliens in the movie *Close Encounters of the Third Kind*). "People were going apeshit over these funny electronic sounds," Moog recalled.

"I heard Walter Carlos doing *Switched-On Bach*," rock keyboardist Keith Emerson said, "and on the cover of the album was this thing that looked like a telephone exchange."[11] Fascinated, Emerson made enquiries, and managed to borrow a Moog synthesizer for a live rendition of the theme music from the movie *2001: A Space Odyssey*.

The extraordinary noises the synthesizer made baffled the audience to such an extent that Emerson decided he had to have a Moog synthesizer of his own to play on stage. So the rock star called the inventor and told him what he wanted to do. Moog replied that he would not recommend it—his synthesizers were only meant to be studio equipment.

Nonetheless, Emerson insisted, eventually shelling out £30,000—a princely sum—for a massive, modular system. He was very proud of his new acquisition. "Trouble was it arrived with no instruction book—three oscillators, a reverb unit, trigger controls, filters, mixers, and a load of strange wires and plugs, and I couldn't even switch the damn thing on. You needed to be a rocket scientist."

Such problems were typical of products made by early U.S. synthesizer firms, all of which suffered from bad management and chronic underfinancing. "We were always in the red," Moog lamented, "we had no capital. None. Zero." They would stumble along from one National Association of Music Manufacturers show (where instrument dealers gather to place orders) to the next. If you didn't have a hit at one year's show, then you had better have one at the next, or you were dead."

A second problem was quality. According to Moog, "In the late sixties and early seventies, you could put five pounds of shit in a box, and if it made a sound you could sell it." In addition to poor manufacturing, another recurrent vexation was the inherently unstable nature of these early, analog synthesizers.

The oscillators that generated the sound were controlled by electrical voltages. To boost an oscillator's pitch up an octave took a commensurate increase in voltage. The trouble was that the damn things wouldn't stay in tune–their pitch was notorious for drifting. A ripple in the power supply, a change in temperature as the hall heated up or as the components themselves became warmer, almost anything was enough to set them adrift, necessitating a retune.

"The tuning was a nightmare," Emerson recalled, "I had a frequency counter built into my system which I had to keep an eye on, plus I was playing the Hammond and two other instruments. When I look back now, I don't know how I got through it, I really don't."

An expanding market, undercapitalized firms, poor manufacturing, and unreliable components–this was a scenario that was virtually tailor-made for the Japanese, with their deep pockets, superb production skills, and long-term commitment. Japanese firms began to make their presence felt in the synthesizer market from the mid-seventies on. Initially, it was the smaller outfits–Korg and Roland–that made most of the running. Lagging behind came Yamaha.

This tardiness was not for want of trying. But Yamaha had chosen a hard row to hoe. By 1966, Mochida had concluded that the only way to produce consistent, high-quality sound was via digital rather than analog means. Converting continuously varying analog waveforms into digital pulse trains of ones and zeros was a cumbersome process, but once accomplished, it offered some compelling features, most notably the ability to check for and correct errors in the instrument's output.

Programming a digital oscillator to stay in tune would be simply a matter of defining numerically what "in tune" meant, then instituting a continuous checking routine on the oscillator's output. If, during the previous microsecond, the output value had drifted a smidgen off spec, then it could be instantaneously caught and brought back into line. *Et voilà:* high reliability!

Digital was wonderful in theory, but implementing it in practice required digital chips. And not just any chips, either—off-the-shelf integrated circuits would not do. Yamaha would need custom chips fast enough to produce sound in real time—in other words, the instant a musician pressed a key. And, if the chips were to be applicable to consumer products, they would also have to be cheap. But who would make such chips for them?

"We went to our semiconductor suppliers," Mochida recalled, "and asked them if they would be prepared to make digital chips to our specifications." But everywhere the Yamaha team went, it was the same story: "They told us to stop thinking about something so difficult, that it'd be a nuisance to have to make chips specially for us. 'What you're talking about is what they do in computers,' they said, 'but you make consumer products, so it'd be too expensive for you, it'll never become a business.' We tried to persuade them to help us. But at that time, the calculator boom had begun, and it was obvious that electronic instruments wouldn't grow as fast, so we weren't such good customers anymore."

Mochida contemplated the problem. He decided that if Yamaha wanted to get integrated circuits made, then they would have to make them themselves. At a time when giant firms like Toshiba had yet to enter the chip business, this was an extraordinarily ambitious decision. But it was made out of sheer necessity: "It wasn't as though we had several choices and picked one—the only way left was that we had to do it ourselves."

Having resolved that Yamaha had to go it alone, Mochida then faced the daunting task of trying to persuade the company's management to take the plunge. A board meeting chaired by Kawakami was held to discuss the matter. Aware that his proposal was unlikely to be well received by his fellow directors, Mochida outlined his plans hesitantly.

Not surprisingly, the reaction of his codirectors—men from the company's dominant piano group, most of them—was overwhelmingly negative. Mochida must be mad, they complained, to propose something as risky and expensive as making chips. Especially since the firm had no prior experience of producing semiconductors, nor any qualified staff.

Kawakami had been listening to them in silence. Then, suddenly, he erupted. "Why are you all ganging up on him?" Kawakami thundered, "I'm not going to sit here all day listening to your arguments—I'm the boss, and I stick up for the underdog." Then he rounded on Mochida and shouted at him, "And as for you—if you're so sure that your idea is correct, how come you're so hesitant? You should speak more clearly." Then, having let both sides have a piece of his mind, Kawakami gave Mochida the go-ahead.

"If we can make the best musical instruments in the world," Mochida remembered Yamaha's president declaiming, "then no matter how difficult it is, no matter how much money it takes—we'll do it." And perhaps Kawakami did say this, or something like it; the Japanese do have a penchant for the melodramatic.

What matters is the fact that Yamaha did make the investment in semiconductor production facilities. It was a huge sum of money, the initial amount invested being about equivalent to the company's paid-in capital at that time. But, as with the giant automated wood-drying kiln, Kawakami had the vision—and the guts—to take such a big risk.

When a Western company elects to go into a new business, the usual approach is to go out and hire people with the requisite experience. But in neofeudal Japan, hiring mid-career staff is extremely difficult. In addition, ever beguiled by the challenge of the new, Mochida was against the idea of bringing in outsiders.

For some years, at Kawakami's instigation, and at considerable expense, Yamaha had been recruiting young graduates from top Japanese universities. Here was a chance to make use of this talent. The chip industry was itself still only a few years old—surely it was possible to catch up? So around 1969, Mochida and a hand-picked team of six bright young graduates, all of them in their twenties, set out to learn from scratch how to make semiconductors.

They adopted a two-pronged strategy. Basic skills would come from sending engineers for instruction at Tohoku University, to the laboratory of Nishizawa Jun'ichi, one of Japan's leading authorities on semiconductors.[12] Meanwhile, manufacturing techniques would be transferred under license from the U.S. firm Philco, a subsidiary of Ford (which would quit the microelectronics business shortly thereafter). Within 18 months, Yamaha's engineers had designed their first digital integrated circuit. In April 1971, around the same time as Sharp and Seiko, they began volume production of chips in a factory at the company's main Hamamatsu plant.

These first efforts were simple circuits, not what Mochida needed to build digital instruments. At that time, Yamaha had two candidate designs for a digital system. Both of them required chips that would work at 3 megahertz, that is, would be able to accomplish 3 million instructions a second (the speed at which a digital circuit operates is governed by the frequency at which its crystal clock ticks).

Japanese semiconductor manufacturers had demonstrated their reluctance to attempt anything so advanced, but perhaps some U.S. companies might have the capability to build such designs? In January 1972, Mochida dispatched his sidekick, Ishimura Kazukiyo, to the United States to find out. And that is why Ishimura happened to be in Yamaha's Los Angeles office when the call came through from Niels Reimers of Stanford University's Office of Technology Licensing.

And what was Mochida's reaction when an enthusiastic Ishimura phoned to tell him about FM? Did he hop on the next plane to San Francisco hot to sign a contract? No, he did not. Mochida would not make the "pilgrimage"—his word—to Stanford until December 1972, eleven months later. The reason for the delay was that in early 1972 he was concentrating on an idea of his own. This was a hybrid system that fudged the speed barrier by implementing control of the instrument's keyboard in digital while using conventional analog means to generate the sound. Marketed as PASS (for "*p*ulse *a*nalog *s*ynthesis *s*ystem"), this instrument sold respectably, but did not exactly set the world on fire.

Mochida was sufficiently humble to admit the possibility that there might be better ideas out there somewhere. In late 1972 he set off on a tour of music departments at U.S. universities, one of which was Stanford. As it happened, Chowning was not there at the time.

Having taught at the university for the requisite seven years, the composer had applied for an important promotion: tenure, the academic equivalent of a full-time job. To this end, Chowning had submitted a paper describing FM, together with *Turenas* and another piece written using his synthesis system. And, to their great discredit (and subsequent embarrassment), the stuffy Stanford review board had turned his application down. So the now jobless Chowning had been forced to leave Stanford for Berlin, where he spent an impoverished year in exile.

Thus it was left to SAIL director John McCarthy and Niels Reimers to demonstrate Chowning's FM samples of brass and percussion to Mochida. The impetuous Mochida was so impressed that he decided to license the technology on the spot. "As an engineer, you are very lucky if you ever encounter a simple and elegant solution to a complex problem," he said later. "FM was such a solution, and it captured my imagination. The problems of implementing it were immense, but it was such a wonderful idea that I knew in my heart it would eventually work."

Mochida also knew that there was no way FM synthesis would work using existing technology. But Reimers insisted that the contract stipulate that Yamaha would make products using FM within a given time limit (understandably so: without products to market, there would be no royalties for the university). And having once again persuaded a reluctant Yamaha board that the company should go ahead and develop this extremely difficult technology, Mochida kept his promise—just.

The GX-1, the first product to use FM technology, was a kludge. Introduced in 1978, instead of a single FM integrated circuit, it had over fifty chips lined up in parallel. It also cost $20,000. This effectively put it out of the reach of everyone except rock stars like Keith Emerson.

The objective was a chip that would run fast enough to perform several million calculations a second to produce sounds in real time the instant a key was pressed (which Chowning's software-based system had not been able to do). To achieve this, Yamaha had continually to update their semiconductor production technology, keeping abreast of the state of the art. For example, Ishimura, who was in charge of this aspect of development, recalled that Yamaha was perhaps the third or fourth Japanese company to purchase a stepper, a key piece of production equipment used to reproduce microscopic circuit patterns on top of silicon wafers.

At the same time, while transforming Chowning's algorithms into hardware, boiling them down onto ever smaller slivers of silicon, Yamaha's engineers were also developing the software that would create the actual sounds. This, as Mochida pointed out, also takes a long time to produce. It stems from a gradual accumulation of knowhow, from endless cut-and-try until they finally achieved something that sounded like a regular instrument.

During those years, Chowning (now reinstated at Stanford) made regular visits to Hamamatsu, where he would work closely with small groups of Yamaha's engineers on the development of prototype instruments. He came away imbued with a lasting admiration for their dedication, their skill and inventiveness, and—interestingly—their remarkable lack of ego. "That's the Japanese way," he commented, "they express themselves anonymously through the products they make."

In particular, a bond developed between Chowning and Mochida, despite the fact that neither could speak the other's language. When Chowning was penniless during his exile in Berlin, Mochida persuaded Kawakami to channel some funds to the young composer, enabling him to continue his work. While on a trip to California, Mochida came down with a kidney stone. Chowning gained the Japanese admission to the Stanford hospital and got the top urologist there to remove it.

It took more than seven long years of effort, but eventually Yamaha came up with the goods. In 1983, the company introduced the DX-7, the first synthesizer to incorporate the brand-new FM chip. Much to the surprise of Yamaha's sales people, it was a huge commercial success, catapulting the Japanese firm to the top of the electronic keyboard industry.

According to English music writer Clive Bell, "The DX-7 was immensely popular because it was the first synth with a hard, sparkly sound, it was very cheap—which meant that almost anybody could afford one—and it was very reliable." The first models of the DX-7 sold for around $2,000, less than half the price of a comparable contemporary U.S. instrument like the Sequential Prophet.

Yamaha sold over 200,000 DX-7s (Moog's most popular synthesizer, the Minimoog, had sold around 13,000 units during its ten-year lifetime), making it by far the best-selling synthesizer ever. The instrument became part of every self-respecting keyboard player's setup.

Offering myriad preset sounds at the touch of a button, plus the possibility of hundreds more from third-party suppliers, the DX-7 was effectively an orchestra in a single box. During the 1980s "it was used on loads of records," Bell said, "usually mixed with other things—its fluffy, flutey calliope sounds, and its fake Fender Rhodes electric piano were particularly popular." Interestingly enough, though almost everyone used it, there is no single classic DX-7 track. (In fact, you can argue that there is no classic track for any synthesizer; flexibility rather than distinctiveness is the characteristic of the instrument).

The DX-7 was by no means the only synthesizer that was powered by FM chips. Yamaha leveraged its massive investment in the technology by applying it across the product range, in everything from small portable keyboards to high-end, top-of-the-line electronic organs.

After the introduction of the DX-7, Mochida lost interest in musical instruments. Ever in search of new things to do, he decided that since he now had a digital chip, and since digital chips were the stuff of computers, he would use his chip to build a home computer. It would be a multimedia computer, no less, complete with state-of-the-art sound and graphics. And that was where he made his first big mistake.

From the outside, Japan may appear a homogeneous country whose corporations all pull together, under government guidance, in pursuit of a common goal—domination of world markets. Inside Japan, however, it is hard to avoid noticing how little cooperation there is between rival groups, and how fierce in fact is the competition between them.

This is particularly true of the electronics industry. Indeed, one of the main reasons why the personal computer revolution was so slow to get off the ground in Japan was that manufacturers simply didn't appreciate the importance of industry standards and the need to encourage independent software vendors.

Only NEC twigged this need, and walked off with a near monopoly of the domestic market as a result. But did other firms then recognize the NEC standard, like Compaq et al. had with the IBM PC, and crank out clones accordingly? Certainly not. Instead, they all opted to make

Yamaha's DX-7 synthesizer.

personal computers to their own proprietary design, fragmenting the market and stunting its growth.

Thus, in deciding that Yamaha would have to develop everything–including operating system, applications software, processors, and peripherals–for their multimedia computer themselves, Mochida was making a characteristic Japanese error. To his credit, though, he was quick to recognize it. "Within a year of commercializing the computer [i.e., around 1985], I realized that we had made a mistake. So I went straight to Kawakami-San, and I told him that we should stop at once, that the more we went on, the more money we would lose."

Mochida paid a stiff price for his failure. He was demoted from managing director to director, and his authority was curtailed. He suffered a cut in salary, and most serious of all, he was reassigned from his beloved R&D to manage Yamaha's audio equipment division. This was a job whose responsibilities included manufacturing and marketing and sales as well as development. But Mochida was not a businessman, and his last years at Yamaha were not happy ones.

Burned by their failure, Yamaha decided to pull out of the computer business, electing instead to pursue the less risky option of selling its chips to outside customers. Kawakami assigned Ishimura, Mochida's long-time deputy, to run this business. Among the first customers for FM chips were arcade game companies like Sega and Bally.

A version of the chip developed for arcade game machines subsequently found its way onto a plug-in sound board that IBM developed in 1986 to go with its new PS/2 personal computer. But this was an expensive chip, the board wound up costing $499, and back then there was little in the way of market pull for personal computer sound. "We only sold about 10,000 units," Ishimura recalled ruefully. He added with a laugh that "perhaps the only people who bought them were IBM employees."

So Yamaha withdrew from the board business too, clearing the way for the entrance of a most unlikely entrepreneur from the other side of the world. Credit for the creation of the sound board market goes to Martin Prével, a soft-spoken French Canadian professor of music at Laval University in Quebec.

Prével was originally interested in the use of computers for teaching music, for training the ear to hear. In the early 1980s he developed a specialized 8-bit computer and founded a company called Ad Lib to market it. This first machine was not a success, but with the advent of more advanced personal computers, Prével decided to have another go.

This time, Ad Lib designed a sound board that would plug into one of the expansion slots provided on the IBM PC. "We were looking for a low-end technology for sound boards," Prével recalled, "and that's where we came up with the Yamaha sound chip."

The chip in question was a cut-price version of FM synthesis that Yamaha had designed to provide audio for an ill-fated (Japanese-government-sponsored) teletext terminal project. The chip was not on the market, and when Ad Lib first contacted Yamaha, the Japanese were leery of selling it to outsiders.

The reason for this reluctance was that Yamaha were worried that FM chips might end up in cheap knockoff keyboards made by Korean firms. But eventually Prével persuaded Yamaha to supply him with chips. Ad Lib's FM-based sound board made its début at the Chicago Consumer Electronics Show in June 1987.

Ad Lib was still aiming primarily at the music education market. But the Canadian company's board turned out to be the solution to another, hitherto unseen problem. PC game companies like Sierra On-

Line were looking to add sound to their games to make them more attractive. Suddenly, here was this board that enabled the computer to generate music. Of such serendipitous matches are niche markets made.

The sound board market would blossom into much more than a niche market. But alas for Ad Lib: The Canadian company would not be the beneficiary of this explosive growth. If Yamaha had been responsible for Ad Lib's success, the Japanese would also be responsible for the Canadian firm's failure.

Game developers were soon demanding more than music. That merely turned their products into the equivalent of a silent film with piano accompaniment. Now what they wanted was the ability to include in their games voices and sound effects as well. For those the developers needed a converter that would take chunks of sound stored by the computer as digital data and turn them into analog audio. Instead of designing a chip that would do this by themselves, Ad Lib elected to work with Yamaha.

Bad decision. If you glance at a map of the world, you will see that Quebec is about as far away from Japan as it is possible to get on the North American continent. In addition to the difficulties of communicating over vast geographical distances, there were also cultural differences to be taken into consideration. Ad Lib was a small start-up, Yamaha a big corporation; and in Quebec, they prefer to speak French, a language almost unknown among Japanese engineers.

It seemed like everything that could go wrong did go wrong. Ultimately, Ad Lib was seventeen months late in coming to market with its second-generation board. That opened up an opportunity for another unknown company from even further out of left field. Creative Technology, a Singaporean outfit run by a shy but aggressive young entrepreneur named Sim Wong Hoo, came in and grabbed the sound board market with its best-selling SoundBlaster board while Ad Lib watched helplessly from the sidelines. The Canadian firm subsequently went bankrupt.

Yamaha was not hurt by Ad Lib's demise. Happily for the Japanese, thanks to Ad Lib's early efforts, it was necessary for sound board makers to concern themselves with providing backward compatibility. Hundreds of games had been written for the Ad Lib board: If this software was to continue to run on new hardware, then the hardware had to be compatible. In effect, it meant that for the foreseeable future sound boards would have to be based on Yamaha's FM synthesis chip and its derivatives. By good fortune, Yamaha had become to sound boards what Intel was to personal computers: the possessor of a de facto monopoly.

Yamaha could conceivably have had the sound board market all to itself. Especially if the old double act of Kawakami and Mochida had still held the reins at the company. But Kawakami retired as chairman of Yamaha in 1983, and Mochida was no longer in charge of new product development. Ishimura, who by 1994 had become Yamaha's managing director, was philosophical about the issue: "If we had been successful in the sound board business," he said, "maybe we wouldn't have been successful in the chip business—it's very difficult to do both."

In May 1994, Stanford held a dinner to mark the expiry of the FM patent. Attendees at the meal included John Chowning and Ishimura Kazukiyo. Among many causes for celebration that night was the fact that, more than twenty-five years after Chowning first heard his oscillators making interesting noises, FM synthesis was well on its way to becoming ubiquitous in the personal computer marketplace. That year, analysts predicted, sound boards would pass the billion-dollar mark, making them the first bona fide multimedia market. Millions of boards would be sold, all but a handful of them carrying Yamaha chips.

At the same time, computer makers were beginning to incorporate sound chips in their basic designs, ensuring even more business for Yamaha.[13] Indeed, the only cloud on the horizon for the corporation's chip business was the expiry of the patent, hence also Yamaha's exclusive license on the technology. And even this was not as bad as it sounded for, over the years, Yamaha had built up a wall of twenty-eight of its own patents surrounding FM technology. Ishimura was confident that this would survive challenges from other chipmakers.

Mochida's vision of a quarter of a century ago that survival as a musical instrument industry leader would require the ability to design and make chips had proved prophetic. The cream on the cake was that chip making had grown into a big business in its own right for Yamaha.

Even Mochida's ill-starred venture into the computer business had not been a complete disaster. The expertise the company developed in computer graphics as a result would stand it in good stead when a small company called Sega asked Yamaha to develop graphics and sound chips for a video game machine it was developing. In the mid-1990s, Yamaha continued to be Sega's chip supplier of choice.

Compared with well-known Japanese chip-making giants like NEC and Toshiba, "Yamaha is not recognized," said Bernie Vonderschmitt, president of leading Silicon Valley firm Xilinx, which has most of its chips made for it in Japan, "but in reality they have some of the finest [chip production] capability—they're up with the best in Japan. It's just amazing what those people have done."

In 1993, Yamaha Corporation [which does not include Yamaha Motor] had total sales of over $2.8 billion. Of these, "digital musical instruments" was the single largest category, accounting for almost $600 million. Almost level with pianos in second place was a category entitled "metal products and electronic equipment," which included semiconductors, worth $465 million. Significantly, this was the only category enjoying decent growth that year. Electronics-related products accounted for almost 54 percent of the company's overall sales. By any standard, Mochida's mission had been a smashing success.

As for the man himself, Mochida left Yamaha in 1988 to join Ricoh, exchanging the world of consumer musical instruments for that of professional office equipment. It was a surprising move in a country where lifetime employment is the norm for workers in big companies.

But the irrepressible Mochida is anything but a typical Japanese. Rather, he is a man who describes himself as an outsider. Once again, the lure was the opportunity to do something new (in this case, to develop a recordable compact disc).

In 1992, Mochida retired from Ricoh to take up a position as a professor in the electrical engineering department of Kogakuin University, a Tokyo-based private school. In the mid 1990s, you could find him there, in an open-plan office cum laboratory, surrounded by young students, teaching a course in multimedia. His eyes still twinkled, he laughed a lot, and he appeared to be delighted with his latest career.

Financially, as is the Japanese way, Mochida received no reward for his efforts other than his regular salary and bonus. He was, he confessed, happy with his achievements. For him, however, "the greatest satisfaction is when the people around you are also happy . . . it's not a question of 'I did that,' because if you're just by yourself, no matter how hard you try, you can't succeed, you're just a small part of it. In order to produce a success, what you need to have is people with all sorts of different talents, and then you combine them to make a team."

Yamaha minus Kawakami and Mochida is a different company. In 1983 Gen'ichi's son Hiroshi took over from his father as president. But the younger Kawakami did not make a success of the job and in 1992, he resigned.

As Mochida pointed out, very few people possess the special blend of vision, guts, and charisma needed to produce a great leader. Effort and diligence are not enough. "What you really need," he laughed, "is a gift from heaven." Or a genius, as Kawakami might have put it.

But, though in the mid 1990s, the company was going through a difficult patch, with many of its product lines mature or declining, it would be premature to write off Yamaha yet. For one thing, the company had recently introduced a revolutionary new line of synthesizers based on a technology licensed from . . . where else, but Stanford University.

Mochida Yasunori.

In the seemingly endless debate that rages over whether the United States is selling its birthright by licensing technology to Japan, the prevailing view is that both sides are engaged in a zero-sum game. In the case of FM synthesis at least, this is a difficult argument to sustain. Without the revenue stream that flowed from Yamaha to Stanford, there would have been no new generation of synthesizer technology, because there would have been no place to incubate it.

Of course, you can argue that Yamaha was smart enough not to kill the goose that laid the golden egg. But the fact is, this time round, the license that the Japanese firm has on the technology is nonexclusive. This time, there are also half-a-dozen U.S. firms with a chance to get in on the act.

After his year in exile, largely as a result of the notice that Pierre Boulez took of his work, Chowning was reinstated at Stanford as a professor. No doubt the review board figured that if Chowning's algorithms were of interest to such a famous composer—a European eminence who was then conductor of the New York Philharmonic—perhaps there was some merit in them after all . . . In 1975, Chowning founded the Center for Computer Research in Music and Acoustics, a mouthful which quickly became known to all and sundry as "Karma" (this is California, remember).

Karma is a conscious attempt to carry on the great multidisciplinary tradition of research as practiced at Bell Laboratories and the Stanford AI Lab. The center is housed in the former President's House, a beautiful Spanish Gothic mansion which sits on a knoll at the back of campus, giving it a panoramic view over Silicon Valley.

A visitor to Karma in the mid-1990s could meet historians, roboticists, psychoacousticians, electrical engineers, all of whom were also accomplished musicians and composers. He might also encounter Max Mathews, the father of computer music, who came to Karma as a professor of music after taking retirement from Bell Labs in 1987. And if he was really lucky, perhaps also Mathews's former boss, the legendary J. R. Pierce, now in his mid-eighties but still writing, lecturing at Stanford, and inventing.[14]

Today, the focus of the center's work is the development of new tools to aid composers and performers. Advances in electronic technology have opened up all sorts of new possibilities.

John Chowning (left) and Julius Orion Smith III outside Karma.

One of the reasons FM synthesis was so attractive was that it was a very efficient technique. It was able to produce a wide variety of sounds without recourse to memory, an almost prohibitively expensive commodity back in the late 1960s and early 1970s. But as memory chips continued to double in capacity every 18 months even as they dropped in price, by the 1990s a new type of synthesis had become feasible. This was sampling, a technique which draws on a database of frozen snapshots of sounds recorded from actual instruments then digitized and stored.

Though samples sound more realistic than the approximations produced by FM, because frozen, they lack the expressiveness that composers crave. Ergo waveguides, a technique invented at Karma in 1985 by an intense young electrical engineer named Julius Orion Smith III. Waveguides are computer-generated models of strings vibrating and of air resonating in tubes, just like it does in brass and woodwind instruments. Waveguides sound uncannily realistic. At the same time, because generated dynamically from sets of equations, they are also richly expressive.

Waveguides are the basis of the new range of high-end "virtual acoustic" synthesizers that Yamaha launched, to rave reviews, in November 1993. A complex technology, waveguides have yet to reach mass markets. But with memory prices dropping still further, waveguide chips from U.S. firms were expected to appear on sound boards well before the turn of the century.[15] Game developers were excited about the prospect of being able to draw on these new and more natural sounds.

Can waveguides pull off the double for Stanford? In mid-1996 Joe Koepnick, an official at the university's technology licensing office, clearly thought so. "Because of multimedia, the potential is clearly there for waveguides to eclipse FM in terms of market impact," he enthused. "My ten-year-old daughter Jennifer will be playing with waveguides."

At the 1939 World's Fair in New York, Laurens Hammond unveiled his latest creation, the Novachord, an all-electronic organ that could produce the sounds of an entire dance band or even an orchestra. The Novachord never caught on, was way ahead of its time, and Hammond would never again attempt anything so ambitious.[16] After 1939, said organ dealer Doug Jackson, "It was all money—he saw he had a winner on his hands, and he rode the wave like a pro."

(The Novachord was influential, albeit in an entirely unexpected way. The instrument, which contained some 230 tubes, served as an inspiration for J. Presper Eckert, when he and others at the University of Pennsylvania were about to embark on the building of ENIAC, generally regarded as the world's first general-purpose digital computer. At the time, it was widely believed that a large machine based on vacuum tubes could not be made reliable. For Eckert, Hammond's organ was proof that one could.)

The last Hammond Model B-3 rolled off the company's Evanston production line in 1975. In the mid-1970s, Hammond Organ was acquired by a conglomerate called the Marmon Group. "During this high-tech era," as a history of the firm issued in 1984 to celebrate its half-century in business put it with unconscious irony, "the advantages of being a part of a large conglomerate were realized." With advantages like these . . .

Today, all that remains of Hammond Organ, like RCA, is a brand name. In 1986 the company was sold to Suzuki, a small firm based in Yamaha's home town of Hamamatsu. Suzuki (which is unrelated to the motorbike maker of the same name) is best known in Japan for melodions, small wind-blown keyboard instruments developed for Japanese kindergarten and primary school children, who dislike the metallic taste of harmonicas.

These days, Hammond Suzuki produces the Super-B, an all-electronic instrument that, the company claims, "captures that great Hammond sound and adds a whole new array of voices and playing features." Organ fanciers grumble that the Super-B sounds a little too perfect. For the real B-3 sound, they say, there's no substitute for the old tone wheels.

PART THREE

CD Players & Printers; Cars & Lights

8

Many Hands Make
Light Work

*It took men of vision to bring the laser from the laboratory to the
living room.*

—Akio Morita[1]

THE SOUND OF CHAMPAGNE CORKS popping was an unusual
one at Bell Laboratories. Like any company that did business with
the U.S. government, the labs were not permitted to have alcohol on
the premises, at least not for drinking. On this occasion, however, top
brass at the labs deemed the momentous nature of the achievement
worth making an exception to the rules.

Celebrations began on Tuesday, 2 June 1970, the day after the
Memorial Day holiday. That morning Morton Panish, a chemist in
Area 20, the device research department at Murray Hill, arrived at his
desk to find a handwritten note from his Japanese colleague, Hayashi
Izuo. It read simply:

C.W. definite!!! at 24° C

A cryptic message, but Panish knew exactly what his partner meant.
After three long years of effort, the pair had finally succeeded in persuading a semiconductor laser, a tiny fleck of material not much bigger
than a grain of salt, to emit a continuous wave of light at room temperature. Though the actual invention of the semiconductor laser had oc-

curred almost eight years previously, this was the first indication that the device was something more than just a physicist's toy–that it might actually have applications in the real world.

The laser that Hayashi and Panish built was the direct antecedent of the light sources used in today's optic fiber communications systems, in laser printers, in supermarket bar-code readers, and above all, as the *sine qua non* in hundreds of millions of compact disc players and CD-ROM drives.

In addition to making this early breakthrough, Bell Labs would also play a key role in the development of the process technology used to manufacture semiconductor lasers. For the most part, however, Japanese entrepreneurs would capitalize on these breakthroughs, not AT&T. Had they known the embarrassments that lay in store, Bell Labs brass might have been a little less effusive in the toasts they drank that day.

The idea for the laser originated in 1957, over lunch in a Bell Laboratories cafeteria. Columbia University professor Charles Hard Townes, a consultant at the Labs, and Art Schawlow, a former student of Townes who had become a researcher at Murray Hill, coauthored the initial, theoretical paper on the subject.[2] Its publication in December 1958 was in effect the starting gun for a race to build the first laser, a race in which some of the brightest minds in the scientific community participated. Bell Labs attorneys were not impressed. They did not think the idea worth patenting, filing an application only after Townes insisted.[3]

The race to build the first laser was won by a rank outsider. Ted Maiman was a brash young scientist working alone, on a shoestring budget, at the Hughes Research Laboratories in Malibu, California. Maiman entered the competition about a year behind the well-funded teams at Bell, Columbia, and elsewhere. Nine months later, on 16 May 1960, he surprised everybody–including his own management–by making a laser work. "Maiman simply took a really potent flashbulb, wrapped it around a ruby rod and Zap!–he got his laser going," recalled Bill Boyle, who was then himself attempting to build lasers at Bell Labs, "and we all thought, Gee, why didn't we do that?" Particularly surprised was Schawlow, who had gone into print with the unfortunate assertion that ruby was not a suitable material for laser action.

Bell Labs researchers were quick to recover from this early setback, though. In December 1960 another of Townes's students, Ali Javan, an Iranian who had joined the Labs two years previously, came up with the first gas laser, a quartz tube filled with a mixture of helium and neon.[4] This was an improvement on Maiman's ruby laser in one crucial respect. Ruby would only operate in pulsed mode, emitting brief flashes of light every time you whacked it with current. The helium–neon laser, by contrast, was capable of putting out a continuous, pencil-thin beam of infrared light. This ability had commercial implications. Javan's gas laser would become the light source of choice for many practical applications–until the advent of a semiconductor counterpart that could do the same job, in a far smaller package, and at a fraction of the price.

Lasers were now all the rage. Everybody was talking about them, everybody was excited about them, and everybody was wondering what would be the next material to lase. In this heady atmosphere it was only natural that people would ask Bob Hall, a quick-witted General Electric researcher who had acquired a reputation for inventing new devices, When are you going to make a laser out of semiconductors?

The idea struck Hall as nonsense–the lasers he was familiar with all had to be made out of transparent materials like ruby. He didn't pay any attention to the suggestion. Hall had better things to do–in particular, he wanted to make tunnel diodes.

Hall was by no means the only one beguiled by Esaki Leona's recent invention at Sony. Another was the coinventor of the transistor (and by this time Nobel Prize winner), Bill Shockley. When Esaki announced his invention at a semiconductor conference held in Brussels, Belgium, in May 1958, Shockley singled out the 34-year-old Japanese's work for special mention in his keynote speech. A hard man to impress, Bell Labs vice president Jack Morton was also full of praise. He called the tunnel diode "a wonderful development . . . [Esaki] deserves all the honor the industry can give him."[5]

A diode is an electrical gate that allows current to pass through it in one direction, but not in the other. It can thus be used, like a transistor, as a switch. The main difference is that the diode has only two terminals whereas the transistor has three. The third terminal enables the transistor to function as an amplifier (a small current on this terminal opens the gate, allowing a much larger current to flow through the device]. Amplification makes it possible to preserve the integrity of a signal as it passes through many switches. Having a third terminal also makes the switches easier to control. This explains why transistors, not diodes, are used as the basic building blocks of most electronic systems.

The Esaki diode was of enormous interest to scientists and engineers alike. Until the discovery of the tunnel diode it had been possible to account for the operation of semiconductor devices like transistors purely in terms of Newtonian mechanics. Electrons were particles that bounced through solids in a more or less predictable fashion. In an Esaki diode, however, electrons behaved not like particles, but like waves, tunneling through barriers, popping up unexpectedly on the other side. To explain this sort of behavior, scientists had to resort to the counterintuitive logic of quantum mechanics.

For their part, engineers were more interested in the unprecedented speed at which the electrons tunneled. To many, it seemed that the Esaki diode was destined for a brilliant future in computers. But before this potential could be realized, it would first be necessary to overcome a crippling limitation.

Esaki had fashioned his devices from germanium. Soon others began fabricating tunnel diodes out of silicon. The problem was that in both materials the devices would only work over a very narrow range, just a few tenths of a volt, not enough to be of practical use. A possible solution to the problem was to try other semiconductor materials that looked as if they might be persuaded to go to higher voltages.

Germanium and silicon are both elements. They are called semiconductors because they sit midway in the spectrum of materials between conductors like metal, and insulators like glass. The atoms of germanium and silicon each have four free electrons in their outermost shell, compared with conductors, which have eight, and insulators, which have none. In addition to such elemental semiconductors, it is also possible to synthesize compound semiconductors out of two elements, one having three free electrons, the other five.[6] The one with five donates an electron to the one with three, so that both have four, just like the elemental semiconductors. The best known of these compound semiconductors is gallium arsenide or "gally-ally" as the British sometimes called it.

(I had always assumed that gallium, a bluish-gray metal that in liquid form turns a beautiful shade of silver, was named after *gallia*, the Latin word for France, by analogy with germanium, which was named for Germany by a nationalistic German chemist called Clemens Winkler in 1886. Turns out that gallium was actually discovered in 1875, before germanium, by an egotistical French chemist called Lecoq de Boisbaudran, who named it for himself–*gallus* being the Latin word for cock. However, since the cock also happens to be the French national bird, I suppose nobody minded.)

Around the time Maiman was inventing his laser, Hall and his colleagues at General Electric were making samples of gallium arsenide tunnel diodes that were capable of oscillating at frequencies of up to 5 billion cycles a second. Such speeds, *Business Week* enthused, were "high enough to make it possible to build computers with the logical capacity of the human brain." GE's researchers were less sanguine; their diodes failed with dismaying rapidity. However, as one of them later wrote, "whether we realized it or not, we were on the road to something much more important."[7] The experience they gained in working with the heavily doped materials used to fabricate tunnel diodes would be vital when it came to making semiconductor lasers.

In addition to GE, a small group of researchers at MIT's Lincoln Laboratory were making a particularly detailed examination of the high-speed computer devices that you could make out of gallium arsenide. Bob Rediker, the group's jolly, independent-minded leader, had decided that the chances of doing something interesting in gallium arsenide were much better than in silicon, the direction in which most semiconductor researchers were heading. In 1958 Rediker had gone so far as to visit the compound's developer, Heinrich Welker, at the Siemens laboratories in Erlangen, Germany, to ask his advice. On returning to the United States, he obtained from RCA some gallium arsenide material on which to begin experiments.

Two common processes used to make semiconductor devices were alloying and diffusion. In fabricating their diodes, the Lincoln Lab group tried both. To help determine how the electrical properties of the two types differed, Rediker suggested hooking up a prism spectroscope to see if there was any light coming out of the devices. The alloy diode didn't emit much, but when spectroscopist Bob Keyes stuck the dif-

fused diode in front of the prism, the pen on his instrument's recorder
shot right off the page. To get the reading back on the scale, Keyes had
to reduce the amplitude of the signal by more than a thousand times.
Clearly, something unexpected was going on.

Keyes reported this dramatic result at the Solid State Device Research Conference held in Durham, New Hampshire, in July 1962. His
calculations showed that the diffused diode was converting electric
current to infrared light with an efficiency of as high as 85 percent. An
RCA researcher in the audience retorted that, if this finding was correct, then it violated the second law of thermodynamics (by which he
presumably meant that it is theoretically impossible to convert completely one form of energy into another). Taken aback, Keyes stroked
his chin and tried to make a joke out of it. "I'm sorry about that," he
said. At which point Bob Hall, who was also in the audience, jumped
up and explained that, because conversion efficiency was less than 100
percent, the result did not in fact violate the laws of physics.

The race to build the semiconductor laser had begun. And, as with
the first laser, this contest too was won by an outsider. In the early
stages, Rediker and his group were the clear favorites. They had a head
start, and they knew exactly what they had to do. Lincoln Lab theorist
Herb Zeiger, another former student of Charles Townes, told them exactly how to go about making a laser.

But the group suffered from a distraction: The lab's management believed it important to demonstrate to their military sponsors the communications potential of the light-emitting diodes that Rediker and his
colleagues had produced. On the roof at Lincoln Lab the group rigged
up a receiver for television signals transmitted by light from Mount
Wachusett, some 30 miles away. The TV demos were great fun: Rediker
would grab the sponsors' attention by re-broadcasting a channel "on
which," he recalled with a chuckle, "there was a very buxom lady doing
exercises." Then, to show that the signal was indeed being transmitted
by light, he would ask someone to block it by standing in front of the
receiver.

The results were sufficiently newsworthy to be written up in *Time*
magazine.[8] But the Lincoln Lab group wasted precious time that, in retrospect, Rediker believed would have been better spent on building a
laser. "We had underestimated the competition!" he lamented.[9]

(Though ultimately overtaken by his rivals, Rediker would remain good friends with them, and maintain a humorous perspective on the heady events of 1962. In December that year, a few weeks after the first semiconductor laser papers were published, Rediker placed a blinking laser on the top of his group's Christmas tree. Thereafter he would tell everyone who asked him about priority that his group was undoubtedly the first to have a Christmas tree with a laser on it.)

Three other groups were hot on the heels of the Lincoln Lab group. All three were based in upstate New York. One was led by Marshall Nathan at IBM's recently established research center in Yorktown Heights.[10] A second group worked at General Electric's electronics laboratory in Syracuse.[11] There, Nick Holonyak was determined to win the race working with a more complicated material, gallium arsenide phosphide. He chose this alloy because it promised to produce a laser whose light would be visible. But using a custom material which he and his group had to make themselves, in preference to off-the-shelf gallium arsenide, would cost Holonyak precious time.

As we shall see in the next chapter, Holonyak went on to champion a closely related development to the laser, the visible light-emitting diode. But as far as the semiconductor laser was concerned, it would be the third group, led by Holonyak's GE colleague Bob Hall, who would come from behind to pip the others at the post.

Hall had been shaken up by the revelations made by Rediker's people at the New Hampshire conference in July 1962. "They talked about tremendously intense radiation coming from these little diodes," he recalled. "There was like a kilowatt per square centimeter ... and they also said that you could even *see* this radiation. Well, you know, the radiation's well out in the infrared and your eye's not sensitive there, but they said you could look at these things and see something that looked like a red color."

This was quite astonishing. Previously it had been thought that diodes might be capable of emitting light with an efficiency of perhaps a hundredth of a percent. Now here were Rediker's people talking of an efficiency of close to 100 percent. If the things really were that efficient, what could you do with them? Above Hall's head, a light bulb went on.

On his way back from the meeting, Hall did some back-of-the-envelope calculations, figuring out how he might go about making a laser.

Then he went to his boss, explained what he and his colleagues wanted to do, and asked for permission to go ahead. And Hall's boss said "That sounds like fun," gave them his blessing, and off they went. In those faroff days, it was that simple.

General Electric was at this time by far the biggest company in the electronics industry, twice as large in terms of sales as its nearest rival, Westinghouse, and four times the size of RCA and IBM. GE produced more semiconductors than anyone other than specialist firms like Texas Instruments.

GE's Research and Development Center, where Hall worked, was located on a wooded bluff overlooking the Mohawk River. A venerable institution founded in 1900, it was the first industrial laboratory in America devoted to basic research. In the early years of the century, GE's lab was where the tungsten filament—the key component of the modern incandescent light bulb—had been invented. By the early 1960s, the lab had become a scientist's paradise, where a bright spark like Hall was free to seize an opportunity and move quickly to capitalize on it.

"It must have been July or August when we started," Hall recalled, "but you can make things move fast if you set your mind to it, and know what you want to do. So within a month, I guess, we had some diodes and began testing."

The diodes that Hall and his group made were tiny sandwiches consisting of two types of gallium arsenide. One layer of the sandwich was heavily doped with impurities, like a tunnel diode, to give it an excess of negatively charged electrons; the other layer was similarly treated, to overload it with positive-charge carriers called holes. Injecting a current into such a device increases the population of electrons and holes, sending them rushing into the active region—the no-man's-land where the two layers meet. There, the electrons and holes combine and annihilate each other, giving up the ghost in the form of a photon, i.e., light.

The light is then amplified in an "optical cavity" within the device. This is a misleading term for the layman, because there is no hole or hollow in the material. The ends of the cavity are highly reflective mirrors that bounce the photons back and forth, causing them to hit other electron-hole pairs, which in turn stimulates the emission of further photons. Hence the acronym "laser," the initials standing for "*l*ight *a*mplification by *s*timulated *e*mission of *r*adiation."

Light from a laser is different than that emitted by other sources. Illumination from a fluorescent lamp, for example, is a mixture of many different frequencies and intensities. Laser light by contrast is coherent, consisting of waves of a single frequency that radiate in lockstep with each other. Coherence gives laser light its unique purity. And, as we shall see, coherence also has important commercial implications.

One edge that Hall had over his rivals was that, as a high school student in Alameda, California, he had been a keen amateur astronomer. So much so, that he had actually built his own telescopes. For this purpose, Hall had learned how to polish mirrors, a key skill as it turned out. "I had a mental image of what would be a reasonable structure," he remembered, "that would pass the light back and forth in the plane of the junction . . . and I could put mirrors on it, I had the knowhow myself of polishing little strips of semiconductor."

The first fruits of this expertise simply exploded. "We socked [them with] so much current that they'd blow right up," Hall said. "Once in a while we'd get a whiff of light out, but nothing very exciting." Then one Sunday, after the project had been underway for about two months, came an exciting phone call. A member of the team who had spent the weekend in the lab testing diodes saw an unusually bright image on his snooperscope which he could not interpret. Clearly something unusual was going on. The following day, the rest of the team piled back into the lab, ran some more tests, and were rewarded with images that could only mean one thing. The diode was emitting coherent light.

They had built a laser.

Hall remembers the next few weeks as a frantic period during which the team worked day and night. They improved their results, gathered more evidence, put together a paper to make the announcement to the scientific community, and scheduled a press conference to tell the world what they had done.

Before they could announce anything, however, it was necessary first to file a patent. Hall flew down to Washington to deliver the bundle of plans they had drawn up to the Patent Office. It was October 1962, the time of the Cuban missile crisis. "The papers were full of it," Hall remembered, "and I went to bed that night in a hotel wondering if we'd be obliterated in the morning, and I would never have the satisfaction of announcing the laser."

But next day Hall managed to file his patent application and fly back to Schenectady unscathed. Ultimately several patents were granted to the various groups that built the first semiconductor lasers. Applied for in late 1962, they were issued in 1966. A patent expires after seventeen years and, as Bob Rediker would take a perverse delight in pointing out, 1966 plus 17 equals 1983, the year that the compact disc player, the first mass market application for the semiconductor laser, took off.

The Hall group's paper was published in the November 1962 issue of *Physical Review Letters*. In the same issue was a paper from the IBM group reporting something that was very close to a semiconductor laser. Rediker and Holonyak published papers describing their lasers the following month. It had been a very close finish.

From conception to invention had taken no more than three months. For the scientists involved, it had all been great sport. "There's always the fun of doing something new for the first time," Hall said. "You get to publish a paper, you get recognition, you can talk about it at a meeting, and everybody goes, Gee, this is tremendous what this guy's done! So it's fun to do these things, that's the main motivation."

But whether the laser diode would ever be good for anything useful was a very different question. Of course, compared with gas lasers, the diode offered the same advantages as the transistor had over the vacuum tube. It was compact and promised to be durable, reliable, and easy to mass-produce. The trouble was the gas laser was itself a recent invention. There was thus no existing market equivalent to the vacuum tube into which the tiny laser could plug.

Certainly nobody in any of the operating departments at GE could see any applications for the things. "People used to scoff at lasers," Hall recalled, " 'So you've got stimulated emission: What are you going to do with it—make a light bulb?' "

One possibility was communications. But Hall's laser, like Maiman's, worked only in brief pulses, lasting a fraction of a second. Even then, only when dunked in a flask of liquid air, to avoid what practitioners called "catastrophic heating"—going phut, as you or I might say—as huge amounts of current poured through a tiny fleck of material.

Cryogenically cooled and prone to catastrophe—such devices were far from being practical. In addition to which, GE's stock in trade was electric power and appliances, not communications—that was still the monopoly of the Bell System. To be sure, GE was also a leading military contractor, but you couldn't blind people with a semiconductor laser, nor could you use them to shoot down airplanes, so the military didn't seem terribly interested, either.

In December 1962, GE offered semiconductor lasers for sale. These were the visible light-producing diodes made by Nick Holonyak at GE's Syracuse lab. They were priced at $2,600, because, according to Holonyak, "since Texas Instruments offered gallium arsenide infrared emitters (incoherent) for $130, someone in GE thought that a gallium arsenide laser was worth $1,300 and a gallium arsenide phosphide laser (visible) even more, $2,600." It was, he reckoned, "a crazy way of doing things, but nonetheless, that was the madness that prevailed." But such low-level commercial activity was not of interest to the company. "GE has trouble managing something that's less than a multimillion-dollar business," Hall commented. "So it was decided that this was too negligible a business to invest company funding in."

Not long after the excitement of the initial discovery had died down, Hall, unable to find a home for laser diodes at GE, turned his attention to some of the many other things he wanted to do. He dropped out of laser research, never to return.

Twenty-some years later, Hall would confess that he felt "not quite ashamed of myself, but as though I had abandoned the field, and had all the fun of discovery without sweating out the hard work of . . . rearing the baby."

Rearing the baby was hard work indeed. From the outset optical communications had been one of the most obvious applications for the laser. Ted Maiman himself had mentioned the possibility at the press conference held to announce his ruby device. The idea was after all very well established: The heliograph-using mirrors to reflect sunlight—had been known in ancient times. Modern equivalents provided signaling between ships at sea.

In 1880 Alexander Graham Bell had adapted the principle to invent the photophone, a device capable of transmitting the human voice using a movable mirror and sunlight. This was supposedly the invention of which Bell was most proud. "I have heard a ray of sun laugh and cough and sing," the great man enthused. The photophone was ahead of its time. Now, however, many decades later, the laser's ultrashort wavelengths of coherent light promised to deliver a much more efficient form of transmission, one with truly dazzling information-carrying capacity.

In 1961 and 1962, right around the time when Bob Rediker was captivating his military sponsors by using light-emitting diodes to transmit television pictures of buxom ladies, Bell Labs began conducting its first experiments in optical communications. A link between the main grounds at Murray Hill and a nearby hilltop was established using Ali Javan's new helium-neon gas lasers. Transmission on this link was carried out under all sorts of weather conditions and, as new types of laser became available, at various wavelengths. The experiments showed that reliable transmission through the atmosphere could not be obtained. Fog, in particular, was a killer.

By the middle of the decade, early optimism about the laser's utility in the communications field had given way to skepticism. As far as the semiconductor laser was concerned, the twin goals of continuous wave operation at room temperature seemed as remote as ever. The field had become more or less moribund.

To be sure, some groups were still doing good work. In particular, RCA, which had been an also-ran in the race to develop the first semiconductor laser, rallied to develop what would become the standard method of fabricating the tiny devices. RCA's aim was to make lasers for use as the trigger in a proximity fuse for bombs. Since this application required room-temperature operation, continuous wave was obviously not a problem.

Which makes it all the more remarkable that one hot day in July 1966 John Kirtland Galt, a senior manager in Area 20 at Murray Hill, should have summoned Morton Panish and Hayashi Izuo into his office and asked them whether they would be interested in trying to crack the semiconductor laser problem.

The pair were not an obvious choice for the assignment. For one thing, neither of them knew the first thing about semiconductor lasers. But

Galt told Hayashi that he thought that experts in a field are not always the best to start research of something new, because they have so much experience of the past.[12] For another, they were both relatively old to be embarking on a new field of exploratory research. Hayashi, a nuclear physicist from Tokyo University, was 44; Panish, a chemist from New York specializing in thermodynamics, was 37. Finally, it was most unusual for a chemist to be paired with a physicist working on a problem on an equal footing. But the physical chemistry worked very well–the reticent Japanese and the voluble New Yorker hit it off right away.

In setting up this apparently quixotic project, what was Galt up to? Panish believed that the manager's goals were relatively modest. He remembered Galt saying that he did not expect the pair to succeed, but that he wanted someone working on the continuous wave problem, so that when it was solved, Bell Labs would not get left behind.

For his part, Hayashi was skeptical: "What was the problem?" he wrote in his notebook. "Is it worth pursuing?" But Galt managed to convince him of the work's importance. "Galt was a good director for a research laboratory," Hayashi said, "always thinking ahead," encouraging people to do new and different things.

In 1966, one new and different thing was a proposal made by Charles Kao and G. A. Hockman of the Standard Telecommunications Laboratory in England that glass fibers could in theory be made to carry signals over long distances with relatively low losses. Glass fibers had been used for many years, especially in medical instruments, but the loss of signal in them was so great–amounting to a decibel per meter at best, which would have meant thousands of decibels per mile– that they were clearly unsuitable for long-distance communications. It was a proposal that scientists at Corning Glass Works would vigorously pursue. However, whether Galt was aware of the STL researchers' suggestion is not clear.

It took Hayashi and Panish more than three years of painstaking effort and over a thousand experimental wafers, but eventually they came up with the goods. They did it by including in their laser an extra pair of layers, made from a slightly different material. Compared to Hall's simple two-layer laser, the one that the Bell Labs team put together was a club sandwich that they dubbed a "double heterostructure."

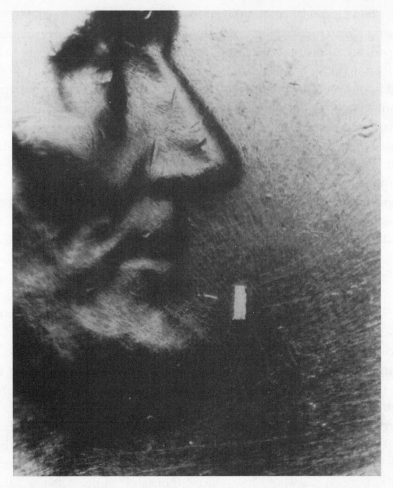

First practical semiconductor laser, 1970. (Photo courtesy of Bell Labs)

The key to this new configuration's success was the realization that, by tuning the refractive index of the layers so that the index of the ultrathin active layer in the middle of the sandwich was higher than that of the ones on either side, you could *confine* the light within that layer. (The refractive index of a material indicates how fast light travels within it.) The result was a laser that would operate at much lower currents—a dry cell battery would do the trick—while producing much greater light amplification.

Panish grew the lasers; Hayashi worked on ways of getting rid of the heat they generated. The pair crept up on their target gradually, wafer by wafer, until at last, they were able to switch the thermometer measuring the temperature of the laser from degrees-below to degrees-above zero. "It's a historic moment," murmured Hayashi's assistant, Philip Foy. Not long after, on the Monday morning of the Memorial Day holiday, they tried another diode, which put out a continuous wave of infrared light at 24°C–room temperature.

And it came to pass, by a coincidence that in retrospect seems well-nigh miraculous, that in 1970, the same year that Hayashi and Panish developed the first reliable laser light source, Corning Glass Works announced a reliable transmission medium–the first low-loss glass fibers. And by an even stranger coincidence, Corning's fibers exhibited their lowest losses at the same wavelength as the light put out by Hayashi and Panish's laser.

Hayashi Izuo (left) and Morton Panish at Bell Labs. (Bell Labs)

The consequence of the near-simultaneous announcement of these ideally matched technologies would seem to be obvious. Having seen the light, as it were, surely researchers in the communications field must have immediately switched their allegiance to this new and more powerful combination, this technological instance of manifest destiny? But that is not what happened at all. The route which optic fiber communications traveled on the way to eventual triumph over rival approaches was anything but linear.

Indeed in 1970, after almost a decade of hard slog, so far from being boundlessly enthusiastic, proponents of optical communication were in fact deeply pessimistic. "Today . . . it is hardly an exaggeration to say that there is, as yet no *practical* optical communication system in existence," lamented Nilo Lindgren in the special issue on optical communication of a journal published in October that year.[13] "Moreover," Lindgren continued, "the best judgement today is that practical optical communication systems lie still far in the future."

This pessimism was no doubt partly due to the fact that the initial heterostructure lasers degraded very rapidly. Most devices lasted just a few minutes before succumbing to catastrophic failure; some only seconds. To be of practical use in the phone system, components obviously had to last for many years. There was no guarantee that the laser's operating life could be improved, but Hayashi told skeptics that he believed that he and Panish could do it. By April 1971, they had pushed the record for the lifetime of a semiconductor laser up to 80 hours.

But the main reason that Bell Labs did not immediately initiate a crash program for the development of optical communications technology was that AT&T management were already heavily committed to an existing technology: This was called millimeter waveguides.

Progress in communications can be seen as a relentless march down the electromagnetic spectrum towards ever shorter wavelengths, electromagnetic waves being the medium phone companies use to carry their signals (be they voice, fax, data, or whatever). Prewar, shortwaves were used for radio telephony; postwar, shortwaves were superseded by microwaves, a derivative of radar. Millimeter waves are a subset of microwaves, the name deriving from the fact that the length of their waves is around 1 millimeter. Shorter still are the wavelengths of light, which range from infrared all the way down through the visible spectrum to ultraviolet.

Shortwave and microwave were wireless forms of transmission. Millimeter systems, development of which began at Bell Labs around 1968, required waveguides. These were copper pipes up to two inches in diameter–a far cry from the delicate, hair-thin strands of glass that would eventually preempt them. A single millimeter pipe could have a capacity of more than a quarter million voice channels.

Plans called for the installation of a heavy metal transmission system of super trunk lines initially linking big East Coast cities like Boston, New York, and Washington. This investment, however, was predicated on a favorable public response to AT&T's great leap forward, Picturephone. Requiring about one hundred times the capacity of an ordinary line, Picturephone was the only possible justification for the huge increase in information-carrying capacity that millimeter waveguides would deliver.

As we saw in chapter 6, however, Picturephone turned out to be a nonstarter commercially. Its failure put rollout plans for millimeter waveguides on indefinite hold. But even before this setback, there were those at Bell Labs who had doubts about the feasibility of laying down clunky great copper pipes in the already overcrowded cable ducts of large cities. They began to ponder alternatives to millimeter waveguides. Chief among the doubters was a Japanese engineer in the Bell Labs development department called Kurokawa Kaneyuki.

In April 1971 Kurokawa visited Hayashi in his lab. He subjected his fellow countryman to a barrage of questions, focusing in particular on the working life of the laser. Hayashi assured Kurokawa that the lifetime could be improved.

Kurokawa initiated the first optical fiber experiments at Bell Labs more or less in his spare time. Gradually, he became convinced that fiber optics did indeed represent the future of communications. By the end of the year, Kurokawa had managed to convert others to his view. Finally, he obtained permission from Jack Morton, the Labs' vice president, to go ahead with the development of a prototype fiber optic communications system.

By early 1973, lasers were running for several hundred hours without degradation. At the end of that year, despite considerable opposition within the Labs, Kurokawa convinced the Transmission Council–a top-level decision-making committee at the phone company–to authorize a full-scale test.

The first formal field experiment with lightwave communication—the Bell System's preferred term—took place at Western Electric's Atlanta facility in 1976.[14] The success of this experiment led to the installation of a 1.5-mile optical fiber system in an actual telephone system under downtown Chicago streets in 1977. This experiment, too, was successful. Nonetheless, support for the further development of lasers from the transmission systems group was not forthcoming. A frustrated Kurokawa quit Bell Labs, returning to Japan to work for Fujitsu.

By this time, his fellow countryman Hayashi was long gone. Dismayed by Bell Labs' lack of enthusiasm for semiconductor lasers, he had gone back to Japan to join the laboratories of Nippon Electric Company (the company now known as NEC) in the fall of 1971. Hayashi was the first of many disenchanted researchers to leave the Bell Labs laser group.

Hayashi's colleague, Panish, soldiered on for another six or seven years. But he, too, felt bitter about the systems people's indifference to their work. "At that time, the connections between the research area and the development area tended very often to be strained," Panish recalled. As a result, "it was not unusual for people in the research area to come up with something and find that they couldn't interest other parts of Bell Laboratories in what they'd done."

Nippon Electric was perhaps the most advanced of several Japanese companies which had been doing research on semiconductor lasers prior to Hayashi and Panish's breakthrough with continuous wave, room temperature devices.

NEC's preeminence was due largely to the encouragement of the company's visionary president, Kobayashi Koji, who had got the story about lasers from the horse's mouth. In his autobiography, Kobayashi wrote that he first heard about lasers during a visit to Hughes Aircraft in 1960. He was told confidentially about Maiman's invention at the company by Hughes's executive vice president Lawrence Hyland: "Most important inventions take twenty years before they can be put to use, but lasers are different," Hyland told Kobayashi. "They are so remarkable, it will only be a matter of a few years before they are in practical use. Hughes is already organizing for laser research, production, and sales." Kobayashi wasted no time in acting on this information. "I took his words as a kind of warning," he wrote. "As soon as I returned home I had NEC begin research on lasers. In 1961 we succeeded in attaining pulse operation of a ruby laser."[15]

Following the momentous announcement from Bell Labs, Japanese enthusiasm for lasers surged. Hayashi's subsequent return to Japan added fuel to the fire. His presence had a major impact, not just at Nippon Electric, but across the entire field.

One of nature's true gentlemen, Hayashi managed to introduce in Japan something of the atmosphere—of free discussion, of interaction, and of the exchange of information beyond the barriers of individual companies—that he had been used to in the United States. A participant in these exchanges, Rangu Hiroyoshi of NEC recalled that "it was very rare for Japanese researchers from different companies, and national laboratories and universities, forgetting about their affiliations, to get together and really discuss the details of the problems they were facing."

In this stimulating environment began a third contest—the race to make long-lasting gallium arsenide lasers. For the first few years—from 1972 until about 1975—Bell Labs was well ahead of the Japanese. The target was a million hours operation at room temperature, a figure the Japanese reported at more or less the same time as the Americans. Having drawn level, the Japanese began to pull ahead.

During this period Rangu made several visits to Bell Labs. The reason for the Japanese success, he believed, was their different style of research. "In semiconductor lasers," he explained, "you need crystal growth, semiconductor processing, metalizing, and also high-speed testing and characterization to find the defects. This requires many good people, and in Japan, it was natural for us to do teamwork—'You grow the crystal, you evaluate it, and I'll do the design.' "

To illustrate the Japanese willingness to subsume individual identity in the interests of achieving the goal of the group, Fujitsu's ace computer designer, Ikeda Toshio, used the metaphor of the *mikoshi*—the portable shrines that on festival days are carried around the streets of most Japanese neighborhoods on the shoulders of local residents. "In Japan," he said, "you just plop down a *mikoshi* and shout, 'Hey, everybody, it's a party! Let's carry this thing!' . . . and before you know it, the *mikoshi* is up and away."[16]

"Things were very different at Bell Labs," Rangu said, "individual researchers were great, but individuals do their own thing. The individual comes first, joining together to develop the device comes second, and I think this is the difference that allowed Japan to catch up and overtake."

This difference in style combined with the lack of funding from the transmission systems group eventually resulted in considerable embarrassment for both Bell Labs and Western Electric. On 16 November 1983, AT&T was awarded a $250 million contract to design and develop the first transatlantic optic fiber submarine cable.[17] Bringing up a submarine cable from the bottom of the ocean if anything goes wrong is what engineers call a nontrivial problem. (You have to send out a ship.) It was therefore imperative to use as the key component in the system a laser that had been tried and tested. Also, it had to be one that operated at the new, longer wavelengths that corresponded to the minimum losses in Corning's latest glass fibers. And Bell Labs did not have such a laser ready to go.

AT&T was forced to send a delegation cap in hand to Japan. They went first to Nippon Electric and Fujitsu, but both companies were fully occupied supplying NTT. So the Americans ended up buying lasers from Hitachi's Central Research Laboratory, which in 1984 had developed a new laser with a lifetime of more than 1 million hours.

The same year also marks the appearance of one of the first mass-market applications for the laser. This was the Hewlett-Packard Laser-Jet printer, which would become HP's most successful product ever and a familiar fixture in offices all over the world. It too used a Hitachi laser.

The way research is done in Japan differs considerably from company to company. Large firms like Toshiba often rely on committees to make decisions on which themes to pursue. Hitachi, Japan's biggest manufacturer of electronics products, prefers to rely on key individuals, and let them decide their own direction. Nakamura Michiharu was one such individual.

Nakamura worked at Hitachi's Central Research Laboratory, an island of greenery located in the otherwise unremarkable Tokyo suburb of Kokubunji. The lab was established in 1942 by Hitachi's founder, Odaira

Namihei. Odaira had given the center a twofold mission: "to create new technologies for the coming ten to twenty years, as well as pursuing development work for [Hitachi's] current business." To this latter end, the lab kept a close relationship with the company's nearby Takasaki works. This ensured a smooth transition from development to production.

With lasers, however, it was a different story. In the late 1970s, making semiconductor lasers was still an art. In addition, it was not yet clear what—if any—mass markets there would be for the devices. For both these reasons, it was premature to think of transferring the technology to the factory.

At the same time, there was pressure to get devices into production. "In the U.S.," Kurokawa (the former Bell Labs researcher) said, "inventors are respected. Here [in Japan], it's different. If you're a scientist in the U.S., and you discover something, that's all. Here, unless it goes into the marketplace, you're not a big guy."

Nakamura's solution was to use the laboratory as a base for manufacturing and marketing. "We sold our products to very advanced system customers," he recalled. From them, "we accumulated information about new requirements and so on—we had very good interaction, and we revised our technologies based on it. So laboratory production was one of the very important schemes for Hitachi's success in the laser area."

Laboratory production, Nakamura thought, was like a sort of Japanese-style venture business. The first step was to find prospective buyers. An obvious target was Hitachi's best customer, Nippon Telegraph & Telephone. But NTT always followed AT&T's lead, and in the late 1970s, the public corporation was still pushing millimeter waveguides, not fiber optics. Mainline communications applications for lasers were still ten years away.

Then, in 1978, a group of senior executives from Canon stopped by Kokubunji for a tour of the laboratory. The visit had been arranged via a technical exchange committee that the two companies maintained. Nakamura showed the Canon people his latest lasers. The latter seemed very interested, peppering him with questions about the devices. They asked Nakamura if they could have some lasers to take away with them. It appeared that Canon knew of an application for which the tiny devices might come in handy.

Hitachi and Canon are both nominally members of the same *keiretsu*, the Fuyo group of companies. *Keiretsu* are often cited in the West as a prime example of Japanese-style exclusionary capitalism. The complaint is that group members typically prefer to do business with each other than with outside firms. So was the Canon–Hitachi technical exchange committee an example of a *keiretsu*-style, keep-it-in-the-family practice? Former Canon deputy chairman Yamaji Keizo was disposed not to think so, seeing the committee more as a simple exchange between component vendor and user.

Yamaji explained that the Fuyo group is much more loosely knit than groups such as Mitsubishi, Mitsui, and Sumitomo. He went on to point out that Canon also maintains close relations with many non-Japanese companies, most notably Hewlett-Packard. Other examples include Texas Instruments, from whom Canon buys chips and with whom it runs a chip fabrication plant in Singapore; Motorola, the company that provided the microprocessor used in the AE-1 camera, with whom the relationship is particularly close; and Eastman Kodak. In Japan, the company has joint development projects with companies from other *keiretsu*, including a long-standing one with Mitsubishi Kasei (raw materials for copiers) and Mitsubishi Electric (X-ray sources for photolithography). At the same time, Yamaji conceded that, as in other *keiretsu*, the presidents of the Fuyo group get together for lunch once a month, "and perhaps intimate relationships do develop as a result."

Among Japanese companies, Canon is an out-and-out maverick. The firm's uniqueness can be traced back to its origins. Most technology outfits are founded by engineers. Canon's first president, Mitarai Takeshi, was by contrast a doctor, a gynecologist who worked at Tokyo's Red Cross Hospital. "He didn't know much about business," his son Hajime recalled, "and he didn't care much about money, either."

What Dr. Mitarai did know and care about was people. He was a shrewd judge of character and he didn't give a hoot about age or educational background, the normal criteria for advancement in Japan. He had an uncanny knack of picking the right man for the job. When Mitarai joined the fledgling Canon in 1937, the company's dream was to make the best cameras in the world, competing with German firms like

Leica. "Even the microscopes we used at school were made in Germany, Mitarai said, "I thought this kind of business was right for Japan."[18] Cameras, along with radios and motorbikes, were one of postwar Japan's first boom industries. In 1962, the year of the semiconductor laser's invention, Japan passed Germany as the world's largest manufacturer of cameras, with production that year of almost 3 million units.

Mitarai's dream came true in 1976, just before Canon's visit to the Hitachi laboratory. The Canon AE-1 was the first 35mm camera equipped with autofocus, a feature that depended on the incorporation of highly sophisticated electronics, most notably a microprocessor, a camera industry first. The easy-to-use AE-1 quickly became the best-selling camera in the world. But this success was just one bright spot in an otherwise bleak picture. Fierce competition in an overcrowded marketplace kept profit margins uncomfortably slim. In addition, saturation of the camera market loomed.

In 1962, Canon made a long-term plan to diversify from cameras into office machines, where the prospects for growth seemed much rosier. To lay the groundwork for diversification, the company established a laboratory called the New Product Center. To head the center, Mitarai picked a forthright young engineer named Yamaji Keizo.

Not long afterwards, during a visit to the headquarters of Eastman Kodak in Rochester, New York, Yamaji had an epiphany. The filmmakers had given him a very friendly reception. The reason for this warmth soon became clear. "You know what we call cameras?" a Kodak executive asked Yamaji. When the Japanese shook his head, the American replied with a smile, "Film burners!" It was a lesson that Yamaji never forgot. He passed on the comment to his colleagues back at Canon. They determined that in the future, in addition to the burners, their company would also make the fuel.

Canon's first major diversification was calculators. In this brutally competitive market the company finished a distant third behind Sharp and Casio. But in parallel with calculators, the company also targeted copiers.

Why copiers? Perhaps the stimulus was the 1962 announcement by Fuji Photo Film, which dominated the Japanese market for photographic film, that it was tying up with Xerox. With characteristic apprehension, some Japanese camera companies saw xerography as a potential rival to film, hence a threat to their core business.

Yamaji obtained a report on the copier market prepared by the U.S. consultancy Arthur D. Little. One item caught his attention. It asserted that the wall of patents that Xerox had erected around their copier technology was so strong that it would never be broken. Like Seiko's Nakamura Tsuneya when confronted with Bulova's Accutron patents, Yamaji had objections to the notion of an unbreachable wall. He said, "Let's try to break it."[19] Canon's R&D chief was then just 37 years old. It was, as he himself described it, "a challengeable age."

Breaking Xerox's monopoly on copiers took Canon six years, but break it they did. The Japanese developed their own original technology named the "New Process." The first alternative to xerography, it was announced in 1968. The New Process copier drum had an insulating layer that permitted a more photosensitive chemical than Xerox machines of those days.[20]

In 1980, ten years after the introduction of their first copier, Canon came up with a revolutionary idea. This was a personal copier, an entirely new category of machine that even the smallest home office would be able to afford. Conventional copiers were always breaking down. So much so, in fact, that the Xerox business model was based on making money from servicing them. But a personal copier, to be successful, would have to be virtually service free. The key to achieving this was to pack all the bits that were liable to break into a relatively inexpensive, disposable cartridge. This was the fuel that Canon's machines would burn.

Though originally intended for copiers, the cartridge idea worked even better when applied to laser printers. Canon had been toying with lasers since the early sixties, since soon after their invention in fact. "In those days," Yamaji recalled, "there were just six engineers at our New Product Center, so it was like Kurosawa's *Seven Samurai,* except that there were only six of us." Back then, "we liked to play around with new things," Yamaji continued. "I did research on ruby lasers, and I concluded that this type of laser wouldn't do." But intuition told him that sooner or later lasers would improve.

The early 1970s found Canon seeking further diversification. "We felt that using our technology just for copiers would be a waste," Yamaji explained, "we wanted to apply it to all kinds of other things, too. And one of those happened to be printers."

The first approach to printing computer output that Canon's researchers tried was copying the image from the computer's monitor screen directly onto the copier's photosensitive drum. The trouble with this method was that the light from the monitor was not very bright. In the United States, meanwhile, 3M was scanning an electron beam across photosensitive paper, using the digital output from the computer to switch the beam on and off. The problem here was that you had to put the paper into a vacuum tube, which was very difficult to do. It seemed unlikely that an affordable product could be made using 3M's method.

Mulling over these problems, it occurred to Canon's engineers that a laser might be the solution. For one thing, laser light was from ten to twenty thousand times brighter than light from a cathode ray tube. For another, you could scan the beam through air, you didn't need a vacuum. "That's how we came up with the idea of scanning a laser beam," Yamaji said. "So we did experiments making lines on an actual copier drum, and when we got a black line, we were really delighted—I remember we drank a toast. And that was in 1972 or '73."

But credit for building the first laser printer goes to Gary Starkweather of Xerox, who had a prototype printer running in the fall of 1971. (I had assumed that, because of a patent cross-licensing agreement between the two firms, Canon had been aware of Starkweather's work. However, when I asked Yamaji whether this had in fact been the case, he replied, "No, we didn't know anything about [Xerox], our development was completely independent." There seemed no reason to doubt him; the history of technology is full of instances of similar inventions being made simultaneously by two or more different groups.)

The Canon researchers combined the laser with a revolving mirror that would scan the light across the drum, and built the combination into an engine to print text out from a computer. What to do next? Canon was not sure; the company had no experience in the computer market. To get feedback, in May 1975, Canon rented a small booth at the National Computer Conference held that year in Anaheim, California. Many attendees at the show visited their booth. Most impressed among them was Bill Hewlett, chief executive officer of Hewlett-Packard.

At the time, HP had itself been in the computer business only a few years. But Hewlett always had been extremely interested in new ideas. At his urging, HP licensed the laser technology from Canon. HP used it to build a printer for their minicomputers. The machine, which was about the size of a refrigerator, listed for $100,000. Not surprisingly, it was not a big seller. But at least HP now knew what laser printers could do. They also had a partner who could help them do it.

The lasers in these first printer engines were helium-neon jobs, which in the mid-1970s were more or less the only reliable type of laser you could buy. But it was obvious to all concerned that gas lasers were not an ideal solution. They were big and bulky, they needed high-voltage power supplies, and they cost several thousand dollars each.

Which explains why Yamaji and Co. were so excited when they discovered that Hitachi had figured out how to make reliable semiconductor lasers. The devices were a fraction of the size, used virtually no power, and—like all semiconductors—could (in theory) be made cheaply.

Nakamura gave Yamaji three diodes to go away and play with. Soon, Canon's R&D chief was back with a wish list consisting of four modifications. He wanted Hitachi to shift the wavelength of the laser's light slightly so that it matched the sensitivity of Canon's drum (the part of the machine that transfers the image onto the paper). He also requested devices that put out more light and that were impervious to changes in temperature.

The most important item on Yamaji's list was price. "We want to use your lasers in a mass-market application," he told them, "so please reduce the cost." Delighted to have such good feedback, Hitachi pulled out all the stops in order to oblige their customer. The result was that in 1979, Canon was able to build a prototype laser printer engine small enough to fit on a desktop.

Meanwhile the Japanese firm was also pouring millions of dollars into developing a cartridge for the personal copier, reducing the price of the guts of the machine by a factor of ten. The first personal copiers were introduced in 1982. By the following year, Canon had adapted the cartridge for use in laser printers. Yamaji flew to the United States to show the machine to Hewlett-Packard's printer people in Boise, Idaho. For Dick Hackbourne, the manager in charge of HP's printer business, it was love at first sight. "Hackbourne saw the engine," recalled one of his people, "and immediately said, 'I want it.' "

The attraction of the laser printer was that it knocked spots off both the conventional approaches to desktop printing. Dot matrix printers, the descendants of the output devices Seiko had used for its Olympic chronometers, allowed users to adopt different fonts and to print graphics. But their resolution—the number of dots per inch—was poor, they were slow, and they made an irritating racket. Daisy-wheel printers offered fine print quality, but only of one font at a time, they couldn't do graphics, and they were even slower than dot matrix machines.

The laser printer, by contrast, combined the font and graphics capability of the dot matrix with the print quality of the daisy wheel. Canon and HP set up an informal joint venture. The Japanese would provide the engine and manufacture the machine, while the Americans would develop the formatting software for the beast.

The first LaserJet retailed at $3,500. As Dave Packard wrote, "The first LaserJet created a totally new market (similar to what handheld calculators had done twelve years before)." The LaserJet made its debut in spring 1984 at Comdex, the computer industry's largest convention, held in Las Vegas. The machine stole the show. "It really was a once-in-a-lifetime experience as an engineer, to see something like this," HP's Jim Hall told *PC Novice* magazine, "something that people really wanted to rip out of your hands and buy. And that was the experience at Comdex. It was absolutely amazing."[21]

It was also bitterly disappointing for Gary Starkweather, the engineer at Xerox's Palo Alto Research Center who had pioneered the laser printer. Accustomed to selling to large corporate clients, Xerox had been unable to imagine why individuals would want to have printers in their offices.

Not that anybody could have imagined that it would be HP—which, after all, until the advent of the LaserJet, was still primarily a scientific instrument company—that would emerge as the big kahuna in the desktop printer market. Starkweather gave HP's management credit for their willingness to take the risk. "They probably couldn't guarantee that they'd sell a million of these [printers] either," he said, "but *they were willing to try,* and that's the key."

The same could also be said for Canon. The company went on to supply the laser engines for many other printers, most notably Apple's LaserWriter. And, of course, the cartridges. In 1996 revenues from sales of cartridges overtook those from laser printers. Kodak's lesson about burners had been well learned.

The semiconductor lasers used in printers were difficult to make, and Hitachi was able to charge for them accordingly. "High specifications and high price," Nakamura reckoned, "that is the area where Hitachi can make a business." This was especially true of the lasers used for telecommunications. In an application like a submarine cable, the semiconductor laser was a small part of a huge system, so there was little incentive for price reduction. Phone companies didn't care if the device cost thousands of dollars—their main concern was that it should function reliably.

There were those in Hitachi, however, who thought that the laser people should concentrate on making devices for a very different sort of application, one that in 1978 was being readied for the consumer market. This was as an optical pickup for the compact disc player, a radical new approach to hi-fi audio. Nakamura stuck to his guns: Hitachi would continue to focus on making high-end, communications-use semiconductor lasers for which they could charge as much as they liked.

Of course, Hitachi tried to make lasers for compact discs. In the beginning, they were quite successful in that area, too. Soon, however, the big firm was elbowed out of the way by companies who understood the economics of the consumer market, who would reduce the price of a semiconductor laser from $1,000 in 1979 to $1 a decade later. The first of these companies was not as you might expect, Philips or Sony, the codevelopers of the CD player, but Sharp.

The idea that light from a laser could be used as an exceptionally sharp playback stylus in place of the diamond tips used in magnetic pickup cartridges originated in the late 1960s. The great virtue of this method lies in the absence of any contact between laser pickup and disc surface. No more wince-inducing scratches, no more dust contamination, no more wear and tear from friction. As one inspired British television presenter demonstrated, you could spread strawberry jam on an optical disc, and it would *still* play.

Like many good ideas, optical discs had two more-or-less simultaneous inventors. One was DiscoVision, a Southern Californian start-up financed by the movie studio MCA. The other was LaserVision, which was the brainchild of the giant Dutch electronics firm Philips. Both were analog technologies intended to play back prerecorded video. In the mid-seventies the two camps decided to join forces. The best features of each were combined into a single format, DiscoVision, with Philips manufacturing the hardware and MCA supplying the software titles.[22]

"Observers questioned the practicality of Philips' plan to use lasers in a player designed for the home," wrote historian Margaret Graham, "and they were particularly skeptical of the contention that lasers could be mass-produced."[23] RCA, which was itself working on a video disc player, scoffed that it was better to aim for "a simple, low-cost, easily serviced player in the home, and to keep the space age technology in the factory." But Philips would have the last laugh. In 1984 RCA discontinued its VideoDisc player, taking a crippling $580 million write-off. That same year laser disc players switched from long helium-neon tubes to tiny semiconductor lasers made by Sharp.

The first laser discs and players went on sale in December 1978 at three stores in Atlanta, the city that by coincidence two years earlier had hosted Western Electric's initial test of optical communications. Unfortunately, the product came late to a market that was already occupied. The video cassette recorder had been launched some four years earlier. In the interim VCR manufacturers had begun to achieve formidable economies of scale.

Philips saw defeat coming. To salvage something from their investment in optical disc technology, the Dutch decided to substitute digital audio for analog video. Optical playback works by tracking ("reading") the reflection of light off the disc's silvery surface. The basic difference between analog and digital records is that, in the former, the information is encoded in the form of a continuously varying groove, while in the latter, it is stored in the form of tiny pits or dimples in the disc's surface, each pit representing a bit of digital data.

To help them establish a new standard, thus avoiding the kind of squabbling that had led in the late 1940s to two rival formats, the 33rpm album (proposed by CBS) and the 45rpm single (backed by RCA), Philips sought a partner. In 1978, Philips technical executive L. F. Ottens invited Sony's then deputy president Ohga Norio to visit the Dutch company's head office in Eindhoven. Sony was an excellent choice of partner because, in addition to their formidable development and marketing skills, the Japanese also owned a record company.[24] And like Philips, Sony was also smarting from a recent failure: By 1978, the writing was on the wall for its Betamax video cassette recorder.

Deciding on the size of the disc was easy. Philips was the originator of the compact cassette, introduced in 1963. For their part, Sony had always been keen on portable products, as the enormous success of the Walkman personal stereo, introduced in 1979, would serve to emphasize. The disc would be a compact 5 inches in diameter. This would provide more than enough room for the 40 minutes of music which was all that both sides of a conventional 12-inch long-playing record could hold.

Deciding on the maximum playing time was more difficult. The Dutch thought that an hour of recording time would suffice. Ohga disagreed. Trained in Germany as an opera singer, friend of classical musicians like Herbert von Karajan, and himself an occasional conductor, Ohga argued decisively that the compact disc should be long enough to hold an entire symphony. And not just any symphony either, but Beethoven's monumental Ninth symphony with its rousing choral finale.

Dai-ku ("Number 9"), as the Japanese call it, is by far the most popular piece of Western classical music in Japan. For some reason, the work has become inextricably linked with New Year's Eve celebrations there. No self-respecting Japanese orchestra would dream of omitting *Dai-ku* from its December 31 concert program.

Thus the playing time of the compact disc was fixed as 74 minutes 42 seconds, long enough to accommodate Beethoven's Ninth. With these two basic parameters, size and time, in place, it was now a matter of simple arithmetic to calculate the width of the optical stylus that would be required. This turned out to be 780 nanometers. The trouble was that, in 1979, there *were* no semiconductor lasers available that operated at that (infrared) wavelength.

Publication of the specs for the CD set off yet another laser-building race. This time, in addition to Philips and Sony, the contestants included Hitachi, Matsushita, Mitsubishi Electric, NEC, and Toshiba. And yet again, the race was won by a dark horse.

Sharp had begun a program to develop light-emitting devices from compound semiconductors back in 1966. It was headed by Fujimori Akira, whom Rocket Sasaki had brought with him to Sharp from Kobe Kogyo. This program culminated in the deployment in May 1969 of what the company claimed was the world's first weather information system for motorists. Huge display boards were installed by the side of the new highway linking Tokyo and Nagoya to warn drivers to slow down because of high winds or slippery road conditions.

Having succeeded in this application, the onus at Sharp—as ever in consumer electronics—was to leverage their investment by extending the technology into other areas. Following the announcement of Hayashi and Panish's breakthrough at Bell Labs, lasers seemed like a good bet. Sharp started development of lasers in 1971.

What did the firm intend to do with such things? Since Sharp was not a member of NTT's family of suppliers, communications did not seem like a good bet. One possibility that interested Sasaki, as head of the company's industrial equipment division, was a new machine intended for use in point-of-sale applications, the bar-code reader. The standard for today's ubiquitous bar codes was adopted in 1973. But by 1978 only 1 percent of U.S. stores were equipped with readers, in large part because the helium-neon lasers the machines used made them very expensive indeed.

In October 1979, Fujimori's team developed its first semiconductor laser. This device put out infrared light with a wavelength of 870 nanometers. Lacking any obvious application, it was not a commercial success. But at least it was a start. Sharp's next laser, developed in 1981, was a different story. This device emitted light at the CD wavelength of 780 nm, and it was very reliable. Which was more than you could say for any of the other diodes that Sony had tried, including their own.

Nakajima Heitaro was the digital audio pioneer who headed compact disc development at Sony. He realized that without a source of reliable semiconductor lasers, Sony would miss their target introduction date for CD players of 1 October 1982, in time for that year's crucial Christmas season.

Nakajima swallowed his pride. He traveled down to Sharp's R&D Center at Tenri to see the tiny device with his own eyes. Satisfied that it worked, he asked Fujimori to make lasers for Sony. Fujimori promised Nakajima that the first one would be ready in six months. It was hard going, but the Sharp researcher kept his promise.

Sharp's first, sample diodes sold for ¥200,000 ($800) each. By the development stage, spring 1982, the company had brought the price down by an order of magnitude to ¥20,000 ($80). By May, when Sharp began mass production, the price in batches of 10,000 was just ¥4,500 ($18). This was still too expensive. "We'd like you to reduce the cost of lasers to ¥1,000 ($4)," Sony's procurement people told Fujimori, "when can you do it by?" With mass production, came the reply, within five years.

Thanks to the efforts of Fujimori and his group at Sharp, Nakajima met his target introduction date for the CD player. Though few people noticed it at the time, this first mass market application came almost exactly twenty years after the invention of the semiconductor laser by Bob Hall at GE back in 1962. In the interim, many firms had managed to make semiconductor lasers in the lab, but Sharp was the first to put the devices into volume production.

Depending on a rival firm for a key component in an important product is not a comfortable situation. On the bullet train back to Tokyo after his visit to Sharp's R&D center, Nakajima quizzed his development people anxiously. "How about our laser efforts?" he fretted, "Are we going to be all right?" "Don't worry," they reassured him. "We'll catch them up in a year or two."

Their confidence was based on a new production process that Sony was working on at its Central Research Laboratory in Yokohama. The key step in the production of infrared semiconductor lasers is the growth of thin films of crystalline material on wafers of gallium arsenide. The method that Sharp used was to load precisely measured quantities of the materials required for the various layers into tiny wells scooped out of a carbon container called a boat. The boat is then launched into a quartz tube over which a furnace is positioned. Heat from the furnace causes the contents of the wells to melt into a liquid solution. As the wafer is slid across the boat from solution to solution, the materials precipitate in the form of a film on its surface. When the wafer cools, metal contacts are applied, and it is cut up and cleaved into individual devices.

This method, known as liquid phase epitaxy, was invented at RCA in 1963. (Epitaxy simply means crystal growth in which each newly grown layer of crystal exhibits exactly the same structure as the layer beneath.) Though tried and tested, there were limits to its applicability. In particular, it took tremendous skill to fabricate the laser's active layer, which was just a few thousand atoms thick. Thus researchers were on the lookout for a process that would give them more precise control over crystal growth. By the late 1970s, two possible approaches had emerged.

At Rockwell, Russell Dupuis had demonstrated the potential of a technique called metal–organic chemical vapor deposition. In this process, gases–including highly toxic arsine–flowing over a heated wafer react on the wafer's surface to form thin films of material only a few atoms thick. In 1977, Dupuis made the first semiconductor lasers grown using MOCVD. But his company couldn't figure out what to do with them. "There was no clear path of technology insertion at Rockwell," Dupuis said. Two years later, he quit to join Bell Labs.

At Murray Hill, Dupuis worked down the corridor from Won Tien Tsang. For the past couple of years, Won had been telling anyone who would listen that if you wanted to mass-produce semiconductor lasers reliably, then molecular beam epitaxy was the way to go. In this method, materials are loaded into cells attached to an ultrahigh vacuum chamber. They are then heated to evaporation point. Snapping open the lid of a cell causes a beam of molecules of the evaporated material to come whizzing out and onto the awaiting wafer. Thin films of material are built up, one atomic layer at a time. It's like spray painting with atoms.

Inverted stainless-steel udders with wires shooting out of them in all directions, MBE systems looked like the very stuff of high technology.

But they were also balky beasts, and would only run with several Ph.D.'s in constant attendance.

Sony decided to leave MBE to university professors, opting instead for MOCVD, toxic gases and all. The director of the firm's research center, Kikuchi Makoto, initiated a full-scale program to turn the technology into a production process. Top management wondered what was the point of investing so much money in such a complex technology, when Sharp had succeeded in making lasers using a much simpler method.

Kikuchi responded by giving them a history lesson, showing how the trend in the semiconductor industry had always been towards greater controllability of crystal growth. When management persisted in grumbling about the cost, safe in the knowledge that he had the full support of Iwama, the company's president, Kikuchi would shut them up by asking: "Which would you rather have—a winner technology or a loser technology?"

By 1984 Sony had tamed MOCVD technology sufficiently to begin mass production of semiconductor lasers at its Atsugi plant in West Tokyo. With the introduction of the Discman portable that October, the market for CD players took off.

In 1985, sales of laser diodes topped $100 million. That year, in what one observer described dryly as "a surprising development," a little-known Japanese component supplier called Rohm began selling semiconductor lasers fabricated using MBE, the method supposedly best left to university professors.[25] In 1995, Sharp, Sony, and Rohm would between them account for 90 percent of the 100 million semiconductor lasers manufactured that year.[26]

Molecular beam epitaxy started life at Bell Labs in the late 1960s as a tool for basic science. Then Al Cho, an ebullient Chinese American electrical engineer who liked to make things happen, blew into Murray Hill. Cho began growing layers of crystal material that were just a few atoms thick. At a crystal growth conference in England, Cho was stung by a skeptical question from the audience: "These layers are very nice, but what can you do with them?" Cho returned to Bell Labs determined to make some actual devices. At that time, Hayashi and Panish had just made their first room temperature lasers. The pair had had a hard time making the active layer of their lasers thin enough—5,000 angstroms was about the best they could manage. (One angstrom is roughly equal to the width of one atom.) "And I said, Whoof!, what is this 5,000 angstroms?" Cho laughed. "It's like a mammoth size, right? I can make 10 angstroms, I can control the layers!"

The first device Cho made was a laser. But it didn't work, and the young scientist was teased by his fellow researchers. "A lot of people laughed at me," he recalled. "They said: 'Al Cho, this'll never become a production thing—it's just a toy in the laboratory.' " The same thing had been said of the laser itself. But Cho was stubborn, and he stood his ground. In 1976, he grew the first room-temperature continuous-wave lasers by MBE.

But it was his younger compatriot and colleague Won Tien Tsang who demonstrated that MBE could cut the mustard on the factory floor as well as in the lab. During the period 1978–82, Won published a torrent of technical papers arguing the case for MBE. It seemed like there was a report from Won in *Applied Physics Letters* almost every week. One paper was particularly explicit. It was entitled "High throughput, high yield, highly reproducible aluminum gallium arsenide lasers grown by MBE."

It seemed to Won that no one was interested.[27] The silence that greeted his outpourings was deafening. Years later he discovered that at least one person had taken him seriously: Tanaka Haruo, a resourceful young chemist at a company called Rohm.

Rohm is based in the ancient Japanese capital city of Kyoto. The firm was founded in 1954 by Sato Ken, a remarkable entrepreneur, when he was just 23. As a student at one of Kyoto's less well-regarded universities, Sato faced an unusual choice of career: whether to train as a concert pianist or to exploit an invention he had made and patented while still at school. After failing to win first prize in a competition for young pianists, he opted for the latter.

Sato's invention was a new method of manufacturing resistors, tiny nozzles that restrict the flow of electrical current and one of the basic building blocks of all electrical circuits. Resistors made the Sato way were smaller than conventional ones. The invention came just in time to catch the first mass-market product that could use such tiny components—the transistor radio. Forty years later, Rohm would be the largest maker of transistors in the world.[28]

Started in the Japanese equivalent of a garage, Rohm—the name is compounded from "R" for "resistor," and "ohm," the unit in which electrical resistance is measured—went on to dominate the world market for resistors. In large part this dominance came about through a mastery of automated production and an extraordinary devotion to customer satisfaction. The word is that whenever there is a problem with one of their products, Rohm flies someone out with a replacement. This is the kind of service that owners of Rolls Royces expect. It is unheard of among resistor makers, whose products typically sell for fractions of a cent.

Like other Japanese suppliers who eke out a precarious existence a few links down the food chain from the giants who lord it over the electronics industry, Rohm is ceaselessly on the lookout for promising new markets. This way, the company avoids competition with the big guys. "Rather than the mainstream, I prefer to swim by the banks of the river," Sato said.[29]

In 1969, Sato assigned Tanaka to work on light-emitting diodes. As a result of Tanaka's efforts the firm was successful in developing the tiny red lamps. But as we saw in chapter 3, during the late 1970s, LEDs lost out in the watch and calculator marketplace to LCDs, sales of LEDs plunged, and Rohm was forced (temporarily) to discontinue production.

In 1982, while wondering what their next step should be, Tanaka came across Won Tien Tsang's papers insisting that MBE could be used to make wonderful lasers. Five years later, when Won visited Tanaka in Kyoto, he asked his Japanese host, "Why the heck did you pick MBE for mass production when everyone else thinks the right way to do it is with MOCVD?" The Japanese replied jokingly that he had decided that, "if you could use MBE to mass-produce papers, then I could use MBE to mass produce lasers!"

With the compact disc player on the verge of becoming a commercial product, laser diodes were of some interest to a specialist component maker. But at the same time, Tanaka realized that entering in the laser market would mean taking on the likes of Hitachi, Mitsubishi, NEC, and, in particular, Sharp, all of whom had already amassed considerable experience in making the devices. Using the same production process that they used, there was no way an insignificant little outfit like Rohm could hope to succeed. After reading Won's reports, however, Tanaka concluded that "even though we are behind, if we use MBE, there's a possibility that we can beat the big guys."

Applying MBE to the mass production of lasers was a risky decision. Years later Won Tien Tsang would applaud Tanaka for having been brave enough to take it. "No question," Won said, "I think that took tremendous courage."[30] Crucial to Tanaka's success was the support of Rohm's top man. "Our president is an entrepreneur," Tanaka explained, "and he has lots of experience with technology. So he understands the need to take a long-term approach to technological challenges, and that was a great help."

Another crucial factor in Rohm's triumph was the company's wealth of experience with production equipment. When the MBE machine that Tanaka ordered—a system that Al Cho had helped design, made by the French company Riber—arrived in 1982, Rohm's engineers took it apart and put it back together the way they wanted it. Tanaka gleefully recalled that "we got a drill and made holes in the pipes of a machine that cost ¥100 million [$400,000]!"

Among the many improvements that Rohm's engineers made, the most important one was enabling the machine to run continuously over a long period of time. This was key because once you open up an MBE machine, baking off the contaminants that coat the walls of its reaction chamber then bringing it back up to ultrahigh vacuum again can take several weeks. Rohm's current machine can run for over three months with one loading. And, like all of Rohm's production equipment, it runs automatically—no need for Ph.D.s in attendance. The company also operates a highly automated laser packaging line, a key requirement in producing low-cost devices. This line, too, is entirely home grown.

Once mastered, molecular beam epitaxy offers two great advantages as a production method. One is that lasers grown by MBE have extremely thin active layers and thus are easily coaxed into emitting light. The devices draw less current, which means that a set of batteries on your portable CD player will last you longer—all the way from, say, Osaka to San Francisco.

The other good thing about MBE is that there is almost no variation in the uniformity of crystal growth across the wafer. This means that if you can make one good laser, then you can have confidence that all the other lasers on the wafer will be good, too. Eliminating the need for expensive testing makes it possible to produce the devices extremely cheaply.

A single 2-inch wafer can yield up to 30,000 lasers. If annual world demand for the devices is 90 million, then all you need is 3,000 wafers. Compared with resistors, of which Rohm produces around 100 million *per day*, this is peanuts.

By the gargantuan standards of the semiconductor industry, lasers have thus far been a niche market. Most have gone into CD players, CD-ROM drives, video game machines, and laser printers. In the late 1990s, however, as optic fiber moves ever closer to the consumer—from the local loop, to the kerb, and thence to the home—demand for lasers will increase dramatically, and they will become a bona fide volume market. This was a prospect which greatly pleased Tanaka.

In the meantime, however, another type of semiconductor light source has already made it into high-volume production. Each year, according to some estimates, at least 30 *billion* light-emitting diodes are produced. That is five each for every man, woman, and child on the planet. But this is only the beginning. Huge markets for LEDs remain untapped. And, as we shall see in the next two chapters, in the drive to open up these markets, in LEDs as in lasers, entrepreneurial Japanese companies are setting the pace.

9

Doctor Nishizawa, I Presume?

There are innovative people in Japan, but there is no one to show them the way.

—Nishizawa Jun'ichi[1]

WHEN TESHIMA TORU CAME BACK to the family farm, his mother was overjoyed. She had not expected to see her younger son alive again. During the last months of World War II Teshima had been training as a transport pilot, and casualty figures for these pilots were appallingly high—almost as bad as for *kamikaze* pilots. But luckily the war had ended before Teshima could graduate from flying school. Returning home to rural Aichi, in central Japan, he could become a country boy again.

However, it was soon apparent that young Teshima was not cut out for life on the farm. For one thing, he was always having ideas about how things could be done better. Farming was a bad business, Teshima told his brother as they splashed around the family rice paddies. You were always at the mercy of the elements. For example, a typhoon could come along and wreck the harvest. Why not roof over the fields, Teshima proposed, and, in fact, why not put in underground heating? That way, even typhoon rains or frosts wouldn't do the crops any damage.

Decades later, the style of farming that Teshima proposed—enclosing crops in heated greenhouses made of transparent vinyl—would become hugely popular among Japanese farmers. In 1945, however, before the Occupation's reforms took effect and turned tenant farmers into owners, most farmers still only rented the land that they worked, giving them little incentive to innovate.

Japanese fields are small compared to Western ones. The neighbors could hear Teshima raving on about his ideas to his brother. "Poor Teshima-San's son has gone crazy since he came back from flying airplanes," they said, shaking their heads. In the country, word travels quickly. Soon Teshima's mother heard that people were saying her son had a screw loose. She became worried. "Toru," she advised him, "perhaps you'd better give up the idea of becoming a farmer."

Teshima was glad, because he didn't really want to be a farmer. General MacArthur had put flying off limits for Japanese, so the youngster couldn't finish his pilot's training. But although the Supreme Commander closed off some avenues, he opened up others. For example, it was now possible for the Japanese to listen to shortwave radio, which during the war the military had banned to prevent people tuning in to foreign news broadcasts. Teshima thought that radio sounded like a promising business, so he went back to school to study electrical engineering.

But though he had switched vocations, Teshima would continue throughout his career to have ideas about how things could be done better. Nor would he ever be shy about telling others how to implement those ideas, and pestering them until they let him have his way.

It would be a hard row to hoe, but Teshima would ultimately succeed in his biggest challenge. In 1976, his company, Stanley Electric, developed the brightest semiconductor lights the world had ever seen. In so doing, Teshima helped set in motion a revolution. Today, these lights are used mostly in niche markets like indicator lamps. But in the future, semiconductor lights will replace conventional light bulbs in an ever-increasing number of applications—including the home.

Nick Holonyak's origins were as humble as those of Teshima Toru. Holonyak's father, a Carpathian immigrant, was a miner in the coalfields of Southern Illinois. Two days down the mine during his summer vacation were enough to convince Holonyak junior that his destiny lay aboveground. Good high school math grades got him into electrical en-

Teacher and pupil: Over tea at the Electro-Technical Laboratories in Tokyo in 1956, Nick Holonyak, Jr., and Kikuchi Makoto discuss a silicon transistor.

gineering at the University of Illinois at Urbana-Champaign. His timing was impeccable. When transistor pioneer John Bardeen came to Illinois from Bell Labs in 1951, Holonyak was his first student.

After receiving his doctor's degree, Holonyak went to Murray Hill. There, he was a member of the team at Bell Labs that laid the foundations for the semiconductor industry's switch from germanium to the more versatile silicon, work that ultimately led to the integrated circuit. In 1955, much to the annoyance of vice president Jack Morton, Holonyak gave up his Bell Labs deferment and was drafted into the U.S. Army. He was posted to a Signal Corps base in Yokohama.

In Japan, through an introduction from Bardeen, he met Kikuchi Makoto, later Sony's research director. The two scientists became lifelong friends. Every other Saturday for the nine months that Holonyak was in Japan, the young American would give all-day seminars at the Electro-Technical Laboratory in Tokyo, where Kikuchi was then working. Then the pair would head off to a coffee shop someplace in Ginza, discussing semiconductors all the way.

A photograph exists of Kikuchi and Holonyak deep in discussion at the laboratory, the tousle-headed Japanese eagerly quizzing the crew-cut American about some arcane aspect of transistor lore. At Kikuchi's request, Holonyak managed to get hold of some ultrapure silicon from Bell Labs through the U.S. Army mail system (which was much faster than the regular post). This, he reckoned, was probably Japan's first piece of device-grade silicon.

Holonyak was thus a rare American witness of early Japanese efforts in the semiconductor era. He visited the labs of companies like Hitachi, Kobe Kogyo, Matsushita, and Sony, and saw how primitive conditions were there. "Third world" was a description that came to mind.

Holonyak nonetheless came away from this encounter with an enduring respect for Japanese creativity. Almost forty years later he would insist that "the idea that the Japanese never do anything original is nonsense, and it has been nonsense from the beginning. They never just copied–they replicated to learn what others had done, then they would always add something more, their own nuances, and go off on tangents."

On his return to the United States in 1957, Holonyak could have gone back to Bell Labs. But the disagreement he had had with Morton over the deferment of his military service still rankled. Besides, Holonyak came from the wide open spaces of the Midwest and he was not crazy about the prospect of living in overcrowded New Jersey again. "I felt that you went from one town to another, and you haven't left any town," he said, "even the clumps of trees have houses inside them." Instead, Holonyak signed up with General Electric's device laboratory in Syracuse, New York. He spent six happy years there, doing more or less exactly as he pleased.

As we saw in the previous chapter, at GE Holonyak investigated Esaki diodes. This led him to work with the compound semiconductor gallium arsenide, and subsequently a derivative alloy, gallium arsenide phosphide. He was thus ideally qualified to participate in the great race to build the first semiconductor laser, which culminated in late 1962 with the narrow victory of his friend and GE colleague Bob Hall. But unlike the other participants, whose devices all output infrared light, from the outset Holonyak targeted *visible* light emitters. He firmly believed that "our concentration should be where the eye is, because that's where the human is and that's what he needs." This consideration had also motivated Ted Maiman, the inventor of the laser: "I was intrigued by the fact that, if it worked, ruby would emit visible light," Maiman said. "I would be able to see it. Essentially, all of the other proposals were in the infrared and so were the subsequent early successful lasers, including helium-neon." [2]

Though this focus cost Holonyak the laser race (in which he was slowed down by the need to make his own material), it also meant that he was well ahead of everybody else in producing a visible light-emitting diode, a device that in many ways resembled the laser. As practical components, the first lasers were sorely lacking. Holonyak's LEDs were, by contrast, of almost immediate commercial significance. Holonyak told a reporter from Reader's Digest that, whereas it might be ten years before lasers were ready for widespread use, "within a year we should have [LEDs] ready for computer indicators and many other electronic devices, where they should be very useful because of the small size and speed of action." [3] Units made in his lab were offered for sale in the 1965 edition of the Allied Radio catalog.

There was also a further difference between Hall and Holonyak regarding the outcome of their work. Within a year of his discovery, Hall would leave the field and turn his attention to other topics. Holonyak, on the other hand, would stay with light emitters throughout his long career. And, in addition to his own contributions, to help push back the boundaries of the field Holonyak would also train several generations of students.

A peculiar thing about the light-emitting diode was that there seemed to be no basic patent on the device. "The phenomenon we call luminescence was perhaps first observed by Aristotle as light emitted by the scales of decaying fish." [4] Modern investigation of the subject dates back to 1907. Experimenting with possible detectors for radio waves, H. J. Round of New York reported that carborundum crystals gave out a yellowish light when current was passed through them. Russell Ohl's 1940 demonstration at Bell Labs of the photovoltaic effect, the basis for solar cells, proved that light could be directly converted into electricity. The light-emitting diode was the inverse case, converting electricity directly to light.

The 1947 invention of the bipolar transistor demonstrated that you could increase the population of electrons and holes in a device by injecting current. This key concept was identified by Bardeen. During the 1950s, Egon Loebner worked on light emission at RCA. Westinghouse had some early results with silicon carbide, a compound which contained naturally occurring positive-negative junctions, the basis for light emission.

This sort of thing was all very interesting scientifically. But it was not until 1962, when Nick Holonyak came up with his red gallium arsenide phosphide alloy diode at General Electric, that light emission by semiconductor devices became of commercial interest.

Two regular visitors to Holonyak's lab around that time were Robert Ruhrwein and Forest "Frosty" Williams of Monsanto, the giant St. Louis, Missouri, -based chemical company. Monsanto's chemists hoped that gallium arsenide wafers would turn into a market for them. They would send Holonyak samples of materials that they had synthesized for him to check. Since the Air Force was supporting the GE researcher's work, it was quite acceptable for him to entertain visitors from other companies and to discuss his results with them.

On one such visit, Holonyak showed Ruhrwein and Williams how he was growing gallium arsenide phosphide in a sealed-off test tube. The two chemists were astonished. "Williams was a Southerner from Kentucky," Holonyak recalled, "and he just rubbed his cheek and went, 'My Gahd, my Gahd—if you can do that [in a] closed tube, I can do that [in an] open tube.' " In an open tube, Monsanto's researchers would be able to control the flow of the chemicals more precisely. They would also be able to scale the process up to industrial levels.

The pair went back to St. Louis, where Williams set up a reactor to replicate what Holonyak was doing. Meanwhile Ruhrwein sat down and wrote a patent application that was as extensive as he could make it, listing every reaction he could imagine taking place in a reactor of that kind.

While Monsanto was getting excited about the potential of semiconductor light emitters, General Electric couldn't have cared less. Holonyak's boss had no interest in the exotic compounds that the young researcher was working on. As far as this manager was concerned, silicon could do everything he needed. He told Holonyak that if the latter couldn't find alternate sources of funding for this work, then there was the road. Not long afterwards, Holonyak took the hint, quitting GE to take up an offer from Bardeen to return to the University of Illinois. He has been there ever since.

Thus, in one of the history of technology's great ironies, the same company that half a century previously had invented the gas-filled, tungsten filament incandescent light bulb—and had made huge profits on its manufacture—turned its back on a development that promised to produce a successor to that lamp.

Solid-state light sources represent in principle an ideal form of lamp. They offer all the same advantages as the transistor did over the vacuum tube. Semiconductor lights are small and, because they do not have to heat a filament to a temperature high enough to make it glow, use almost no power. As time went by, they would moreover become long lived and cost relatively little to produce. Indeed, Holonyak confidently predicted that while he himself would not live to see it, LEDs would eventually come to threaten much of the world's $50 billion light bulb industry.

To be sure, it required a leap of faith in the 1960s to imagine such a future for these early red LEDs, whose output was more than a hundred times dimmer than that of a 60-watt incandescent lamp. But successive breakthroughs over the next twenty years would see LEDs becoming progressively brighter, and acquiring the ability to produce more and more colors. To the point where anxious executives from GE's huge lamp operation in Cleveland, Ohio, would call Holonyak's former students to ask about the long-term implications of solid-state light sources for their business.

"You can look at that and say, Are those people crazy that they didn't see that the semiconductor had a future in light emission?" Holonyak reflected bitterly.

Monsanto would also let Holonyak down. The firm was founded in 1901 by John Queeny to produce the artificial sweetener, saccharin. Evidently a gallant entrepreneur, Queeny named the company not for himself, but for his wife, Olga Monsanto. Queeny's son Edgar took over the company in 1928. He embarked on a program of expansion that would ultimately see Monsanto's activities embrace everything from the production of chemical fertilizers to the refining of plutonium for America's nuclear weapons. Edgar Queeny stepped down as Monsanto chairman in 1960, leaving a flourishing international firm whose revenues in 1962, the year of the LED's invention, passed $1 billion for the first time. Further expansion was set to follow, and the new field of electronic devices seemed particularly promising.

According to one observer, Monsanto's motivation for getting into compound semiconductors was that "they were in the phosphorus business, the phosphorus they used for phosphates, and for fertilizer . . . and they thought, Gee—there must be some use for phosphorus in all this emerging electronics stuff. Basically, they had a phosphorus mine, and they ended up in the LED business, which is a pretty bizarre chain of events."[5]

At the University of Illinois Holonyak became a consultant for Monsanto, helping them start their LED business and sending them four of his best graduate students—in particular, George Craford. Craford arrived in St. Louis in 1967 and a year later made the next major breakthrough in LED technology.

Thus far, semiconductor lights resembled the Model T Ford in that you could have them in any color—so long as it was red. They were also so dim that, to gain their full effect, you basically had to be in a dark room. Seeking to improve the performance of the device, Craford doped gallium arsenide phosphide with nitrogen. It was a mixture that researchers at Bell Labs had asserted would not work.

Craford would never forget the surprise he got when he turned on his new LED for the first time: "Man, it was a yellow device and it was *vastly* brighter than anything we had seen before. So that was neat, a real nice moment. . . . I don't remember saying anything, just being kind of stunned that these crazy ideas actually worked, because there was certainly some noise in the system that said they weren't going to work, and we were kind of forging ahead anyway."

But the significance of Craford's breakthrough was not recognized within Monsanto. "We had this great stuff with all these colors," he recalled, "and some of our marketing people went around talking to customers. Basically they came back with the feedback that, Gee, our customers are using red, and they like red, and they don't much care if it gets brighter, unless it gets cheaper."

"Well, that may be right," Craford remembered thinking, "but it doesn't sound right." Certainly, that kind of feedback didn't do much for his group's morale. During the early 1970s, following the invention of the yellow LED, he and his colleagues were struggling for funding to do any kind of development work. As so often in electronics R&D during this period, the only way to get support for the group turned out to be through government contracts.

Worse was to follow. Monsanto was fundamentally a chemical company, more comfortable with selling bulk stuff in big sacks than fiddly little devices in plastic bags. Like everyone else in the components industry, Monsanto attempted to reduce costs by shipping production offshore, building dirt-floor plants in places like Jakarta and Kuala Lumpur. But these factories failed to live up to expectations, reinforcing the company's doubts about whether it really wanted to be in the electronic components business in the first place.

Another thing that upset the Midwesterners about the business was its roller-coaster cycles. But even by the volatile standards of the semiconductor industry, few products took off faster, or came down harder, than LEDs. As we saw in chapter 3, in the early 1970s LEDs became the display of choice for calculators and watches. During the middle of the decade, as assemblers turned to the cheaper and more efficient liquid crystal displays, these markets dried up. In 1977, according to market researcher Dataquest, sales of LEDs plunged 40 percent to just $50 million.

Around this time, Monsanto started hiring consultants to investigate what Craford and his colleagues were doing. Sometimes these people came from other parts of the company, other times they were consultants brought in from outside. Craford saw the surveys as "Gestapo squad kind of things." It seemed to him that what was going on was that "basically, somebody at a high level decides that this business isn't a good idea. So he hires a consultant to come in and look at the business, and pays the consultant to give him the answer he wants to hear, so that he can say, We've had this outside appraisal, and [as a result] we're going to sell the business."

According to Craford, "the guys that came in were like one or two years out of MBA, and they spent a week or two looking us over." Their verdict: Monsanto should pull the plug on its LED device business. The justification for making this recommendation was that Monsanto could not hope to compete with the Texas Instruments juggernaut. TI was this big semiconductor manufacturer, went the rationale, and the Texans also made calculators, so they had all the pieces needed to win. In 1978, Monsanto sold its optoelectronics operation, lock, stock, and barrel. Not long after, Texas Instruments also pulled out of the LED business.

The device business was sold to General Instrument, the materials business to Mitsubishi Metal. With hindsight, Craford was surprisingly philosophical about Monsanto's decision to quit. "I don't actually fault the high-level people from a strategic point of view," he said. "They pointed the company in a different direction and got rid of those things that didn't fit in with that, and Monsanto's basically done pretty well. I mean, it didn't sink Monsanto to get rid of them."

At the time of its tail-between-legs exit, Monsanto was by far the dominant producer of compound semiconductors in the world, with a huge factory west of St. Louis that ran some 100 furnaces for synthesizing gallium arsenide. But Monsanto and TI were by no means the only big U.S. companies to drop out of the LED field after making much of the early running. Bell Labs, too, had been much interested in the potential of little semiconductor lights.

This research was initiated by a chemist called David Thomas, an Englishman who had arrived at Bell Labs in the mid-1950s, more or less by accident. While vacationing in New Jersey, Thomas bumped into Richard Bozorth, an authority on magnetism, at a dinner party. On learning that Thomas was a chemist, Bozorth asked him if he had ever visited Bell Laboratories. Thomas replied that he had never even *heard* of Bell Laboratories. A bemused Bozorth arranged a visit to Murray Hill. There, under the misapprehension that Thomas was looking for a job, the director of one of the labs interviewed him, and subsequently he was hired.[6]

In attempting to produce a visible light-emitting diode, Thomas worked with a different material than Holonyak, gallium phosphide.[7] By 1970, in addition to red emitters, Thomas had also made efficient green lights out of this compound. There were immediate practical applications for such lights within the Bell System.

The main one was providing low-powered indicator lamps for phone sets with illuminated pushbuttons. The incandescent lamps with which conventional sets were equipped required thick cables. To power them, the phones had to be plugged into the wall socket. Using LEDs, the same dribble of current that came over the line to power the phone would also suffice for the lamps. Another application for solid-state lights was a dial with lamps under each button. This enabled the caller to see the numbers glowing, even at night. LEDs were also used by the phone company in the early days of optical communications to transmit signals. However, it eventually became apparent that the future in this application lay mostly with lasers.

The gallium phosphide technology that Bell Labs developed is still widely used for the production of LEDs, especially green ones. So, too, is the gallium arsenide phosphide technology pioneered by Monsanto. Indeed, these 1970s technologies still dominate the market for red, green, and yellow light emitters. From where I sit in my office, I can see over twenty examples of this simple type of LED, incorporated in my computer, modem, printer, phone, tape recorder, security system, and speakers.

Western Electric put gallium phosphide devices into production at the company's facility in Reading, Pennsylvania. But for several reasons, the phone company ended up abandoning the business. One was the usual Bell System problem with transferring technology from the labs to a production environment. Another was a limitation with the technology itself.

Gallium phosphide was very slow to switch on and off. That was not a problem for telephone pushbutton call directors and illuminated dials. But it effectively put the devices out of contention for any kind of digital display. The U.S. company that best understood the display market, and that would stick with LED technology through thick and thin, was Hewlett-Packard.

Hewlett-Packard's involvement with light-emitting diodes began around the same time as Monsanto's. But HP had a very different reason for developing LEDs. Whereas the Midwesterners saw electronic devices as an emerging market opportunity, the Californians got into solid-state displays because they were crucial to HP's core business.

Look at the front panel of any one of the scientific instruments that were Hewlett-Packard's stock in trade in 1962, the year of the LED's invention, and you will see an array of Nixie tubes. Nixies, as we saw in chapter 3, were gas-filled glow tubes containing filaments in the shape of the numbers 0 through 9. Open up the instrument's back panel, however, and you will see that the guts of the machine had gone completely solid state. By the early 1960s, the tubes had been replaced by transistors, perhaps even a few small-scale integrated circuits.

Nixies were thus an anachronism, the last remnants of an otherwise obsolete technology. More to the point, they were electrically incompatible with the tiny amount of current required to drive the semiconductors. This need for compatibility was the primary motivation behind HP's effort to build solid-state displays for its instruments business.

Developing LEDs took HP over six years. The effort, which was led by former RCA researcher Egon Loebner, proceeded in parallel with LED development at Monsanto. Indeed, for three years during the mid-sixties, the two companies actually teamed up. It was an unusual arrangement, brought about by pressure from the Air Force, which was funding much of this research. But the joint effort appears to have worked well. Or at least, as former HP lab director Paul Greene remarked dryly, "nobody sued anybody, which is the best you can ask for."

Monsanto's expertise in materials nicely complemented HP's knowledge of devices and systems. When both companies had managed to make LEDs that were reasonably efficient, they split up and went into business on their own.

In addition to motivation, a second obvious difference between Monsanto and HP in their approach to LEDs was the attitude of top management at the two firms. Monsanto's chiefs, as we have seen, were less than totally committed. At HP, by contrast, Bill Hewlett understood the need for LEDs as a replacement for Nixies, and was from the first a strong supporter of the research.

After HP's researchers had produced practical light emitters, a meeting was held in the company's boardroom to decide on whether to proceed with commercialization. Investment on the order of several million dollars would be required, a serious matter for a company whose 1965 sales totaled just $200 million. The presentation was made jointly by Bob Burmeister, a young physicist fresh out of Stanford on his first project at HP, and Burmeister's boss, Paul Greene.

They outlined the applications for LEDs. Displays were clearly the most important of these, but there were also others, such as pilot lamps, the little indicators that tell you at a glance whether an appliance is on or not.

When Burmeister and Greene had finished, HP's vice president of marketing did his best to pick holes in their proposal. This executive was particularly skeptical of the notion that they would ever be able to meet the cost targets for such applications. At the time, pilot lamps sold for roughly 10¢ each—"Do you think you could make them for that?" the marketing man wanted to know. Burmeister replied that he thought it might be possible some day, a suggestion that his antagonist promptly dismissed as ridiculous.

But Bill Hewlett was in the room listening to the discussion. Recognizing the importance of the research, he intervened to give the project his personal OK. "In another company," Burmeister reckoned, "without such a strong individual, I would say that the marketing person might have squashed it right there."

No wonder HP's technical staff loved their CEO. Hewlett the hands-on engineer liked nothing better than to wander around HP's labs, leaving his partner Dave Packard to take care of the company's external relationships. In the lab, Hewlett would chat with researchers, asking them questions, finding out whether they had any problems with their projects, suggesting solutions if they did. He was always eager to hear about the latest technologies. And, as we saw in chapter 8 with the laser printer, to propose new applications for them.

It was Hewlett's idea to develop a handheld scientific calculator. This project began in the fall of 1970, while Packard was off in Washington on a tour of duty as Deputy Secretary of Defence. Hewlett defined the objective as a product that you could " 'put in your pocket and attend a meeting without having to haul out some damn thing that isn't convenient.' An engineer drew up rough sketches for a calculator the size of a Benson & Hedges cigarette package. . . . When Hewlett returned from a month-long trip, a plastic model had been created. Hewlett slipped the model into his shirt pocket. It fit, and development of the HP-35 was underway."[8]

"Time was of the essence, for the field of handheld calculators was already blooming, albeit calculators with only four functions and

mostly using discrete components. It was agreed that a concrete proposal should be readied by Groundhog Day in February 1971, at which
time a final decision would be made. The day arrived, a proposal was
submitted, and it was approved." [Once again, Hewlett overruled the
objections of HP's marketing people, who asserted that no one would
pay $400 for an electronic slide rule.] "By September of that year, pro-
totype working models were available, and two months later manufacturing was underway."[9]

HP thought they would do well to sell 10,000 of the $395 product in
its first year of production. In fact, they sold over 100,000 units. Programmable calculators turned out to be one of the most successful
products Hewlett-Packard ever made. By 1994, the company had sold
over 15 million of them.

LED displays were critical to the success of the HP-35. To produce
thousands of displays a month required tooling up for mass production,
which in turn represented a significant capital investment. But for
Hewlett and Packard, "there was no question," Burmeister recalled.
"You gave them the numbers, [told them] we're going to have to build
five or more reactors, hire people and rent space, and that's going to
cost an awful lot of money. And [they said], 'No problem, just tell us
what you need.' We did, and the plans were approved."

By 1979, with Monsanto pulled up and out of the running, HP had
emerged as the clear leader of the LED market. That year, estimated
Business Week, although much of HP's production would be used in-
ternally, sales to outside customers would total $75 million.[10] The secret
of HP's success, the magazine suggested, was that as a company in the
systems business, it had a good sense of potential applications in the
outside market. The director of a rival firm's optoelectronics operation
was quoted as saying that he saw HP as "the Cadillac of the industry."

HP would shortly be thinking of Cadillacs itself. Not as a term of
self-approval, but as a new market that would emerge as a result of the
next breakthrough in LED technology. But this breakthrough would
not be initiated by Hewlett-Packard. In 1982 George Craford,
now happily translated from Monsanto to the bosom of the Palo
Alto–based firm, would make a trip to Japan. In Yokohama, he visited
the laboratories of Stanley Electric, where he met with the company's
R&D chief, Teshima Toru.

Despite not being able to speak each other's languages, the two men got on well together. As a parting gift, Teshima gave the American a couple of his company's latest red LEDs. They were by far the brightest that Craford had ever seen.

Stanley Electric was founded in 1920 by an entrepreneur called Kitano Takaharu to manufacture light bulbs for automobiles. Kitano had read about the adventures of the great nineteenth-century journalist and African explorer Henry Morton Stanley. Inspired by the great man's exploits, Kitano decided to adopt Stanley as his company's brand name. He vowed that, just as Stanley the man had brought light to the Dark Continent, so Stanley the firm would bring light to the dark highways of the world.

This was an ambitious vision. In 1920 cars were being produced in Japan, but only on a very limited basis. Local manufacturers were unable to compete with a flood of imports, mostly from the United States (such as the chauffeur-driven Buick owned by Morita Akio's father). It was not until 1933–the year that saw the establishment of both Nissan and Toyota–that annual domestic Japanese production of cars passed the 1,000 mark. Nineteen thirty-three was also the year of Stanley's incorporation.

By the time Teshima arrived for a job interview at Stanley in 1949, the company had perhaps 250 employees. But the firm was proud of its status as Japan's largest specialist manufacturer of automobile light bulbs. The job interview did not go well. Fresh out of school, the 24-year-old Teshima fancied himself as something of an expert on vacuum tubes used in radio communications. As he saw it, tungsten lamps–Stanley's stock-in-trade–represented a much lower level of technology.

"If you do vacuum tubes, I'll join," he told the interviewer jauntily, "if you don't, I won't." How long had Teshima been studying vacuum tubes? the latter wanted to know. "Three years," came the response. The interviewer was nonplussed, wondering how the young man could be so cocksure of himself with so little experience.

Despite this inauspicious beginning, Teshima was hired. In Japan in 1949, with the economy in recession and thousands of demobilized soldiers looking for work, jobs were extremely scarce. Teshima's modest qualifications would probably not have been enough to get him into a blue-chip firm like Nippon Electric or Toshiba.

Production of Japanese passenger cars resumed in 1952. Initially, taxi fleets accounted for most of the demand. But with the coming of the income-doubling 1960s, sales of cars to Japanese consumers took off. In 1967, the number of automobiles produced in Japan passed the 10 million mark. As a supplier of lights to most of Japan's major car makers, Stanley rode the boom all the way.

By 1969, the company was flush enough to be able to celebrate its fiftieth anniversary in business by establishing that corporate status symbol par excellence, a research center. As a factory manager and with other, better qualified people on the company's payroll, Teshima was an unusual choice to run this laboratory. But somehow, he got the job. What themes should he and his young charges pursue? It was left entirely up to Teshima to decide.

As a nation, the Japanese are martyrs to anxiety. They suffer from a chronic sense of insecurity that they call *fuan*. Teshima was no exception. But in his case, the apprehension had a specific cause. Edison had patented his carbon-filament incandescent light in 1880. Thirty-five years later, GE substituted tungsten wire for carbon as the filament material and filled the globe with inert gas. In the ensuing half century, there had essentially been no major changes in lamp technology.

But Teshima was well aware that there were plenty of talented scientists in the world. What would happen, he used to fret, if one of them were to come up with a better way of producing light? If that happened, it could mean the end of the road for Stanley, whose entire business was based on the manufacture of tungsten bulbs for car lamps. Tortured by the prospect, he would lie awake nights, tossing and turning.

Teshima's uneasiness was further fueled by a visit he made during the 1960s to the engineers in Toyota's design group. At that time, transistor radios were beginning to be installed in cars. Transistors were eminently suitable for automotive applications because they used almost no power. But the radios needed an indicator light to show whether they were on or off. For this application, a miniature incandescent lamp was used. The trouble was that the indicator lamp used ten times more power than the radio.

"What's the point in trying to save power," the Toyota engineers complained, "when you have to waste it on something you don't really need?" And Teshima could only bow his head and humbly apologize: Very sorry, customer-san, but tungsten lamps are the only kind there is.

Then one day, not long after Teshima became Stanley's technical director, came word from a friend in the United States. It concerned a new kind of light that the Americans had begun using for the indicator lamps in their satellites. These new lamps had no filaments, didn't produce heat, used little power, were strong against vibration and shock, and apparently had very long lives. They were, in short, everything that the tungsten lamp was not.

Teshima's recurring nightmare had come true. The long-feared threat to Stanley's core business was at hand.

In a flash, the news clarified the problem of what research theme to pursue at Stanley's new lab. It was immediately obvious to Teshima that what they had to do was find out how to make light-emitting diodes, whatever they might be. The only question was, How to go about it? There were two possible avenues to explore. One was to license the technology from an American firm. The other, more risky, approach was to look for a local source of technology. To increase his chances of success, Teshima decided to pursue both courses in parallel.

Licensing the technology from the U.S. turned out to be a disaster. Stanley contracted with a start-up that claimed to have the technology for making Monsanto-style LEDs. Two years later, after Stanley had invested a lot of cash in the venture, it turned out that the Americans had promised more than they could deliver. The failure of this approach left Stanley totally reliant on local technology and, in particular, on Japan's best-known—and most controversial—semiconductor specialist, Nishizawa Jun'ichi.

Nishizawa was born in 1926, into a family of academics. His father had been dean of engineering at Tohoku University, where he and his younger brother would both become professors.[11] The university had racked up an enviable reputation, unusual in Japan, for original research. Earlier in the century its engineering faculty had boasted the likes of Honda Kotaro, the developer of high performance steel, and Yagi Hidetsugu, the inventor of the television antenna. At the same time, however, Tohoku is also located some 250 miles north of Tokyo, and as much again from Osaka. A long way, in other words, from where corporate Japan makes its decisions.

When the transistor was invented at Bell Labs, Nishizawa was just 21 years old. Two years later, while still a graduate student at Tohoku, he came up with his first invention. This was a PIN diode, a device that had significant commercial potential in microwave and power applications (the initials stand for *positive-intrinsic-negative*). As with many of his inventions, there is controversy over the extent of Nishizawa's contribution. Nishizawa filed for a patent on the diode in Japan a few days before Bob Hall of GE lodged an application on a similar device in the United States.

Despite the existence of a local alternative, Japanese electronics companies preferred to license the technology from GE, even though doing so cost them far more in royalty payments. Nishizawa couldn't understand this at all. He went to visit the makers to ask them the reason for their preference. Their answer was instructive: "If we put 'Made under license from General Electric of the U.S.' on the box, then Japanese customers will buy them," he was told, "whereas if we put 'Made under license from Nishizawa Jun'ichi of Tohoku University,' they won't."

This use of foreign technology for marketing purposes shocked the proud young scientist.[12] It also set the pattern for what was to come, a struggle for acceptance that would last the next thirty years. Inventions continued to pour out of Nishizawa's creative mind. He took out dozens of patents on his ideas. They included one of the earliest patents on a semiconductor laser (1957) and another that predated work elsewhere on optical fibers (1964). But many of these patents are controversial because they do not explain how the ideas could be reduced to practice, as engineers say. In other words, how working devices could be made based on them.

As far as the Japanese electronics industry was concerned, Nishizawa's inventions were unproven. Though more expensive, it was safer to rely on tried-and-tested technologies imported from the United States. Nor did Nishizawa's attitude help his cause. He was irrepressibly outspoken about the merit of his own ideas. At the same time, Nishizawa was also contemptuous of companies that, unwilling or unable to come up with anything original themselves, were forced to license from abroad. They were, in his bitter words, "contaminated by U.S. technology."

Some sense of Nishizawa's attitude can be gained from the following story about the comments Nishizawa made circa 1979, at the mandatory public review MITI held on the completion of its VLSI project. Asked to grade the initiative, Nishizawa said he gave it ninety out of a hundred. This was a surprise, since everyone knew what a dim view Nishizawa held of the VLSI project, whose basic aim had been to catch up with the U.S. in microchip production technology. He was then asked to explain how he had arrived at such a figure. Nishizawa was happy to oblige, saying that he had awarded the ninety marks for those parts of the project that had attempted to mimic U.S. technology, which had been entirely successful. He added that he had deducted ten points for those parts that had attempted to do something original, which in his view had been a complete failure.[13]

Whenever Nishizawa thought that companies were infringing his patents, he would threaten to sue. This upset Japanese firms, which were not accustomed to dealing with uppity young academics. To be sure, they were happy enough sending their people up to Tohoku to get laboratory practice in handling semiconductors. But as far as Nishizawa's grand ideas were concerned—Japanese industry simply didn't want to know.

In his struggle to gain acceptance, however, Nishizawa did have some supporters. Most notable among them was Chiba Genya, a young physicist who returned to Japan in 1961 from graduate studies at New York's Columbia University. Looking around for something to do, Chiba became involved in technology licensing agreements. "What I found was a very sad situation," Chiba recalled. "Those contracts [with U.S. companies like Fairchild, GE, IBM, RCA, Texas Instruments, and Western Electric] were so *unfair*."

The percentage of royalties paid to individual firms was not so high. But in order to manufacture a single chip, a Japanese manufacturer might have to make payments to several different U.S. companies—2 percent to Western Electric for the use of its diffusion patents, 3.5 percent to Texas Instruments, and a further 4.5 percent to Fairchild for access to the Kilby and Noyce basic microchip patents. With the result that by the end of the 1960s, Japanese integrated circuit producers were paying 10 percent of their semiconductor sales as royalties to U.S. firms.[14]

Nor was the cost of licensing only financial. The contracts stipulated that any subsequent improvements to the technology made should belong to the owner, not to the originator. Reading such one-sided documents made Chiba angry. But licensing U.S. technology was the accepted practice among top management at big Japanese firms like Matsushita or Toshiba. After all, electronics was a highly competitive business—who could afford to waste years reinventing the wheel?

An exacerbating factor was the attitude of government. In their efforts to restructure the Japanese economy during the 1950s and 1960s, bureaucrats at the Ministry of International Trade & Industry encouraged Japanese firms to buy in American technology. They did this for two reasons. On the one hand, MITI had no confidence that local firms could compete on the basis of home-grown technology. On the other, the ministry exercised control over the companies via its monopoly on allocation of foreign exchange, which gave the bureaucrats the power to decide who licensed what. This factor led to a very ironic situation: MITI was supposed to support domestic firms. At the same time, however, the ministry was reluctant to do anything that would weaken its control over them. (To be fair, however, one should also add that, in encouraging Japanese firms to license technology, MITI was also attempting to prevent the Japanese economy from domination by foreign investment.)

For the domestic Japanese research community, overwhelming imports of technology were bad news indeed. When top management decided to eschew their work in favor of buying technology from the outside, researchers at Japanese companies inevitably became discouraged. By the late 1950s, concern among industrial and academic circles had grown to the point where there were fears that if wholesale imports continued, this would undermine the entire structure of the Japanese research establishment. In this gloomy atmosphere the Research & Development Corporation of Japan was established in 1961, as an offshoot of one of MITI's main rivals, the Science & Technology Agency.

The nonprofit corporation's charter was to bolster the precarious state of local research. In particular, the JRDC was intended to cater to the needs of small and medium-size companies. The big boys could afford to do their own research. Chiba became one of the new organization's first employees. His initial task was to try and break the stranglehold that the web of U.S. patents had on local chip makers. It was in this context that Chiba first came across the work of Nishizawa. Nishizawa had filed some early (1950) patents on a technology called ion implantation, which is used to dope semiconductors with impurities. Ion implantation would eventually replace Western Electric's diffusion technology, which in turn meant that the Japanese companies that adopted the new technique no longer had to pay Western Electric 2 percent on every chip they produced.

The founding of the JRDC happened to coincide with Nishizawa's elevation to professorhood, at the remarkably early age–for Japan–of 36. Nishizawa celebrated this newly acquired independence by setting up his own laboratory at Tohoku, the Semiconductor Research Institute, using the money that companies gave him to train their people. Several of Nishizawa's students would go on to make a name for themselves–most notably Toshiba's Masuoka Fujio, the inventor of "flash" memory, who spent six years at Tohoku. "Almost all Japanese companies followed U.S. technology," Masuoka said, "but Professor Nishizawa did not. He taught me that the most important thing for an engineer is not to follow another's technology. Since I joined Toshiba, in every case, I have tried to do original technology."

Now, with his own institute, Nishizawa was finally free to develop devices based on his ideas. The first of these was the static induction transistor.

The SIT was an independently arrived-at variant on Bill Shockley's field-effect transistor. Conceptually, both types of device date back to the early 1950s. Like the FET, the SIT could not be produced using the relatively primitive technology of that time. At his new institute, Nishizawa proceeded to build the first actual static induction transistors. They turned out to be, in at least one respect, superior to other solid-state devices. Conventional transistors were not suitable for use in audio amplifiers. The reason was that, at higher frequencies, their response flattened out, distorting reproduction and producing a tinny sound. Whereas, at the same frequencies, the response of vacuum tubes continued a graceful upward trajectory. (This is one reason why, even today, salesmen in some audio equipment shops continue to praise tubes and pooh-pooh transistors.)

Nishizawa's static induction transistor behaved exactly like a tube—as the inventor himself was the first to notice. An avid fan of classical music—Gregorian chants and Bach being particular favorites—Nishizawa built an amplifier incorporating SITs. With characteristic modesty, he noted that there were only two people in the world who could listen to music on transistors that they had developed—Shockley and himself. He announced his discovery at a technical meeting in Japan. As usual, Japanese industry greeted Nishizawa's claims with indifference.

Eventually, however, word of Nishizawa's results reached Mochida Yasunori, technical director of Yamaha. Mochida went up to Tohoku to see Nishizawa. After their meeting, an excited Nishizawa called Chiba. At long last, someone from industry had showed an interest in his ideas.

As we saw in chapter 7, Yamaha's goal was to make electronic musical instruments. But the firm was having trouble persuading Japanese semiconductor firms to manufacture chips to their specifications. It had become clear to Mochida, and to Yamaha's president Kawakami Gen'ichi, that if they wanted special devices, then they were going to have build their own factory and manufacture the chips themselves. But in the early days, digital FM chips proved too difficult for them to make. The first semiconductors that Yamaha produced were static induction transistors.

The development of the static induction transistor by Nishizawa and Yamaha was underwritten, at Chiba's urging, by the JRDC. The corporation invested the money on the understanding that, if the venture was successful, Yamaha would repay the principal together with modest royalties on the technology. If it failed, then Yamaha would not be obliged to repay the loan.

Within the JRDC, there was an argument about whether to invest in Yamaha, because of the risk involved. After all, the firm had no prior experience of making semiconductors; it was entirely possible that they might give up in the middle. Chiba visited Kawakami to see whether Yamaha's president was serious about the whole business. He was.

The development was successful. The resultant products—SIT-based amplifiers and preamps for audiophiles—delivered exceptionally good sound reproduction. Though several times more expensive than conventional hi-fi systems, Yamaha's products sold well for a few years, until large companies like Matsushita managed to come up with rival devices whose response was almost as good as that of the SIT.

Then came the audio boom of the late 1960s when, post–*Sgt. Pepper*, pop music made the transition from low-fi mono to hi-fi stereo. From a specialist market, stereo sets exploded into something that no well-equipped living room could be seen without.

The fact that Yamaha had had no prior experience with semiconductors was one reason that the relationship between Nishizawa and Mochida's people had gone so well. Engineers who had been educated–"contaminated"–in the United States would argue with Nishizawa based on what they had learned at MIT or Stanford or wherever. But to Yamaha's young engineers, who knew nothing else, Nishizawa *Sensei* was the be-all and end-all of semiconductor technology. From the professor's point of view, such eager novices were much easier to educate.

"You had to be a believer in what Nishizawa said," Chiba recalled laughing. "That was the important thing." Another supplicant who made the pilgrimage to Tohoku to see the professor was Teshima Toru of Stanley. With Stanley, it would be the same story. Knowing nothing whatsoever about LEDs, Teshima put his trust one hundred percent in Nishizawa. And this relationship, too, would work very well.

It began in 1969, when several Japanese companies were already making LEDs on a trial basis, Toshiba being the front runner. A Toshiba researcher had recently returned from Bell Labs, bringing with him the phone company's gallium phosphide technology. Other large companies, including Matsushita, Nippon Electric, Sanyo, and Sharp, were developing light emitters based on the Monsanto (gallium arsenide phosphide) model. As yet, however, there was no clear idea of what the markets for the devices would be, and therefore no commercial production.

The presence in the field of so many big and active rivals heightened Teshima's already well-developed sense of crisis. "I felt that we might get left behind," he said. Failure to enter the LED market could have a disastrous impact on Stanley's sales of car lights and small lamps. At the same time, Teshima was well aware of the fact that "because we were starting from zero, we were taking a big risk."

Nishizawa had recently come up with an original way of making LEDs out of a new, slightly different alloy, aluminum gallium arsenide. This was not an entirely new development. Aluminum gallium arsenide was first reported at a 1967 device conference in Santa Barbara by Jerry Woodall of IBM. But IBM was not initially interested in visible-light emitters. According to HP's George Craford, "What Nishizawa did, and then Stanley capitalized on, they basically came up with a growth system that worked, that produced a little higher efficiency, and that could be turned into a mass production technology. So it was kind of an evolutionary thing. [Nishizawa] certainly made a major contribution, then Stanley picked that up from him and turned it into a business, and they were the first out there with commercial aluminum gallium arsenide devices, no question about it. So I give them credit for doing that."

The new method promised to yield lights that would be both cheaper and brighter than ones made the conventional way. Once again, at Chiba's urging, the JRDC reluctantly (because of the risk) underwrote the transfer of the technology from Nishizawa's lab to Stanley. In addition to this government funding, the company was expected to invest considerable amounts of its own money.

Stanley's top management left the decision on whether to go ahead with the development up to Teshima. "They knew that I was a nuisance," Teshima said, "and I think they were worried that if they didn't let me have my own way, I'd keep bothering them until I got it."

Development of the technology lasted four years. For the first three years things did not go well at all. "We kept going round in circles," Teshima recalled, "and we kept making mistakes." For these, the research director was penalized. "When it came to spring salary rises, and to midsummer and year-end bonuses, it was 'Teshima-San, you've lost so much money, and the company's results are poor, so you're not getting much of a rise or a bonus this time.' "

Teshima protested that losing money during the development phase of a project was only natural. It was after all being spent for a good reason. "But I was the only one out of sixteen directors who thought that. . . . [Meanwhile] the union complained that the company was losing money because one person was doing research that no one asked him to do. That was the sort of thing that was said, and there were all sorts of other painful things, too."

But although nobody within the company was rooting for Teshima, nobody was actually advocating that he should quit, either. "The board of directors never took a vote on whether we should continue with LEDs," Teshima recalled. "That was one good thing about the Stanley people."

After three years' work and nothing to show for it, Stanley's researchers finally figured out what they had been doing wrong. The problem, ironically, was that for all their protestations of devotion, the disciples had not been following their teacher's instructions closely enough.

Nishizawa had insisted that the key to success in growing LEDs was that the reaction should take place while the temperature in the furnace was extremely stable. But Stanley had been cutting corners. The company did not have the deep pockets of a conglomerate like Toshiba. In addition, Teshima had lost a lot of money on the failed attempt to bring in technology from the United States. So his researchers had tried to be as economical with their equipment purchases as possible, and in so doing, they had made their reaction chamber too small. Inserting materials into such a small space caused wild fluctuations in the temperature of the furnace. The result: dud devices.

Now they knew what they had to do—scale up the furnace as close to the size of the actual production equipment as possible. But the development deadline was almost upon them. Teshima went to Chiba to see whether the latter would allow development to be extended by a further six months. "I thought Chiba-San would tell us off for not having done things properly, because he was a government official." But Chiba was well aware that it would take them more than six months just to build the furnace. He told Teshima that the JRDC would postpone the deadline for a year. And Teshima was delighted, because a year was what he'd secretly wanted all along.

But though reprieved, Teshima was still under fire from all sides within the company. He told Stanley's owner, Kitano Takaharu's son Takaoki, that he would accept full responsibility for the performance of the expensive new furnace. Teshima even went so far as to hand Kitano an undated letter of resignation, to be used if things went wrong.

Teshima's faith in Nishizawa finally paid off. When the very first batch of devices grown in the new, enlarged furnace were hooked up,

Teshima Toru (left) and Nishizawa Jun'ichi at Stanley, c. 1975 (Teshima Toru)

they emitted a really bright light. This was in 1973. Three years of technology refinements later, Stanley was producing the brightest LEDs in the world.

Teshima was not out of the woods yet. They had made LEDs, but at first Stanley could not sell them, even though they were so bright. The first hurdle Teshima had to overcome was convincing his own salesmen of the product's merit. This was not easy. "You could line up Stanley's lamps next to LEDs made by other companies and when you switched them on, anyone could tell that Stanley's were twice as bright as the others," Teshima recalled, "but Stanley's salesmen still thought that Toshiba or Matsushita lights were better."

The problem, Teshima explained, was that "in Japan, brand image is too strong. There's much less of that sort of thing in the U.S. and Europe; they evaluate things fairly there—if something's good, it's good. But in Japan, people think that if something is made by a big company, then it must be good; but if it's made by a small company, then there must be something wrong with it."

The first time Stanley showed their LEDs outside Japan was at a trade fair, the 1976 Wescon show in Los Angeles. The initial reaction was one of skepticism. Visitors marveled at the brightness of Stanley's LEDs, but presumed that since the devices were twice as bright as conventional lights, they would surely need twice as much current to drive them? Teshima assured them that Stanley's devices drew no more current than regular LEDs.

The next question was, Well, isn't the operating life half as long? Teshima replied that, since the devices had only just been developed, he didn't honestly know how long their life would be. What he could say was that, compared to other LEDs, Stanley's gave off much less heat, because the efficiency with which they converted electricity into light was so high. So—who knew?—perhaps their lifetime would be twice as long.

The third thing most visitors wanted to know was, From which American company had Stanley licensed the technology? And Teshima would tell them proudly, "We didn't license it from an American company, this technology came from Professor Nishizawa of Tohoku University."

Impressed by the devices, some Americans told Teshima that Stanley should give the LEDs a suitably sexy name—like "super-bright," or something like that. And Teshima was very happy about such comments, because Stanley's sales manager was standing at his side, listening to everything that was said. There would be no more doubts as to the superiority of Stanley's LEDs when they got home.

But having overcome the in-house credibility problem, Stanley now faced a sterner challenge. When his researchers first succeeded in making LEDs, Teshima expected to be able to sell the devices for ¥250 ($1.25) each. But Stanley embarked on production only to find the industry engulfed in a price war. The result was that Teshima wasn't even able to get ¥50 (25¢) for his devices. And the situation continued to deteriorate; fierce competition drove prices down until they finally bottomed out at around ¥10 [5¢]. At this level, Stanley were losing ¥100 [50¢] on every device they produced.

What was happening was that companies like Monsanto and Texas Instruments were applying the logic of the learning curve to their prices. The more you cut prices (went the argument), the more devices customers would buy, the more experience in production you gained, enabling you to cut your prices further. This strategy had worked wonderfully well in expanding markets for transistors and integrated circuits. With LEDs, however, it had a fatal flaw: No matter how much makers discounted, customers simply weren't buying. But though their sales weren't increasing, U.S. makers kept on discounting. The result was that by 1980, quite a few companies had either gone bankrupt or, like Monsanto and TI, quit making LEDs.

The cause of this madness, Teshima thought, was that market studies had promised too much, and as a result, people had become greedy. "They used to decide the unit price based on nothing more than mental arithmetic," he recalled, "like, If we can sell so many tens of thousands of units, how much do we charge for them?" Among U.S. firms only Hewlett-Packard refrained from selling below cost in order to gain market share. Teshima was full of admiration for the way HP had behaved. The U.S. firm had moved ahead steadily, improving the technology as they went along.

As the price war raged on, for a second time it looked as if Teshima would have to quit Stanley. The technology on which he had bet his career was costing the company a fortune. Then, just as Teshima was about to throw in the towel, Monsanto abruptly quit, followed shortly afterward by Texas Instruments. With two of the biggest producers out of the way, Stanley's LEDs started to sell well. Ten years after LED development at the company began, things were finally looking up.

To be sure, there was still competition. Ever on the lookout for emerging markets to which to apply its formidable expertise in volume production, Matsushita swooped down upon LEDs. Toshiba, which had temporarily suspended manufacture of the devices because they were not profitable, resumed production. But even against such giants Stanley was able to hold its own.

The fierce price wars of the late 1970s had honed the company's competitive edge. Better than most, Teshima now knew how to make LEDs at low cost and still make a profit. And Stanley's LEDs were much brighter than Matsushita's, or anyone else's for that matter. At the same time, the market for the devices was expanding into new and unexpected areas ... like graphic equalizers, for example. Now commonplace in consumer stereos, these devices divide up the audible spectrum, enabling listeners to selectively boost or reduce individual frequency bands. Equalizers were originally invented in the late 1930s as an aid to medical diagnosis. Several microphones were attached to the patient's chest, and the doctor would don a pair of headphones to listen to the heartbeat. The equalizer enabled him to filter out certain frequencies and boost others, to detect otherwise hard-to-hear abnormalities such as heart murmurs.

The leading manufacturer of equalizers was a British company, BSR. This firm had made a name for itself in audio gear such as pickup cartridges and speakers. But it was not until the mid 1970s that two BSR employees—Roger Allen and Vic Amador—took what had hitherto been a piece of scientific equipment and turned it into a consumer product. Equalizers had been used in recording and broadcast studios. But no one had ever thought of using them in a home environment before.

BSR called their products Sound Shapers. Early models mounted on their front panels an array consisting of forty-one plastic sliders—little plastic knobs, one for each frequency band, that you could move up and down. On the end of each knob was a white line. The idea was that, once you'd set the sliders, you could see the equalization curve. Trouble was, the curve was hard to make out from across the room. Or in the dark, for that matter. Brooding on this shortcoming in the BSR booth at the 1975 Chicago Consumer Electronics Show, Allen came up with a solution. He asked Amador, "Can you imagine all these things with *lights* on them?"

To realize this application, BSR chose Stanley's LEDs. Not only were they the brightest, the Japanese firm's lights were also small enough to fit into the end of the sliders. Teshima was delighted. Prior to this point, LEDs had mostly been used as power on–off indicator lights, which meant that products only needed one or two of them. Now here were these crazy Brits who wanted to put dozens of LEDs in a single product.

And this was just the beginning. Subsequent generations of equalizers incorporated all sort of LED-driven features, like lights that switched themselves on and off in time with the music. The new-look graphic equalizers took the market by storm. "We blew people away with them," Allen recalled. "The purists went bananas ... people saw these things and they just had to have them, so that they could sit and watch the dancing lights."

Graphic equalizers went on to become a standard component in audio systems. Today, you even see them in cars. To be sure, LEDs have long since been replaced in such systems by cheaper types of displays, notably vacuum fluorescents. But as it turned out, there were also other things that you could do for cars with light-emitting diodes.

LED makers had had their eyes on the auto market right from the beginning. An early Monsanto advertisement showed—thirty years prematurely—LEDs being used for the exterior lighting on an automobile. In the 1970s General Motors had attempted to hire George Craford away from Monsanto, because the car company suspected that LEDs might end up being used all over cars.

Interior applications, like the radio on–off indicator that had embarrassed Teshima at Toyota, came first. But it was not until the early 1980s that LEDs became sufficiently bright to allow their application to the lights on a car's exterior. By 1983, over three generations of technology, Stanley had increased the brightness of their lights by ten times. The company's LEDs were now brighter than incandescent lamps. So bright, in fact, that if you looked at them for too long, they'd hurt your eyes. The tiny red lights could be clearly seen in direct sunlight. That meant they could be used outdoors. And the obvious outdoor application was cars. In addition to mounting some 30 bulbs inside its dashboard, the average automobile uses up to 20 lamps in external applications like headlamps, indicators, and brake lights.

But it turns out that automobile makers are among the most conservative companies on the planet. Concerns about safety and price deter them from rushing into new technologies. Much of the credit for the introduction of LEDs as exterior lights on cars belongs, not to an automobile company, but to the U.S. government—more specifically, to the National Highway Traffic Safety Administration.

Statistics had long shown that rear-end collisions constitute about a quarter of all multivehicle accidents. "Therefore, it is not surprising that over the past 25 years, much research has been devoted to evaluating alternative vehicle rear lighting, signaling, and brake systems that would enhance their conspicuousness and visibility, thus inducing quicker accident avoidance maneuvers from following drivers. This line of research culminated in the development, evaluation, demonstration of effectiveness, and finally, implementation of the Center High-Mounted Stop Light."[15] These lamps have been standard equipment on U.S. passenger cars since 1 September 1985.

The problem from a design standpoint was, How to implement center high-mount brake lights? To be sure, you could simply stick a large, red-filtered tungsten bulb (or bulbs) plus bulky enclosure in the back window. Many designers chose, and continue to choose, this option. But by using a long, thin strip of LEDs there was now also the possibility of installing the brake light in a car's spoiler, or along the rim of the rear window. Since LED strips are less than an inch thick, they can be attached directly to the sheet metal of the car body.

There was a precedent for this application. During the 1950s, researchers at General Electric had come up with the halogen lamp to accommodate demand for tiny, powerful lights that could fit within the razorlike wings of supersonic jet aircraft. Forty years on, halogen bulbs finally became cheap enough for use in desk lamps and domestic lighting.

But were LEDs reliable enough for use in cars? Safety standards for cars are extremely tough, and they were based on tungsten lamps. Teshima sent engineers to Washington three times, to make the case for Stanley's LEDs at hearings and discussions held by federal agencies and the Society for Automotive Engineers. He came away impressed by the procedure. "So long as you satisfy people that you can deliver the goods, I think America is a place that evaluates new technology very fairly, even if it comes from a Japanese company," Teshima said. Getting regulatory approval for safety standards for a completely new type of light in Japan would have taken much longer. "With the Japanese government, it's always, There's no precedent—what shall we do?" he said. "Changing the law in Japan takes a long time."

Having overcome the regulatory hurdle in the United States, Teshima's final challenge was to get LEDs designed into cars. The first company to pick up on the possibility was General Motors. The firm dispatched a team of engineers from its Detroit technical center to visit Stanley in Tokyo. The Americans told Teshima that they wanted to use the Japanese firm's LEDs, and suggested that engineers from both companies should do joint research. The first GM car to be equipped with LED center-mounted brake lights was a Corvette, a prototype that was tried out in the U.S. The rationale behind the choice of the Corvette as test bed, according to one industry analyst, was that "cost would not necessarily be a factor for an upmarket vehicle, and the high-techiness would be a differentiator for Chevrolet's 'image car.'"[16]

Having satisfied themselves that Stanley's lamps passed muster for practical use, GM installed them in its 1993 model Cadillac. This, however, was not the first commercial vehicle to mount LEDs as brake lights. "Unfortunately, GM is an extremely large company," Teshima explained, "and it took a long time for them to reach the practical application stage." Other companies moved faster. The first production model to hit the roads with LED center high-mount brake lights was a Nissan Fairlady. And after that, most Japanese auto makers started using LEDs in models that were equipped with spoilers. The first production car to use Hewlett-Packard's high-brightness LEDs, which were developed in response to Stanley's, was the 1995 Thunderbird.

This was vindication indeed for Teshima. His premonition that solid-state lights would replace tungsten bulbs in cars—albeit, initially, on a limited basis—had turned out to be completely accurate. Teshima had challenged a big dream and he had been successful. But there was also some cream on his cake. During the extensive tests they performed, GM's engineers discovered that in addition to offering twice the brightness of incandescents and more flexible styling, LEDs also conferred a much more important advantage.

With tungsten bulbs there is a lag between the time your foot hits the brake pedal, and the brake light coming on. The filament of the light needs time to heat up. With LEDs, by contrast, you get 100 percent output instantaneously. Driving down the highway at a speed of 60 miles per hour, the driver of the car behind gains about four yards of extra reaction time from the ultrafast turn-on of the LEDs on the car in front. Or, to put it another way, about the length of a car. The notion that his little lights might reduce the number of lives lost in rear-end collisions made Teshima very happy indeed.

In 1985, as a reward for his success with LEDs, Teshima became president of Stanley. He was then faced with a very difficult decision. Thanks to their existing relationships with car makers, Stanley was able to dominate the market for automotive-use LEDs, winning a share of around 80 percent. But because LEDs for automotive use were still more expensive than tungsten bulbs, and because of the innate conservatism of the auto makers, Teshima could not rely on sales to the car industry. He concluded that, if the company was to continue to grow, they would have to look for new markets further afield.

For example, one attractive prospect was information display boards. Visit an airport or a train station, especially in Japan, and you will see dozens of such boards. Or, the stock price displays that are prominently located in the retail outlets of brokers. Or, outdoor advertisement billboards, like the ones you see outside gas stations. Or, again in Japan, *pachinko* parlors, gaudy pinball arcades that advertise their existence through copious use of Las Vegas style neon. In the 1990s, the craft of neon-tube bending was in decline. LEDs offered an attractive replacement, one which moreover could be *programmed* to display messages. Each of these applications uses thousands, if not hundreds of thousands, and, in some cases, millions of lights. As of 1995, the world's largest outdoor display board was the Sky Screen, located in Tianjin, China. Built by Hewlett-Packard, the full-color screen measures 40 meters long by 14 meters high and uses over 3 million LEDs.[17] (In 1997 this was topped, at least temporarily, by the massive 52m by 19m screen used by the rock band U2 on their PopMart tour.)

But to challenge such new markets, Stanley needed large injections of capital to finance the expansion. That meant selling stock, and that in turn brought Teshima into conflict with Stanley's chairman and owner, Kitano Takaoki. The more stock they sold, the more diluted were Kitano shares, the less influential the family became. And Kitano wanted his son, Takanori, to inherit the firm. Chairman and president clashed. In 1990, Teshima retired from Stanley.

That year, semiconductors accounted for around a quarter of the company's overall sales, a business worth some $200 million. Automobile LEDs represented a relatively small chunk of that, at about 20 percent of the total. Looking back over twenty years of effort, Teshima was entitled to feel a sense of satisfaction. "Starting from research and development of a new technology, to the best product in the world, and even with someone like me as a manager," he reflected, "Stanley's done quite well, really."

Though retired and nearly 70 years old, the irrepressible Teshima still found that he had plenty of energy and passion. He set up a one-man technology development consultancy called I-HITS. "I chose 'I' for international," Teshima explained, "'H' for human relations, the next 'I' for innovative industry, 'T' for technology transfer. That made 'HIT', and I thought, that's good, but a double hit is better than a single hit, so I added an 'S' for system or science, or whatever." He also came up with a motto for his new venture: "Out of mistakes come opportunities."

In April 1995, for the first time in almost forty years, Nick Holonyak journeyed to Tokyo. He came to receive the Japan Prize, Japan's highest award for scientific achievement. Established in 1982 with funds donated by the great Japanese entrepreneur Matsushita Konosuke, the award differs from the Nobel Prize in one significant respect. To win the Swedish award, you have to make an important discovery. But to win the Japan Prize, your discovery must also be of practical use.

The criterion of usefulness certainly applies to Holonyak's work. In his speech following the prize giving, he talked about the LED's progress over more than thirty years, from the origins of the tiny device in his lab at GE to the worldwide, multibillion-dollar industry of today. As he rehearsed this progress for the audience, Holonyak took particular pride in pointing out the achievements of his former students.

In the early 1990s one alumnus of Holonyak's lab, Fred Kish, working at Hewlett-Packard under the direction of another, George Craford, came up with a further addition to the family of light-emitting alloys. Aluminum-indium-gallium-phosphide deposited on a transparent substrate extended the range of high-brightness LEDs, from the red to the orange to the yellow, and down into the green. These latest colors opened up new opportunities for replacing incandescent bulbs. For example, the ability to produce bright orange meant that LEDs could now function as the turn signals on automobiles.

Beyond such uses lay the biggest application of all—interior illumination. Light bulbs, in other words, as used in houses, schools, offices, factories, and everywhere else for that matter. "I'm not going to live to see it," Holonyak predicted, "because I'm 65 going on 66, but in the time scale of 100 years, all this lighting we've got around us, along with the other kinds of stuff—the semiconductor is going to do it all."

But if LEDs were going to replace the light bulb, then they had to be capable of producing *white* light. This, as every schoolchild learns, is formed by combining light of the three primary colors: red, green, and blue.[18]

People had been trying to make bright blue LEDs for twenty-five years. The quest for this particular grail had at one time or another included researchers from many of the biggest firms in the electronics industry. They included RCA, Hewlett-Packard, and Matsushita. But, as Holonyak pointed out in his speech, the grail had recently been claimed.

Astonishingly, the claimant turned out to be not just an outsider, but someone who came from so far outside the normal boundaries of the electronics world as to strain credulity to the breaking point. The man who made the breakthrough, Nakamura Shuji, was an obscure researcher working alone at a hitherto unknown Japanese company called Nichia Chemical.

10

The End of Edison

Nothing that we've done that's very good has been done very quickly—it's just too hard, too complicated. You study for a long time, you learn for a long time, and you work for a long time. But there is something worth doing.

—Nick Holonyak, Jr.

WHEN NAKAMURA SHUJI FIRST SET EYES on Nichia Chemical, his heart sank. It was not a pretty sight. A jungle of pines almost hid the company's ramshackle facilities. But though hard to see, Nichia was easy to smell. Such a stench could only come from a chemical factory. Clutching his nose, Nakamura wondered: Can I survive in a company like this?

For his part, Ogawa Nobuo, Nichia Chemical's founder and president, did his best to discourage the young man. "This is not the kind of company that someone like you should join," he warned Nakamura. "Think hard before you make up your mind." But fresh out of school, the electronics engineer didn't have much choice. He needed a job, it had to be local, and Nichia was the only firm around.

There was no way Nakamura could have known it, but in choosing Nichia he was making the best decision of his life. At Nichia, Ogawa would give Nakamura the kind of chance that researchers at larger firms could only dream about. And Nakamura would make the most of that chance. Fourteen years later, in 1993, he scooped the electronics industry by producing the world's first bright blue LED.

In the momentous late-twentieth-century shift from gross bulbous objects made of evacuated glass and hot metal to the nanoscale thin films of the microcosm, the final element was now in place. For Edison's electric light bulb, it was the beginning of the end.

Light-emitting diodes and lasers produce light by bringing together in a confined space energized electrons with positively charged holes. The wavelength, or color, of the light depends on the amount of energy the electrons must give off in order to recombine with the holes. Constrained by their basic physical properties, different materials give off different amounts of energy, hence emit different wavelengths of light.

Having produced first red, then green solid-state light emitters, it was only natural that researchers should also shoot for the third of the primary colors, blue. From the earliest days of the technology it was clear what the advantages of having all three primaries would be. In theory, you could use them to build solid-state televisions and general-purpose lamps.[1] But the wavelength of blue light is shorter than those of the other primaries, beyond the range of the physical properties of the two original LED materials, gallium arsenide phosphide and gallium phosphide. So researchers turned to other materials to see whether they could go the distance.

The first of these was silicon carbide, a bluish-black compound that contains naturally occurring positive-negative junctions, the basis for light emission. Silicon carbide has been known as an emitter of light since 1907. Work done at the Signal Corps Engineering Laboratories in New Jersey in the early 1950s clarified the mechanism of emission. Westinghouse made some of the early running in silicon carbide. General Electric was also involved. By 1968, GE was marketing silicon carbide diodes that emitted yellow light. Shortly afterwards, the material was persuaded to produce blue, too. But silicon carbide LEDs were only a fraction as bright as red and green ones, and there were good physical reasons to suppose that this would always be the case.[2]

A second possibility was semiconductors like zinc selenide, which were compounded from materials in columns II and VI of the periodic table. These "cunning alloys," as David Thomas dubbed them, promised to be more efficient emitters than silicon carbide. But they proved devilishly difficult to make. In particular, for a long time it was impossible to fabricate positive-type zinc selenide, ruling out the construction of a p-n junction, the basic structure required to make an LED. But their potential as shorter-wavelength light emitters made the II–VI compounds the focus of the bulk of research in this field for the next twenty-five years.

The third candidate was also the least likely. Gallium nitride was first synthesized in 1969 at RCA's David Sarnoff Research Center in Princeton by a young researcher called Paul Maruska. His boss was Jacques Pankove, a senior scientist at the center.

Born in Russia, Pankove grew up in France. In 1942, he was lucky to escape the Nazis, eventually ending up at the University of California at Berkeley, where he graduated in 1944. Pankove spent the next four years doing a stint in the military, then getting his master's degree. In 1948, he arrived at the Sarnoff Center, where he would spend the next thirty-seven years.[3]

Pankove's first job at RCA was to work on a new invention, the transistor. To obtain the necessary germanium, he would crack open Western Electric diodes. Many years later, Pankove would claim that "my work on making the prototype of the first commercial transistor is what launched RCA into the transistor business." Pankove stayed with transistors until 1956, winning many patents in the process. Then a sabbatical spent at the Ecole Normale Supérieure in Paris set Pankove thinking about the possibility of making a semiconductor laser. Seeing no commercial potential in this idea, RCA management told him not to bother.

Despite this lack of encouragement, Pankove persisted. In 1961, while studying the luminescence of gallium arsenide, he made one of the first p-n junction LEDs. But when the great race to make semiconductor lasers commenced, Pankove was handicapped by having to work alone. Following the announcement by the groups at GE and IBM that they had succeeded in producing lasers, RCA management woke up and rallied round with support. Two weeks later, Pankove demonstrated his first laser. But from a scientific point of view, that was already too late.

Nonetheless, during the 1960s Pankove continued to work on light emitters. In 1969, he went back to his alma mater, Berkeley, where he wrote a book on lasers that became a set undergraduate text on the subject. On his return to Princeton, Pankove asked Maruska what the young scientist had been up to while he had been gone. Maruska told him that he had synthesized a new material called gallium nitride.

Theory predicted that the compound should have been a good light emitter. But in trying to measure its luminescence, Maruska had drawn a blank. It was not until several months later that Pankove discovered the reason for this puzzling negative result. The window of the measuring equipment his protégé had been using was coated with a protective layer. This layer blocked light at precisely those wavelengths that gallium nitride was most likely to emit.

Pankove replaced the coated window with one made from a transparent material, and *zut alors!* "I got a sample of gallium nitride," he recalled, "and the signal was tremendous—it pinned the needle. So we were quite excited about that, and at that point I decided to work on gallium nitride."

RCA management grudgingly gave Pankove approval to go ahead. "I was told, 'Well, it's an interesting material, but there's no commercial value to it, so don't make a big project out of it.' " Pankove's first step was to try and make a p-n junction. But as with zinc selenide, frustratingly, it proved impossible to make gallium nitride positive type. So Pankove fell back on an alternative, less efficient device structure, known as metal-insulator-semiconductor, which did not require positive-type material.

In 1971, after a year's research, he made gallium nitride MIS LEDs of several colors—including blue. "And RCA said, 'Oh, that's very nice—we should make a study of what the market is for [blue light emitters].'" The survey was conducted by an executive who was about to retire from one of the corporation's manufacturing divisions. "And he didn't want to get involved with anything new at all," Pankove recalled. The survey concluded that what customers wanted was not a different color, but a cheaper LED. Monsanto's marketing people had said exactly the same thing when George Craford presented them with a yellow LED. Since it was unlikely that Pankove's LEDs could be made cheaper than the conventional ones, there would thus be no market for them.

Pankove continued to work on gallium nitride, devising alphanumeric displays made out of the material and ways of producing them.

"But there was no interest, and I was asked to stop." Pankove soldiered on against mounting resistance from RCA management. "Every time the vice president of the laboratories saw the words 'gallium nitride' in my progress reports, his face would turn red and [he would say], 'What!—are you still working on this?' " In 1973, the pressure finally got to Pankove. He gave up and moved on to other topics.

Elsewhere, by the mid-1970s, it was the same story. Gallium nitride was regarded as a hopeless case: It was hard to grow, you couldn't make a p-n junction out of the material, so why waste time working on it?

The idea that he might have been wasting his time seems not to have occurred to Akasaki Isamu. On graduating from Kyoto University in 1952, Akasaki joined Kobe Kogyo. There he worked in the laboratory of Arizumi Tetsuya, the scientist who the previous year—together with Rocket Sasaki—had brought back transistor technology from RCA. It was a heady time. In 1953, thanks to the efforts of Arizumi and his team, Kobe Kogyo became the first Japanese company to develop a transistor. But the good days would not last. By the early 1960s, Kobe Kogyo was in deep financial trouble. In 1963, Arizumi quit to become a professor at the newly established department of electronic engineering at Nagoya University. He took Akasaki with him.

In Japan's go-go sixties, universities were not the only places establishing new labs. As we have seen elsewhere, Japanese companies, too, were investing in research centers. Matsushita already had a big lab at its headquarters in Osaka, but the focus of this facility was development, not research. The company decided to set up a second center, in Tokyo, with a brief to investigate new concepts. The lab was headed by Koike Yujiro, a well-known professor from Tohoku University. Around him Koike gathered a staff drawn from national universities, consisting mostly of assistant professors in their mid- to late thirties, reckoned to be the most creative age for a researcher. Among them was Akasaki.

At Matsushita's new lab, around 1969, Akasaki began work on compound semiconductors, a novel theme in Japan at that time. His research led him naturally to light emitters. Akasaki began by developing red, Holonyak-style, gallium arsenide phosphide diodes. This work was successful, but there was a problem—Monsanto's all-inclusive patent on crystal growth technology. Somehow Akasaki found a way of producing LEDs that did not infringe the U.S. patent. Matsushita commercialized the devices, but the LEDs did not sell well, because they were difficult to make.

Undaunted, Akasaki proceeded to grow green diodes using nitrogen doping, à la George Craford. In this, too, he was successful. "And because in a sense I'd done that, I wanted to move on to the next thing," he said. "So in 1973, I began work on gallium nitride." He thus picked up the baton that Pankove had recently been forced to drop at RCA.

For the rest of the 1970s, Akasaki experimented with techniques for growing gallium nitride films. The work culminated in 1981 with Matsushita announcing plans to commercialize a blue gallium nitride MIS-type LED. But in fact, the quality of the crystal was not up to snuff, and the device never shipped.

By this time, Akasaki was back at Nagoya University. There, throughout the 1980s, he continued to work on gallium nitride. Progress was painfully slow, but Akasaki refused to quit. In Japanese universities, professors are a law unto themselves. If they wish to pursue a particular line of research, there is nothing anyone can do to stop them going on until they retire. Thus it was with Akasaki. He hung in there and slugged it out. Eventually, his persistence paid off. He succeeded in taming the recalcitrant material.

Akasaki made two crucial breakthroughs. The first was to improve the quality of the crystal. A difficulty peculiar to gallium nitride is the lack of a good base material on which to grow it. Light-emitting devices are sandwiches consisting of many layers. If the devices are to work, the crystalline lattice of the layers needs to be as near defect free as makes no difference. This in turn necessitates that the structure of each successive layer be almost exactly the same as the previous one. It's like building a house out of different-colored Lego™ bricks, where the top and bottom of each brick are designed to snap onto their neighbors.

Other compounds had bases that matched the bricks. With gallium nitride, however, it was like trying to stack Lego bricks on top of a base made by a rival company. There was no compatible material on which to grow it. The closest match was sapphire. But the structure of sapphire crystals was considerably different from that of gallium nitride. The inevitable result was lots of tiny dislocations—defects in the crystal structure. Such dislocations are anathema to optical devices because they trap electrons and holes, preventing them from getting together to produce light.

Akasaki's solution to this problem was to insert a buffer layer of a third material (aluminum nitride) between the sapphire base and the gallium nitride device. This improved the quality of the material somewhat. But the resultant crystal was still full of dislocations.

Indeed, subsequent analysis would show that gallium nitride LEDs typically exhibit more than *10 billion* dislocations per square centimeter. That is an amazingly large number, especially when compared to conventional gallium arsenide– and phosphide-based light emitters. One hundred thousand dislocations per square centimeter is enough to severely degrade the ability of such LEDs to produce light. With 10 billion dislocations, they simply would not work.

At this point no one suspected what would later prove to be the astonishing truth: namely, that gallium nitride would behave very differently than all other known light-emitting materials. Even the best gallium nitride that researchers could grow would continue to be full of defects. Yet it would be capable of producing spectacular devices. Shaking their heads, theoretical physicists would eventually conclude that defects can sometimes play a helpful role. For the moment, however, Akasaki's pioneering work was overlooked.

With one exception, the same would also be true of his second, even more important breakthrough. In 1989, while examining a sample of doped gallium material in an electron microscope, Akasaki noticed something odd going on. The light the sample was emitting was getting brighter and brighter. He removed it from the equipment and measured its conductivity. To his astonishment, Akasaki discovered that somehow, bombardment by electrons in the microscope had turned the material into positive type.

The significance of this accidental discovery was immediately obvious to Akasaki. With p-type material, it would at last be possible to make a p-n junction out of gallium nitride, and hence a proper LED.

But from then on it would not be Akasaki, a senior professor on the verge of retirement, who would make most of the running. (Not that Akasaki, like so many successful Japanese researchers, would retire completely. In 1991 he moved to take up a position at Meijo University, a private school located in Nagoya.) Rather, it was a much younger, more highly motivated challenger who snatched the baton from out of the old campaigner's hands. And as we shall see, Naka-mura Shuji was uniquely qualified to take advantage of Akasaki's work.

Nakamura's company, Nichia Chemical, is located outside Anan, a small city (population: 60,000) by Japanese standards. Anan is located on Shikoku, the smallest of the four main islands that make up the Japanese archipelago. Until the recent completion of a chain of bridges linking the island with Honshu, the main island, where most Japanese live, Shikoku was effectively a backwater. "[H]igh mountains and steep slopes severely limit agriculture, habitation, and communication. . . . Much of the island is a thinly populated agricultural region, with few natural resources and little industry."[4]

Mention Shikoku to most Japanese, and what they think of is danc-ing in the streets. During the dog days of August, the kimono-clad citi-zens of Tokushima dance the *Awadori* along the avenues of their city, Mardi Gras style. A chant accompanies the *Awadori*. It goes, "You're a fool whether you dance or not, so you might as well dance."

Rustic hinterland though it might be, Shikoku has produced at least one major-league industrialist. Starting in 1947 with seventeen work-ers, Otsuka Masahito built up his family pharmaceutical firm into an empire that in 1995 had a turnover of around $10 billion. In Japan, the company is best known for its health drinks, notably one that rejoices in the name of *Pocari Sweat*.

Nichia Chemical's founder, Ogawa Nobuo, also started out in phar-maceuticals. At Tokushima technical college, he was Otsuka's senior by several years. Born in Anan in 1912 to a family of dirt-poor farmers, Ogawa went to school on a military scholarship. During World War II, he worked as a pharmacist, supplying drugs to front-line troops of the Japanese Imperial Army. Ogawa served at Guadalcanal, the battle in which—he told visitors proudly—John F. Kennedy also fought. Not con-tent merely to dispense, Ogawa also concocted a new formulation for Ringer's solution, a medication used to treat dehydration.

After the war, Ogawa returned to Japan to find an impoverished na-tion. "We didn't have anything," he recalled. "No houses, no beds—nothing." After working briefly as a manager for an oil company, he went back to Anan. There, in 1948, Ogawa founded his own company. Grandly entitled Kyodo Pharmaceutical Laboratory, the firm was actually nothing more than a drugstore. It had just three employees. But in the store's back room, Ogawa set up a workbench on which to do research. There in 1951, he developed anhydrous calcium chloride, a compound used in the production of the antibiotic streptomycin.

First isolated in 1944, streptomycin was a vital drug used in the treatment of what was then Japan's number one killer, tuberculosis. Ogawa's formulation was of higher quality than the conventional compound. But gaining recognition for his achievement was an uphill struggle.

Eventually, "[a]fter the expenditure of great personal effort and the endurance of significant personal hardship," Ogawa managed to get his product approved by Kyowa Hakko, at the time Japan's leading producer of streptomycin.[5] But it seems that Kyowa Hakko muscled in on the development of the compound, so that by the time it was finally commercialized, Ogawa was left with slim pickings. Burned by this experience he vowed that, henceforth, he would do independent development.

Streptomycin's success in virtually eradicating TB forced Ogawa to look around for something else to make. He decided to focus his attention on calcium phosphate, a phosphor powder used to coat the insides of fluorescent lamps.

Commonplace objects today, in the early 1950s the long, thin illuminating tubes were still something of a novelty. The first practical fluorescent lamps were marketed in the United States in 1938. Their ability to produce more light for the same amount of electricity as incandescent lamps made them particularly attractive for offices and factories. Ogawa saw his first fluorescent lamp in Mindanao during the Japanese occupation of the Philippines. "That's interesting," he thought, and he promised himself that, "after the war, I'll make something like that."

In his approach to development, Ogawa drew on what the Japanese call a "twisted navel"—a perverse streak. He believed that the key to doing good research was to rely on one's instinct and experience rather than on formal training. "If you study books, you only believe what is written in them, and you can't go on to the next step," he said. "Reading books, then copying what's in them, that's no good at all."

The approach Ogawa favored was to "read the books, then stop and think. Once you've thought, you'll be able to do something better than what's in the book." The Nichia company slogan encapsulates his philosophy thus: "Let's study, let's think hard and work hard, then let's make the world's best products."

When coated on a fluorescent tube, the calcium phosphate that Ogawa developed gave out about 20 percent more light than conventional phosphors. In 1956, having succeeded in development, Ogawa founded Nichia Chemical to manufacture and sell this new product. He started with just twenty-two employees, for the most part local people whose previous occupation had been making charcoal. Ogawa came up with a motto that would thenceforth characterize Nichia's mission: "Ever researching for a brighter world."

But finding Japanese customers for the world's best product proved impossible. Companies such as Toshiba had already begun production of fluorescent lamps using technology licensed from the United States. Nichia's location in the middle of nowhere counted against the fledgling firm. "Japanese companies wouldn't buy [our phosphors]," Ogawa said. "They had this fixed idea that something as good as that couldn't be made in the country."

The reaction of foreign lamp makers was very different. They evaluated the samples that Nichia sent objectively, without prejudice. Nichia's first customer was the U.S. firm Sylvania. Then representatives from Europe's biggest light-bulb maker, Philips, made the trip to Anan. They bought one and a half tons of phosphors, which came to ¥700,000 ($2,000). Ogawa recalled gleefully that it cost the Dutch firm ¥900,000 ($2,500) in air freight charges to ship the stuff from Osaka to Amsterdam.

But despite these early successes, raising the capital to support his little company was always tough. "Back then, Japan didn't have any money, and banks wouldn't lend to me," Ogawa recalled, then grinning broadly he added, "so we had to work using the strength of the gods."

As it happened, several top executives of local banks died of cancer one after another. Ogawa was able to turn this melancholy circumstance to his advantage. He hinted to their superstitious successors that the deaths were a punishment from heaven for not having lent Nichia money. Overnight, their attitude changed. "Not because I did anything, or because I put a curse on them," Ogawa explained. "They just said, 'I'd better lend him money or else I might die of cancer, too.'" Subsequently, when he bumped into senior bank managers, Ogawa would reassure them, "Don't worry—you'll live long!"

Ogawa was resourceful in raising funds by other means, too. During the late 1980s, when Japan's bubble economy was close to bursting, an Osaka restaurant owner named Onoue Nui gained national notoriety by conning Japanese banks into lending her vast sums of money to buy shares, which she then used as collateral to purchase more shares. By the time the bubble burst, Nui was reckoned to be worth around $15 billion. Then she went bankrupt.

Ogawa developed a pitch for banks that had lent Nui money. He told them, "If you're prepared to lend hundreds of billions of yen to someone like her, surely you can spare my company a few billion?" According to Ogawa, the embarrassed bankers would always agree to lend Nichia money.

In 1971, Nichia branched out into the manufacture of red, green, and blue phosphors for coating the inner screens of color TV tubes. Eventually, this would prove to be a successful undertaking. Nichia would become the largest independent manufacturer of phosphors, with 50 percent of the domestic Japanese market and around 25 percent of the world market.

In the short term, however, the timing of this diversification was extremely unfortunate. The recession that followed OPEC's decision to raise oil prices in late 1973 almost bankrupted the company. By the summer of 1974, Nichia was having difficulty meeting its payroll. Characteristically, Ogawa managed to turn adversity into advantage. He gave his workers four weeks' vacation, telling them to go home and enjoy themselves. This gave him the respite he needed to scrape together enough cash to weather the storm. But though the company returned to profitability, Ogawa retained the long summer break. Nichia became known for offering its employees longer holidays than any other Japanese firm.

Ogawa himself took advantage of the break to indulge in his passion for climbing mountains. He claimed that good ideas came to him while he was ascending the slopes. A framed photograph on the wall of the main meeting room at Nichia's spartan head office showed Ogawa in climbing gear setting off up Mount Kilimanjaro, Africa's tallest peak. In the mid 1990s, aged over 80, having handed day-to-day running of the company to his son, Eiji, he was still at it. "But I don't climb the really high mountains like Everest because I'm too old," Ogawa said. "These days, 3,000 meters [10,000 feet] is about my limit."

All small Japanese companies have trouble recruiting good people. Young high school and college graduates tend to prefer the security of working for a large firm. Nichia is no exception to this rule; indeed, the firm's location way out in the sticks makes hiring even more difficult. Offering potential recruits long holidays helps, but it is not a sufficient incentive. Few employees join Nichia because of the kind of work the company offers. Mostly people sign on because they live locally, and it is convenient for them to find work nearby. In this respect, Nakamura Shuji was entirely typical.

Nakamura was born in May 1954 in neighboring Ehime Prefecture, where his father worked for the island's power company as a maintenance engineer. As a kid, Nakamura wanted to be a scientist; at high school, physics was his favorite subject. But Nakamura's grades weren't good enough to get him into a top university like Tokyo, and his teacher recommended that rather than science the youngster should go in for engineering. Reasoning that electronics engineering was close to physics, Nakamura agreed, though not with any great enthusiasm. "If you really wanted to do electronic engineering," he said, "you would go and study under a famous professor like Nishizawa *Sensei* at Tohoku." But Nakamura ended up enrolling at nearby Tokushima University, where there were no famous professors.

There, he took a four-year course followed by a master's degree. What happened next, Nakamura related, was that "I got married while I was doing my master's—which is unusual in Japan—and we had a baby. But big companies like Sony and Matsushita only take unmarried recruits. So I had a family, and from when I was a kid, I didn't like big cities, I preferred the country—life is better here, especially if you have a family ... plus my wife is from Tokushima, and she wanted to stay here."

So when the time came to find a job, in time-honored Japanese fashion, Nakamura asked his professor to make an introduction for him somewhere. The professor responded that Nichia Chemical was the only company in the Tokushima area that he knew. Nakamura asked what kind of company Nichia was. The professor told him that they made phosphors. "And I knew absolutely nothing about phosphors," Nakamura recalled, laughing. "All I knew was electronics." Nonetheless an appointment was made, and Nakamura went out to Anan with his professor to meet Ogawa.

As we have seen, the young man's first impressions were anything but favorable. But despite his qualms about surviving in a company like Nichia, and in spite of all of Ogawa's efforts to dissuade him, Nakamura came to the conclusion that he had no option but to join. He called Ogawa to tell Nichia's president that he had thought it over and that he had decided to come and work for Nichia. And Ogawa replied, "Well, in that case, it can't be helped—you're hired."

When Nakamura joined Nichia Chemical in April 1979 the company had perhaps 200 employees. From day one, he worked on topics related to semiconductor light emitters. Ogawa initially assigned Nakamura to refine high-purity metals, such as gallium, the starting material for LEDs. His development efforts went well, and a production line was established. Next came the growth of compound semiconductors such as gallium arsenide and indium phosphide. These too became products. But though a technical success, Nakamura's materials were a commercial failure. The problem was that the market for them was already dominated by giant suppliers like Sumitomo Electric.

Nonetheless, Nakamura proceeded with the next step, the production of wafers for use in manufacturing LEDs. But here, too, Nichia ran into a brick wall. Big competitors like Toshiba were already well established in the marketplace selling equivalent products.

By 1988, almost ten years after joining the company, Nakamura was a deeply frustrated man. He had succeeded in everything he had been asked to do, but there had been little or no commercial reward for his efforts. Technical success didn't cut much ice in a company which depended on sales for its survival. Nor did it do much for Nakamura's salary and bonuses, not to mention his standing within the company.

But though frustrated, Nakamura was not the type to give up. Thus far, he himself had not been responsible for choosing the development themes on which he worked. These had typically come from Nichia's salesmen returning from customers with suggestions about what they would like Nichia to develop for them. Next time, Nakamura decided, he would ask Ogawa for permission to decide his own research theme.

As a result of his experience in the light-emitting field, Nakamura knew exactly what he wanted to shoot for. "Everything I'd done was LED materials," he explained. "So from way back I knew that there was no blue [LED]. Everybody was doing research on this theme, and the fact that there was no blue was the number one topic at conferences."

Having decided to shoot for the blue, Nakamura's first step was to choose a crystal growth method. Judging from what he had heard at conferences, metal–organic chemical vapor deposition sounded like the way to go. At that point, Nakamura had little idea what MOCVD was, or how it was done. But at least he knew someone who could tell him. Sakai Shiro, an assistant professor who had been two years his senior at Tokushima University, was using the technique in his research. Sakai was then at the University of Florida. When the academic came back to Japan during the summer vacation that year, Nakamura invited him out to Nichia.

The idea was that Sakai should persuade Ogawa that MOCVD was the way of the future in light-emitter production technology. Also, that Nichia's president should buy a machine for Nakamura, and pay for him to learn how to use it.

The presentation went according to plan. Ogawa gave Nakamura his blessing. "Unless you let your young researchers do whatever they like, they can't do research," Nichia's president would later explain. "So if they ask you for a machine, then you have to give it to them."

Ogawa allowed Nakamura to spend a year at the University of Florida learning how to do MOCVD. On his return, to enable the researcher to build himself a machine on which to grow devices, Nichia's president allocated Nakamura ¥300,000,000 (approximately $3.3 million), an amount equivalent to 1.5 percent of the company's annual sales.

This was a gesture on a grand scale. "It is rare for a large company to spend in the region of $3.3 million within essentially one year on a single blue-sky type research project of a single researcher, when the probability of success is unknown," wrote Gerhard Fasol, a German scientist based in Tokyo.[6] "It is even rarer that 1.5 percent of annual sales would be spent on a single blue-sky R&D project of initially unknown outcome."

Nakamura Shuji (left) and Ogawa Nobuo at Nichia Chemical, Anan.

Fasol went on, "Large companies such as NTT or AT&T spend in the region of $250,000 to $400,000 per researcher per year on average. The approach of large companies is usually to provide small budgets until commercial success is within reach, or at least until the risk is easier to assess . . . "

But as Ogawa would counter, "We're not like a big company with a fixed R&D budget." And Nichia's president would be impatient with those who chided him for taking such a big risk: "Of course it was a big risk," he responded warmly, "but risk is synonymous with research." Ogawa gambled on Nakamura because he had faith in the young researcher's ability. "He's good at thinking," Nichia's president said, "so my policy was, if I let him get on with it, he'd probably be able to come up with the goods." Ogawa knew nothing about crystal growth techniques. The important thing was that the down-to-earth industrial chemist had himself had first-hand experience of developing successful products.

This was not the first time Ogawa had made a risky bet on an individual. Some years earlier, Nichia backed a technology developed by another of its researchers. Following Sharp's lead, the company made electroluminescent backlights for the LCD displays of personal computers. Based on phosphors, EL was a natural technology for Nichia to try and exploit. The company put a lot of effort into the product—Nakamura recalled that at one point Ogawa had between fifty and sixty people working on EL backlights. But though the technology was commercialized—most notably in some of Toshiba's Dynabook laptops—there were problems with reliability, and PC makers abandoned EL in favor other types of backlights.

When Nakamura arrived in Florida he got a nasty shock. He had gone there to learn how to do MOCVD, but the machine in the laboratory to which he had been assigned was a long way from being operational. Nakamura and his fellow students pitched in to help build the equipment. It took them ten months. "So we didn't have it ready until about a month before I was due to go back to Japan," Nakamura recalled, laughing. "And because there were about ten other students as well as me, and we all wanted to use the machine, I was only able to use it about three times before I returned."

Waiting for the machine to be ready left Nakamura with plenty of time to think about which material he was going to work on. As we have seen, he had three choices. There was the conventional technology, silicon carbide, which was already commercialized but physically not capable of producing bright light. Then there was zinc selenide, on which almost everyone at companies and universities, especially in Japan, had placed their bets. And finally there was the hopeless case, gallium nitride, on which hardly anybody (except old Akasaki at Nagoya University) was working.

Nakamura chose gallium nitride. The logic behind this seemingly foolhardy choice was quite simple: "The most important thing was that no one else was doing gallium nitride," Nakamura said. "It wasn't that I was confident that I would succeed; it was because I'd had this bitter experience that, if you do the same thing as everyone else, when it comes to commercializing products, you can't sell them."

In April 1989, on his return from Florida, Nakamura began his quest in earnest. The first step was to build a reactor. Thanks to his efforts in the United States, he knew exactly what to do. But not everything went smoothly. In particular, the machine's heater kept cutting out. It took about a year to get rid of all the bugs. Nakamura perforce acquired an intimate knowledge of the workings of his machine, one that he would draw on to make crucial improvements to the growth process.

Then, just as Nakamura had persuaded his machine to grow good films, exciting news arrived from Nagoya. Akasaki had managed to make positive-type gallium nitride, thus solving what had always been the material's biggest drawback. For Nakamura, this was a fantastic stroke of luck. The timing of the breakthrough could hardly have been better if he had scheduled it himself.

The race to build a bright blue LED was on.

It was a race with only two entrants. It was also one that from the outset, Nakamura felt confident he could win. "[Akasaki] was at a university, and I was at a company," Nakamura explained, "and in Japan, when a university professor and a company compete, the company usually wins."

(In fact, Akasaki was working with a company, Toyoda Gosei, a member of the Toyota group specializing in rubber and resin products. This development, like that of Nishizawa Jun'ichi's high-brightness red LEDs by Stanley, was sponsored by the Japan Research & Development Corporation. But Toyoda Gosei was committed to old-style MIS LEDs, and seems not to have been able to take immediate advantage of Akasaki's p-type breakthrough.)

Nakamura was younger and better equipped than his rival. He had the full support—moral as well as financial—of his president. In addition to which, after ten years of failure, he was doubly determined to succeed.

But Nakamura did not merely replicate Akasaki's work. Independent development was Nichia's guiding principle, as laid down by the company's founder. In addition to which, copying would inevitably have led to patent problems a few years down the track. It made good commercial sense for Nakamura to stake out his own intellectual property.

Akasaki had discovered that you could convert gallium nitride into positive type by zapping the material with electron beams. Nakamura did not buy the professor's explanation of the reason for the transformation. He noticed that, when exposed to electron beams, the temperature of the sample rose significantly. Working on the hypothesis that it was the heat rather than the electron beams that caused the change in electrical properties, Nakamura tried baking the material in an atmosphere of nitrogen. His much simpler method worked. This was good news, because e-beam equipment was cumbersome and expensive. And there was an added bonus: With e-beams, the temperature only went up on the surface of the material; whereas with annealing, the whole film became p-type.

By the summer of 1991, Nakamura had established the technology for producing uniform films of p-type material. He was feeling really pleased with his progress. Just then came unsettling news from the Midwest. A group working at 3M's Corporate Laboratories in St. Paul, Minnesota, announced that they had succeeded in making a blue-green laser out of zinc selenide.[7]

This breakthrough was quickly replicated by several other groups working at U.S. universities and at Japanese companies, including Sony. As yet, however, none of these devices was anywhere near being practical. The 3M laser for example could only produce brief pulses of light, and even then only when cooled to a temperature of −9°F. ("Some people say that's a nice day in St. Paul," quipped one of the company's researchers.)[8]

The sudden progress of his rivals dented Nakamura's confidence. "Compared to lasers, LEDs are simple, because they don't use much current," he explained. "So because they'd done a laser, I thought that they'd be able to make an LED out of zinc selenide, too."

But obstacles continued to dog the development of zinc selenide. The biggest was that the material was soft, making it difficult to work with. Plus, it was hard to hook up devices made of zinc selenide. Contacts—on which to solder the wires for connecting the device to its power supply—simply wouldn't stick.

With regular LEDs, you attached contacts at a temperature of between 300° and 400°C. This was not a problem for a hard material like gallium nitride, which is grown at around 1,000°C. For zinc selenide, however, which had a growth temperature of just 280°, it was a potential showstopper. The only materials that would stick had high electrical resistance. This meant that to get zinc selenide lasers to emit light, you had to pump them with about 20 volts, a huge amount for tiny solid-state devices, which normally operate on 3 volts or less. As a result, early zinc selenide lasers seldom lasted longer than a few minutes before succumbing to catastrophic overheating.

But in addition to giving Nakamura a nasty shock, the 3M announcement also served as a useful inspiration. Thus far, the devices he had made had all been simple p-n junctions. They emitted some light, but not enough to compete with silicon carbide. The 3M laser was a double heterostructure—a multilayered device directly descended from the ones that Hayashi and Panish had made at Bell Labs in 1970.[9]

The key feature of a double heterostructure is that light in the active layer of the device is confined between two layers of slightly different material. As we have seen, the payoff from confinement is more light for less current. Nichia's salesmen wanted to rush Nakamura's first efforts into production. But Nakamura refused. He insisted that unless he could make a double heterostructure, the devices would never get brighter. And unless the LEDs got brighter, there would be no market for them.

The work proceeded smoothly. In September 1992 Nakamura succeeded in growing a double heterostructure out of gallium nitride. At about four o'clock one afternoon, he touched the tiny chip with the tip of a probe and . . . blue light came out. It wasn't very bright, but Nakamura was delighted all the same. He dashed off to Ogawa's office to tell Nichia's president about his breakthrough. Pausing only to pick up his camera, the latter hurried back with him to the lab. When Ogawa saw Nakamura's first light, however, the old man was distinctly unimpressed. "Dim, isn't it?" he said, adding, "Can we sell something that's as dim as that?"

Nakamura was not so concerned about his little light's lack of brightness. Experience told him that making gradual improvements to the structure of the device would likely increase the amount of light it produced. What worried him was its lifetime. To be a viable product, a gallium nitride LED would have to last for thousands of hours. Would the huge number of defects in the crystal prove a fatal weakness? Since no one had ever commercialized such a device, this was completely unknown. Before he could go any further, Nakamura had to find out.

It took him about four days to set up the equipment to perform the lifetime test. During this period, Nakamura was a bundle of nerves, continuously worrying about whether his device would go the distance. On the fifth day, he began the test. He went home, leaving the LED lit. All through that night he fretted, adrenalin keeping him awake. Nichia

Chemical's working day began at 8:30 A.M., but Nakamura couldn't wait that long. Next morning he came in at seven o'clock, praying silently that the device would still be working. He went to his lab, to the black-shrouded portion of the room where optical measurements were made. Heart in his mouth, Nakamura drew back the curtain.

The little light was still on.

It was Nakamura's happiest moment. Quickly, he measured the device to see how much light it was putting out. The result showed that output was almost 100 percent—it hadn't dropped at all. Then Nakamura thought to himself, "Maybe this'll do."

Indeed it would. By the beginning of 1993, as the result of many improvements to the process, Nakamura had succeeded in producing an LED that was about a hundred times brighter than previously available silicon carbide ones, and comparable in brightness to Stanley's super-red LEDs. During the hectic months that followed, Nichia scrambled to consolidate their advantage, scaling up the process and establishing production facilities. By November that year, the company was ready to make its momentous public announcement.

A few days beforehand, Ogawa and Nakamura made a pilgrimage up to Tohoku University, to lay the device at the feet of Nichizawa Jun'ichi. Japan's foremost semiconductor specialist was himself no stranger to the quest for blue light emitters. Ten years earlier, he had struggled to make zinc selenide do his bidding, but to little effect. Now, confronted with Nakamura's extraordinary success, Nichizawa was inclined to be magnanimous. He praised Nichia for their efforts. And to encourage them to continue, on the back of an envelope, he penned a poem:

> Looking at the light of the blue light emitter,
> After the success of the first step, there is a second step.
> After the success of the second step, there is a third step.[10]

In the months to come, this was advice that Nakamura would take to heart.

On 29 November 1993, Nichia announced their achievement to the Japanese media. Not surprisingly, the initial reaction was one of sheer disbelief. "Everyone thought it wasn't true," Nakamura recalled, laughing loudly, "and one reason was that as far as the semiconductor industry was concerned, Nichia Chemical was a completely unknown company." Another was that Nichia was based in no-tech Shikoku. In American terms, it was as if a hot new microprocessor had been developed by a start-up hailing from Newfoundland.

But as Nichia began sending out samples of its blue LED for evaluation by customers, the realization gradually dawned that these upstarts from the back of beyond had caught the rest of the industry with their pants down.

In the wake of Nakamura's dramatic achievement, companies around the world initiated crash research programs to develop blue gallium nitride light emitters. In the U.S., the government's Advanced Projects Research Agency led the way, sponsoring no fewer than three research consortia. Their corporate members included huge firms like AT&T, Hewlett-Packard, Kodak, Philips, and Xerox.

Despite all this effort, three years after the Nichia announcement, no one had managed to duplicate Nakamura's results. This was not for want of trying. But unlike the case with so many previous laser and LED technologies, there was no beneficent Bell Labs to publish papers showing everyone else the way. Understandably for a small firm with a posse of giants in hot pursuit, Nichia had been very careful not to reveal the essentials of its growth process.[11]

The company also had established a strong patent position, one which it was defending aggressively. For his part, Nichia's chairman was against licensing gallium nitride technology. Ogawa was more interested in providing work for the people of Anan. Commercial production of blue LEDs by Nichia had already created over a hundred new jobs.

Meanwhile Nakamura was not resting on his laurels. From his lab proceeded a stream of improvements. The blue LED got brighter, and it was joined by a bright green gallium nitride light emitter. This too was commercialized. By then Nakamura had moved on to a more ambitious target. His new aim was to build a blue laser.

In January 1996, he succeeded. His laser produced a blue-violet light. The world's first gallium nitride laser, it emitted the shortest wavelength ever reported for a semiconductor device. Although it operated at room temperature, the laser was as yet only capable of producing pulses of light. The same month, researchers at Sony responded with an announcement that they had grown a zinc selenide blue-green laser that was capable of continuous operation at room temperature for 100 hours.

By the end of the year, Nakamura hit back by persuading gallium nitride lasers to operate continuously at room temperature for 35 hours. He predicted that commercialization of this laser would probably take place by the end of 1998.[12] Meanwhile, researchers at Toshiba announced that they had made a pulsed mode gallium nitride laser.

Competition was fierce because the stakes were high. Riding on the development of the blue laser was the future of optical data storage. The amount of information an optical disc can store is determined by the wavelength of the light emitted by the laser pickup. The shorter the wavelength, the smaller the pits (on the surface of the disc) the focused spot of laser light can read.

The infrared lasers that CD players use enable a capacity of 74 minutes of digital audio, enough to store Beethoven's Ninth Symphony. The red lasers of the Digital Video Disc players that went on sale in late 1996 can hold 133 minutes of digital video, enough for most feature-length movies, or 4.7 giga (billion) bytes of information. When blue laser–based players arrive, perhaps as early as the turn of the century, they will enable a single disc to store *all nine* of Beethoven's symphonies; or a three-hour, high-definition movie; or, as a multimedia computer peripheral, 17 gigabytes of information. Or, in the military view of things that provides the justification for Pentagon funding of blue laser development, enough information to allow pilots to store "the information on where the SCUDs were last seen, and to then turn off their radar and enter into the battle arena in a complete stealth mode, relying only on stored information."[13]

The revolution in lighting triggered by the bright blue LED will take much longer to occur. Displacing a technology as deeply entrenched as the incandescent bulb will not be easy. The first priority is to reduce the cost of production by increasing the volume. In 1996, blue LED lamps were priced at between $1 and $1.50, compared with red and green LEDs, which sold for less than 10 cents.

As it happens, though, there are several applications that, between them, should represent enough demand to push blue light emitters into high-volume production. One, as we saw in the previous chapter, is large outdoor displays—the kind that sports stadiums use to show action replays. Another is color copiers and scanners, which currently rely on fluorescent light with red, green, and blue filters. But the biggest niche market where LDs are likely in the near future to replace incandescents is traffic lights.

Estimates put the number of traffic signals in use worldwide at around 12 million. The lights cost about a billion dollars to run, plus they have to be replaced about once a year, at a cost of about $2 per bulb. They are also inefficient: Red traffic signals are produced by filtering light from an incandescent lamp, wasting about 85 percent of the emitted light. To obtain green and amber, nearly 30 percent of the light must be filtered out. In addition to which, the visibility of incandescent traffic lamps in direct sunlight is not good, and when they fail, they fail totally.

LEDs by contrast use a fraction as much power, and they offer lifetimes of up to 10 years. With no filter to reflect sunlight their visibility is excellent, and when they fail, they do so gradually.

Indeed, the logic of LEDs is so persuasive that many municipalities around the U.S. have begun to install red emitters in their traffic lights. Notable among them was Philadelphia, PA, which by mid 1995 had converted some 10 percent of its intersections to red LEDs. Each lamp consists of between 500 and 750 individual LEDs connected in strings. In 1995 a typical lamp cost $200, about one hundred times more than an incandescent bulb. Yet because of the energy savings they offer, LED traffic lights pay for themselves in about three years.[14]

In Japan, the total energy consumption for traffic lights alone is estimated to be in the gigawatt range. Following the trail blazed by red devices, in mid 1995, blue-green LED traffic lights were undergoing tests at many locations. The Japanese expect that the energy savings accrued from decreased replacement and service costs will be very substantial.

The extrapolation from traffic lights to household lights is irresistible: "It has been shown that switching from incandescents to LEDs in signal lights reduces energy consumption by up to 85 percent. If this same value held for an LED-based white light, the energy savings in U.S. households would approach $35 billion a year. This is an application that would require trillions of units . . . "

Who would make those trillions? Would a small firm like Nichia be able to compete in such a market against the giants of the electronics industry? Ogawa thought that they might. He himself would probably not live to see his company take on the competition. "But I'll be urging them on from heaven," he laughed. "That's why I'm so keen on climbing mountains—I'm practicing looking down!"

II

Nails That Stuck Up

*... progress and achievement are the unpredictable result of indi-
vidual will and faith, diligence and ingenuity ... in business as in
art, individual vision prevails over the corporate leviathan; the
small company—or the creative group in the large firm—confounds
industrial policy; the entrepreneur dominates the hierarch. The
hubristic determinisms of the academy and the state ... give way
to one man working in the corner of a lab or a library.*

            —George Gilder[1]

L AUNCHED IN THE SUMMER OF 1994, it became the fastest-
growing product in the history of the U.S. consumer electronics
industry—faster than color television, VCRs, or CD players.

In this book, we have become accustomed to a familiar pattern: U.S.
firm invents semiconductor device, fails to follow through, Japanese
company picks device up, commercializes product based on it. But in
the case of direct broadcasting by satellite, DBS, most notably the
product known as DirecTV, the pattern seems to be reversed.

Critics warned would-be investors that DBS stood for "Don't Be
Stupid." But by early 1997, nearly 5 million American households were
subscribing to direct broadcasting by satellite services. Pundits predicted that by the turn of the century, DBS would sign up a further 10
million subscribers. Most of these new viewers would come from rural
areas not served by cable TV. Others would be won over by the crystal-clear images and CD-quality sound that the satellite signals delivered.

At a conference in Tokyo that year, News Corporation chairman Rupert Murdoch said he believed that "DBS—not cable—will be the linchpin of mass communications in the twenty-first century."[2]

The big difference between DBS and earlier generations of satellite television is the size of the antenna used to receive the signals. Conventional satellite dishes were monstrous metal-mesh objects several meters across, expensive to buy, unsightly to the eye, and requiring a large backyard to install. The new antennas were just 18 inches wide—the size of a pizza dish or, in oblong versions, a turkey tray. They were cheap enough for almost everybody to afford, and so light you could fix them to the rail of a balcony.

Key to this enormous reduction in size and cost is a device called a high electron mobility transistor, or HEMT. Perched in front of the dish, it picks up the almost unimaginably faint microwave signals that beam down from satellites parked in geosynchronous orbit 22,300 miles above the Earth, then amplifies those signals into usable form.

DirecTV was developed by Hughes Electronics, a division of General Motors. The first batch of receivers for the service were manufactured by Thomson Consumer Electronics, a French-owned company, and marketed under its RCA brand. The high electron mobility transistor was invented in 1979 by Mimura Takashi, a researcher at the Japanese computer and communications equipment maker Fujitsu.

A direct line connects Mimura's HEMT with Japan's first commercial transistor, produced a quarter of a century earlier. The first Japanese transistor was developed by Kobe Kogyo, Rocket Sasaki's old firm. In 1968, Kobe Kogyo merged with Fujitsu. Two years later Mimura joined Fujitsu's Kobe facility. There all his seniors were former Kobe Kogyo researchers—in particular, the scientist who became his boss, Fukuta Masumi.

"Kobe Kogyo was a really interesting company," Fukuta recalled. "Technically, the firm was very aggressive, the first in Japan to come up with new technology, or to bring it in from abroad." But by the time Fukuta came aboard in the mid 1960s, as a result of bad management, the firm was nearly bankrupt. Luminaries like Sasaki, Esaki, and Arizumi were long gone. Still, much of the company's let's-challenge-something-new-and-different culture remained. "It may sound strange,"

Fukuta said, "but rather than pursuing sales or profit, researchers at Kobe Kogyo preferred to try and be the first in the world to do something."

This was an attitude that greatly appealed to the young Fukuta. At the time, the prevailing approach in Japan was still to look overseas–especially to America–for new ideas, then to copy those ideas as quickly as possible. "I hated that sort of thing," Fukuta said. "To me, copying was mortifying. In my first two or three years after joining Kobe Kogyo, I felt very strongly that I should try and do something different. It didn't matter what it was–I just didn't want to copy if I could help it. So if there was someone somewhere else doing it, then I didn't want to do the same thing."

Fukuta quickly realized that if he focused on silicon, the theme that the vast majority of semiconductor researchers had chosen, "it would be very difficult to find interesting things to do." He turned instead to investigate compound semiconductors like gallium arsenide. "For me," Fukuta said, "the idea that something new might come out of compound semiconductors was an extremely strong motive force."

Gallium arsenide was attractive because of its theoretical advantages over silicon; namely, higher speed of operation (and hence, the ability to operate at higher frequencies). Fukuta chose as his target a high-power transistor made from gallium arsenide, a device that looked promising for microwave transmission applications. At the time, theoretical case studies indicated that such a device was an impossibility. The problem was getting rid of heat: Gallium arsenide suffered from extremely poor thermal conductivity. When you cranked up the power, the resultant heat would cause the device to shut down or, in extreme cases, to melt.

After many failed attempts, Fukuta finally figured out a way to solve the heat problem. He announced his results at a conference in 1973. "The Americans were interested in [the high-power transistor]," Fukuta said, "because there was a big demand for it in military applications like radar. In Japan, there's no connection with the military, and we weren't thinking about that kind of application, so there was a lot of discussion about what it could be used for. But Fujitsu had no immediate use for it, and that was a problem."

(Twenty years later, Fukuta's transistors would find a consumer application in the shape of power amplifiers for the Personal Handyphone, a low-cost digital mobile phone system introduced in Japan in mid-1995 that quickly became a huge hit, especially among young consumers. This was a development that made Fukuta very happy, and he paid tribute to Fujitsu management for the consistent support they had given him over two decades. "Our top managers understood what I was trying to do, and bit by bit sales increased and some profit came out of it, so I was never told to stop, even though I was doing something that was very difficult and, to put it bluntly, something that Fujitsu didn't have to have.")

In addition to high-power transistors, a second theme at Fukuta's lab was gallium arsenide metal oxide semiconductor field-effect transistors. Microwave systems people were keen to get their hands on a transistor that would operate at higher frequencies, and with lower noise, to replace the vacuum tubes they were using in their receivers. (Noise is unwanted electrical disturbance in circuitry. In communications systems, noise interferes with or prevents signal reception.)

Mimura Takashi joined Fukuta's group in the early 1970s. The young engineer soon impressed his boss with his analytical approach to tackling problems. "When working on something new, he has the ability to think," Fukuta said. "He's not very good at experimental work; his strength lies rather in using his head, analyzing data, getting to the heart of the matter." In 1975, Fukuta assigned Mimura to develop a gallium arsenide MOS FET.

Three years later, having hit a brick wall, Mimura was about ready to quit. Accumulating sufficient electrons in the oxide layer of gallium arsenide to make a viable device proved impossible. He went to Fukuta and told him that there was no point in continuing with research on this type of transistor. "I understood that he wanted to stop," Fukuta recalled, "so I asked him to come up with some new type of device."

In June 1979, Mimura traveled to the University of Colorado at Boulder to give a paper at the Device Research Conference held there that year. It was to be his swan song before quitting MOS research. After giving the paper, Mimura discussed his work with other researchers in the field. And it was during these discussions that an idea for a new type of device burst into his head. The stimulus for this idea was a paper by a group at Bell Labs that Mimura had read in a recent issue of *Applied Physics Letters*.

The leader of the group at Murray Hill was an Australian called Ray Dingle. In the early 1970s Dingle's starting point had been not transistors, but light-emitting diodes and lasers like the ones Hayashi and Panish had recently developed down the corridor at Bell Labs.[5] Dingle was not interested in the devices per se, but rather in the fundamental physics on which their operation depended. In particular, he was trying to understand the optical properties of excitons, combinations of electrons and holes. For this, Dingle needed very thin layers of material.

"We got down to a point where we just couldn't make the wretched stuff any thinner by conventional methods like polishing and etching," Dingle recalled. Eventually, he realized that "the only way I would ever get to understand what the exciton properties in gallium arsenide were all about would be to actually create a thin crystal, rather than get a thick piece of material and etch it away to make it thinner."

The answer was molecular beam epitaxy, the high-precision crystal growth method that Al Cho had recently pioneered at Bell Labs. For their experiments, Dingle and his people grew materials consisting of thin films of gallium arsenide sandwiched between aluminum gallium arsenide. This system worked wonderfully well. So much so that Dingle was encouraged to move on from excitons to electrons, and to investigate the possibility of making actual devices.

As we have seen, to produce semiconductor devices, you have to dope the material with impurities to make it electrically positive or negative. The trouble with compound semiconductors was that the atoms of dopant that donated the extra electrons got in the way of the electrons as the latter sped through the crystal lattice. The result of this phenomenon, known as electron scattering, was to lower the mobility of the electrons. So much for gallium arsenide's much-vaunted speed.

The solution to the electron scattering problem was a revolutionary idea. Why not put the donor atoms in the aluminum gallium arsenide layer, and leave the gallium arsenide layer undoped? Thanks to the slightly different physical properties of the two materials, the conduction electrons should tend to drop into the undoped layer where, completely unobstructed, they would whiz along like gangbusters.

Bell Labs technicians modified that MBE machine so that the beams of dopant atoms could be turned on and off from one layer of crystal to the next. Modulation doping, as the technique came to be known, worked first time out. In October 1978, Dingle and his colleagues published a paper describing their work.[4]

This was the paper whose implications exploded like a time bomb in Mimura Takashi's head. In modulation doping, the Bell Labs group had come up with a way of accumulating electrons in gallium arsenide–the very thing that Mimura had spent three fruitless years trying to do. On his return to Japan, he got down to some serious thinking. By July 1979 Mimura had mapped out the basic idea for an ultrahigh-speed transistor. In August he applied for a patent on his idea. That same month he teamed up with some MBE specialists in a different section of the company.

Fujitsu had been the first Japanese company to invest in an MBE machine. As former Fujitsu chairman Kobayashi Taiyu recounted, "In 1975 there was talk at Fujitsu Laboratories of purchasing molecular beam [epitaxy] equipment. We made some inquiries and discovered that there was not even one of these machines in Japan at the time. The cost was somewhere around ¥1 billion [approximately $3.5 million]. . . . I knew that the previous year at Bell Labs they had attracted worldwide attention by developing a semiconductor with aluminum, gallium, and arsenic using this type of machine. Still I had reservations. There were quite a few questions to be answered. But sympathizing with the tremendous energy of the young engineers, I decided to go ahead and provide the money just as they had asked."[5]

By December 1979, Mimura and his colleagues had built the first high electron mobility transistor. Mimura was then 34 years old.

Mimura's HEMT caused a minor sensation among scientists. His first paper on the new transistor, published in the *Japan Journal of Applied Physics* in 1980, went on to become a "citation classic." That is, it was cited as a reference by other researchers in several hundred publications. The HEMT was especially popular with astronomers, because the extremely low noise characteristics of the device made it a natural for picking up very faint signals from deep space. The first application of a Fujitsu HEMT came in 1986, in the radio telescope at the Tokyo University Observatory. But the next application—direct broadcasting by satellite—took Fujitsu completely by surprise.

Japan is three-quarters mountains, a feature that makes it tough for television stations to broadcast nationwide. But in its charter NHK, Japan's national broadcasting corporation, is charged with providing TV programs to the entire Japanese population. Hence the logic of direct broadcasting by satellite, which can beam signals wherever they need to go, regardless of the terrain. During the early 1980s, NHK conducted DBS trials working with its traditional equipment suppliers, consumer electronics companies like Sony and Matsushita. The service was slated to go into operation in 1987.

For the suppliers, DBS represented a wonderful opportunity to sell new equipment. However, success in the marketplace would depend largely on whether the dish antennas were small enough to fit on the roof or the veranda of the average Japanese home. The fortuitous appearance on the scene of the HEMT was a godsend, because it made possible a dish diameter of just 30 centimeters, about half the size that would otherwise have been required.[6]

Consumer electronics firms were thus quick to understand the commercial significance of the device. But Fujitsu's mission was to stay in the forefront of computers and communications. The company had not historically been much concerned about broadcasting and consumer electronics, with the result that the people in Fujitsu's business divisions were slow to see what the HEMT was good for. Thus, "although Fujitsu was the first to do HEMTs at the research level," Mimura said, "Sony and Matsushita were the first to announce products. And that caused a problem within the company."

Fujitsu's origins were, literally, elemental. In 1877, the year after Alexander Graham Bell invented the telephone, a 45-year-old entrepreneur named Furukawa Ichibei bought his first copper mine. Soon Furukawa was mining and smelting half of Japan's copper. From there it was a short hop downstream to rolling wire and cable. Next came a joint venture, Fuji Electric, formed in 1923, with the giant German firm Siemens, to produce heavy electrical equipment like transformers. In 1935, the company spun off the division making Siemens-style telephone switching equipment to form Fuji Tsushinki ("Fuji Communications Machinery"), a name later abbreviated to Fujitsu.

In the vast literature that deals with the Japanese computer industry, Fujitsu is invariably depicted as a bastion of Japan, Inc. This is understandable, given that the company was a loyal member of the Fuyo *keiretsu*, one of Nippon Telegraph & Telephone's exclusive family of equipment suppliers, and the cornerstone of MITI's drive to keep IBM at bay.

And yet, not so long ago, Fujitsu had been an altogether different beast, employing two of the brightest sparks ever to adorn the Japanese industrial firmament. One was Inaba Seiuemon, who pioneered numerical controls for machine tools. His firm, FANUC (Fujitsu Automated Numerical Controls), spun off from the parent in 1972. By the mid 1980s, FANUC had become the most profitable company in Japan. The other was Ikeda Toshio, the architect who designed Fujitsu's first computer.

Ikeda was a dynamic individual whose unusual habits used to startle his colleagues. For example, Ikeda preferred to work at home during the day, showing up at the office toward evening. And he would not hesitate to call people in the middle of the night to discuss his latest ideas. In 1972, Ikeda bailed out the company started by his American friend and kindred spirit Gene Amdahl, IBM's former chief computer designer. But in 1974 Ikeda was felled by a stroke and, with his death, Fujitsu lost its visionary leader.

By the time of the introduction of direct broadcasting by satellite in 1987, Fujitsu had become a very bureaucratic firm, dependent for an uncomfortably high proportion of its business on the grace and favor of the Japanese government. Yet something of the spirit from the old days evidently remained.

When the company's then president, Yamamoto Takuma, heard that Sony and Matsushita had beaten Fujitsu to market with DBS products, he was very angry. "What do you people think you're doing?" Mimura remembered Yamamoto berating the business division. "Other companies coming out before us with a Fujitsu invention—that's no good!"[7]

On the president's instructions, resources were allocated for a crash catch-up program. This was highly successful. In the late 1980s, DBS had become a hit both in Japan and the U.K. By 1994, when marketing of DirecTV began in the United States, Fujitsu had fought back to dominate the HEMT market, with a share of around 70 percent. That year, unable to compete on price, Sony pulled out of production and sales of HEMTs.

To be sure, low-noise devices for the consumer market were not Fujitsu's only interest in HEMTs. During the latter half of the 1980s, the company mounted a big (partly government-sponsored) effort to develop ultra-high-speed integrated circuits based on HEMTs for application to its mainframes and supercomputers. However, conventional C-MOS silicon technology advanced faster than anyone expected, and this effort was not successful commercially.

It is instructive to compare and contrast the reaction of Fujitsu's top management to the challenge from Sony with the reaction of the Bell Labs management to the challenge from Fujitsu.

Following their discovery of modulation doping, Dingle's group at Murray Hill immediately realized that the technique could be applied to make a high-speed transistor. Indeed, they had actually filed for a patent on such a device, which was subsequently granted. There ensued a legal battle between AT&T, Fujitsu, and several other parties, which seems to have ended up in a division of the rights. But regardless of the disputes over who owned what, "I don't think anyone would detract from the Fujitsu work," Ray Dingle said magnanimously. "[The fact] that they did it, and they did it independently."

But in mounting an effort to develop the technology, the phone company did not proceed with much enthusiasm. As Art Gossard, the MBE specialist in the group, recalled: "What we did in Bell Labs was we hired Chris Allen, who was a new Ph.D. from Penn, to come and have a joint appointment spending 50 percent of his time in Area 10 [the research department] and the other fifty in Area 20 [the device development department] . . . and his project was to make the modulation-doped transistor.

"So Bell Labs did pursue making a modulation-doped FET, but it was a small effort, basically just this one person, who had never made a transistor, never done MBE, a new student straight out of graduate school, so it proceeded more slowly. So the way I see it is that Fujitsu just proceeded more vigorously."

The publication of Mimura's results finally stung Bell Labs into action. Dingle was transferred to Area 20 to lead a development group. But from the beginning, this group was hamstrung by a lack of resources and by internal debates over direction. In 1983, Dingle left Bell Labs to form a start-up called Gain Electronics, taking the gallium arsenide device technology with him. "My goal" he recalled, "was to commercialize the scientific and technological advances that had been made at AT&T, because they clearly weren't going to."

The principle investor in Gain Electronics was Mitsui, one of Japan's largest trading companies, which poured more than $30 million into the Somerville, New Jersey, based start-up. But the timing was not right and Dingle had no experience of business. In October 1988, Mitsui pulled the plug, leaving the company to enter receivership.

"At Bell Labs," a former member of Dingle's group commented, "after [you'd done something] and published a couple of papers, it was like: Well, what's your next big wonderful thing going to be?" In Japan, by contrast, according to one former Fujitsu researcher, "the ideal path to success is not to finish by writing a paper in *Applied Physics Letters*. The ideal path is, you join the company, you do a bit of research, you write some papers, you find something that sells, you make lots of it, and you become manager of a factory somewhere."

The factory in this particular case is located in the outskirts of Kofu, a small city in the heart of Japan's grape-growing region, about sixty miles west of Tokyo. There, Mimura's former colleagues are cranking out compound semiconductor devices for use in mobile phones, satellite broadcasting, communication and navigation systems, and high-speed broadband networks. The market for such devices is currently growing at about 30 percent a year. Fujitsu expects sales to reach the billion dollar mark by the year 2000.

Half a century on from the invention of the transistor, Japan finds itself desperately in need of a new miracle. The situation is grim: The bubble has long since burst, the economy is stagnating, financial institutions are faltering, unemployment is reaching historic highs, while confidence plummets to all-time lows. Clearly something must be done, but what?

The point of this book has been to demonstrate that, though unseen and undervalued, there are entrepreneurs in Japan and that such individuals have played a key and hitherto unrecognized role in Japan's rise to prominence as an economic power. Until very recently, however, such creative forces have been stifled by ineffective government policy. Now the time has come to release their talents.

The Japanese financial system has been chronically overregulated. Prior to recent changes in the law, the average time from company founding to initial public offering in Japan was 21.4 years, compared to 3.6 years in the United States.[8] It is unreasonable to expect venture capitalists to wait more than two decades for a return on their investment.

The freeing of restraints on new issuances in the last few years should lead, eventually, to the development of an environment that can sustain American-style venture capital–driven entrepreneurship. But in the short term, a lack of infrastructure–in particular, of experienced venture capitalists–and a risk-averse culture, in which capital has more or less dried up, are combining to make life very hard for would-be Japanese entrepreneurs.

In the cases studied in this book, the companies all had sufficient cash flows from their existing business to finance the development of new technology. In other words, they had what my friend Hiro Negishi of Canon calls "a platform for generosity." It seems likely that reliance on in-house funding will continue to be the dominant style of Japanese entrepreneurship for some time to come.

Can companies still afford to finance costly internal developments? The answer for firms such as Sony, Canon, and Rohm (and for other entrepreneurial Japanese high-tech outfits like Kyocera, Murata, Omron, and TDK) is undoubtedly, yes. In the context of a Japanese stock market that has recently lost a quarter of its value, all these so-called nifty stocks have gone through the roof. They are, in short, extremely profitable.

Outside of the financial press, the phenomenon of the nifties is not much noticed by Western commentators. They mostly prefer to focus on Japan's economic woes, trotting out the usual stereotypes, ignoring any contrary indications. Japanese-style capitalism, so fashionable in the late 1980s, has been found wanting. The American way has triumphed.

The result is widespread complacency. But as Eric Bloch, chairman of the National Research Council's Committee on Japan, recently warned, "Japanese companies are just as strong as ever in many key technologies, such as electronic hardware, areas of advanced materials, and high-quality manufacturing.... If the United States is complacent and underestimates Japan's ability to bounce back," Bloch continued, "we could find ourselves facing some of the same problems we faced in the early 1980s when complacency was rampant."[9]

Sooner or later, Japan will bounce back. In the past, the Japanese have repeatedly demonstrated their resilience—especially when their backs are against the wall. Today many Japanese companies—including not a few mentioned in this book—find themselves in difficult straits. They have enormous cash flow problems and their shareholders are demanding a higher return on investment. If such firms are to survive, they must come up with new strategies. In particular, if they are to develop new products, they must encourage their employees to be more entrepreneurial and stop discouraging entrepreneurial employees.

Japanese culture tends not to support individual endeavor. Indeed, as a famous Japanese saying warns, "Nails that stick up will be hammered down." Step out of line, in other words, and you're in trouble. But a lesser-known variant of the saying goes, "Nails that stick up too far cannot be hammered down." This book has told the story of a handful of such nails. Japan needs hundreds more like them.

TIMELINE

1935   Yukawa Hideki, 28, predicts the existence of the meson, a new elementary particle.

1939   Bill Hewlett (26) and Dave Packard (27) found Hewlett-Packard.

1940   Russell Ohl demonstrates (and John Bardeen witnesses) the photoelectric effect on an ingot of pure silicon.

1943   Tomonaga Shin-ichiro, 37, publishes theory of quantum electrodynamics (shares 1965 Nobel Prize physics with Richard Feynman).

1945   Bill Shockley conceives field-effect transistor.

Pacific War ends.

1946   Bell Labs begins research project that leads to invention of transistor.

Kashio Tadao (29) founds Kasio Seisakujo (Casio)

Ibuka Masaru, 38, and Morita Akio, 25, found Tokyo Tsushin Kogyo (Sony).

Iwama Kazuo joins Tokyo Tsushin Kogyo.

1947   New Japanese Constitution goes into effect.

Sasaki Tadashi visits Bell Labs, meets John Bardeen.

John Bardeen, 39, and Walter Brattain, 45, invent the first point-contact transistor.

Bardeen and Brattain demonstrate the transistor.

W. Edwards Deming arrives in Japan.

Esaki Leona joins Kobe Kogyo.

Sanyo Electric Works established.

1948   Bell Labs publicly announces the invention of the transistor.

Bill Shockley, 37, invents junction (bipolar) transistor.

1949   Justice Department initiates antitrust suit against AT&T.

Teshima Toru, 24, joins Stanley Electric.

Yukawa becomes first Japanese to win the Nobel Prize in physics.

1950   Korean War begins.

Deming, speaking in Tokyo, predicts Japanese quality will be the best in the world.

Kawakami Gen'ichi, 38, succeeds his father as president of
Yamaha.

Nishizawa Jun'ichi invents static induction transistor.

1951   San Francisco Peace Treaty, first United States–Japan Security
Treaty

Union of Japanese Scientists and Engineers establishes Deming
Prize (legend on prize medal reads: "The right quality and
uniformity are foundations of commerce, prosperity, and
peace").

Invention of gallium arsenide compound semiconductor material

Rashomon, directed by Kurosawa Akira, wins Grand Prix at
Venice Film Festival.

Invention of shadow-mask TV picture tube at RCA Laboratories.

1951–52   Procurement orders to Japanese manufacturers from U.S. military
peak at nearly $800 million. (By end of 1954, "Divine Aid" to
Japan will total nearly $3 billion.)

Kobe Kogyo concludes technical cooperation agreement with
RCA.

RCA Princeton Laboratories renamed David Sarnoff Research
Center.

Bell Labs holds five-day ("properties and applications") transistor
symposium; three hundred attend from universities, military,
and industry.

Sasaki Tadashi and Arizumi Tetsuya go to U.S.

1952   On their return, Kobe Kogyo begins transistor R&D.

Original transistor licenses issued (licensees include TI).

Ibuka Masaru makes three-month trip to U.S.

Western Electric transistor technology ("cookbook") symposium
for licensees, 25 U.S. companies; 12 foreign, mostly European
attend.

Occupation ends, Japan regains sovereignty.

1953   International conference on theoretical physics held in Tokyo;
Bardeen presents paper, gives lectures.

FCC approves NTSC national television standard.

NHK begins TV broadcasts in Japan.

Hayakawa Electric begins producing Japan's first televisions, under
licence from RCA.

Korean War ends.

Kawakami of Yamaha embarks on three-month round-the-world
trip.

Morita travels on to United States to sign transistor license.

1954   MITI allocates foreign currency to Totsuko (Sony) for transistor license.

Regency announces first transistor radio.

Kobe Kogyo begins production of transistors for car radios.

Justice Department files antitrust suit against RCA.

Bell Labs produces first practical silicon photovoltaic cells.

Bell Labs begins development of Picturephone.

Casio develops first electric calculator.

1955   Totsuko (Sony) makes transistor, builds prototype transistor radio.

North American Aviation forms Autonetics ("automatic cybernetics"); by 1960, Autonetics is the company's largest division, employing 26,000.

1956   Shockley, Bardeen, and Brattain win Nobel Prize in physics.

Shockley leaves Bell Labs, founds Shockley Semiconductor in Palo Alto.

AT&T consent decree agrees to license all patents free of charge to domestic competitors, also agrees not to sell semiconductors.

Western Electric symposium on diffusion, oxide masking (key semiconductor process technologies); Iwama attends

IBM forms research division.

Esaki Leona joins Tokyo Tsushin Kogyo (Sony).

1957   Esaki, 32, invents tunnel diode.

Sony introduces first pocket-type transistor radio; ships half a million units.

Mochida Yasunori joins Yamaha with a brief to build a transistorized organ.

U.S.S.R. launches *Sputnik*, first artificial satellite.

Fairchild Semiconductor founded.

Ampex introduces first videotape recorder.

Westinghouse begins liquid crystal research program.

1958   RCA consent decree agrees to make all color TV patents available to domestic competitors.

Charles Townes and Art Schawlow publish laser proposal.

Jack Kilby, 35, invents integrated circuit.

1959   Bob Noyce, 32, invents integrated circuit.

1960   Ted Maiman invents first (ruby) laser at Hughes.

David Sarnoff arrives in Japan.

Bulova begins sales of Accutron watch.

Sony introduces first all-transistor TV.

	John Atalla builds first MOS field-effect transistor.
1961	Xerox ships first copier.
	John F. Kennedy proposes Moon Landing project.
	North American Aviation wins contracts to build Apollo command and service modules ("the most complex industrial project ever undertaken").
	Ikeda Hayato introduces Income Doubling Plan, to double national income in the decade 1961–1970 (goal will be reached in 1968).
	Japan Research & Development Corporation established.
1962	AT&T launches Telstar, first communications satellite.
	Cuban Missile Crisis
	Bob Hall, 40, builds first semiconductor laser (beating IBM, MIT Lincoln Lab, and GE colleague Nick Holonyak).
	Paul Weimer publishes work on thin-film transistors.
	Nick Holonyak, 34, builds first visible (red) light emitting diode.
	Canon begins diversification from cameras to office machines.
	Frank Wanlass of Fairchild elucidates sodium contamination problem; clears way for mass production of MOS devices.
1963	Frank Wanlass patents first C-MOS circuit.
	Invention of liquid-phase epitaxy at RCA
	Suwa Seiko produces first quartz timepiece.
1964	Hayakawa markets first transistorized desktop calculator.
	Inauguration of Tokyo–Osaka *Shinkansen* bullet train
	Tokyo Olympic Games begin.
	George Heilmeier, 28, invents dynamic scattering liquid crystal display.
	Researchers at University of Illinois develop AC plasma display panel.
	AT&T demonstrates Picturephone at New York World's Fair.
	Sony demos first solid-state desktop calculator at New York World's Fair.
	Sasaki Tadashi, 49, joins Hayakawa Electric.
1965	David Sarnoff hands reins of RCA over to his son, Bobby.
	NEC makes first Japanese integrated circuits.
	Casio introduces first electronic calculator.
	Kilby and colleagues at TI begin work on handheld calculator.
1966	Hayakawa produces first calculator with ICs.
	Invention of vacuum fluorescent display, production by Ise Electric.

1967   John Chowning, 33, discovers FM algorithm.
       RCA begins sampling C-MOS devices.
       TI completes prototype of first handheld calculator.
       Sony markets Sobax desktop calculator.
       Rockwell-Standard merges with North American Aviation to
           become North American Rockwell.
1968   FCC rules that non-AT&T equipment can be attached to phone
           network.
       Intel founded.
       RCA holds press conference to announce LCDs.
       Sony introduces Trinitron.
1969   Rockwell and Hayakawa announce biggest-ever contract to build
           MOS circuits.
       Invention of MOCVD by Hal Manasevit at Rockwell.
       Commercial introduction of (red) LEDs by HP and Monsanto.
       First gallium nitride crystals grown at RCA.
1969   Sharp announces $277 MOSLSI calculator at IEEE show in New
           York City.
       The *Eagle* lands at Tranquility Base: first human beings land on
           Moon in the *Apollo II* lunar module. (The Apollo program
           purchased more than 1 million integrated circuits.)
       Invention of molecular beam epitaxy by John Arthur and Al Cho
           at Bell Labs.
       Seiko introduces first quartz watch.
       Suwa Seiko begins research on C-MOS.
       Bill Boyle, 45, and George Smith, 39, invent CCD.
       Teshima becomes R&D director of Stanley, begins work on LEDs.
1970   Kent State massacre.
       Hayashi Izuo, 48, and Morton Panish, 41, invent continuous wave
           room-temperature semiconductor laser.
       Hayakawa builds semiconductor factory, changes name to Sharp.
       Esaki and Chu propose superlattice at IBM
       Intel makes first D-RAM.
1971   Intel introduces 4004, first microprocessor (2,700 transistors).
       Pocketronic calculator marketed (by Canon).
       "Dollar Shock": Released from fixed rate, yen rises in value from
           ¥360 per dollar to ¥308.
       Hamilton markets Pulsar LED watch, priced at $1,500.
       Xerox demonstrates first laser printer.
       Jacques Pankove demonstrates GaN-based LED.

RCA exits computer business, taking $490 million writeoff.

David Sarnoff dies, aged 80.

1972   Hewlett Packard introduces first scientific calculator, the $395
            HP-35.

James Fergason demonstrates twisted nematic LCD.

Intel markets 8008, first 8-bit microprocessor.

Toshiba begins manufacture of C-MOS calculator chips.

Western Electric halts production of Picturephone sets.

Bernie Vonderschmitt becomes GM of RCA's Solid-State Division.

1973   Suwa Seiko builds semiconductor factory.

Sharp introduces first LCD calculator.

Sony begins development of CCD.

Yamaha licenses FM synthesis patent from Stanford.

Esaki wins Nobel Prize in physics for tunnel diode.

Seiko introduces first digital LCD watch.

OPEC announces 21-percent hike in price of crude oil.

1973–74 Prolonged recession following oil embargo.

1974   Justice Department files new antitrust suit against AT&T.

Sharp introduces bright thin-film EL display.

Peter Brody and colleagues at Westinghouse apply TFTs to LCDs.

Kikuchi Makoto joins Sony as Director of R&D Center.

Matsushita overtakes RCA to become largest TV producer in the
            world.

Sixty-three Japanese companies make calculators; Busico, the
            company for which Intel designed the first microprocessor, goes
            bankrupt.

Dave Carlson, 32, and Chris Wronski, 34, invent amorphous-
            silicon solar cell at RCA.

1975   Walter Spear and Peter LeComber of Dundee University
            demonstrate that amorphous silicon can be doped.

Sharp's calculator sales pass 10-million mark.

Sony markets Betamax VCR.

Emperor Hirohito travels to U.S., visits Disneyland.

Canon demos laser printer at National Computer Conference.

1976   Pat Haggerty retires from TI.

Lockheed scandal

Iwama becomes president of Sony.

JVC markets VHS.

Al Cho grows first semiconductor lasers by MBE (at Bell Labs).

	Bell System's first full-scale experiment in optic fiber communications at Western Electric's Atlanta Works

Bell System's first full-scale experiment in optic fiber
    communications at Western Electric's Atlanta Works

Stanley develops world's brightest red LED.

1977   Introduction of 16K D-RAM

Russell Dupuis grows first laser diodes by MOCVD (at Rockwell).

1978   Hitachi announces fast C-MOS Static RAM.

Philips and Sony agree on specifications for compact disc.

Monsanto sells LED business.

Sharp demonstrates prototype EL wall-hanging TV.

DiscoVision laser disc players marketed in Atlanta.

1979   Spear and LeComber propose amorphous silicon for TFTs.

Bernie Vonderschmitt leaves RCA.

Sony introduces Walkman.

Mimura Takashi, 34, invents high electron mobility transistor at Fujitsu.

1980   Masuoka Fujio, 35, invents flash memory at Toshiba.

Sony installs CCD in ANA jumbo jet (first commercial application).

Japanese automobile production overtakes that of the U.S.

Hayakawa Tokuji dies, aged 88.

Sanyo introduces first commercial a-Si solar cell.

1981   Breakup of Bell System.

RCA introduces Selectavision VideoDisc.

1982   Iwama Kazuo dies of cancer, aged 63.

Sony and Philips introduce CD player.

1982   Suwa Seiko develops monochrome Dick Tracy wristwatch TV.

Yamaha introduces DX-7 keyboard.

1983   Suwa Seiko announces 3-inch poly-Si TFT TV.

Sanyo shows prototype a-Si TFT display.

1984   To settle federal antitrust suit, AT&T agrees to spin off regional Bell operating companies.

HP introduces LaserJet printer.

RCA discontinues VideoDisc player, total loss: $580 million.

1985   Teshima becomes president of Stanley.

Following the Plaza Accord, yen appreciates steeply.

Suwa Seiko and Epson consolidate to form Seiko Epson.

GE acquires RCA for $6.28 billion.

1986   Direct Broadcasting by Satellite (DBS) begins in Japan.

1987   Hattori Ichiro dies, aged 55.

Introduction of CD-ROM.

1988	Akasaki Isamu makes p-type gallium nitride.
	Washizuka Isamu demonstrates 14-inch TFT LCD at Sharp.
1989	Emperor Hirohito dies, aged 88.
1990	Teshima retires from Stanley.
1991	3M reports zinc-selenide blue laser.
	Nakamura Shuji, 36, of Nichia Chemical makes his first blue LED
1993	Nichia announces world's brightest blue LED.
	W. Edwards Deming dies, aged 93.
1994	Nichia begins mass production of blue LEDs
	Hughes Electronics introduces DirecTV.
1996	Nakamura announces room-temperature, pulsed mode bluish-purple laser diode.
	Nakamura succeeds in developing room-temperature, continuous-wave blue laser.

PEOPLE

Japanese

Akasaki Isamu	Developed gallium nitride growth technology at Matsushita/Nagoya University.
Arizumi Tetsuya	Made first commercial Japanese transistor at Kobe Kogyo.
Chiba Genya	Promoted indigenous technology development at JRDC.
Esaki Leo(na)	Invented tunnel diode at Sony; proposed superlattice at IBM.
Fujimori Akira	Developed laser diode for CD player at Sharp.
Fukuta Masumi	Pioneered gallium arsenide devices at Fujitsu.
Harigaya Hiroshi	Led C-MOS development at Suwa Seiko.
Hattori Ichiro	Son of Shoji; invested in semiconductor production at Suwa-Seiko and Seiko Epson.
Hattori Kentaro	Son of Kintaro.
Hattori Kintaro	Founded Seiko.
Hattori Shoji	Sponsored C-MOS development at Suwa Seiko.
Hayakawa Tokuji	Founded Hayakawa Electric, later Sharp.
Hayashi Izu	Codeveloped first practical semiconductor laser at Bell Labs.
Ibuka Masaru	Cofounded Sony.
Ikeda Hayato	Initiated income-doubling plan while prime minister of Japan
Ikeda Toshio	Pioneered computers at Fujitsu
Inaba Seiuemon	Pioneered numerical controls at Fujitsu
Inoue Hiroshi	Led C-MOS development at Sharp
Ishimura Kazukiyo	Led C-MOS development at Yamaha
Iue Toshio	Founded Sanyo
Iwama Kazuo	Initiated CCD development at Sony
Kashio Tadao	Founded Casio
Kawakami Gen'ichi	Sponsored development of electronic keyboards at Yamaha
Kawakami Kaichi	Father of Gen'ichi

Kawana Yoshiyuki	Led CCD development at Sony
Kikuchi Makoto	Made first Japanese transistor at Electro-Technical Laboratory; directed research at Sony
Kitano Takaharu	Founded Stanley Electric
Kitano Takaoki	Son of Takaharu
Kurokawa Kaneyuki	Pioneered optical fiber communication at Bell Labs
Kuwano Yukinori	Pioneered amorphous silicon solar cells at Sanyo
Masuhara Toshiaki	Coinvented fast C-MOS memory at Hitachi
Masuoka Fujio	Invented flash memory at Toshiba
Matsushita Konosuke	Founded Matsushita
Mimura Takashi	Invented high electron mobility transistor at Fujitsu
Mitarai Hajime	Son of Takeshi, former president of Canon
Mitarai Takeshi	Founded Canon
Mochida Yasunori	Developed keyboards based on FM synthesis at Yamaha
Morita Akio	Cofounded Sony
Morozumi Shinji	Pioneered active matrix LCDs at Suwa Seiko
Nishizawa Jun'ichi	Invented static induction transistor; super-bright red LED at Tohoku University
Nakamura Michiharu	Pioneered semiconductor laser at Hitachi
Nakamura Shuji	Invented super-bright blue LED at Nichia
Nakamura Tsuneya	Led development of quartz watch at Suwa Seiko
Ochi Shigeyuki	Pioneered CCD at Sony
Ogawa Nobuo	Founded Nichia
Ohga Norio	Succeeded Iwama as president at Sony
Saeki Akira	Supported Sasaki at Sharp
Sasaki Tadashi	Championed calculator technologies at Sharp
Sato Ken	Founded Rohm
Tanaka Haruo	Pioneered lasers grown by MBE at Rohm
Teshima Toru	Led development of super-bright red LED at Stanley
Tomonaga Shin'ichiro	Proposed quantum electrodynamics at Kyoto University
Tsukamoto Tetsuo	Reengineered Western Electric transistor at Sony
Uenohara Michiyuki	Directed R&D at NEC
Wada Tomio	Pioneered LCD development at Sharp
Washizuka Isamu	Led active matrix LCD development at Sharp
Watanabe Hiroshi	Directed Central research Lab at Hitachi
Watanabe Seiichi	Succeeded Kikuchi as research director at Sony
Yamaha Torakatsu	Founded Yamaha
Yamaji Keizo	Led laser printer development at Canon
Yamazaki Yoshio	Pioneered LCD development at Suwa Seiko
Yasui Tokumasu	Coinvented fast C-MOS memory at Hitachi
Yukawa Hideki	Discovered meson at Osaka University

Americans and Others

Amelio, Gil	Championed CCD at Fairchild
Bardeen, John	Coinvented point contact transistor at Bell Labs
Boyle, Willard	Coinvented CCD at Bell Labs
Brattain, Walter	Coinvented point-contact transistor at Bell Labs
Brody, Peter	Developed TFT flat-panel displays at Westinghouse
Buchla, Don	Built first modern synthesizer
Burmeister, Bob	Developed first LEDs at Hewlett-Packard
Carlson, Dave	Coinvented amorphous silicon solar cells at RCA
Castellano, Joe	Developed LCDs at RCA
Cho, Al	Pioneered MBE at Bell Labs
Chowning, John	Invented FM synthesis at Stanford University
Craford, George	Developed first yellow LEDs at Monsanto
Dingle, Ray	Invented modulation doping at Bell Labs
Dupuis, Russell	Pioneered MOCVD at Rockwell
Early, Jim	Initiated CCD research at Fairchild
Eyestone, Fred	Initiated MOS production at Rockwell
Fergason, James	Invented twisted nematic LCDs at Kent State University
Galt, John	Initiated development of semiconductor laser at Bell Labs
Gibson, Rod	Worked with Spear and LeComber at Dundee University
Hackbourne, Dick	Championed laser printers at Hewlett-Packard
Haggarty, Pat	Initiated transistor development at Texas Instruments; sponsored chip calculator
Hall, Bob	Invented semiconductor laser at General Electric
Hammond, Laurens	Invented Hammond Organ
Heilmeier, George	Invented dynamic scattering LCDs at RCA
Herzog, Gerry	Initiated C-MOS development at RCA
Hoerni, Jean	Invented planar transistor at Fairchild; pioneered C-MOS chips at Intersil
Holonyak, Nick	Invented visible light-emitting diode
Javan, Ali	Invented helium-neon laser at Bell Labs
Kahn, Fred	Pioneered LCDs at NEC, Hewlett-Packard
Kalish, Israel	Developed first C-MOS circuits at RCA
Kao, Charles	Proposed optical fiber communications
Kilby, Jack	Coinvented integrated circuit; designed first pocket calculator
Kish, Fred	Invented super-bright orange LEDs at Hewlett-Packard
Kosonocky, Walter	Developed CCD at RCA

Kovac, Charlie   Marketing vice president at Autonetics

LeComber, Peter   Coinvented amorphous silicon solar cells and TFTs at Dundee University

Maiman, Ted   Invented first (ruby) laser

Mathews, Max   Pioneered computer music at Bel Labs

Merryman, Jerry   Worked on pocket calculator at Texas Instruments

Moore, Gordon   Cofounded Intel

Noyce, Bob   Coinvented integrated circuit; cofounded Intel

Ohl, Russell   Discovered photoelectric effect in silicon at Bell Labs

Ovshinsky, Stanford   Pioneered amorphous materials at Energy Conversion Devices

Panish, Morton   Codeveloped first practical semiconductor laser at Bell Labs

Pankove, Jacques   Pioneered gallium nitride at RCA

Prével, Martin   Pioneered sound boards at Ad Lib

Pierce, J. R.   Named transistor; encouraged computer music at Bell Labs

Rediker, Robert   Pioneered LED/laser at Lincoln Labs

Ruhrwein, Robert   Scaled up LED production technology at Monsanto

Sarnoff, David   Invented RCA

Schawlow, Art   Coproposed laser at Bell Labs

Shockley, Bill   Coinvented transistor at Bell Labs

Sim Wong Hoo   Developed sound boards at Creative Labs

Smith, George   Coinvented CCD at Bell Labs

Smith, Julius   Invented waveguides at Stanford University

Spear, Walter   Coinvented amorphous silicon solar cells and TFTs at Dundee University

Starkweather, Garry   Invented laser printer at Xerox Palo Alto Research Center (PARC)

Tannas, Larry   Pioneered LCDs at Rockwell

Thomas, David   Invented gallium phosphide LEDs at Bell Labs

Townes, Charles   Coproposed laser at Columbia University

Vonderschmitt, Bernie   Managed semiconductor production at RCA

Wanlass, Frank   Solved sodium contamination, invented C-MOS at Fairchild

Weimer, Paul   Pioneered thin-film transistors at RCA

Williams, Forest   Scaled up LED production technology at Monsanto

Williams, Richard   Invented LCD at RCA

Won Tien Tsang   Championed MBE for growing lasers at Bell Labs

Wronski, Chris   Coinvented amorphous silicon solar cells at RCA

SOURCES

References to books, magazines, and other printed sources are given as they occur, in footnotes in the text. An overall source I used extensively was *Japan: An Illustrated Encyclopedia* (New York: Kodansha, 1993). In addition to being a mine of useful information, this is also the most beautiful book I own. My main sources were interviews with the actual participants in the drama, of whom the following is a more or less complete list.

Interviews

Chapter One

Esaki Leo	6	September	1994
Ichikawa Keizo	4	August	1995
Charlie Kovac (phone)	26	May	1994
Jerry Merryman (phone)	24	October	1994
Takashi Mitsutomi (phone)	6	September	1995
David Rubinfien	2	July	1996
Sasaki Tadashi	1	February	1994
Sasaki Tadashi	6	April	1995
Sasaki Tadashi	14	November	1995
Yawata Keiske	11	March	1994

Chapter Two

John Hall (phone)	6	March	1996
Gerry Herzog	28	June	1994
Harigaya Hiroshi	21	January	1994
Jean Hoerni (phone)	27	February	1996
Inoue Hiroshi	14	July	1994
Israel Kalish	18	April	1994
Kawanishi Tsuyoshi	16	November	1994
Nakamura Tsuneya	4	February	1994
Makimoto Tsugio	23	March	1995
Masuhara Toshiaki	17	March	1994

Bernie Vonderschmitt	1	November	1993
Frank Wanlass	3	July	1996
Yasui Tokumasa	17	March	1994

Chapter Three

Joe Castellano (phone)	25	April	1995
James Fergason	28	June	1994
George Heilmeier (phone)	8	March	1994
Masaya Hijikigawa	26	April	1994
Fred Kahn (phone)	22	April	1995
Larry Tannas (phone)	15	July	1995
Wada Tomio	10	May	1995
Richard Williams	19	April	1994
Yamazaki Yoshio	2	February	1994

Chapter Four

| Morozumi Shinji | 3 | August | 1995 |
| Paul Weimer | 19 | April | 1994 |

Chapter Five

David Carlson (phone)	6	November	1995
Rod Gibson	19	September	1995
Kuwano Yukinori	18	November	1994

Chapter Six

Gil Amelio	27	June	1994
Bill Boyle (phone)	30	May	1995
Jim Early	29	June	1994
Kawana Yoshiyuki	9	August	1994
Kikuchi Makoto	18	November	1993
Kikuchi Makoto	23	February	1995
Walter Kosonocky	19	April	1994
Miyaoka Senri	9	August	1994
Ochi Shigeyuki	23	March	1994
Ogawa Mutsuo	13	September	1994
George Smith (phone)	21	August	1994

Chapter Seven

John Chowning	3	November	1993
John Chowning	1	July	1994
Ishimura Kazukiyo	22	December	1993
Joe Koepnick	3	July	1996
Max Mathews	3	November	1993
J. R. Pierce	1	July	1994
Niels Reimers	4	November	1993
Mochida Yasunori	7	November	1993
Mochida Yasunori	20	December	1993

Chapter Eight

Al Cho	20	April	1994
Fujimori Akira	16	March	1995
George Hall	13	April	1994
Hayashi Izuo	27	October	1994
Kurokawa Kaneyuki	10	November	1994
Mitarai Hajime	30	November	1994
Mori Yoshihisa	20	September	1994
Nakamura Michiharu	10	August	1994
Nakajima Heitaro	16	May	1994
Morton Panish (phone)	27	January	1995
Bob Rediker	15	April	1994
Rangu Hiroyoshi	18	July	1996
Gary Starkweather (phone)	25	May	1994
Steve Simpson (phone)	8	June	1994
Tanaka Haruo	1	November	1994
Won Tsien Tsang (phone)	11	November	1994
Yamaji Keizo	8	December	1994

Chapter Nine

Roger Allen (phone)	13	September	1996
Bob Burmeister	1	July	1994
George Craford (phone)	18	August	1994
Chiba Genya	4	March	1994
Chiba Genya	26	July	1995
Paul Green (phone)	29	October	1994
Nick Holonyak (phone)	5	March	1994

Miyuki Minoru	15	July	1994
Teshima Toru	31	March	1994
Teshima Toru	6	September	1994

Chapter Ten

Akasaki Isamu	22	May	1995
Nakamura Shuji	16	April	1994
Nakamura Shuji	16	May	1995
Ogawa Eiji	16	April	1994
Ogawa Nobuo	16	May	1995
Jacques Pankove	29	September	1994

Chapter 11

Ray Dingle (phone)	20	January	1995
Fukuta Masumi	21	November	1994
Art Gossard (phone)	7	November	1994
Masuoka Fujio	8	December	1993
Mimura Takashi	17	November	1994
Misugi Takahiko	21	November	1994
Sakaki Hiroyuki	18	January	1995

GLOSSARY

Active matrix liquid crystal display (AM-LCD) Flat-panel display screen driven by thin-film transistors, usually made of amorphous silicon. Produces a brighter picture than passive matrix LCD.

Amorphous silicon Brown-colored, randomly ordered material used to make solar cells and thin-film transistors.

Bipolar transistor Transistor that uses both negative- and positive-charge carriers. First type of transistor to go into mass production. Also known as junction transistor.

Bubble memory Early form of magnetic storage for digital data. Superseded by D-RAM.

Cadmium selenide, sulphide Photoconductive compound semiconductor materials used in early thin-film transistors.

Capacitor Passive device used for temporary storage of electrical charge.

Cathode ray tube (CRT) Funnel-shaped bulb of evacuated glass used to display television pictures and as a computer monitor screen.

Charge-coupled device (CCD) Solid-state image sensor used in video cameras and filmless digital still cameras.

Complementary Metal Oxide Semiconductor (C-MOS) Combines negative and positive type transistors on a chip. Low power and high speed make C-MOS the dominant process in the semiconductor industry.

Compound semiconductor Semiconductor material consisting of two or more elements. Gallium arsenide, used in lasers, LEDs, and microwave devices, is the best known example.

Core memory Obsolete form of magnetic storage.

Diffusion High-temperature process used to change the electrical characteristics of semiconductor materials by doping them with positively and negatively charged impurities.

Diode Two-terminal semiconductor device that allows current to flow in one direction only.

Doping Adding trace amounts of impurities to semiconductors to make them positive or negative type.

Double heterostructure   Abrupt transitions between three different semiconductor materials forming a sandwich structure. Used to make lasers and LEDs. Also known as double heterojunction.

Dynamic random access memory (D-RAM)   Most commonly used form of semiconductor memory. So called because, unlike static memory, **D-RAM** must be periodically refreshed to preserve its contents.

Dynamic scattering   Obsolete form of LCD characterized by milky-white letters and numerals.

Electroluminescent (EL) display   Flat panel based on electrically excited phosphors. Characterized by yellow-colored readout.

Field-effect transistor (FET)   Transistor that uses only one kind of charge carrier: electrons or holes. Superseded bipolar and other types of transistor in almost all types of applications.

Flat-panel display   Any of several types of screen, including electroluminescent, liquid crystal, and plasma display panels.

FM (frequency modulation) synthesis   Method of producing sounds by combining the outputs of two or more oscillators.

Gallium aluminum arsenide   Compound semiconductor used to make red light–emitting diodes

Gallium arsenide   Compound semiconductor used to make infrared lasers and light–emitting diodes, and high-speed devices.

Gallium arsenide phosphide   Compound semiconductor used to make red and orange light–emitting diodes.

Gallium nitride   Compound semiconductor used to make green, blue, and violet lasers and light-emitting diodes.

Gallium phosphide   Compound semiconductor used to make red and green light–emitting diodes.

High electron mobility transistor (HEMT)   High-frequency gallium arsenide transistor used as an amplifier in dish antennas of direct broadcasting by satellite systems.

Integrated circuit (IC)   Various transistors, diodes, resistors, etc., contained on a single piece of (usually) silicon. Commonly known as a chip, or microchip.

Ion implantation   Precise method of doping semiconductors using beams of energized impurities. Superseded diffusion.

Laser diode   Semiconductor device that emits coherent light of a particular frequency. Used in laser printers, CD-ROM drives, and compact disc players.

Light-emitting diode (LED)   Semiconductor device that emits light of a particular color. Used in indicator lamps, displays, and brake lights.

Liquid crystal display (LCD)   Flat screen that operates by alternately blocking light and allowing it to pass. Extremely low power makes this form of display suitable for portable, battery-driven applications.

Liquid phase epitaxy (LPE)   Method used to grow films of semiconductor material for making lasers and LEDs. Superseded in advanced applications by MBE and MOCVD.

Magnetron   Power tube used to generate radio frequency signals for such applications as radar and microwave ovens.

Metal insulator semiconductor (MIS)   Alternate structure to p-n junctions formerly used to make light-emitting diodes and other devices.

Metal–organic chemical vapor deposition (MOCVD)   Method of growing extremely thin films of semiconductor materials by flowing gases over a heated wafer.

Metal oxide semiconductor (MOS)   Structure used to make field-effect transistors.

Modulation doping   Process for selectively varying the dopant in a device such as a HEMT grown by either MBE or MOCVD.

Molecular beam epitaxy (MBE)   Method of growing extremely thin films of semiconductor materials in an ultrahigh vacuum chamber by directing beams of elements at a target wafer.

Nixie tube   Obsolete form of neon-filled display used in early computers and scientific instruments.

Passive matrix liquid crystal display (PM-LCD)   Flat-panel display screen driven by a simple grid of electrodes. Produces a dimmer picture than active matrix LCD.

Planar transistor   Transistor on which all elements are laid down flat with respect to each other. Precursor to the integrated circuit.

Plasma display panel (PDP)   Flat screen based on ionized gas. Characterized by red-orange readout, though full-color screens have recently become available.

Phosphor   Material with luminescent properties used in lamps and display screens.

p-n junction   Structure formed by combination of positive and negative type semiconductor material. Used in diodes (including light emitters) and bipolar transistors.

Point-contact transistor   Original form of transistor, now obsolete.

Polycrystalline silicon   Blue-colored semiconductor material used to make solar cells and as wiring on chips

Resistor   Passive device used to limit current flow in electrical circuits.

Semiconductor   Class of materials, including silicon, germanium, and gallium arsenide, whose electrical properties lie midway between those of conductors, such as metal, and those of insulators such as rubber.

Semiconductor laser   Solid-state device that emits a beam of coherent light at a particular wavelength. Used in laser printers, compact disc players, and CD-ROM and DVD drives.

Single-crystal silicon   Silver-colored semiconductor material used to make chips.

Solar cell   Silicon device that converts sunlight into electricity.

Thin-film transistor (TFT)   Amorphous silicon device used to control active matrix LCDs.

Transistor   Three-terminal semiconductor device used as an amplifier in analog applications, and as a switch in digital ones.

Tunnel diode   Heavily doped device in which electrons tunnel through potential barriers. Also known as Esaki diode, after its inventor.

Twisted nematic   Dominant form of LCD, characterized by black letters and numerals on a gray background.

Vacuum fluorescent display (VFD)   Blue-green display device used in cars, point-of-sale terminals, and other mains-powered applications.

Vacuum tube   Evacuated glass device used as an amplifier. Replaced by transistor in almost all applications.

Vidicon   Image pick-up tube used in television cameras.

Wafer   Thin, polished slice of semiconductor material on which devices and integrated circuits are fabricated en masse, then diced up.

Zinc selenide   Compound semiconductor used to make green and blue lasers and light-emitting diodes.

Zone refining   Method used to purify ingots of semiconductor crystal.

ACKNOWLEDGMENTS

The seeds for this book were sown during a year (1990–91) I spent in the Knight Science Journalism Fellowship Program at the Massachusetts Institute of Technology. In particular, much stimulation came from discussions during regular walks to and from MIT with the program's director, Victor McElheny; also, from a most enlightening seminar on the history of technology given by the inestimable Tom Hughes. Vic subsequently became an enthusiastic supporter of the book, suggesting its title, and providing all sorts of help, in particular in finding a publisher. To him, more than anyone else, I give thanks.

Researching and writing this book over the past five years have been an exciting and often intensely pleasurable experience. A large part of that pleasure was the opportunity to meet and talk with many extraordinary individuals. The bulk of the book is derived from about one hundred such interviews. I am deeply grateful to these people, many of them senior executives, for taking time out of their busy schedules to talk to me, in some cases on several occasions.

In particular, I am grateful to two outstanding individuals. Kikuchi Makoto, one of the pioneers of semiconductor technology in Japan, was exceptionally generous with his time, in face-to-face interviews, in responding to my queries by letter, and in reading and commenting on early drafts of some of my chapters. He was also unstinting in his support for this project. Chiba Genya has been an inspiration to all who know him. In this project, in addition to filling me in on developments in which he participated personally, he was also an invaluable source of background information.

In addition to the interviewees, I would also like to express my heartfelt gratitude to the many people who helped support this project. Living in Japan made the logistics of doing interviews in that country relatively simple. On frequent visits to Northern California, I was lucky enough to be able to stay with good friends. I am deeply grateful to

Gavin Bourne and Leslie Davis for their gracious hospitality in Palo Alto. In addition, I owe Gavin special thanks for numerous insights into the history of Silicon Valley; also, for arousing my curiosity as to the nature of the mechanism via which C-MOS technology was transferred from the United States to Japan. I would also like to thank Bill and Lynn Clark for looking after me so well in the tranquillity of their Marin County eyrie. On the other side of the country Ruth and Victor McElheny kindly opened their doors to me in Cambridge, as did my good friend Tom Murtha in New York.

I am indebted to two other good friends, Michael Chinworth and Scott Callon, for reading early drafts of the manuscript, for their thoughtful comments and suggestions, and for their unflagging encouragement over the course of the project.

In addition, I must mention Dick Samuels, for whose enthusiastic support I have long been grateful. Dick runs the MIT Japan Program, under whose aegis an early version of chapter 7 appeared as a working paper.

I am also much obliged to Dan Okimoto and Jim Raphael for giving me the opportunity to air some of my themes in public for the first time in a seminar at the Stanford University Asia/Pacific Research Center; also, for their stimulating comments and criticisms.

In New Jersey, I want to thank Phyllis Smith at the David Sarnoff Research Center for setting up a most memorable visit, and for allowing me to delve into the archives at the David Sarnoff Library. Sincere thanks also to several generous individuals at AT&T Bell Laboratories, in particular to Donna Cunningham, virtual PR person extraordinaire, for (among other things) organizing a thrilling day for me at Murray Hill; to special projects writer Dick Hofacker for his unstinting patience in taking the time to set me straight about many things; and to Sheldon Hochheiser at AT&T Archives for his unfailing efficiency in digging up reference material for me.

Many thanks are also due to the Queen of the Silicon Bayou, Gayle LeDoux at Wilson McHenry Company and, latterly, Silicon Graphics, for her generosity in helping me on numerous occasions; in particular for her resourcefulness in tracking down people I needed to interview.

In Japan, for their help in setting up interviews, and their diligence in finding answers to my not infrequently arcane questions, I would like to thank the following corporate PR officers: at Canon, Egawa Nakaba; at Casio, Omura Taro; at Fujitsu, Mike Beirne; at Hitachi, Takase Emi;

at NEC, Mark Pearce; at Ricoh, Sakagami Hiroshi; at Rohm, Yoshimi Shinichi; at Sanyo, David Lee; at Seiko Epson, Kanamori Satoru; at Sharp, Minamihori Nobuo, at Sony, Georges Gérard and Aldo Liguori; at Toshiba, Ohashi Akira; and at Yamaha, Unno Kenji.

I am also grateful to Alexander B. Magoun, curator of the David Sarnoff Collection, Inc., for kindly granting permission to quote from Hans Straus's letter describing David Sarnoff's visit with Hayakawa Tokuji in October 1960.

Embryonic versions of chapters 7 and 9 appeared in *Wired* magazine. I am grateful to Louis Rossetto, Kevin Kelly, and John Batelle for indulging my curiosity and for printing the results.

I would especially like to thank George Gilder, for the inspiration of his writing and for his personal encouragement on several occasions.

I owe a particular debt of gratitude to my agent, William Miller of the English Agency in Tokyo, whose faith in my work kept my spirits up, and who has consistently pointed me in the right direction.

I was flattered that Mike Bessie thought my book worthy of publishing. Mike has been a delight to deal with from start to finish. At Basic Books, Tim Bartlett has been very efficient with the book and very gentle with me. Many thanks also to project editor Richard Fumosa and in particular to copy editor Ruth Davis for her delicate touch and exquisite judgment.

Above all, I am most grateful to my wife, Nakaki Setsuko, for her support. Not only for putting up with a monumental obsession over the course of several years, but also in practical terms, for helping me with translation and transcription, and for explaining the mores of her native land.

This research was assisted by a grant from the Abe Fellowship Program of the Social Science Research Council and the American Council of Learned Societies with funds provided by the Japan Foundation Center for Global Partnership.

I am deeply grateful not only to the Program and its officers past and present, notably Mary-Lea Cox and Sheri Ranis, but also to Jim Bartholomew, Kikuchi Makoto, and Mike Nelson for their generous support of my Abe Fellowship proposal.

Needless to add, all errors of fact and judgment in the text are mine.

Melbourne, July 1998

NOTES

Preface

1. Makoto Kikuchi, *Japanese Electronics: A Worm's-Eye View of its Evolution* (Tokyo: Simul Press, 1983).

2. At the Edinburgh Academy, Maxwell was reviled as a bookworm and nicknamed "dafty" (source: Philip J. Smith).

3. Hayato was, I think, the prime minister who on a visit to France was contemptuously dismissed by French President Charles de Gaulle as a mere "transistor salesman."

4. *MITI and the Japanese Miracle: The Growth of Industrial Policy, 1925–1975* (Stanford University Press, 1982).

5. *Business Week*, 14 December 1981, p. 36. The assertion appeared in a special feature entitled "Japan's strategy for the '80s." To be fair, one should also mention that ten pages later the same survey sensibly added, "But viewing MITI as the controlling hand behind Japanese companies' every move ... is too simplistic." Indeed.

6. VLSI stands for "very large scale integration," which in turn means tens of thousands of transistors on one chip.

7. The term "Japan Inc." entered the lexicon in the late 1960s. In a speech before the Industrial Committee of the OECD, MITI vice minister Ojimi Yoshihisa defined it as follows: "... recently some people have expressed the opinion in relation to Japan's industrial policy that Japan in its entirety is like a corporation ('Japan Inc.'), that the Japanese Government, particularly MITI, is the corporate headquarters, and that each enterprise is a branch or division of the corporation. Some view the relationship between government and industry as being that between hand and glove."

But the vice minister went on to pooh-pooh the idea: "... the postwar period being as it may, today there is no such thing as unilateral MITI direction of business activity of individual enterprises or passive acceptance by business of government judgment."

Eugene J. Kaplan, *Japan: The Government-Business Relationship* (U.S. Government Printing Office, 1972), pp. 14–15.

8. Jim Martin, Chair, Competitiveness Task Force, National Research Council, 28 July 1997.

9. In *Japan vs. Europe: A History of Misunderstanding*, by Endymion Wilkinson (London: Penguin, 1983).

10. Scott Callon, *Turf Wars: Bureaucratic Conflict in Japanese High Technology Consortia* (Stanford: Stanford University, Asia/Pacific Research Center, Draft Working Paper, 1994).

Industrial policy aficionados are encouraged also to read Callon's devastating full-length critique, *Divided Sun: MITI and the Breakdown of Japanese High Tech Industrial Policy, 1975–1993* (Palo Alto: Stanford University Press, 1995).

11. Anecdote quoted in *Genryu: Sony Challenge 1946–1968*, p. 108, a collection of columns from the company's management newsletter published in Tokyo to commemorate Sony's 40th anniversary in 1986.

12. Akio Morita, *Made in Japan: Akio Morita and Sony* (Tokyo: Weatherhill, 1987), p. 66.

13. Between MITI and the Market: Japanese Industrial Policy for High Technology, Daniel I. Okimoto, Stanford University Press, 1989, p. 65.

14. John W. Dower, *War Without Mercy: Race and Power in the Pacific War* (New York: Pantheon, 1986), p. 30.

15. This anecdote comes from an article by Michael Wolff in IEEE *Spectrum*, "The secret six-month project" (date unknown). The first transistorized computer was probably the UNIVAC Solid State 80, introduced in August 1958 (source: Paul Ceruzzi). As late as 1991, according to Electronic Industry Association of Japan figures, consumer equipment accounted for 42.5% of Japanese semiconductor demand, compared to 32% for computers.

16. *Japanese Innovation Strategy: Technical Support for Business Visions*, by Lewis M. Branscomb and Fumio Kodama (Cambridge, Mass.: Harvard University Center for Science and International Affairs, 1993), pp. 12–13.

17. "Gordon Moore's Crystal Ball," *Business Week*, 23 June 1997, p. 66.

18. A good example of this phenomenon is the laser printer. In his book, *The HP Way* (New York: HarperBusiness, 1995), p. 116, David Packard related: "With LaserJet printers, we decided that each revision would offer our customers greater capability at a lower price than its predecessor."

19. David F. Noble, *Forces of Production: A Social History of Industrial Automation* (Oxford: Oxford University Press, 1984).

Introduction

1. Akio Morita, *Made in Japan: Akio Morita and Sony* (Tokyo: Weatherhill, 1987) p. 214.

2. *Made in Japan*, p. 66.

3. Richard Storry, *A History of Modern Japan*, rev. ed. (London: Penguin, 1982), p. 42.

4. This figure comes from Noel Perry's delightful and instructive monograph, *Giving Up the Gun: Japan's Reversion to the Sword, 1543–1879* (Boston: David R. Godine, 1979), p. 10.

5. *Modern Japan*, p. 31.

6. *Giving Up the Gun*, p. 17.

7. Anonymous Japanese trade journal, quoted in Maureen Erbe, Aileen Antonier, and Roger Handy, *Made in Japan: Transistor Radios of the 50s and 60s* (San Francisco: Chronicle Books, 1993), p. 29.

8. *The Engineer*, 16 December 1960.

9. Quoted in T. R. Reid's indispensible book, *The Chip: How Two Americans Invented the Microchip & Launched a Revolution* (New York: Simon & Schuster, 1984), p. 181.

10. Esaki insists that Leona (a Japanized variant of Leonard) is his given name, and not, as is often thought, Reona. The confusion arises because Japanese has no "L" sound. When Esaki decamped to the United States to work for IBM in 1960, he became known as Leo.

11. Quoted in "The transistor: Two decades of progress," a special report in *Electronics* magazine, 19 February 1968, p. 81.

"What Bell hoped to do was to improve the transistor so that it might become a really valuable device, particularly for the communications system, by encouraging other firms to tackle the problem. By publishing, holding seminars and licensing widely, Bell did its utmost to stimulate others to play a part in developing the device. This accorded well with Bell's coveted image as a public utility, but it made good practical sense, too. The more Bell appeared to be performing a public service, the less the danger from the anti-monopoly lobby" (Ernest Braun and Stuart Macdonald, *Revolution in Miniature: The history and impact of semiconductor electronics,* [Cambridge: Cambridge University Press, 1978], p. 48).

12. Ibid. "After 1956, Bell's early transistor patents earned royalties only from foreign companies."

13. Margaret Graham, *The Business of Research: RCA and the VideoDisc* (Cambridge: Cambridge University Press, 1986), p. 41.

14. Unpublished speech.

15. The conventional wisdom is, as T. R. Reid put it in *The Chip*, p. 169, "The Japanese aggressively purchased patent licenses in the West." RCA's behavior suggests that a corrective along the lines of "The Americans aggressively peddled patent licenses in Japan" is necessary.

16. *War Without Mercy*, p. 123.

17. Government researchers operated at a particular disadvantage, as Kikuchi Makoto relates: "Our friends in companies obtained much information through license agreements with American industrial partners. Once, I wrote to a U.S. company saying that I wished to purchase a high-frequency generator and a temperature controller, and requested some ratings. Their answer refused to provide any information to a Japanese government employee. We simply had to work on our own and collect knowledge and experience ourselves" ("How a Physicist Fell in Love with Silicon in the Early Years of Japanese R&D" [unpublished paper]).

18. These anecdotes about Japanese semiconductor pioneers are taken from the excellent television documentary by Japan's national broadcasting corporation NHK, *Denshi Rikkoku Nihon no Jijoden* ("Autobiography of Japan, a Country Based on Electronics") directed by Aida Yutaka, 1992.

19. *Made in Japan*, p. 68.

20. Personal communication with the author, 31 January 1996.

Chapter One

1. Akio Morita, *Made in Japan: Akio Morita and Sony* (Tokyo: Weatherhill, 1987), p. 160.

2. The name "Silicon Valley" was coined by Don Hoeffler, editor of *Microelectronics News*, in 1971.

3. This version of the story is the one that Sasaki tells. Charlie Kovac, then vice president of marketing at North American Rockwell, offers the following—somewhat different—version: "At the time, Autonetics, being the military facility that it was, required approval from the Department of Defense and the Department of Commerce to even host these guests. We had an international division, and I think that Dr. Sasaki and a few of his protégés were sitting in the lobby of that international division waiting for the clearances from DoD and DoC for three days. The clearances didn't arrive, and this caused them to reschedule to go back to Japan. So they went back to the Los Angeles airport and were waiting in the JAL lounge to catch their flight. And lo and behold that morning

their clearances came through from DoD and DoC to allow us to talk to them, and to cut a long story short, they canceled their flight and came back, and our relationship started."

4. Quoted in the July 1946 edition of "195 Bulletin," a Bell System newsletter (named for the address of AT&T's head office, 195 Broadway in New York City).

5. The transistor was actually invented on 16 December 1947. The official birthday came a week later, when the device was first demonstrated to the Bell Labs brass in the form of a circuit that could amplify sound.

6. Kobe Kogyo supplied subminiature tubes to the Galvin Manufacturing Company of Chicago, the firm now known as Motorola.

7. After graduating from MIT in 1953, Mitsutomi worked for the Electronics Research Division of Autonetics for eighteen years. In 1971, with support from Sasaki, he formed a company called Hycom, a 50–50 joint venture with Sharp. In 1989, the Japanese bought the other 50 percent, and Hycom became Sharp Digital Information Products, a wholly owned subsidiary.

8. In Sasaki's office hangs a drawing, a present from North American Rockwell, captioned "Rocket Sasaki." It depicts him, a big grin on his face, sitting astride a (Minuteman?) rocket labeled "Sharp."

9. "A Distant Star," staged in Osaka in 1973.

10. The description comes from an unpublished letter to Sarnoff's brother, Irving, written by Hans Straus, an RCA executive based in Japan.

11. Robert Teitelman, *Profits of Science: The American Marriage of Business and Technology* (New York: Basic Books, 1994), p. 59.

12. Other than the name, which it purchased from the original firm, the contemporary personal computer company trading as Packard Bell is unrelated.

13. According to an article by Nick Valéry, "Coming of age in the calculator business" (*New Scientist Calculator Supplement*, 1975), the first electronic calculators containing discrete semiconductors wired to printed circuit boards were produced in 1963 by another British firm, the Bell Punch Company. This machine was apparently made under license in Japan.

14. Genryu, *Sony Challenge 1946–1968*, p. 198.

15. *Made in Japan*, p. 115.

16. At Hayakawa, Sasaki would also head a successful project to develop copiers.

17. A marvelous ongoing source of information about electronic calculators is *The International Calculator Collector*, the official newsletter of the International Association of Caculator Collectors, 14561 Livingston Street, Tustin, CA 92680-2618.

18. Tadao Kashio, "Creativity and Contribution" (Casio Computer Company [internal company production], 1991), p. 45.

19. According to T. R. Reid, "Moore was asked in 1964–when the most advanced chips contained about 60 components–to predict how far the industry would advance in the next decade. 'I did it sort of tongue-in-cheek,' Moore recalled later. 'I just noticed that the number of transistors on a chip had doubled for each of the last three years, so I said that the rate would continue.' To his dismay, that off-the-cuff remark was widely quoted and soon came to be known as 'Moore's Law' " (*The Chip: How Two Americans Invented the Microchip and Launched a Revolution* [New York: Simon & Schuster, 1984], p. 123).

20. "Creativity and Contribution," p. 54.

21. At the time of writing, prototype chips containing over a billion transistors have recently been fabricated.

22. See chapters 2 and 4.

23. Quoted in Michael S. Malone's excellent book, *The Big Score* (New York: Doubleday, 1985), p. 104 (now, alas, out of print).

24. T. R. Reid (quoting Bob Noyce) in *The Chip*, p. 119.

25. *Aviation Week*, 13 June 1960, p. 95.

26. Thanks to such unprecedented rates of reliability, "[l]ate in 1962 . . . the largest single order ever written for transistors will probably be forthcoming for the Minuteman missile," speculated *The Engineer*'s American editor.

27. *The Chip*, p. 121.

28. According to the revisionist caption of this photograph, which appears on p. 42 of the corporate history of Sharp, "Eighty Years of Sincerity and Creativity" (1992): "Saeki decided that Sharp must get involved in the semiconductor industry when he saw the Apollo spacecraft command module during a visit to North American Rockwell."

29. *Business Week*, 18 September 1978, p. 67.

30. Bankruptcy among small firms is by no means unusual in Japan. In fact, as George Gilder points out in his book, *Recapturing the Spirit of Enterprise* (San Francisco: Institute for Contemporary Studies, 1992), p. 164, the Japanese rate of bankruptcies is actually far higher than that of the United States. "It is from this domestic crucible of intense competition," writes Gilder, "with scores of rivals in every field, that the great Japanese companies have emerged." I think Gilder is correct in this assessment. After all, as anyone who has spent any time in Japan knows, the Japanese are exceptionally competitive in almost everything they do. It would be odd if the field of commerce were to prove an exception to the rule.

Chapter Two

1. Prior to that, the Japanese day was divided into 12 two-hour periods, each period being designated by both a number and an animal (the same ones as in the Chinese 12-year calendar cycle).

2. Source: Pieter Doensen, on the Web: *http://www.iit.edu/~matleri/bulova.html.*

3. The Engineering Department of Western Electric was spun off as Bell Telephone Laboratories in 1925. The Laboratories were originally located at 463 West Street in New York City.

4. Margaret Graham, *The Business of Research: RCA and the VideoDisc* (Cambridge: Cambridge University Press, 1986), p. 48.

5. This effort was ultimately successful, but Weimer's thin-film image sensors were no match for the charge-coupled device (see chapter 6).

6. G. B. Herzog, "COS/MOS—from concept to manufactured product" (paper published by the RCA Corporation, 1976).

7. Richard Turton, *The Quantum Dot: A Journey into the Future of Microelectronics* (New York: Oxford University Press, 1995), p. 55.

8. The scientist who would subsequently head MITI's VLSI Project.

9. In mid-1994, when this interview was conducted, Inoue was the general manager of Sharp's IC group; Harigaya meantime had become Seiko Epson's managing director in charge of consumer products.

10. Battelle Memorial Institute.

11. According to an officially sanctioned corporate history, *"Shirarezuru Kigyo Shudan Seiko Gurupu"* (which, literally translated, means: "Unknown Industrial Group Seiko," an accurate description that for some reason is rendered in English as "The Other Sides of the Seiko Group"), Nihon Kogyo Shimbun [date unknown], Shoji assigned separate projects to each of the three manufacturing companies within the group. Seikosha was to build photo-finish equipment; Dai-ni Seikosha, stopwatches; and Suwa Seiko, chronometers. However, several sources agree that there was competition between the companies over chronometers.

12. In 1984, according to the 12 November 1984 issue of *Fortune,* Suwa Seiko and Epson invested more than $100 million in semiconductor production, "about 10% of the two companies sales."

Chapter Three

1. *Electronic Engineering Times*, 19 December 1994. The high point of powder EL displays, wrote Larry Tannas in his book *Flat Panel Displays and*

CRTs (New York: Van Nostrand Reinhold, 1985), was in the Apollo and lunar module space vehicles, where eleven displays were used "in seven different functions, from event timers to guidance and navigation displays. In 1964, they were sunlight readable and had a life (to one-half luminance) of 2,000 hours."

2. The Nixie was also the immediate precursor of a third type of flat-screen display technology, the plasma panel (source: Joseph A. Castellano, *Handbook of Display Technology* [New York: Academic Press, 1992]).

3. The last Nixies I can remember seeing were in an elevator in Tokyo, in the old NEC offices near Tamachi Station. NEC, ironically enough, is the third-largest manufacturer of vacuum fluorescent displays, the devices that replaced the Nixie.

4. Steven Depp and Webster Howard, "Flat Panel Displays," *Scientific American*, March 1993, p. 43.

5. George W. Gray, *Molecular Structure and Properties of Liquid Crystals* (New York: Academic Press, 1962).

6. This basic LCD patent was granted in 1967.

7. George Heilmeier, "Liquid Crystal Displays: An Interdisciplinary Experiment that Worked" (IEEE review paper, 1976).

8. Westinghouse had passed up on television, too. After emigrating to the U.S., Vladimir Zworykin, the Russian inventor who pioneered television, worked at Westinghouse for more than a decade before being hired by David Sarnoff in 1930.

9. Optel LCDs were apparently applied to watches that were marketed in 1971 by Seiko's old nemesis, Bulova.

10. The figure is quoted by Sasaki in Hedrick Smith's book, *Rethinking America* (New York: Random House, 1995), p. 22.

11. See chapter 9.

12. Recalled in "By George," Rotsky's excellent weekly column in *Electronic Engineering Times*, 30 November 1995.

13. The Pulsar brand name was eventually acquired by Seiko.

14. Sasaki sent Takashi "Mits" Mitsutomi, a Japanese American whom he had met while the latter was working at Rockwell, to find out what was going on in Ohio.

15. Figures and anecdote quoted in Mike Malone's excellent book, *The Microprocessor: A Biography* (Santa Clara, Calif.: The Electronic Library of Science, 1995), p. 133.

16. With the arguable exception of IBM, which later reentered the LCD arena via a Japan-based joint venture with Toshiba.

17. See chapters 6 and 8.

Chapter Four

1. *Electro-Technology*, January 1970.

2. This account of Brody's work is based on his paper, "The Thin-Film Transistor—A Late Flowering Bloom," *IEEE Transactions on Electron Devices*, November 1984.

3. Letter to the *New York Times*, 8 January 1991.

4. David Rubinfien.

5. *Fortune*, 12 November 1984, p. 38.

6. See chapter 5.

7. *Fortune*, p. 38.

8. See chapter 6.

9. *Electronic Engineering Times*, 26 June 1991.

10. Lawrence E. Tannas, Jr., ed., *Flat Panel Displays and CRTs* (New York: Van Nostrand Reinhold, 1985), p. 242.

11. Mito is known to his American friends as Paul, the name given to him at baptism by his Christian parents.

12. By mid-1994, Hijikigawa had risen to become the deputy general manager of Sharp's LCD group.

13. Joseph A. Castellano, *Handbook of Display Technology* (New York: Academic Press, 1992), p. 188.

14. In 1994, Yamazaki estimated that Seiko Epson had LCD sales of between ¥25 and ¥30 billion ($250 to $300 million), out of total company sales of around ¥450 billion ($4.5 billion); in the same year, Sharp's LCD sales were ¥187.5 billion ($1.8 billion) out of total company sales of around ¥1.2 trillion ($12 billion). By 1995, Sharp's LCD sales had risen to ¥240 billion ($2.9 billion). The company predicted sales of ¥1.5 trillion ($12 billion) by the end of the century.

15. My friend, Tokyo-based journalist Dennis Normile.

16. In late 1996, it looked as though LCDs were being overtaken in large-area applications, at least in the short term, by another display technology invented in the U.S. and developed in Japan—the plasma display panel, a descendant of the Nixie tube. Fujitsu and NEC both announced that they had begun manufacturing 42-inch plasma screens. In 1997, both firms expected production of PDPs to grow to 10,000 units a month. At the 1998 Tokyo Business Fair, Sharp demonstrated a massive 60-inch LCD screen.

Chapter Five

1. The jam was made by the firm Keillor's, the journalism came from D. C. Thompson, a company headquartered in the city whose flagship publication,

the local daily newspaper, the *Courier and Advertiser*, provided the springboard for several journalists who subsequently became well known in Fleet Street.

2. Matsushita is better known outside Japan by its brand name, Panasonic.

3. Jeremy Bernstein, *Three Degrees Above Zero: Bell Laboratories in the Information Age* (Cambridge: Cambridge University Press, 1984), p. 74. For a more detailed account, see Michael Riordan and Lillian Hoddeson, *Crystal Fire: The Birth of the Information Age* (New York: W. W. Norton, 1997), pp. 94–95.

4. *Business Week*, 26 March 1960, p. 7.

5. The culprit in this case being H. M. Hubbard, author of "Photovoltaics Today and Tomorrow," *Science*, 21 April 1989, p. 300.

6. In October 1997, Toshiba announced that it planned to spend ¥50 billion ($400 million) at its Fukaya plant near Tokyo on production facilities to make next-generation, low-temperature polycrystalline silicon LCDs.

7. In "The Commercialization of Amorphous Silicon-Based Photovoltaics," an invited paper published in *Optoelectronics–Devices and Technologies*, September 1994 (Tokyo: Mita Press).

8. In 1993, in terms of output, Solarex and Sanyo were running neck and neck. The U.S. firm produced solar cells capable of generating a total of 6.5 megawatts; the Japanese firm, 6.2 megawatts.

9. The effects of this and other, similar programs in Germany and elsewhere are already making themselves felt. In 1997 the solar cell industry passed a significant milestone, with residential, grid-connected applications overtaking remote applications (such as telecommunications and water pumping) as the largest single sector of the photovoltaic market.

10. Genesis is one of those highly contrived acronyms so beloved of Japanese companies. The initials stand for "*G*lobal *E*nergy *N*etwork *E*quipped with *S*olar cells and *I*nternational *S*uperconductor grids." Kuwano first made the proposal at an international photovoltaics conference in Sydney, Australia, in 1989.

11. Walter Spear had a long-standing consultancy with Xerox.

Chapter Six

1. In an article entitled "From Research to Technology," *International Science and Technology*, May 1964.

2. Boyle and Smith, "The Inception of Charge-Coupled Devices," *IEEE Transactions on Electron Devices*, July 1976.

3. Michael Noll, "Anatomy of a Failure: Picturephone Revisited," *Telecommunications Policy*, May/June 1992.

4. *Bell Laboratories Record*, June 1978.

5. Noll, "Anatomy of a Failure."

6. Under the terms of the 1956 consent decree, Western Electric was not permitted to sell its products on the merchant marketplace.

7. On the subject of when research on the CCD at Bell Labs was wound up, recollections differ. Amelio reckoned that "in 1971, despite a flurry of patents all over the place, interest started to wane. George Smith decided he wanted to do something else, Mike Tompsett started to get bored ... and so the team started to drift apart as other questions came up, and we all felt like, Gee, this is an interesting concept, but could not conceive of how we could come up with a viable, a really and truly practical device, which is what we were looking for, to replace the [MOS] image sensor."

Boyle and Smith vigorously disagreed with Amelio's reckoning on both the timing and the extent of research. Boyle said, "I think George pushed [the CCD] up until 1973, and demonstrated a pretty good working model of the whole thing." This model, which was capable of a resolution of about 270 lines, can be seen in a set of photographs released by Bell Labs in December 1974 to commemorate the issuance of the basic patent on the CCD. In the photo on p. 183 Smith is seen focusing a TV camera about the size of a tea caddy on Boyle's face, while the latter tunes a small television receiver. In 1975, Bell Labs announced a prototype CCD camera capable of meeting broadcast resolution (525 lines) standards.

CCDs did actually enter commercial use in the Bell System, albeit in a much more modest application as the filters used for tone detection in push-button telephones.

8. The contract was the largest of three awarded as a result of presentations made to a special meeting of a subgroup of the Advisory Group on Electron Devices, the same committee that around this time was giving Peter Brody and his thin-film transistors such a hard time. The other contracts went to TI and RCA.

9. Ricoh was able to maintain this early lead; in 1994, the company was the top seller of faxes in the Japanese domestic market. CCDs continue to be used as the image sensor in all high-speed, high-resolution fax machines.

10. Iwama was president of Sony of America from May 1971 to September 1972.

11. Akio Morita, *Made in Japan: Akio Morita and Sony* (Tokyo: Weatherhill, 1987), p. 160.

12. Ibid., pp. 13, 15.

13. *Genryu: Sony Challenges 1946–1968*, p. 39.

14. The quotation comes from James Lardner's indispensable book, *Fast Forward: Hollywood, the Japanese and the VCR wars* (New York: Mentor, 1987), p. 42.

15. Nick Lyons, *The Sony Vision* (New York: Crown, 1976), p. 45.

16. *Genryu*, p. 100.

17. See the Introduction.

18. Quoted in *Genryu*, 1996 edition, p. 243.

19. A position Iwama assumed in January 1976.

20. Watanabe Seiichi, who succeeded Kikuchi as director of Sony's research center in 1989.

21. Hatoyama Michio, Kikuchi's former boss at ETL, had been the first director of the Sony center.

22. Michael Riordan and Lillian Hoddeson, *Crystal Fire: The Birth of the Information Age* (New York: W. W. Norton, 1997), p. 219.

23. Now trading as Nippon Silicon.

24. According to Watanabe Seiichi, the CCD development budget from 1974 to 1983 consumed from 0.1 to 0.36 percent of total company sales, a very high percentage for a single-product program. *Japanese Innovation Strategy* (Cambridge, Mass.: Harvard University Center for Science & International Affairs, 1993), p. 59.

Chapter Seven

1. M. V. Mathews, "The Digital Computer as a Musical Instrument," *Science*, Nov. 1, 1963, pp. 553–57.

2. Much of this history of Hammond comes from "Fifty Years of Musical Excellence," a commemorative brochure put out by the Hammond Organ company in 1984. Copies of this fascinating document can be obtained from John C. Drotos, executive director of the The Museum of Hammond Organs, P.O. Box 44, Peninsula, OH 44264.

3. ". . . as early as 1968 . . . General Instrument combined with Hammond to produce integrated circuits for organs" (Ernest Braun and Stuart Macdonald, *Revolution in Miniature* [Cambridge: Cambridge University Press, 1978], p. 103).

4. For much of this history of Yamaha, I have relied on an exemplary (alas, anonymous) review article entitled "Yamaha's First Century," which appeared in the 25 August 1987 edition of *Music Trades* magazine.

5. In 1897, Yamaha incorporated his company as Nippon Gakki ("Japan Musical Instrument"), the name by which the company was formally known until the late 1980s. For simplicity's sake, I have referred to the firm as Yamaha throughout.

6. In 1958 Kawakami sent his son, Hiroshi, an engineer, to work for Sony's tape recorder division, where he spent thirteen years before joining Yamaha in 1971.

7. Nick Lyons, *The Sony Vision* (New York: Crown, 1976), p. 30.

8. These anecdotes about Buchla, Moog, and other U.S. pioneers are taken from *Vintage Synthesizers: Groundbreaking Instruments and Pioneering Designers of Electronic Music Synthesizers* (San Francisco: Miller Freeman Books, 1993), an anthology lovingly edited by *Keyboard* magazine's Mark Vail.

9. The grand-daddy of all electronic instruments was invented by a Russian, Leon Theremin. Powered by what was then a new device, the vacuum tube, the instrument mixed the output from two oscillators to produce its unmistakable tones. In 1929, RCA took out a license to manufacture and sell theremins (Source: Barry Fox, *New Scientist*, 23–30 December 1995, p. 52).

10. In fact, this was not the first use of the name. The RCA Synthesizer was invented by Harry Olson and Herbert Belar at RCA at the corporation's Princeton labs in 1955. A monster made up of banks of vacuum tubes, it would play notes punched into a roll of paper tape. The holes tripped electro-mechanical relays that controlled various aspects of the sound.

11. This and subsequent reminiscences by Keith Emerson are taken from an article in *MOJO* magazine, January 1997, p. 17.

12. There was also a second aspect to this relationship. Yamaha would manufacture a Nishizawa invention, a special type of transistor that the company would incorporate in amplifiers for audio use. See chapter 9.

13. "According to industry watchers, about 80 per cent of the new personal-computer motherboards leaving factories these days have an audio chip on them" (*Electronic Engineering Times*, 20 November 1995).

14. Pierce's inventions included a new musical scale. "It doesn't sound too bad," he said modestly, going on to explain that "it has most of the properties of the diatonic scale—it has 13 instead of 12 keys, it has transpositions, and it's a chance for people who like something orderly in music to do something new without changing their orderly habits."

15. Waveguide licensees include Chromatic Research, Crystal Semiconductor, and Seer Systems.

16. This anecdote comes from Joel Shurkin's highly readable account of the evolution of the computer, *Engines of the Mind*, rev. ed. (New York: W. W. Norton, 1996).

Chapter Eight

1. Akio Morita, *Made in Japan: Akio Morita and Sony* (Tokyo: Weatherhill, 1987), p. 240.

2. "Infrared and Optical Masers," *Physical Review*, December 1958.

3. This and several subsequent anecdotes are taken from *Laser Pioneer Interviews* (Torrance, Calif.: High Tech Publications, 1985).

4. One of Javan's colleagues had brought in a bottle of 100-year-old wine to celebrate their achievement. But when Javan called the director of Bell Labs to invite him to join them in their celebration, the latter told Javan that he would be delighted to, but added that there was a problem he would have to attend to first. The problem was the ban on liquor on the premises, which had been introduced some months earlier. Later that afternoon, a memo was circulated around the labs stating that no liquor was allowed on the premises unless it was over 100 years old. After that, the director came to join the celebrations.

5. *Business Week*, 20 May 1960.

6. Or, as we shall see in chapter 10, two and six.

7. Nick Holonyak, "Semiconductor Alloy Lasers–1962," *IEEE Journal of Quantum Electronics*, June 1987.

8. "Snooperscope Television," *Time*, 19 April 1963.

9. R. H. Rediker, "Research at Lincoln Laboratory Leading Up to the Development of the Injection Laser in 1962," *IEEE Journal of Quantum Electronics*, June 1987.

10. Where, by coincidence, Esaki Leona, or Leo Esaki as he would henceforth be known, had taken up residence in 1960 after Sony had concluded that tunnel diodes were not useful for consumer electronics. After being offered jobs at many U.S. firms and universities, Esaki chose Yorktown Heights–sometimes known as Thomas Watson, Jr.'s gift to the scientific community–in large part because it was a new lab.

11. Unlike his colleagues at Schenectady, Holonyak was interested in the tunnel diode not because it was speedy, but because it was a negative-resistance switch, that is, a device in which an increase in the applied voltage increases the resistance and thereby produces a proportional decrease in current. Holonyak had been working on more complicated negative-resistance devices (work that eventually led to the triac, a commonly used component found in wall-mounted dimmer switches). "When Esaki published his work, and he's talking about negative resistance, he's obviously talking about something that we're working on," Holonyak said. "So we're bound to be interested in what Esaki's talking about, because it's actually something simpler to go to work on."

12. A similarly benign ignorance seems to have assisted Hayashi and Panish's Area 20 neighbors, CCD coinventors Boyle and Smith.

13. Nilo Lindgren, "Optical Communications–A Decade of Preparations," *Proceedings of the IEEE*, October 1970, p. 1410.

14. "We have found from experience," wrote Solomon Buchsbaum, a Bell Labs vice president, "with nonspecialist audiences, that the term 'optical' communication often needs further definition."

15. *Koji Kobayashi Rising to the Challenge* (Tokyo: Harcourt Brace Jovanovich, 1989), pp. 91–92.

16. Makoto Kikuchi, *Japanese Electronics* (Tokyo: Simul Press, 1983), p. 144.

17. Code-named TAT-8.

18. *Canon Chronicle,* May–June 1997, p. 197.

19. This anecdote comes from the estimable and informative book by Gary Jacobson and John Hillkirk, *Xerox: American Samurai* (New York: Collier, 1987), p. 143.

20. *Japanese Maverick: Success Secrets of Canon's "God of Sales,"* by Louis Kraar and Seiichi Takikawa (New York: John Wiley, 1994).

21. *PC Novice,* October 1991.

22. DiscoVision was acquired in 1989 by Pioneer Electric, a leading Japanese maker of laser disc players.

23. Margaret Graham, *The Business of Research: RCA and the VideoDisc,* (Cambridge: Cambridge University Press, 1986), p. 167.

24. A Japan-only joint venture called CBS/Sony. In 1987, Sony went worldwide by buying CBS Records outright.

25. Sam Wood, in a case study published by Stanford University Graduate School of Business entitled "The Development of Laser Diodes at Sony" (January 1995). "Although it was difficult to tell," Wood wrote, "Sony believed it was manufacturing more than half the world's supply of laser diodes for CD players."

26. In 1996, semiconductor laser makers were gearing up for the latest race— the production of red (635nm) devices for use in Digital Video Disc players— billed as "the next important medium for both computer data and home entertainment, especially movies."

As with the CD, the availability of lasers was critical to the commercial success of the players, which were introduced in time for Christmas that year. Once again, it appeared that many firms were having difficulty in putting lasers into volume production. And once again, Sharp claimed to be the first company to have succeeded in making red lasers in quantity.

27. For a while AT&T used an MBE system to produce microwave gallium arsenide transistors at its plant in Reading, Pennsylvania. But business was not very good, so they closed it down. MBE cannot be used to produce the relatively long-wave lasers used in telecommunications because one of the materials used in making such lasers is phosphorus, which ignites when you open up the reaction chamber.

28. Individual transistors, that is, as opposed to ones that are integrated on a chip. In 1995, Rohm was the world's twenty-third largest producer of semiconductors, two places ahead of AT&T, the originator of the transistor (Source: Dataquest)

29. "A Most Un-Japanese Company," *Business Week*, 21 July 1997, pp. 20, 21.

30. For their work in developing and manufacturing compact disc lasers, Tanaka and Won were joint winners of the 1993 IEEE Laser and Electro-Optic Society's LEOS Award for Engineering Achievement.

Chapter Nine

1. Source: Interview with the author, November 1983.

2. *Laser Pioneer Interviews* (Torrance, Calif.: High Tech Publications, 1985), p. 90.

3. Harlan Manchester, "Light of Hope—Or Terror?" *Reader's Digest*, February 1963. (The sensational title reflects the fact that in the early days, much to the annoyance of laser researchers, the popular press, no doubt mindful of Buck Rogers's ray gun, were obsessed with the notion of lasers as death rays.)

4. David Thomas and John Galt, "Luminescence in Semiconductors," *Bell Laboratories Record*, March 1968.

5. George Craford.

6. This delightful anecdote comes from Jeremy Bernstein's book, *Three Degrees Above Zero* (Cambridge: Cambridge University Press, 1984), p. 178.

7. As did IBM, another early dropout from the LED race. The computer company was interested in LEDs for use in optical storage systems.

8. "The HP-35: A big idea in a small package" *R&D Network*, (internal Hewlett-Packard newsletter), November/December 1989–January 1990 issue. The model number 35 was chosen because the calculator had 35 keys.

9. From "Inventions of Opportunity: Matching Technology with Market Needs" (selections from the pages of the *Hewlett-Packard Journal*, 1983).

10. "A comeback for LED displays," *Business Week*, 29 October 1979, p. 162

11. In 1990, Nishizawa would be elected president of Tohoku University, a position from which he retired in 1996.

12. This anecdote comes from NHK's excellent television documentary, *Denshi Rikkoku Nihon no Jijoden* ("Autobiography of Japan, a Country Based on Electronics"), directed by Aida Yutaka, 1992.

13. Source: Chiba Genya.

14. John Tilton, "International Diffusion of Technology: The Case of Semiconductors" (Washington, D.C.: The Brookings Institution, 1971), p. 148. It should be remembered that in addition to such patent licensing agreements,

U.S. firms like RCA would sometimes also sell process knowhow, for which they would charge substantially more.

15. This description is taken from the abstract of a paper by Reuven Koter published by the Society of Automotive Engineers in February 1994, entitled "Advanced indication of braking: A practical safety measure for improvement of decision-reaction time for avoidance of rear-end collisions."

16. My friend Michael Chinworth.

17. Source: Robert Metzger, *Compound Semiconductor*, July/August 1995, p. 27.

18. In fact a second, simpler option may carry the day. In 1997 Nichia Chemical, Toyoda Gosei, and Siemens all announced that they would shortly begin volume production of bright white LEDs. "White LEDs need blue diodes based on gallium nitride to excite either organic dyes or inorganic phosphors in the yellow part of the spectrum. The yellow then mixes with its complementary color, blue, to produce white." Possible initial applications for white LEDs included vanity and glove compartment lights, as well as reversing lights in cars (source: *Opto & Laser Europe*, issue 44, October 1997).

Chapter Ten

1. See, for example, "Light Emitting Diodes," a paper presented by David Thomas of Bell Laboratories at the IEEE Conference on Display Devices in New York, December 1970.

2. Silicon carbide is what is known as an "indirect" semiconductor; that is, compared to "direct" semiconductors like gallium arsenide, it produces light by a more complex process. This means indirect semiconductors are inherently less efficient than direct ones. Nonetheless, blue-light-emitting silicon carbide diodes were commercialized, most notably by a small North Carolina–based firm called Cree Research. Until the advent of Nakamura's bright blue emitters, silicon carbide was the only game in town.

3. When I interviewed him in 1994, Pankove was a professor at the University of Colorado at Boulder.

4. This description is taken from the entry on Shikoku in *Japan: An Illustrated Encyclopedia* (Tokyo: Kodansha, 1993).

5. Nichia Chemical company profile, 1994.

6. Nakamura Shuji and Gerhard Fasol, *The Blue Laser Diode: GaN Based Light Emitters and Lasers* (Berlin: Springer, 1997).

7. In 1990, researchers at the University of Florida and at Matsushita's Osaka research laboratories had succeeded in producing p-type zinc selenide, clearing the way for the fabrication of p-n junctions.

8. Quoted in "True Blue: A zinc compound adds to the laser spectrum," by the estimable Elizabeth Corcoran, *Scientific American*, September 1991, p. 171.

9. See chapter 8.

10. Nichia had the envelope framed. It hangs proudly in the meeting room where the company receives visitors.

11. In 1994 Nichia Chemical had 750 employees and annual sales of $222 million. The company is privately held, with directors holding 23 percent, employees 27 percent, and banks and key customers (such as Sony, which since the mid-1970s has held a 5-percent stake) the remaining 50 percent. It is worth mentioning that employee ownership is rare in Japan.

12. Personal communication with the author, 7 November 1996.

13. *Compound Semiconductor*, July/August 1995, p. 30

14. These and subsequent facts and figures come from Robert Metzger, "Stop!" *Compound Semiconductor*, July/August 1995, p. 14.

Chapter Eleven

1. *Recapturing the Spirit of Enterprise* (San Francisco: ICS Press, 1992), p. 293.

2. *The Australian*, 16 May 1997.

3. John Galt, who had assigned Hayashi and Panish to work on lasers, was also Dingle's director. In 1971 Dingle grew gallium nitride needles which he used to produce ultraviolet laser action at low temperatures.

4. R. Dingle, H. L. Stormer, A. C. Gossard, and W. Wiegmann, "Electron mobilities in modulation-doped semiconductor heterojunction superlattices," *Applied Physics Letters*, 33:665–70, 1978.

5. Kobayashi Taiyu, *Fortune Favors the Brave* (Tokyo: Toyo Keizai, 1983), p. 126.

6. A second factor enabling a reduction in the size of the antenna was the shorter wavelength of the signals. Previous generations of satellite TV had transmitted signals with a wavelength of 4 gigahertz; DBS moved up to the so-called Ku-band, transmitting signals with a wavelength of 12 gigahertz.

7. There is a contemporary parallel between Fujitsu's invention of, and subsequent immediate failure to exploit, the HEMT, and the invention of flash memory at Toshiba in 1980. Billed as a solid-state replacement for magnetic disc memory, flash was commercialized not by Toshiba, but by Intel. The reasons for this were twofold, according to flash's inventor, Masuoka Fujio. One was that the lack of a U.S. precedent made it difficult to convince Toshiba's management to go ahead with the technology. But more important was the fact that in the early 1980s there was a much larger market—D-RAMs—that demanded

all the company's development resources. "Toshiba's position in D-RAMs was very weak," Masuoka recalled, "so every engineer including myself was assigned to develop one megabit D-RAMs." This effort was highly successful: Thanks in part to its expertise in C-MOS, Toshiba went on to dominate the megabit generation of memory chips. And, like Fujitsu, the company would later return to challenge the early exploiters of its invention. At the time of writing, however, Intel remains the dominant player in the market for flash memory.

8. Scott Callon, "Unleashing Japan's Venture Business Sector: Problems and Policies for Reform," Japan Development Bank Discussion Paper Series No. 9403, August 1994.

9. "Maximizing U.S. Interests in Science and Technology Relations: Committee on Japan Framework Statement and Report of the Competitiveness Task Force," public briefing, 28 July 1997.

INDEX